Playful Identities

MediaMatters is a series published by Amsterdam University Press on current debates about media technology and practices. International scholars critically analyze and theorize the materiality and performativity, as well as spatial practices of screen media in contributions that engage with today's (digital) media culture.

For more information about the series, please visit www.aup.nl

Playful Identities

The Ludification of Digital Media Cultures

Edited by

Valerie Frissen
Sybille Lammes
Michiel de Lange
Jos de Mul
Joost Raessens

Amsterdam University Press

This book is published in print and online through the online OAPEN library (www.oapen.org).

OAPEN (Open Access Publishing in European Networks) is a collaborative initiative to develop and implement a sustainable Open Access publication model for academic books in the Humanities and Social Sciences. The OAPEN Library aims to improve the visibility and usability of high quality academic research by aggregating peer reviewed Open Access publications from across Europe.

This work is part of the Humanities research programme Transformations in Art and Culture, sponsored by the Netherlands Organisation for Scientific Research (NWO).

Cover illustration: Photograph of the game *I'd Hide You*, Blast Theory, 2012 (courtesy of Blast Theory).

Cover design: Suzan Beijer
Lay-out: Crius Group, Hulshout

Amsterdam University Press English-language titles are distributed in the US and Canada by the University of Chicago Press.

ISBN 978 90 8964 639 2
e-ISBN 978 90 4852 303 0
NUR 670

Contents

1. Homo ludens 2.0: Play, media, and identity 9
Valerie Frissen, Sybille Lammes, Michiel de Lange, Jos de Mul & Joost Raessens

Part I Play

Introduction to Part I 53
Valerie Frissen, Sybille Lammes, Michiel de Lange, Jos de Mul & Joost Raessens

2. Playland: Technology, self, and cultural transformation 55
Kenneth J. Gergen

3. Spiritual play: Encountering the sacred in *World of Warcraft* 75
Stef Aupers

4. Playful computer interaction 93
Daniel Cermak-Sassenrath

5. Playful identity in game design and open-ended play 111
Menno Deen, Ben Schouten & Tilde Bekker

6. Breaking reality: Exploring pervasive cheating in *Foursquare* 131
René Glas

7. Playing with bits and bytes: The savage mind in the digital age 149
Valerie Frissen

Part II Media

Introduction to Part II 167
Valerie Frissen, Sybille Lammes, Michiel de Lange, Jos de Mul & Joost Raessens

8. Location-based mobile games: Interfaces to urban spaces 169
Adriana de Souza e Silva & Jordan Frith

9. The playful use of mobile phones and its link to social cohesion 181
Rich Ling

10. Digital cartographies as playful practices 199
Sybille Lammes

11. Ludic identities and the magic circle 211
Gordon Calleja

12. Play (for) time 225
Patrick Crogan

13. Playful identity politics: How refugee games affect the player's identity 245
Joost Raessens

Part III Identity

Introduction to Part III 263
Valerie Frissen, Sybille Lammes, Michiel de Lange, Jos de Mul & Joost Raessens

14. Playing out identities and emotions 267
Jeroen Jansz

15. Playing with others: The identity paradoxes of the web as social network 281
Jeroen Timmermans

16. New media, play, and social identities 293
Leopoldina Fortunati

17. Playing life in the metropolis: Mobile media and identity in Jakarta 307
Michiel de Lange

18. The conflicts within the casual: The culture and identity of casual online play 321
Frans Mäyrä

19. Afterplay 337
Jos de Mul

About the authors 347

Index of Names 353

Index of Subjects 359

1. Homo ludens 2.0: Play, media, and identity

Valerie Frissen, Sybille Lammes, Michiel de Lange, Jos de Mul & Joost Raessens

Immense est le domaine du jeu.
Émile Benveniste

Foreplay

A playful specter is haunting the world. Since the 1960s, when the use of the word "ludic" became popular in both Europe and the US to designate playful behavior and artifacts, playfulness has become increasingly a mainstream characteristic of modern and postmodern culture. In the first decade of the 21st century we can even speak of the global "ludification of culture" (Raessens 2006; 2014). Perhaps the first thing that comes to mind in this context is the immense popularity of computer games, which, as far as global sales are concerned, have already outstripped Hollywood movies. In the US, 8- to 18-year-olds play on average an hour and a half daily on consoles, computers and handheld gaming devices, including mobile phones (Rideout et al. 2010, 2-3). This is by no means only a Western phenomenon. In South Korea, for example, about two-thirds of the country's total population frequently plays online games, turning computer gaming into one of the fastest growing industries and a key driver for the Korean economy (Jin 2012).[1]

Although perhaps most visible, computer game culture is only one manifestation of the process of ludification that seems to penetrate every cultural domain (Neitzel and Nohr 2006). In our present experience economy, for example, playfulness not only characterizes leisure time (fun shopping, game shows on television, amusement parks, playful computer, Internet, and smartphone use), but also those domains that used to be serious, such as work (which should above all be fun nowadays), education (serious gaming), politics (ludic campaigning), and even warfare (computer games like war simulators and interfaces). According to Jeremy Rifkin, "play is becoming as important in the cultural economy as work was in the industrial economy" (2000, 263).[2] Postmodern culture has been described as "a game without an overall aim, a play without a transcendent destination" (Minnema 1998, 21).

Sociologist Zygmunt Bauman maintains that human identity has even become a playful phenomenon. In ludic culture, he argues, playfulness is no longer restricted to childhood, but has become a lifelong attitude: "The mark of postmodern adulthood is the willingness to embrace the game whole-heartedly, as children do" (Bauman 1995, 99).

The focus of this volume is on the complex relationship between play, media, and identity in contemporary culture. The chapters in this book investigate, from different perspectives, the role that digital information and communication technologies play in the ludification of personal and cultural identity. The focus on (new) media is not only motivated by the dominant role that digital media play in our present culture, but also by the intuition that "play is central [...] to media experience" (Silverstone 1999, 63; cf. Thimm 2010).

In this introductory chapter, we analyze these three interconnected phenomena that constitute the subject of this volume, offering a conceptual background that enables the reader to situate the contributions to this volume. This introductory chapter consists of three main sections, which correspond to the three parts of this volume, devoted to play, media, and identity.

With regard to the dimension of play in this triad, our starting point is the theory of play developed by Johan Huizinga in his famous 1938 book *Homo ludens*. It is not without reason that *Homo ludens* is regarded as a classic in the study of play. Although published more than seventy-five years ago, Huizinga's central claim, that culture and civilization "arises *in* and *as* play, and never leaves it" (1955, 173), still offers a fruitful framework for the study of the ludification of human identity in our contemporary media landscape, or *playland* as Kenneth Gergen calls it in this book. This claim has found wide acclaim. Thanks to recently developed fields like game and leisure studies, we can even speak of a Huizinga-renaissance. However, we argue that in order to apply Huizinga's theory of play to the world of digital technologies, *Homo ludens* needs a serious "update" because play and technology are almost complete opposites for Huizinga.

In this introductory chapter we will update *Homo ludens* to a "2.0" version that goes beyond the opposition between contemporary play and technologies. In the section on media, we will use the insights from leading scholars in the domains of New Media and Game Studies to substantiate this position further by focusing on the playful dimension of digital technologies. We argue here that both media explicitly designed for play, such as computer games, as well as digital technologies in general, have an inherent ludic dimension. This dimension is closely connected with medium-specific qualities like multimediality, virtuality, interactivity, and connectivity.

In the last section of this chapter, the emphasis lies on the role that these ludic technologies play in the construction of personal and cultural identities. Here the vantage point is Paul Ricoeur's theory of narrative identity. According to this theory, narrative is not only an appropriate metaphor for human identity, but human beings actually construct their identity through stories, ranging from explicit biographies and autobiographies to fictional accounts of human life in novels. In light of the aforementioned ludification of digital culture, we propose to supplement Ricoeur's theory of narrative identity with a theory of *ludic identity construction* that explains how both play and games are currently appropriate metaphors for human identity, as well as the very means by which people reflexively construct their identity.

Phrases like "self-construction" and "construction of cultural identity" might suggest that this process is fully controlled by an autonomous subject. Evidently, this is not the case. The fact that "the self" is not something given, but a construction, does not necessarily imply that the self is the (main) constructor. Commercialization, globalization, and technological homogenization mold the subject's self-construction to the logic of an external system. As the chapters in this volume will demonstrate in more detail, practices of reflexive identity construction constantly take place in a tension between communicative action and commercialization, between localization and globalization, and between heterogenization and homogenization.[3]

Play

Viewing man and world *sub specie ludi* is of course not a new phenomenon. Already early in Western thought, Heraclitus speculated that "the course of the world is a playing child moving figures on a board – the child as absolute ruler of the universe" (Sprague 2001). Ludic accounts of man and the world have been formulated at all times and in all cultures. In Western culture we can witness an important development during the past two centuries. Whereas the Enlightenment did not show a deep interest in play, the Romantic movement heralded a new fascination for this phenomenon. Friedrich Schiller – who can be regarded as the founding father of contemporary ludology – even considered the play drive as the core of humanity since it enables man to reconcile necessity and freedom. As he famously phrased it in *On the aesthetic education of man*: "Man plays only when he is in the full sense of the word a man, and *he is only wholly Man when he is playing*" (Schiller 2004, 80). Alongside reasoning (*Homo sapiens*) and making

(*Homo faber*), playing (*Homo ludens*) now advanced to the center of attention. Philosophers including Nietzsche, Wittgenstein, Heidegger, Gadamer, Marcuse, Deleuze, and Derrida (most of them considered as forerunners or representatives of postmodern culture), followed the ludological footprints of Heraclites and Schiller in their attempts to transform the modern, predominantly rationalistic and utilitarian ontology and anthropology (Axelos 1964; cf. Minnema 1998). Moreover, play and games have gained strong attention in the natural sciences, social sciences, and humanities. One can think, for example, of the implementation of *game theory* in biology (Sigmund 1993), economics (Neumann and Morgenstern 1944; Leonard 2010), and cultural anthropology (Bateson 1955; 1977). In addition to the increased interest in play and games in these already existing disciplines, in the last decades – motivated by the substantial growth of leisure time and the growth of ludo-industry and ludo-capitalism (Dibbell 2008) - several new fields entirely devoted to the study of play and (computer) games have emerged (cf. Mitchell et al. 1934; Avedon and Sutton-Smith 1971; Raessens and Goldstein 2005; Mäyrä 2008; Ritterfeld, Cody and Vorderer 2009; Fuchs et al. 2014).

As mentioned above, one of the most foundational works in the contemporary study of play is Johan Huizinga's *Homo ludens: A study of the play-element in culture*. This book, first published in Dutch in 1938 and later translated into many other languages, can even be considered as "the key modernist statement on play" (Motte 2009, 26). "Richly suggestive and admirably broad in scope, it provides the first full-blown theory of ludics, and it remains moreover, seven decades after it first appeared, an inevitable point of reference for any 'serious' discussion of play" (ibid., 26).

The book is still so impressive because of its grand ambition and scope. Already the book's subtitle – "a study of the play-element of culture"[4] – and foreword make it clear that Huizinga's ambition is no less than to offer a genealogy that explains how "civilization arises and unfolds in and as play" (Huizinga 1955, foreword). In the second to the last chapter – "Western Civilization *Sub Specie Ludi*" – Huizinga summarizes his argument:

> It has not been difficult to show that a certain play-factor was extremely active all through the cultural process and that it produces many of the fundamental forms of social life. The spirit of playful competition is, as a social impulse, older than culture itself and pervades all life like a veritable ferment. Ritual grew up in sacred play; poetry was born in play and nourished on play; music and dancing were pure play. Wisdom and philosophy found expression in words and forms derived from religious

> contests. The rules of warfare, the conventions of noble living were built up on play-patterns. We have to conclude, therefore, that civilization is, in its earliest phases, played. It does not come *from* play like a babe detaching itself from the womb: it arises *in* and *as* play, and never leaves it (ibid., 173).

This summary explicates that *Homo ludens* is not primarily a study of play or games, but rather "an inquiry into the creative quality of the play principle in the domain of culture" (Caillois 2001, 4). The first chapter of Huizinga's book offers a definition of the phenomenon of play, which has been quoted in almost every book on play and games that has been published since.[5]

> Summing up the formal characteristics of play we might call it a free activity standing quite consciously outside "ordinary" life as being "not meant"[6], but at the same time absorbing the player intensely and utterly. It is an activity connected with no material interest, and no profit can be gained by it. It proceeds within its own proper boundaries of time and space according to fixed rules and in an orderly manner. It promotes the formation of social groupings which tend to surround themselves with secrecy and to stress their difference from the common world by disguise or other means (Huizinga 1955, 13).

Let us elucidate the six elements of this definition. First, like Schiller and the Romantics before him, Huizinga defines play as an *expression of human freedom* vis-à-vis both nature and morality (ibid., 7-8). Play, like beauty in nature and art, to which it is closely related, is *disinterested*, distinct from ordinary life, "it contains its own course and meaning" and presents itself as an "intermezzo, an *interlude* in our daily lives" (ibid., 9). Playing is "non-serious"[7] in the sense that it is not characterized by our daily concern for food, shelter, and everything else fragile beings like us need in order to survive. Play takes place "outside and above the necessities and seriousness of everyday life" (ibid., 26). We could also say that play is beyond *profane* seriousness. However, this does not exclude the fact that the activity of playing requires total devotion from the player. Playing is not merely "fun", but earnest, even "holy earnest" (ibid., 23). For Huizinga, this is not (merely) a figurative expression: "In all its higher forms the latter [human play] at any rate always belongs to the sphere of festival and ritual – the sacred sphere" (ibid., 9). In order to distinguish this kind of intrinsic, sacred earnestness from profane seriousness we might call it *sacred seriousness* (on the relation between spirituality and play, see Stef Aupers' chapter in this volume).

Second, playing is "not meant", it refers to an activity of "just pretending". The thing represented in play is not real. Playing is only acting *as if*, pretending. Huizinga calls this "the consciousness that it [play] is 'different' from 'ordinary life'" (ibid., 28).

Third, play is not only immersive in the sense that it is absorbing the player intensely; this state of mind is also "accompanied by a feeling of tension, joy" (ibid.). According to Huizinga, the "play-mood is one of rapture and enthusiasm, and is sacred or festive in accordance with the occasion. A feeling of exaltation and tension accompanies the action, mirth and relaxation follow" (ibid., 132).

Fourth, play is distinct from ordinary life both in terms of locality and duration. It is characterized by specific *limits of time and space:* The *magic circle* ("tovercirkel") of play is not only a spatial circle, but a temporal one as well.[8] It also takes place *in* and *as* what we might call a magic *cycle*: "It can be repeated at any time, whether it be 'child's play' or a game of chess, or at fixed intervals like a mystery. In this faculty of repetition lies one of the most essential qualities of play" (Huizinga 1955, 10).

Fifth, the *rules* that constitute the play-world are crucial to the concept: "All play has its rules. They determine what 'holds' in the temporary world circumscribed by play. The rules of a game are absolutely binding and allow no doubt" (ibid., 11).[9] "As soon as the rules are transgressed the whole play-world collapses" (ibid.). Whereas the cheater still pretends to play and in doing so still acknowledges the magic circle and cycle, "the player who trespasses against the rules or ignores them is a 'spoil-sport'" (ibid.).

Sixth, play "creates order, *is* order. Into an imperfect world and into the confusion of life it brings a temporary, a limited perfection" (ibid., 10). Play is "indispensible for the well-being of the community, fecund of cosmic insight and social development" (ibid., 25).

As Huizinga considers play to be a "primary category of life" (ibid., 3), the play-definition presented in the first chapter of *Homo ludens* has a universal ring. Huizinga explicitly claims that "all peoples play, and play remarkably alike" (ibid., 28)[10], and he distinguishes two basic forms of play: "The two ever-recurrent forms in which civilization grows in and as play are the sacred performance and the festal contest" (Huizinga 1955, 48). In *Les jeux et les hommes* (1958), a critical elaboration of Huizinga's work, Roger Caillois presents a typology consisting of four categories. In addition to the two forms mentioned by Huizinga, including "sacred performance", which Caillois terms simulation (*mimicry*), ranging from children's imitation play to theater, and "festal contest", or competition (*agôn*), referring to free play, regulated sports, contests, and so on, Caillois also distinguishes chance (*alea*), as we find it, for example, in counting-out rhymes and lotteries, and vertigo (*ilinx*), ranging from merry-go-round "whirling" to mountain climbing. Crosscutting this classification of game types Caillois discerns two play attitudes: *paidia* and *ludus*. *Paidia* refers to "free play", improvisation, carefree gaiety and laughter, and spontaneous, impulsive, joyous, and uncontrolled fantasy. *Ludus* on the other hand disciplines and enriches *paidia*, since it refers to "gaming", more explicitly rule-governed forms of play that often involve specific skills and mastery.[11] In each of the four categories, play phenomena are located somewhere between the poles of *paidia* and *ludus*. However, *agôn* and *alea* lean towards the pole of *ludus*, while *ilinx* and *mimicry* tend to lean more towards *paidia*. Taken together, these two classifications are useful tools for the analysis of the ludification of contemporary culture.[12]

Before directing our attention to the playful dimension of contemporary information and communication technologies, we have to return to Huizinga's historical analysis for a moment. Although he emphasizes that all culture "arises and unfolds in and as play", he does not claim that cultures always *keep* playing. Echoing the pessimistic tone of Spengler's *The decline of the West* (1991)[1918-1923], Huizinga argues that cultures are most playful in their youth, and gradually become more serious and lose their playfulness as they grow more mature (Huizinga 1955, 75). For Huizinga, Romanticism was the last period in Western culture that exhibited a playful spirit, while in the 19th century, society "seems to leave little room for play" (ibid., 191). And in the dark-toned last chapter of the book, on the play element in 20th century culture, Huizinga states that the play element in culture is "on the wane": "civilization to-day is no longer played" (ibid., 206).

Huizinga acknowledges that this observation seems to be at odds with the fact that sports and popular culture have become major industries in 20th century culture. However, he discerns two contradictory tendencies with regard to the relationship of play and seriousness that in his view lead to a blurring of boundaries between both play and (profane) seriousness. On the one hand, when referring to professional sports, Huizinga claims play has become more and more serious thereby resulting in a loss of playfulness (ibid., 199; cf. Raessens 2009, 86). On the other hand, he claims that we are witnessing a growing playfulness in the sphere of profane seriousness. For example, he points out in commercial competition: "Sport and athletics showed us play stiffening into seriousness but still being felt as play; now we come to serious business degenerating into play but still being called serious" (ibid., 199).

These developments do not lead so much to a more playful culture, but are instead expressions of cheating – "false play" – and for that reason are undermining (playful) culture as such (ibid., 206). This assertion is actually debated by René Glas later in this volume. According to Huizinga, there are several "external factors independent of culture proper" (ibid., 199) that are responsible for the decay of playful culture. He especially refers to the *global commercialization of culture*[13] and the emergence of *puerilism*: a "blend of adolescence and barbarity which has been rampant all over the world for the last two or three decades" (ibid., 205) that have been "caused or supported by the technology of modern communication" ["veroorzaakt of in de hand gewerkt door de techniek van het moderne geestelijk verkeer"] (Huizinga 1950, 237).[14] In this culture, characterized by an "insatiable thirst for trivial recreation and crude sensationalism, the delight in mass meetings, mass-demonstrations, parades etc." he finds a "[complete lack of] humour, the very idea of decency and fair play" (Huizinga 1955, 205).

We should not forget that Huizinga wrote these bitter words in 1938, with the disconcerting memories of the First World War still fresh, and in terrifying anticipation of the no less outrageous barbarisms of the emerging fascist movements. However, in our view, Huizinga's pessimism is not only motivated by the historical context, but points at real contradictions in his argument. If we want to use Huizinga's penetrating insights into play as a fundamental category of life to gain a deeper understanding of the ludification of contemporary, strongly mediated culture, we first have to come to terms with these contradictions, which point at the fundamental ambiguities of the play phenomenon itself.

Despite its inspiring insights, *Homo ludens* still puzzles the reader because of its many contradictions and ambiguities. Let us mention the four most important ones. First, Huizinga presents play as being both *reality and appearance*. On the one hand, he sees play as a key dimension in human life and even maintains that culture is only possible in and as play. On the other hand, he argues that play entirely takes place outside everyday life and is nothing more than a disinterested "*interlude*" (ibid., 9). While play is "indispensable for the well-being of the community, fecund of cosmic insight and social development", it is at the same time only pretending, "make-believe" (ibid., 25) – and for that reason is inconsequential to real life. Because of its reality, we play "holy earnest", yet our play is completely non-serious. Second, play is both *freedom and force*. According to Huizinga, play is a celebration of human freedom, yet he is of the opinion that it "casts a spell over us" because it demands our complete maddening absorption (ibid., 10).[15] For a critique of this idea, see Gordon Calleja's chapter in this volume. Conversely, although the rules of the game are "absolutely binding", players are also constantly breaking these rules. Third, games are both *determined and changing*. Huizinga emphasizes that the rules of a game are absolute, and at the same time *Homo ludens* is above all a historical narrative about the never-ending transformation of play into various cultural forms. Fourth, play is both an *individual and collective* activity. Although the player is absorbed in his own private play-world, in most cases he plays with or against other players in a shared play-world, often before an audience. Even when one plays a solitary game, it is played before an imagined audience.[16] Moreover, in the case of *mimicry*, the player is pretending to be someone else by creating a community of personae within himself.[17]

Scholars such as Jacques Ehrmann (1968) and Warren Motte (2009) have also pointed out these ambiguities. They have criticized Huizinga for being entangled in contradictions. According to Ehrmann, the "hierarchical dichotomy", in which play is understood as a *re*presentation of a reality existing prior to and independent from play, is highly problematic, as "there is no 'reality' (ordinary or extraordinary!) outside of or prior to the manifestations of the culture that expresses it" (Ehrmann 1968, 33). However, Ehrmann's alternative – "Play, reality, culture are synonymous and interchangeable" (ibid., 56) – is equally problematic since in this case these concepts completely lose their distinctive meaning. And, as Huizinga rightly observes, in our lives we constantly use distinctions as the one between play and non-play. Every culture is based on fundamental distinctions, such as those between nature and culture, profane and sacred, life and death, male and female, good and evil, freedom and constraint (Oudemans and Lardinois 1987, 31). Although these distinctions have a natural basis, they are not simply a given, they are (at least partly) historically and culturally variable constructions (de Mul 2004, 146-52). And often we find ourselves in the uncanny, and sometimes tragic, situation in which we cannot distinguish sharply between these opposites, because things are fundamentally ambiguous or because both opposites turn out to be the case (de Mul 2009).

Moreover, we are often confronted in the case of play with fundamental ambiguities. Sometimes, in case of dangerous sports or war, it is difficult to distinguish between play and seriousness. Or, in the case of game or gambling addiction, between freedom and force. However, within the "separative cosmology" that characterizes modern thinking, including Huizinga's analysis, in the last analysis these ambiguities have no place and have to be exorcized. But in his constant, almost ritual opposing of play and non-play (reality, utility, seriousness, etc.), Huizinga cannot avoid becoming entangled in the insoluble conceptual tensions that we have pointed out above (cf. Motte 2009, 25-6).

Yet, Motte points to the fact that Huizinga, at several places in *Homo ludens,* shows a greater sensitivity towards the "ambiguity of play" (cf. Sutton-Smith 1997, and Jos de Mul's contribution to this volume) than Ehrmann attributes to him. For example, in the last chapter of *Homo ludens*, Huizinga acknowledges that "play can be cruel and bloody and, in addition, can often be false play. [...] War and everything to do with it remains fast in the daemonic and magical bonds of play" (Huizinga 1955, 208-9). And in the same chapter of his book, Huizinga even – reluctantly – acknowledges the blurring of play and profane seriousness in modern culture. However, just because of the aforementioned "separative drive", Huizinga is not able to explain *that* and *how* culture (sacred seriousness) and ordinary life (profane seriousness) can merge *in* and *as* play. Eugen Fink offers an intriguing ontology of play in *Spiel als Weltsymbol* (1960). He maintains that we cannot arrive at such an explanation as long as we stick to the modernist dichotomy of – on the level of attitude – play and seriousness, and – on the ontological level – play and reality (Fink 1968, 19). If we want to grasp this ontological meaning, we should realize that human play never really occurs outside everyday reality. Huizinga is right that the world of play has its own kind of reality. However, the building blocks of the play-world – the playing field, the other players, play objects – are at the same time part of our everyday reality. What distinguishes playing from more serious modes of being on the one hand, and sheer fantasy on the other hand, is that the player is *simultaneously* in the ordinary world and in the play-world. Moreover, as Huizinga acknowledges explicitly, in the playful experience the child, sportsman, and actor are all *aware* of being in both worlds simultaneously (Huizinga 1955, 18).

Here again, the play-experience is very close to aesthetic experience. Aesthetic experience is characterized by a similar double experience. When we watch a horror movie, and are fully immersed in the narrative, we may experience intense fear. At the same time, however, we know that what we are seeing is "just a movie", "only as if". In psychoanalytical terms we can say that the aesthetic experience requires an ego-split that enables us to have two contradictory experiences at once, e.g. the vampire in the movie is experienced as both real and non-real.[18] This ambiguous, double experience is connected with human reflexivity, the fact that human beings not only experience, but are also, and at the same time, able to experience their experience. In the terminology of Plessner's philosophical anthropology: human experience is simultaneously centric and eccentric, in one word:

(*ec*)*centric*. Being (ec)centric not only implies that we can go beyond our private experience and imagine ourselves in someone else's experience, but also that we can mask ourselves and play different roles in social life. However, at the same time we also remain immersed in our own experiences (Plessner 1975, 288ff.; cf. de Mul 2003, 247-66). As a consequence, when we engage into playful activities, we do not, as Huizinga and Caillois suggest, step outside the everyday world into the magic circle of the play-world, but we intentionally and explicitly play with the double existence that characterize human life. As Eugen Fink explains:

> The player who participates in a game executes in the real world an action of a familiar type. Within the context of the internal meaning of play, however, he is taking over a role. Here we must distinguish between the real man who "plays" and the man created by the role within the play. The player hides his real self behind his role and is submerged in it. He lives *in* his role with a singular intensity, and yet not like the schizophrenic, who is unable to distinguish between "reality" and "illusion". The player can recall himself from his role; while playing, man retains a knowledge of his double existence, however greatly reduced this knowledge may be. Man exists in two spheres simultaneously, not for lack of concentration or out of forgetfulness, but because this double personality is essential to play (Fink 1968, 23).

We might further elucidate this double experience of play by referring to Gregory Bateson's analysis of play. According to Bateson, play combines communication and meta-communication (Bateson 1955). Play is always accompanied by the signal "it's just play" or "it's only a game". We already witness this in higher animals, for example, when two dogs are playfully biting each other. When we play, we can enthusiastically immerse ourselves in the play-world, while at the same time keeping an ironic distance towards our playful behavior, which just for that reason can be termed "playful".

This double character of play has several important implications for a correct understanding of the phenomenon of play. In the first place, Huizinga's remark that play creates order acquires a deeper meaning. The order created by play is not so much a temporary order completely outside or beyond everyday reality, but rather a layer of meaning that *during* play is superimposed on everyday reality. That is why we can call the act of playing a "medium" between us and the world outside us in which lived experience is organized as a meaningful whole (cf. Rodriquez 2006). In the act of play, profane reality is enriched by a layer of sacred seriousness.

Augmented reality before technology! But it is just because it is part of our condition to add new layers to our experiences that human experience is so susceptible to all kinds of technological add-ons.

A second implication of the double character of play is that, just because the immersion in the play-world is always accompanied by the experience that "it's just play", the rules that guide the play are necessarily experienced as being contingent, flexible, and changeable. Just because we are both inside and outside the magic circle, we are able to reflect on the rules as "just play rules" and can modify them if we want to. This is in sharp contrast with Huizinga's emphasis on the absolute character of rules. Moreover, playing *with* the rules is inherent to many forms of play. We already see in child's play that playing with the rules – "Now I'm policeman and you are the naughty boy" – is an important part of the fun.

In addition, in children's play the boundaries of the magical circle (and magical cycle) are rather fuzzy. Where exactly are the spatial boundaries located for children's play-world? When exactly does children's play begin or end? And this also counts for many other playful situations, like playing with your pen while making a telephone call, flirting with someone on a train, or joining a pervasive game (Montola 2005; de Lange 2009). The flexibility and changeability of games cannot only be discerned at the micro level (e.g. small changes in the rules of soccer), but also on the macro level. Entirely new domains of playfulness may be disclosed, for example funshopping or serious gaming.

Connecting to the flexibility of play, Lourens Minnema provides an interesting explanation for the growing interest in play in 19th and 20th century culture. Following Luhmann, Minnema points to the fact that since the Modern Age Western culture has transformed the so far hierarchically stratified structure of society into a functionally differentiated structure, consisting of many substructures, such as politics, economy, law, education, science, technology, and art, which each possess relative autonomy and have their own specific roles and rules. This causes a much higher level of societal complexity and flexibility. According to Minnema, the 20th century fascination for play and games is strongly connected with this societal development. We see our postmodern culture "as a complex of games each one having its own framework, its own rules, risks, chances, and charms" (Minnema 1998, 21). Play becomes a *rite de passage*, a room for new (re) combinations of actions and thoughts, a database of alternative models for living (Turner 1969).[19] However, unlike premodern and modern rites, postmodern rites no longer seem to have a clearly demarcated transformational (liminal) period, but have become a never-ending (liminoid) phenomenon, an integral part of the socio-economic, cultural and multimedial systems (cf. Van Gennep 1960; Turner 1982).

When we speak about the ludification of culture we are confronted with the question whether this ludification consists in an increase in playful activities or rather a transformation in perspective, in which we use play as a metaphor to understand entities and domains that in themselves are not necessarily considered playful. We think both answers are correct. On the one hand, and contrary to what Huizinga claims, Western culture has witnessed a remarkable revival of the "ludic worldview" since the Romantic movement, with Huizinga's *Homo ludens* being one of the fruits of this development. On the other hand, this change in perspective has also generated the development of all kinds of new ludic attitudes, practices, and objects, which in turn stimulate the ludification of our worldview. In principle, no single "serious domain" within human life is exempt from "ludification". This even applies to the "serious domain" that Huizinga considered to embody the very decay of playfulness: modern technology.

Ludic media technologies

Not only Huizinga's claim that the ludic worldview has disappeared since the beginning of the 19th century is debatable, the same goes for his claim that play and technology are incompatible. Media archaeologist Errki Huhtamo provides a telling example of the interconnectedness of play and technology. According to Huhtamo, "the introduction of large-scale machine production [in the 19th century] was accompanied by an avalanche of different devices that provided amusement, including game-play" (2005, 3). These so-called "slot machines" prepared the ground for the introduction of computer games in the early 1960s. Moreover, we assert that in our contemporary culture, deeply entrenched with digital technologies, play is the key feature for understanding this culture and "playful technologies" are the very means by which we – as we will see in the next section – reflexively construct our identity.

When we talk about the medium-specific ludic characteristics of digital information and communication technologies, we by no means refer to a set of essentialist qualities (see the chapter by Daniel Cermak-Sassenrath in this volume). As we argued above, playfulness does not reside in a single characteristic, but should rather be understood as a set of characteristics that can appear in activities in various more or less overlapping combinations.[20] The question is what affordances (and limitations) for play are being provided to users by digital media such as computer games, Internet, and mobile phones through their design: "The term affordance refers to the perceived and actual properties of the thing, primarily those fundamental properties that determine just how the thing could possibly be used. [...] Affordances provide strong clues to the operations of things" (Norman 1988, 9; see also the contributions of Menno Deen, Ben Schouten, and Tilde Bekker). A playful affordance is, thus, only "virtual" (in the sense of a potentiality) until it is actualized by the playful attitude of the user and experienced as such.[21] This search for playful affordances goes hand in hand with what we earlier called a transformation of perspective. Regarding digital media as ludic practices enables us to conceptualize them in specific terms, as we will discuss in more detail at the end of this section.

The characteristics of digital media that we are focusing on here are: multimediality, virtuality, interactivity, and connectivity. *Multimediality* not only refers to the multitude of means of expression including images (still or moving), sound (talk, music, and noises), and written text that digital media share with, for example, film and television, but also, and more importantly, the fact that these elements share one common digital code which has all kinds of economic and legal implications. Think of the ease with which computer games can be (illegally) modified, copied, and distributed without any loss of quality.[22] The second characteristic of digital media, *virtuality*, traditionally refers to immersive experiences provided by new forms of simulation technology (think of virtual reality), as well as to metaphorical spaces created by communication networks (think of the space which comes into being when you're talking on the telephone). But, as Michiel de Lange argues, these descriptions were mostly "founded on two ontologies that were mutually exclusive, the *real* and the *virtual*. Much current (mobile) media research questions this separation. Mobile phone 'virtualities' are embedded in 'real life'. Inversely, 'real life' is encapsulated in 'virtual' communication practices" (de Lange 2010, 165). "Virtual reality" has increasingly become "real virtuality".[23] An example of this is the online game *I'd Hide You* by the Brighton (UK) based artist group Blast Theory. In *I'd Hide You*, players see the world through the eyes of a group of illuminated live runners as they roam the city streets trying to film each other, while at the same time challenging their friends online.[24] Due to a third characteristic, *interactivity* (or *participation*), digital media afford different levels of engagement. Next to "cognitive interactivity" (or "interpretative participation") – digital media also share this with other media – users can intervene in a meaningful way within the representation itself. According to Salen and Zimmerman, this intervention can assume two different forms. The first one they call "explicit interactivity: or participation with designed choices and procedures". The second form is "beyond-the-object-interactivity: or participation within the culture of the object" (Salen and Zimmerman 2004, 60; cf. Raessens 2005). We can think, for example, of the co-construction of online games in fan cultures or WEB 2.0 applications which enable their users to co-shape websites. In his contribution to this volume, Frans Mäyrä adds to this debate by zooming in on the casual kinds of play and engagement. An example of the fourth characteristic, *connectivity*, is Facebook, the largest social network site worldwide which now claims to have more than one billion active subscribers. "Due to its make-up, Facebook can be seen both as a site for individual entertainment, and as a tool for maintaining and building communities" (Timmermans 2010, 189).

The concept of play, as elaborated by Huizinga, is a very useful starting point for the analysis of the media experience. Our media and play experiences have many common characteristics. Or, to put it differently, digital media afford users new opportunities to play. To show how the medium-specificity of digital media opens up particular possibilities for play, we have to take into account the six elements of play we distinguished in the section on play (cf. Raessens 2012).

The first element, *expression of human freedom*, can be subdivided in three parts: freedom to play, freedom to make decisions while you are playing, and freedom towards the world (cf. Cermak-Sassenrath 2010, 129-53). What is striking when we take a closer look at how this kind of freedom takes shape in actual media use, is that freedom and force are not as diametrically opposed as Huizinga claims, as we have argued above when discussing the ambiguities in Huizinga's analysis. The freedom to play becomes visible in the player's decision to do so. But when you are forced to play to make a living – as we see in the example of the Chinese gold farmers – play and work, as well as freedom and force, become entangled in the most curious of ways.[25] In relation to mobile phones, this freedom to play is described by Michiel de Lange as "play on, with and through the mobile" (de Lange 2010; see also Rich Ling's chapter in this volume). Play *on* the mobile means that a mobile phone can be used as a platform to play games, anytime and anywhere; while play *with* the mobile means that mobile phone devices have certain properties that elicit play. For example, playing with the mobile phone's camera, in a game called "photo war" with girls competing against boys to get as many opponents as possible in one sharply focused mobile phone photograph (Jarkievich et al. 2008; de Lange 2010, 191). An example of play *through* the mobile would be playful communication. For instance, the use of text messages (SMS): "A text message is less direct and often more playful in character by making creative use of language and smileys" (de Lange 2010, 209).

The freedom to make meaningful decisions refers to the interactive or participatory nature of digital media. As Huizinga states, play is a "free *activity*" (our italics). An example of the rise of participatory culture is the transition from WEB 1.0 to WEB 2.0. Instead of a few producers of media content sending it out to the masses by limited television or radio channels, WEB 2.0 turns anyone with access to the web into a potential content-provider who can report on specific, idiosyncratic topics to a targeted audience. We should realize, however, that media users are only to a certain degree "in control", as we will discuss later on in relation to the rules of play. Leopoldina Fortunati even suggests in her contribution to this volume that ludic culture might be used as a new control mechanism.

To play, finally, also means that you are free from the constraints of the outside world, it goes beyond profane seriousness as we referred to earlier. The claim that play should have "its aim in itself" (Huizinga 1955, 28) seems difficult to maintain in today's gaming culture where items from Massively Multiplayer Online Role-Playing Games (MMORPGs) are being traded on a large scale at online auction and shopping websites such as eBay, and where serious games seem to employ play for educational purposes. But, according to Hector Rodriguez, this is not necessarily the case. Playing serious games can, not only be used "as a vehicle to maximize the 'effectiveness' of teaching", but it can also be used to illuminate "the fundamental nature of the subject being taught. Philosophical games should not, for instance, be merely treated as efficient techniques to make philosophy more appealing or entertaining to students; the act of playing can become a genuine medium of scholarly inquiry into the roots of philosophical activity" (cf. Rodriquez 2006). This means that in serious games, such as *Food Force* and *Darfur is Dying*, profane and sacred seriousness are not mutually exclusive beforehand as claimed by some critics (see Joost Raessens' chapter in this volume).[26]

The second element, *pretending* (not meant), refers to (digital) media use and/or understanding as doing *as if*, or, the double character of media. Like play, "our media culture consists of the acceptance of the 'as-if-ness' of the world" (Silverstone 1999, 59). And in our media culture, too, "we know when we are playing and when we are not" (ibid., 66). The reason for this is twofold. In the first place, it is related to what Jay David Bolter and Richard Grusin call "the two logics of remediation". Even when (digital) media obey the logic of transparent immediacy – which means that it is the medium's purpose to disappear – think of "the promise of immediacy through the flexibility and liveness of the web's networked communication" (Bolter and Grusin 1999, 197) – they, at the same time, obey the logic of hypermediacy. This means that the user is constantly reminded or brought back into contact with the interface (and its constructedness), in the case of the web the filling of the screen with windows, each with a variety of multimedia applications (ibid., 196-210). Media users are, in principle, in a position to realize that the reality they are facing "is just mediated". It is the explicit goal of media education to make media users more aware of the ways in which media try to mask their own constructedness (for example, their own ideological presuppositions) in order to come across as spontaneous and transparent presentations of so-called "reality". In the second place there is a historical argument. According to Gianni Vattimo, the proliferation of digital media today "makes it increasingly difficult to conceive of a *single* reality. It may be that in the world of the mass media a 'prophecy' of Nietzsche's is fulfilled: in the end the true world becomes a fable" (1992, 7). Media realities are just versions of the way the world works, but never the one and only objective reality.

To analyze the *pleasures* (and/or displeasures) of digital media use, the third element, we have to take into account the medium-specific relationships between production, media texts and reception. Consequently, we have to focus on two questions: "how pleasure is generated in the relationship between the rules and scripts developed by producers and how they are experienced and engaged with by users" (Kerr et al. 2006, 64). The suggestion by advertising and marketing campaigns that digital media can offer more fun and pleasure than traditional media seems untenable to us.[27] We do claim that digital media can offer a wide diversity of complex pleasures – dependent on the particular users and contexts – that are partly the same (for example, the pleasure of narrative), partly more intensive (for example, the pleasure of immersion), and partly different from what traditional media have to offer. Specific for digital media are those displeasures and pleasures that are related to interactivity, including computer game addiction, boredom, or frustration ("World Wide Wait"), and the feeling of being in and out of control, the tension of winning or losing, of succeeding or failing, as well as those pleasures that can be experienced by submitting and confirming to the rules, including negotiating or resisting these rules. According to Aphra Kerr, Julian Kücklich, and Pat Brereton, play is "a key concept for understanding the interaction of users with new media" and "the unique pleasure experienced when [the pleasures of] control, immersion and performance are combined" (ibid., 69-70). Players experience the pleasure of immersion, for example, while performing their skills (e.g.

playing Dance Dance Revolution)[28] or while they modify the original goals of the designers by playing with the rules of the system, for example teaching Sony's robot dog AIBO how to dance, as we will discuss later on.

The fourth element, *specific limits of time and space*, seems to be subjected to great pressure in this time of ubiquitous computing. It is, on the contrary, the illimitability of the mobile phone for example that seems to be the defining and at the same time the liberating and the restraining characteristic of today's media culture: "At its introduction it was praised as the ultimate device in terms of mobile communication, the freedom to move and staying 'logged in' at the same time, but it also forced us into a culture of constant reachability, reciprocity in terms of answering phone calls and text messages and an 'always on' mentality" (Timmermans 2010, 134). This does not mean, however, that digital media would not have a separate time and place: "The media have the capacity, indeed they entirely depend upon that capacity, to engage an audience within spaces and times that are distinguished – marked off – from the otherwise relentless confusions of everyday life. There is a threshold to be crossed each time we participate in the process of mediation" (Silverstone 1999, 61). This is evident, for example, when we focus on security issues. Digital media users can, as players do, try out or test or experiment with new identities, something that does not need to have real-life consequences (see the chapter by Jeroen Jansz in this volume). "Both surprises and security. The challenge of the new within the bounds of the familiar. Risks managed. Games, in their endless, electronic recurrence, that, unlike in life, we never really lose" (ibid., 61). The limits also come to the fore at moments when a user wants to continue (the magic cycle), but is forced, by external reasons, to stop using the medium.

The *rules of play*, the fifth element, can either be accepted or played with both on the individual micro level and on the macro level of the media system. On the one hand, digital media require users to submit to their rules. Within specific limits, there is freedom for the user to play. Individual users give what Stuart Hall called "preferred readings" (or in this case preferred play) of a media text, while they explore and/or select one of the many preprogrammed system-internal possibilities of a digital media system (Hall 1996, 128-138). In both cases users play according to the rules. On the other hand, users can play with these rules in – more or less – subversive ways. Here, users are involved in "oppositional readings" of media texts, and, on a macro level try to change the relationship between media producers, distributors and consumers. An example of this is the participatory culture that has been established around online games such as *World of Warcraft*. We are witnessing here again, within certain limits, a disintegration of the traditional distinction between the consumer and the producer. Players become, for example, active participants in the process of *World of Warcraft*'s creation and evolution (cf. Glas 2013). And referring to the aforementioned codification of digital culture, all software-based products can be modified and adapted to the personal needs of a user: "A Microsoft Xbox becomes a Linux computer. Nintendo's GameBoy gets turned into a musical instrument, and Sony's robot dog AIBO learns how to dance" (Schäfer 2011, 12). These examples of playful product modifications are exemplary of the important changes that have taken place in today's cultural industries. But we have to keep in mind that, within a globalizing economy, the basic rule of "industrial temporal objects" (a Stiegelerian term used by Patrick Crogan in this volume) like *World of Warcraft* is that in order to play the game, players – even when they have become "prosumers" – need to buy the game, pay a monthly subscription fee to play it and, on top of that, have to pay for the creative cultural modifications resulting from (sometimes their own) active player participation. So we need to be careful. The concept of participatory culture is in danger of overstating the importance of Do-It-Yourself counterculture, as discussed in the chapter of Valerie Frissen in this volume. As Henry Jenkins phrases it: "Allowing consumers to interact with media under controlled circumstances is one thing; allowing them to participate in the production and distribution of cultural goods – on their own terms – is something else altogether" (Jenkins 2006, 133).[29] This sense of "being-played" is what Michiel de Lange calls play *by* the mobile: "We are not univocal masters over our information and communication technologies. Mobile media also impose their logics on us in a dialectic between freedom and force" (2010, 215).

The sixth element, *order*, is related to the formation of social groupings. A good example of a WEB 2.0 application that creates a community-based temporary order is the so-called green blog. In line with Félix Guattari's analysis of a *post-media age* "in which the media will be re-appropriated by a multitude of subject-groups capable of directing its resingularisation" (2000, 61), people from all over the globe gather online in their struggle for a cleaner environment. The decentralized nature of the Internet "lends itself particularly well to grassroots activism. Disenfranchised segments of society who are fighting against environmental injustices in their communities no longer need to deal with intermediaries in the form of the mainstream mass media and established publishing routes" (Timmermans 2010, 164). These "green blogs" are engaged in forms of "*playful* social resistance and "a *light* dealing with matters that were formerly often seen as 'abstract', 'incomprehensive', or 'too big' for individuals" (ibid., 166-7).[30] Green blogs enrich so to say – like play does – (profane) reality with a layer of (sacred) seriousness.

This example of playful social resistance makes clear that media can be used as part of a political battlefield (*agôn*), as we discussed earlier in relation to Roger Caillois' typology of play. But depending on the specific type of play that is chosen, the world can also be presented as a performance (*mimicry*), a place where chance rules (*alea*) or where people strive for kicks (*ilinx*). In the domain of mobile media, we can provide the following examples. We already referred to the practice of "photo wars" as an example of mobile *agôn* where "girls [compete] against boys to get as many opponents as possible sharply in one mobile phone photograph" (de Lange 2010, 191). The fact that many people in Asia place high value on lucky telephone numbers in the hope that this brings them fortune is a good example of mobile *alea* (ibid., 195). An example of mobile *mimicry* is "stage-phoning": "the presence of the mobile can be used to inform the audience that this is a person with a life, a person of the mobile world" (Plant 2003, 49). Finally, users of iPods dwelling in their own privatized sound "bubble" can be considered a good case in point of mobile *ilinx* (de Lange 2010, 164, 200).

Approaching digital media as playful practices enables us to conceptualize them in terms of the four ambiguities we discerned in the section on play. The first ambiguity refers to the "as-if-ness" character of media; *reality and appearance* are not strictly separated, but are interrelated in meaningful ways. Digital media, at least in principle, afford users the opportunity to become (more or less) aware of the constructedness of their media experiences. This implies a second ambiguity, that of *freedom versus force*. As is the case with play, we are able to reflect on the rules as "just play rules" always open for modifications, both on a basic micro level (the individual user that interacts with a media text and/or technology) and on a macro level (changes in the relationships between media producers, distributors and consumers). There is a dialectic relationship between freedom and force: we can play and are "being-played" (cf. players who suffer from game addiction) at the same time. The third ambiguity is that of *determination versus change*. Each medium pretends to be the final phase of a long-lasting development, think of the Web's claim for immediacy based on its flexible and live network communication possibilities, and the mobile phone's claim to realize the desire for ideal communication (cf. de Vries 2012). But, as history shows, many if not most of these claims are being outdated by the arrival and claims of newer media. The liveness of the WEB, for example, is "a refashioned version of the liveness of broadcast television" (Bolter and Grusin 1999, 197). The fourth ambiguity, *individuality versus collectivity*, deals with the identity of individual media in today's media landscape. This landscape can be characterized by concepts such as "convergence" which represents "an ongoing process or series of intersections between different media systems" (Jenkins 2006, 282) or "remediation" which is "the representation of one medium in another" (Bolter and Grusin 1999, 45). We just need to think of the web's claim to represent or absorb all other media. However, because all the current media – consoles, computers, as well as mobile phones – have play applications and can be used as play devices, they lose a bit of their presumed individual identity and all become part of and play a role in the collective playful media landscape. A mobile phone, for example, has developed over time from a strict communications tool into a multimedia computer you can play on, play with, and play through as we have seen. Moreover, the converging multimedia landscape also provides extremely fruitful soil for crossmedia games and virals, as well as for online game worlds that combine, in various (re)combinations, *agôn*, *mimicry*, *alea*, and *ilinx*, such as *World of Warcraft* and *Second Life*.

Playful identities

Now that we have explored the characteristics and ambiguities of play and "playful media", we would like to explain how this relates to personal and cultural identity. The claim we will defend in this section is that the playful technologies, which have substantially invaded our lives in recent decades, have a profound impact on the construction of our identity. In order to defend our claim, we start with some general remarks on identity and its construction.

The word "identity" has its etymological roots in the Latin concept *identitas*, which in turn is derived from the Latin word "*idem*" referring to "the same". Indeed, the "I" remains the same during my lifetime as far as this word refers to my *numerical unity*: x=x. I am identical to myself and to no one else. It is reasonable to expect that I will still be the same person tomorrow as I am today, and will not, for example, awake as my neighbor. Obviously, this does not mean that we do not change. After all, during our lifetime both our body and our mental life undergo substantial transformations. Due to biological growth and renewal (almost all of the cells in our body are gradually replaced by new ones), our learning processes, new experiences and, finally, decay, our identity changes from birth to death. However, when we talk about *personal identity,* we usually do not refer to some unchangeable entity,[31] but rather to a particular kind of *spatial and temporal continuity*.

Spatial continuity lies in the fact that the elements from which the physical and psychic identity are constructed do not form a loose conglomerate, but rather constitute an internal nexus, in which the parts and the whole are closely connected. This is evident for the physical dimension of our existence, where the various body parts – cells, tissues, organs, limbs, etc. – are integrated into a functional whole. But our embodied thoughts, actions, social roles and desires are also part of a functional and meaningful whole. Of course, this integration is never complete. Human identity consists of many heterogeneous elements that are often more in conflict than not. Moreover, our life shows all kinds of dissociative states, such as (day)dreaming, religious or sexual ecstasy, immersion in a movie or a (computer) game, highway hypnosis, intoxication by alcohol and other drugs, symptoms of bodily and mental disintegration, and so on. When the functional or meaningful nexus is largely or completely destroyed (for example in case of dissociative identity disorders), disintegration or even a total loss of the person's identity may be the result.

Although we change all the time during our lives, the temporal continuity lies in the fact that our bodily and mental changes mostly take place gradually. One does not become an adolescent, adult, or graybeard overnight. And the same counts for our personal relationships, social roles, professions, etc. Memory and anticipation play a crucial role with regard to temporal continuity because they constitute permanence in time.[32] Also in this case, the continuity is never complete; it is characterized by interruptions (sleep) and gaps (forgetting). This is also with regard to the temporal nexus, sometimes radical discontinuities – for example, the loss of memory in the case of dementia, the loss of a limb, a transgender operation, a disruptive addiction, or a radical religious or political conversion – may result in fundamental changes or even total distortion of the temporal (bodily and mental) identity.

Much of what has been said about personal identity also counts for *cultural identity*. A culture or subculture also shows a certain unity of the constituting parts and at the same time can involve interruptions. A Calvinist culture or a hip-hop subculture, to mention two examples, are not only characterized by a particular worldview, but also find expression in the lifestyle of their members, the way they dress, their musical taste, the way they organize their social relations, among other things. In addition, cultures also show temporal continuity. Calvinism and hip-hop enjoy a particular history, which is expressed in collective memories. Moreover, they entail specific aims and ideals that guide future behavior. Just as in the case of personal identity, the spatial and temporal continuity of cultural identities is never complete, but shows all kinds of dissociations and interruptions. And like individual persons, cultures are characterized by a lifespan that ranges from birth to death, and in between they change and influence each other continuously.

A third and crucial aspect of the human identity – next to its numerical unity and spatio-temporal continuity – concerns its *reflexive* character. We came across the notion of reflexivity already in the section on play, when we discussed the double existence that characterizes human play. Reflexivity consists of "the turning-back of the experience of the individual upon himself" (Mead 1934, 134), or, in other words, the ability to "experience our experiencing" (Plessner 1975, 364). In the context of identity, we encounter this reflexive dimension when we pose the question for whom the spatial and temporal continuity characteristic of personal and cultural identity arises. Although other people can ascribe a personal or cultural identity for us (which obviously can have a great influence on the way we experience our selves), we ourselves are the ones who actually finally *experience* our personal and cultural identity. Reflexivity denotes self-awareness, self-reflection, having a self-image. We express ourselves in daily conversations, the way we dress, our lifestyle, and so on, and also experience how others describe or treat us, but what is crucial for our identity is whether we recognize ourselves in these (re)presentations. Whether someone identifies with being female, with Islam, or hip-hop culture (or possibly all three) is not only always, and somewhat arbitrary, determined by physical characteristics, actions, habits, preferences or beliefs, but it also depends on whether this person regards and recognizes themselves as such.[33]

In sum, our personal and cultural identity is not a self-contained and unchanging entity, somewhere hidden in the depths of our "inner self" or "national spirit", but it is reflexively constructed in a social world with the aid of various expressions. According to the hermeneutic philosopher Paul Ricoeur, among these expressions (life) stories play a prominent and even crucial role. This is understandable, as life stories are particularly suitable to express the spatial and temporal continuity of our identity. In a series of publications Ricoeur has developed this insight into a full-fledged theory of *narrative identity* (Ricoeur 1985; 1991a; 1991b; 1992). His starting point is the insight that "Answering the question 'Who?' [...] implies the narration of a life story" (Ricoeur 1985, 335). It is only in the stories we tell others and ourselves about our own lives and about other people's lives (real or fictional) that we are able to adequately articulate our own selves, and only by identifying ourselves with these stories does our own identity come into being. Thus the narrative for Ricoeur is not only a suitable metaphor for human identity, but it is also preeminently the *medium* we use to give our identity form. We might even say that for Ricoeur our identity is contained in our life story.

At first sight, Ricoeur's narrative model offers a good starting point for a theory of *ludic* identity construction. When seen from the perspective of Huizinga's *Homo ludens*, literature entirely belongs to the sphere of play. Huizinga writes in his chapter dedicated to the relationship of play and poetry: "All poetry is born of play: the sacred play of worship, the festive play of courtship, the martial play of the contest, the disputatious play of braggadocio, mockery and invective, the nimble play of wit and readiness" (1955, 129; cf. Raessens 2009, 88). After enumerating the six characteristics of play again that we discussed in the section on play (expression of freedom, as if character, tension and joy, specific time-space limits, rule-governed, creation of order), he even states: "Now it can hardly be denied that these qualities are also proper to poetic creation. In fact, the definition we have just given of play might serve as a definition of poetry" (Huizinga 1955, 132). Actually, in a civilization that becomes increasingly serious, poetry even is play's last haven of refuge: "Civilization as a whole becomes more serious – law and war, commerce, technics and science lose touch with play; and even ritual, once the field *par excellence* for its expression, seems to share the process of dissociation. Finally only poetry remains as the stronghold of living and noble play" (ibid., 134).

How then do stories, in Ricoeur's account, contribute to our identity construction?[34] Ricoeur's starting point is that (life) stories are not pre-given and static, but attain form through our actions and our narrative reflection on them. According to Ricoeur, we can distinguish in this process a threefold *mimesis*. The first level, referred to as *mimesis*$_1$, is connected with the narrative prefiguration of our daily life. In Ricoeur's view this lies in the practical knowledge that guides our actions. We experience our dealings with our fellow human beings in terms of meaning: we distinguish motives and interests, we set standards and ascribe values, and we attempt to realize certain ideals in life. Therefore, in a certain sense, our actions already contain an implicit narrative. Our life is an unremitting "quest of narrative" (Ricoeur 1991a).

Ricoeur designates the expression of the experienced prenarrative coherence in explicit narratives as *mimesis*$_2$. He describes this second stage in narrative construction of our identity in dramaturgical terms, derived from Aristotle's analysis of tragedy in his *Poetics*. According to Aristotle, the notion of the plot (*muthos*) is central for the expression of a series of mutually connected and motivated actions (1984, 2321). For Ricoeur, the plot (in the French original he uses the phrase *mise en intrigue*) can be understood as "a synthesis of the heterogeneous" (1992, 141). The plot unites the heterogeneous elements that make up a story – events, such as actions and happenings, and existents, such as settings and characters (cf. Chatman 1978). The Aristotelian plot can be regarded as a complete whole. It is a whole because all the elements within the plot are linked and there are no elements unrelated to the plot. In the plot, every element has meaning in light of the whole. It is complete because together the elements provide the narrative closure. In a nutshell, a plot endows a heterogeneous whole with a proper beginning, middle, and end (Aristotle 1984, 2321). Ricoeur refers to the meaningful configuration created by the plot as the *concordance*. However, this concordance is no static state, but is continuously jeopardized by *discordance*, such as reversals of fortune that threaten the meaningful closure of the narrative. A story is the representation of an act that is continuously frustrated by more or less unforeseen settings and happenings. This makes the story a dynamic whole. For that reason Ricoeur calls the story a *discordant concordance* (Ricoeur 1992, 141).

The third step in the construction of narrative identity, *mimesis*$_3$, consists of the reflective application of the narrative configuration on the self, resulting in our identification with the characters of the story. In Ricoeur's view, the unity of the story – the plot – is closely connected to the characters figuring in it. Telling a story is telling who does what and why. In the story, we witness how a character develops. Just like with the plot, characters show a dialectic of concordance and discordance. Contingent events receive a narrative coherence through the character. From a psychoanalytical point of view, we could say that the identification that characterizes *mimesis*$_3$, consists in the internalization of the object of desire – the state of concordance obtained by the characters in the story. This is not a simple imitation, but an appropriation or assimilation that results in a change in the identity of the identifying person (cf. Freud 1953, IV, 156). However, just as in the case of the plot, the stability obtained by this internalization is rather shaky, as it is continuously confronted by the return of the heterogeneous, which threatens the concordance of our identity. A sublime love, a personal vendetta, a crisis or addiction, illness and death – such happenings give our life story unexpected turns, and keep challenging the concordance of the character and ultimately may destroy it. Until its very end, the (life) story is characterized by this dialectic between concordance and discordance.

In our view, Ricoeur's theory of narrative identity offers an excellent starting point for a better understanding of identity construction in the age of ludic technologies, as it illuminates the mediated character of human identity construction. However, we have to adapt his theory in order to apply it to popular media culture. Ricoeur's notion of narrative is limited for several reasons.

First, in his work he almost *exclusively pays attention to the art of the novel.* Because of his focus on works belonging to *serious* high culture, he seems to be blind to the often more *frivolous* ways identity construction takes place in everyday gossip and life stories, and in popular fictional accounts, such as movies, soaps, comics, and narrative computer games, among others.

Second, his focus on mostly classical novels also results in a greater emphasis on elements of form that are connected with these kinds of novels, such as *monomediality, linearity,* and *closure.* The kinds of narratives we come across in the aforementioned genres in popular culture often have a different form; they are, for example, *multimedial, interactive, connected,* and *open-ended.* If Ricoeur's presupposition that the structure of the explicit narrative (*mimesis*$_2$) is crucial for identity construction, since it influences the identity that results from its identification with this explicit narrative (*mimesis*$_3$), is true, then narratives that have a different aesthetic form might also result in *different forms of identity.* This is exactly what Ajit Maan argues in *Internarrative identity* where she investigates identity construction in (post)modernist and non-Western novels that are characterized by open endings or multiple openings and/or endings (Maan 1999). And the same can be argued with regard to self-constructions in the domain of narration in digital media. Even when they remain within the domain of *mimicry,* they may result in other "identity effects" than classical narratives.

Third, Ricoeur's focus on *mimicry* is another limitation of his theory. As we noted earlier in this section, for Huizinga, "poetry" encloses much more than narrative accounts of human action. It also includes the play of worship, of courtship, and contests, among other things. Connecting to the division that Caillois has derived from Huizinga, we claim that an adequate *theory of ludic identity construction* should not only take into account the ways classical and contemporary postmodern and/or popular narratives (understood as *mimicry*) constitute and structure our identity, but it should also address the ways other ludic expressions, characterized by *alea, agôn,* and *ilinx,* constitute and structure our identity.

This intended extension of Ricoeur's theory of narrative identity construction is necessary, in our opinion, because in our present culture self-construction via classical narratives is increasingly being complemented, and partly replaced by self-constructions using all kinds of "ludic" digital technologies, as analyzed in the previous section. We realize the need for such a theory, when we consider the fact that identity construction in today's present culture has become rather problematic. This has to do with what sociologist Anthony Giddens has conceptualized as *reflexive uncertainty* (Giddens 1991). Because of the complexity, flexibility and changeability of our present life, and the abundance of media of expression, it has become a real challenge to master the overwhelming discordant character of our lives. Because of their abundance and heterogeneity, as well as their rapid development, present information and communication technologies contribute substantially to this uncertainty. However – and here again we touch upon one of the aforementioned ambiguities of new media – it at the same time also offers us the tools to cope with it.[35] The construction of identity has become a highly reflexive project, and communication media are at the very heart of this reflexivity. Mainly for this reason, we maintain that the playfulness of modern communication technologies is key to understanding contemporary identity construction.

In order to express our adaptation of Ricoeur's theory of narrative identity to include the ludic categories of *alea, agôn*, and *illinx*, we will replace in the following the base term *mimesis* (which is strongly connected to *mimicry*) with *play*. This enables us to reformulate Ricoeur's mimetic triad with $Play_1$, $Play_2$, and $Play_3$. In the remainder of this section we discuss the new insights that this extension of Ricoeur's theory provides in the nature of identity construction in today's culture.

$Play_1$ refers to the ludic prefiguration of our everyday life. This moment consists of our lived experience of the natural and human world as playful. For example, when we notice the play of light or waves or when we watch the play of animals or children. Whereas some of our playful experiences are connected to *mimicry*, as in the example of watching playing children or when we are enjoying a good joke or a funny story told by a friend or colleague, *alea, agôn*, and *illinx* can also offer many playful moments in our daily lives. The dimension of *alea* ranges from counting-out rhymes like children do, to betting who will win the soccer finals with your colleagues. Especially the experience of *agôn* pervades almost every aspect of our lives. The car driver who tries to take the lead when the traffic light turns green, is no less "infected" by the spirit of *agôn* than the student or employee who wants to show that he is the best of his class or the office, the heaviest drinker in the pub, or the most successful womanizer. In sports as well as transportation, to mention only a few domains, the experience of *illinx* always plays a role, ranging from the kicks we derive from speed, from running and cycling, to car racing, high speed trains and aviation or the kicks we get from dangerous activities such as mountain climbing or bungee jumping.

However, in addition to these more or less traditional manifestations of play, the ubiquitous presence of digital media in our everyday life is implicitly prefiguring our experiences and actions in a playful way. For instance, this is happening when our daily tasks, travels, and communications are being aestheticized by fancy apps on our smartphones and tablets, or when we are invited to rank a sportsman, actress, or politician on a fan site, share casual tweets or mobile camera images during our daily interactions with others, or get engaged in the erotic play of seduction when exchanging text messages. In a world full of playful technologies, we are constantly seduced to become more receptive to the ludic dimensions of life. In a world of ludic technologies we are invited to experience this kind of playful movements backward and forward that renew themselves in constant repetition everywhere in the world (Gadamer 1986).

While $Play_1$ refers to the more implicit understanding of our everyday life as playful, and our more or less casual playing (*paidia*), $Play_2$ refers to the expression of this experienced ludic nexus in more or less explicitly articulated and regulated games (*ludus*). In addition to the already overwhelming amount of games in the offline world, the new media afford an abundance of online ludic activities in all four dimensions of play. We can think of online worlds such as *Second Life* and Massively Multiplayer Online Role-Playing Games (MMORPGs), such as *World of Warcraft* and *Star Wars: The Old Republic,* which combine *mimicry*, *agôn*, and *illinx*, and gambling websites and dating sites (*alea*). We already introduced several examples in the previous section and the contributions to this volume discuss many other examples in detail. We will restrict ourselves here to a discussion of just a few other examples in order to explicate some of the most striking tendencies that shape identity construction.

One of the notable characteristics of playful technologies is that they tend to mix the different types of play into one total play experience. In our view this characteristic is connected to the fact that the computer is a "universal machine" that thanks to its digital code is not only able to mix most of our media (hence its multimedial character discussed in the previous section), but can also simulate all possible machines and practices. The computer, tablet, or smartphone easily becomes the "focal device" of our life (cf. Borgmann 1984). Michiel de Lange provides an example of mixed *mimicry, alea* and *agôn* in this volume by analyzing the practice of *gengsi* in urban Indonesia. *Gengsi* refers to the display of prestige or status, originally in terms of family standing and class, but currently used in terms of a self-defined "being modern". De Lange describes how mobile technologies have become an indispensable part of *gengsi*. Possession and proper use of the right device "rubs off its prestigious qualities on the individual bearer". The presentation of mobile phones in highly modern shopping malls, dressing up the phone with danglers and sleeves or leather pockets, the use of "beautiful numbers", and the mastery of the proper use of language and form in communicative practices, all add up to the theatrical and competitive presentation of prestige. Thus mobile phones become the props of actors who present themselves as successful masters of an ever-evolving modern urban life. Furthermore, the use of "beautiful numbers" may be seen as *alea*. Many Indonesians place a high value on these lucky telephone numbers, which they believe will bring good fortune. Of course, they recognize this is only superstition, but still...[36]

Another remarkable characteristic of playful technologies is that they tend to merge completely with everyday life. This takes place, for instance, when we play *FarmVille* with our Facebook contacts and playfully shape and color our social relations. Another good example is also provided by Sybille Lammes in her chapter in this volume, in which she describes the use of mapping applications (like Google Maps) and locative media services (like *Layar* and *Foursquare*) that are becoming increasingly popular nowadays. By using these applications in an explicitly playful way, we are able to experience and give meaning to our everyday lives in a postmodern urban culture, a point also made by Adriana de Souza e Silva and Jordan Frith in this volume. Lammes argues that our playful use of these media transforms us from mere readers of maps to "cartographers on tour". By using these media we create *social maps* that reveal our whereabouts, actions, and the relationships and interests we share with others. Mapping applications and locative media are thus explicitly used to create social and spatial coherence in our everyday movements and actions. In other words, they help us "to navigate through life".

As already mentioned in the previous sections, in the world of playful technologies the strict division between profane seriousness and play gets blurred. All kinds of "serious business" obtain ludic dimensions. The domain of politics offers many examples. Although elections always had a competitive and interactive dimension, the use of online polls and tablets and smartphones as "second screens" during television debates between candidates reveals again how the playful dimension of politics can come to the fore. Without doubt, politics still is an activity in which decisions are made about "the necessities of life" and often even about life and death. The point here is rather that seriousness and play no longer exclude each other. The soldier who guides a drone to its destination resembles the computer player in an often somewhat uncanny way. In other cases, the ludification of politics may also make depressing political issues easier to "digest". A good illustration of this is given in Jeroen Timmermans' *Playing with paradoxes: Identity in the web era*. He describes playfulness as an explicit new feature of the strategy of social movements and political activists. A "green blog" like Treehugger playfully weaves "serious" environmental issues into a more frivolous lifestyle blog. Two features of playful conduct are particularly important in regard to these new forms of activism. First, playing as subversive and critical behavior, and second, play as non-seriousness, as a frivolous manner of raising environmental awareness. Therefore, a blog like Treehugger offers *Spielraum* that is both a platform for "light" critical reflection and a space for subversive action (Timmermans 2010, 148ff.).

In the third moment of the construction of ludic identity, *Play*$_3$, the player *understands* her/himself from the perspective of his expressions, reflectively internalizing their structure and content. Whereas in the case of (classical) narrative expressions, we identify ourselves with a logically structured plot or a causal chain of events, in the case of the ludic technologies, *multimediality*, *interactivity*, *virtuality*, and *connectivity* are inscribed in our identity. This is, of course, no passive determination by the medium (as technological determinists might think), but rather an active appropriation by the player, who might also play with these very structures themselves. Identities that result from the use of playful technologies will have a multimedial character. Whereas narrative identity mainly has a verbal character (although it is important not to forget that language can also evoke, for example, images and music), in ludic identity all inscriptions are multisensorial. Images, music, gestures, they all become part of the internalization. And, whereas in the case of narrative, the inscribed identity has the character of a causal chain of events, in the case of ludic identity the result is rather a play area (*Spielraum*), a space of possible actions. While the narrative, as Roland Barthes points out, "always speaks the language of fate" (1982), ludic technologies always embody freedom. In *Play*$_3$ the space of possible action that characterizes playful technologies is reflectively applied to the self. As Giddens' notion of "reflexive uncertainty" expresses, this experience is not always pleasant. In the movie *The Matrix Revolutions*, Neo succinctly expresses this key experience of late modernism: "Choice. The problem is choice". And whereas the models offered by classical narratives nestle themselves in our imagination, the "virtual reality" offered by ludic technologies easily turns out to be a real virtuality. The gamer who identifies himself with a character in *World of Warcraft* and plays for many hours in a row, experiences how the boundary between imagination and reality gets blurred. "The other" is already part of our narrative identity, because others always play an important role in our life stories, just as we do in theirs, which makes our identities rather a "tissue of stories" than an individual story (Ricoeur 1985, 356). However, in the case of ludic identity the other is a much more real aspect of our identity due to the interactive connectedness with others in social media. The stories and images of others become part of our Facebook pages in a very real and explicit sense.

Although the different types of play tend to merge in ludic technologies, their predominance may vary. The same applies to the resulting playful identities. Depending on the dominant category of play, postmodern identity displays four basic dimensions. The *competitive identity* dimension transforms everything from economic production and consumption to education, scientific research, and even love relationships, into a game with winners and losers. The *simulational identity* dimension expresses itself in theatrical performances rather than in (romantic) inwardness. This postmodern identity dimension finds its expression predominantly in the society of the spectacle (Debord 1967). The *aleatory dimension* highlights how people are "thrown" into certain conditions by birth or during life by a play of fate, in what Giddens calls "fateful moments" (Giddens 1991, 131; cf. de Mul 1994). At the same time it underlines how people may embrace a profound openness to the – fortunate or unfortunate – contingencies of life. For this type of identity the risk society is the "natural habitat". The *vertigo identity* dimension is characterized by thrill seeking. Perhaps here, we might think of the fatalistic, Dionysian behavior regarding the use of drugs or risky sexual behavior that characterizes many youth cultures (cf. Maffesoli 2000; 2004).

However, as is the case with the different types of ludic technologies, the four identity dimensions that characterize postmodern society often merge and connect in various playful ways. For example, in order to deal with life as an aleatory gamble, people may adopt strategies that correspond with one of the other play types. People may try to regain mastery over life's unpredictability by dragging *alea* into the domain of *agôn*[37], they may try to conceal certain conditions by living a life of *mimicry* pretense; or they may attempt to run away from it by escaping in *ilinx* thrill seeking. And the bodybuilder at the school of martial arts is often not only interested in competition with his peers, but may also like to show off his muscles in a public space, and/or may like to play with steroids.

In each of these intertwined dimensions the playful personae are confronted with ambiguities we described in our analysis of play and playful media. First, these playful personae are constantly oscillating between *reality* and *appearance*. They play their role, just pretending that they are identical to them, but at the same time their role-playing is utmost serious and as such becomes a reality *sui generis*. Moreover, the competitions they engage in are not "just play", but they have very profane real-life consequences. Second, playful identities constantly oscillate between *freedom* and *force*. They play with their contingency, but at the same time they cannot escape the factuality of these contingencies. They express themselves in freedom, but are constantly experiencing the constraints exercised upon them by the media that themselves are subject to the homogeneous global forces of the market economy. In the following chapters various examples of these forces will be discussed in more detail. And in a more radical sense than with previous generations, playful identities oscillate between *determinedness* and *change*. Although as playful personae they enjoy the possibility of constantly changing masks, they still feel the ever-lasting longing for rest in the hard core of their subjectivity. Finally, playful identities constantly oscillate between *individuality* and *collectivity*. In our playing they express their inmost subjectivity, but in doing so they constantly follow their mimetic desire to become someone else (Girard 1961). And above all, they embrace the game as whole-heartedly as the game embraces them.

Notes

1. See http://quod.lib.umich.edu/i/iij/11645653.0002.102?view=text;rgn=main.
2. Cf. Julian Dibbell, who claims that we are witnessing "the emergence of a curious new industrial revolution, driven by play as the first was driven by steam" (2006, 297).
3. An overview of the contents of these chapters is provided in separate introductions at the beginning of each of the three parts of this volume.
4. Part of the confusion surrounding the reception of *Homo ludens* is unfortunately due to poor translations. For example, the subtitle of the English translation (Boston: Beacon Press, 1955) – reads "a study of the play-element *in* culture" (our italics), which obviously is a mistranslation of the Dutch subtitle: "Proeve eener bepaling van het spel-element *der* cultuur" (our italics). Moreover, the English translation, based on the German edition published in Switzerland in 1944 and Huizinga's own English translation of the text, is somewhat abbreviated and does not always follow the Dutch original *ad verbum* (this is partly due to the fact that Huizinga rewrote some of the text after the outbreak of World War II). In this volume, we quote from the English edition, but in cases where it is incorrect or incomplete,

we offer our own translations of the Dutch original (1938), as it was reprinted in Huizinga's collected writings published in 1950.

5. Huizinga gives two slightly different formulations of play on pages 28 and 132. Throughout the book he gives further clarifications of the elements, to which we refer in our clarification of this definition.

6. In the English translation the Dutch phrase "niet gemeend" (literally: "not meant") is incorrectly translated as "not serious". For that reason we have replaced the incorrect English translation by the correct one.

7. "Examined more closely [...] the contrast between play and seriousness proves to be neither conclusive nor fixed. We can say: play is non-seriousness [niet-ernst]. But apart from the fact that this proposition tells us nothing about the positive qualities of play, it is extraordinarily easy to refute. As soon as we proceed from 'play is non-seriousness' [niet-ernst] to 'play is not serious' [niet ernstig], the contrast leaves us in the lurch – for some play can be very serious indeed" (ibid., 5).

8. Huizinga only refers to the concept of the magic circle four times in *Homo ludens*: twice as part of an enumeration of different sorts of playgrounds (10, 20) and twice in very general terms (77, 212). However, in Game Studies this concept has become a real buzzword, mostly in the wake of Salen and Zimmerman's *Rules of play* (2004). For a discussion of the reception history of the merits of this and alternative concepts (such as "magic node" and "puzzle piece"), see: Lammes (2008), Juul (2008), Nieuwdorp (2009), and Copier (2009).

9. Although the translation "fixed rules" for the Dutch "naar bepaalde regels" [according to certain rules] in Huizinga's definition of play is obviously not correct, at other places in the Dutch edition of *Homo ludens* which were not translated *ad verbum*, Huizinga explicitly claims that the rules of a game are "onwrikbaar" [irrefutable] and he adds: "The rules of a game cannot be denied. We can vary a game, but not modify it" ["De regels van een spel kunnen niet gelogenstraft worden. Het spel kan gevarieerd, maar niet gemodificeerd worden" (1950, 235)].

10. According to some critics, Huizinga's definition is universalist and essentialist in the sense that it pretends to cover the immense variety of play and games. However, in our view we should understand the six elements we have distinguished in Huizinga's definition of play not as a single characteristic, but rather as a set of criteria that together constitute a family resemblance in the Wittgensteinian sense. An activity belongs to the family of play when it satisfies at least several of these criteria. Wittgenstein uses the word "game" (*Spiel*) as an exemplary case in his argument against essentialism (1986, 31-2).

11. Caillois (2001, 11-36). *Paidia* and *ludus* are often understood to correspond with the English distinction between play and game.

12. Often, in playing and gaming we find combinations of the aforementioned categories. In soccer, for example, there is not only the obvious dimension

of competition, but *alea* plays an important role as well (coin toss, lucky shot), just like *mimicry* (players acting theatrically), and *ilinx* (both with the players and with the exalted fans). Moreover, soccer consists both of strictly rule-governed behavior as well as more spontaneous playful elements, such as, the personal style of an individual player. In addition, the four categories may become each other's object. When writing about contests and representation, Huizinga notes: "These two functions can unite in such a way that the game [spel] 'represents' a contest, or else becomes a contest for the best representation of something" (1955, 13). An example of the first is chess, which represents a battle, while an example of the second we can find already in pre-Socratic culture with the Dionysia festival in which tragedians competed with each other for the prize of the best tragedy.

13. "Technology, publicity and propaganda everywhere promote the competitive spirit and afford means of satisfying it on an unprecedented scale. Commercial competition does not, of course, belong to the immemorial sacred play-forms" (ibid., 199-200).
14. This expression is missing in the English translation. In the Dutch edition, the passage reads: "For a large part it concerned habits that were caused or stimulated by the technique of modern spiritual/mental communication, such as the need for banal entertainment, which is easy to satisfy but actually insatiable, the craving for rude sensation, and the diversion in the display of power." ["Het betrof voor een groot deel gewoonten die hetzij veroorzaakt of in de hand gewerkt worden door de techniek van het moderne geestelijk verkeer. Daaronder valt bijvoorbeeld de gemakkelijk bevredigde maar nooit verzadigde behoefte aan banale verstrooiing, de zucht tot grove sensatie, de lust aan massavertoon"] (Huizinga 1950, 237).
15. Cf. Gadamer's analysis of play, where he emphasizes: "All playing is a being-played" (2006, 106).
16. Every play (*Spiel*) is, at least potentially, a "presentation for an audience" (*Schauspiel*) (Gadamer 2006, 109). See also the chapter by Jeroen Timmermans in this volume.
17. This connects to the notion of identity as developed by symbolical interactionists such as Mead and Goffman (see for example Goffman 1959, 77-104). As de Lange explains: "Goffman's unit of analysis in observing impression management is the 'team': a group of people who assist each other in playing a role together and are bound together by ties of reciprocity. An individual too can be a team. He can be his own audience, or he can imagine an audience to be present" (2010, 59).
18. For a detailed analysis of the double character of aesthetic experience, see Jos de Mul, *Disavowal and representation* (1999, 173-92; cf. Mannoni 2003, 68-92).
19. Cf. Kücklich: "Play liquefies the meaning of signs; it breaks up the fixed relation between signifier and signified, thus allowing signs to take on new

meanings. This is probably also the reason why the metaphor of play has gained such prevalence in the post-modern discourse" (2004, 7-8).

20. See our remark on Wittgenstein's notion of "family resemblance" in note 10 (cf. Ryan 2001, 177).
21. Playful affordances can also not be actualized, think of the Chinese gold farmers who must work instead of having play opportunities. Stephenson reveals that the "Gold farmers are players hired to earn in-game currency. In the off-line world, these players often work in questionable working conditions for long hours at low pay [...] The in-game currency is then sold to other players" (2009, 598).
22. The focus on (the interpretation of) computer code is part of the emerging field of "critical code studies" in the humanities. However, Lev Manovich prefers the more general term "software studies". He writes: "In the end of the 20th century humans have added a fundamentally new dimension to their culture. This dimension is software in general, and application software for creating and accessing content in particular" (2008, 14).
23. Real virtuality "is a system in which reality itself (that is people's material/symbolic existence) is entirely captured, fully immersed in a virtual image setting, in the world of make-believe, in which appearances are not just on the screen through which experience is communicated, but they become the experience [...] The *space of flows* and *timeless time* are the material foundations of a new culture, i.e. the culture of real virtuality" (Castells 1996, 373, 375).
24. See www.blasttheory.co.uk/projects/id-hide-you.
25. In his article about the Chinese gold farmers, Julian Dibbell notices that the opposition of work and play is rather problematic in this case: "What would these young men do now with their precious few moments of free time? How would they amuse themselves? I followed them out of the room and was not surprised to see that some retired to their company dorm rooms for idle conversation while others sat in the break room watching television. But quite a few of them, it turned out – nearly half – headed straight to a nearby internet café to spend the evening doing exactly what their job had required them to do all day: play World of Warcraft. And this I was at a loss to account for" (2008, 84).
26. The term "serious games" "may easily be criticized for its literal meaning, which is an oxymoron: Games are inherently fun and not serious" (Ritterfeld, Cody, and Vorderer 2009, 3).
27. For example, see the television commercial "Restroom Encounter" for Sony's PlayStation Portable (PSP) that shows a man being so immersed in playing a game that he wets his pants while standing in front of a urinal www.youtube.com/watch?v=DWeHlfFKoYc.
28. See www.youtube.com/watch?v=0gh6hzs_7Kc.

29. Cf. van Dijck and Nieborg (2009, 871): "We need to carefully dismantle the claims of *Wikinomics*, 'We-Think' and *Convergence Culture* in order to better understand the kind of brave new worlds to which we are being welcomed".
30. The Dutch environmental weblog *new-energy.tv* has created such a playfully resistant movie clip featuring an actor impersonating the former US President George W. Bush addressing the nation on the subject of climate change. www.new-energy.tv/overig/opwarming_bush_spreekt_natie_toe.html.
31. Our conception of identity differs from the Christian-Cartesian tradition in which the self is understood as the eternal soul. Still, René Descartes, who defines the self as "a thing that thinks" (1968, 106), conceives of this thinking substance as an isolated, timeless, non-corporeal entity. Against this traditional conception, the skeptical tradition within empiricism, of which David Hume was the most important representative, denied the I or self any real substance. According to Hume, consciousness is nothing else than the continuous stream of perceptions and ideas: "I always stumble on some particular perception or other, of heat or cold, light or shade, love or hatred, pain or pleasure. I never can catch myself at any time without a perception, and never can observe anything but the perception. [...] The identity which we ascribe to the mind of man is only a fictitious one" (1956, 252, 259). Or, to use the words of Daniel Dennett, a temporary Humean skeptic, it is "a theorist's fiction" comparable with an *abstractum* such as "the center of gravity" of an object in physics, which "does not refer to any physical item in the world" (1992). Although we agree with this skeptic critique on the Christian-Cartesian conception of the self as a timeless substance, we believe that Hume and Dennett throw away the baby with the bathwater when they deny the self any real existence. Unlike the case of an entity, which does not have a subjective experience as its center of gravity, a person consciously experiences itself. In the passage quoted from Hume, for example, it seems to be undeniable that there is someone who claims to be unable to find himself behind the flow of consciousness. The problem seems to be that both Descartes and Hume seem to agree that the self, if it exists, must be a substance. Along with the phenomenologist and hermeneutical tradition, we hold that the ontological status of human identity is fundamentally distinguished from the ontological status of lifeless objects such as stones, because human beings exist in time (Heidegger 1996; Ricoeur 1992, 128). Existing does not simply mean that we are situated in time (after all, this is also true for a stone), but that our being has a fundamentally temporal character and that we have an awareness of our temporality. Although we always live in the present, unlike the stone, in our acting we are always oriented toward our future possibilities, and we are also always stamped by the possibilities we have realized in the past.
32. In the analytical philosophical tradition since Locke, this temporal continuity, and the implied role of memory, is also central in the theory of per-

sonal identity. In *An essay concerning human understanding* (1690), Locke maintains memory is determinate for our identity: "For, since consciousness always accompanies thinking, and it is that, which makes everyone to be what he calls self, and thereby distinguishes himself from all other thinking things, in this alone consists personal identity, i.e. the sameness of rational being: and as far as consciousness can be extended backwards to any past action or thought, so far reaches the identity of that person" (1975, 335).

33. A phenomenon such as transsexuality shows that the perceived and the experienced reality do not necessarily correspond. Moreover, conflicts with regard to the attribution of identity easily arise. For example, during the Bosnian War (1992-95), many Bosnian citizens who regarded themselves as secular were suddenly assigned a Muslim identity by some ethnic Serbs in Bosnia.
34. The following explanation of Ricoeur's theory of narrative identity is partly adapted from de Mul 2005.
35. In postmodern life, we are exposed everyday to a multiplicity of often-conflicting images and stories that reach us through many different media (Vattimo 1992). At the same time, the very same media offer us the tools to cope with this confusing environment and to interact smoothly with these real and imaginary worlds that are nowadays increasingly intertwined. Digital media enable us to playfully move back and forth between these worlds. This play sometimes resembles a play of fate – or what Caillois would label *alea*. Every new interaction may induce new explorations and new actions and may "open new windows". We no longer plan ahead, but shape our everyday actions by the accidental hunches brought to us through our mediated experiences. At other moments our mediated lived experience is more like a theatrical play, or *mimicry*. We use our imagination and our potential to act "as if" to play the complex game of modern life. When using our mobile phones, for instance, we continuously move between absence and presence and we do this without really reflecting on it (Gergen 2002). We are perfectly able to "remove" ourselves in an imaginary way from the present physical context and become involved in a virtual world that is not available to those around us. We imagine the role that the invisible other is playing at the other side and the settings in which this takes place. The people around us implicitly engage in this play by doing as if they do not take part at all, and at the same time by imagining what is happening in this intriguing play of two actors.
36. See note 18.
37. For instance, Sennett (1998) describes a shift in the late-modern work ethic in which unexpected events like a discharge from work are no longer seen as simply bad luck but understood as the result of one's own actions.

References

Aristotle. 1984. *Poetics*. In *The complete works of Aristotle in two volumes. The revised Oxford translation*, volume II: 2316-2340. Princeton, NJ: Princeton University Press.

Avedon, Elliott, and Brian Sutton-Smith. 1971. *The study of games*. New York: Wiley

Axelos, Kostas. 1964. *Vers la pensée planétaire. Le devenir-pensée du monde et le devenir-monde de la pensée*. Paris: Les Éditions de Minuit.

Barthes, Roland. 1982. Introduction to the structural analysis of narratives. In *Image, music, text*, 79-124. London: Fontana Paperbacks.

Bateson, Gregory. 1955. A theory of play and fantasy. In *Steps to an ecology of mind: Collected essays in anthropology, psychiatry, evolution, and epistemology*, ed. Gregory Bateson. New York: Ballantine.

—. 1977. Play and paradigm. In *Play. Anthropological perspectives*, ed. Michael A. Salter. New York: Ballantine.

Bauman, Zygmunt. 1995. *Life in fragments: Essays in postmodern morality*. Oxford: Blackwell Publishers.

Bolter, Jay and Grusin, Richard. 1999. *Remediation: Understanding new media*. Cambridge, MA: The MIT Press.

Borgmann, Albert. 1984. *Technology and the character of contemporary life*. Chicago, IL: The University of Chicago Press.

Caillois, Roger. 2001. *Man, play and games* [*Les jeux et les hommes*, 1958]. Urbana, IL: University of Illinois Press.

Castells, Manuel. 1996. *The information age: Economy, society and culture. Volume I: The rise of the network soci*ety. Oxford: Blackwell Publishers.

Cermak-Sassenrath, Daniel. 2010. *Interaktivität als Spiel. Neue Perspektiven auf den Alltag mit den Computer*. Bielefeld: Transcript.

Chatman, Seymour. 1978. *Story and discourse: Narrative structure in fiction and film*. Ithaca, NY: Cornell University Press.

Copier, Marinka. 2009. Challenging the magic circle: How online role-playing games are negotiated by everyday life. In *Digital material: Tracing new media in everyday life and technology*, eds. Marianne van den Boomen, Sybille Lammes, Ann-Sophie Lehmann, Joost Raessens, and Mirko Tobias Schäfer, 159-71. Amsterdam: Amsterdam University Press.

Debord, Guy. 1967. *La société du spectacle*. Paris: Buchet-Chastel.

Dennett, Daniel. 1992. The self as a center of narrative gravity. In *Self and consciousness*, eds. Frank Kessel, Pamela Cole and Dale Johnson, 275-88. Hillsdale, NJ: Erlbaum.

Descartes, René. 1968. *Discourse on method and the meditations*. [*Discours de la méthode: Suivi des méditations métaphysiques*, 1637] Harmondsworth: Penguin.

Dibbell, Julian. 2006. *Play money: Or, how I quit my day job and made millions trading virtual loot*. New York: Basic Books.

—. 2008. The Chinese game room. Play, productivity, and computing at their limits. *Artifact* 2 (2): 82-7.

Dijck, José van, and David Nieborg. 2009. Wikinomics and its discontents: A critical analysis of WEB 2.0 business manifestos. *New Media & Society* 11(5): 855-74.

Ehrmann, Jacques. 1968. *Homo ludens* revisited. *Yale French Studies* no. 41, Game, Play, Literature: 31-57.

Fink, Eugen. 1960. *Spiel als Weltsymbol*. Stuttgart: W. Kohlhammer.

—. 1968. The oasis of happiness: Toward an ontology of play. *Yale French Studies* no. 41, Game, Play, Literature: 19-30.

Freud, Sigmund. 1953. *The standard edition of the complete psychological works of Sigmund Freud.* London: Hogarth Press.

Fuchs, Mathias, Sonia Fizek, Paolo Ruffino, and Niklas Schrape, eds. 2014. *Rethinking gamification.* Lüneburg: Hybrid Publishing Lab.

Gadamer, Hans-Georg. 1986. *The relevance of the beautiful and other essays.* Cambridge, MA: Cambridge University Press.

—. 2006. *Truth and method.* London: Continuum.

Gergen, Kenneth. 2002. The challenge of the absent presence. In *Perpetual contact: Mobile communication, private talk, public performance.* eds. James Katz and Mark Aakhus, 227-41. Cambridge, MA: Cambridge University Press.

Giddens, Anthony. 1991. *Modernity and self-identity: Self and society in the late modern age.* Cambridge, UK: Polity Press.

Girard, René. 1961. *Mensonge romantique et vérité romanesque.* Paris: B. Grasset.

Glas, René. 2013. *Battlefields of negotiation. Control, agency, and ownership in World of Warcraft.* Amsterdam: Amsterdam University Press.

Goffman, Erving. 1959. *The presentation of self in everyday life.* Garden City, NY: Doubleday.

Guattari, Félix. 2000. *The three ecologies* [*Les trois écologies,* 1989]. London: The Athlone Press.

Hall, Stuart. 1996. Encoding/decoding. *Culture, media, language. Working papers in cultural studies,* eds. Stuart Hall, Dorothy Hobson, Andrew Lowe and Paul Willis, 128-38. London: Hutchinson.

Heidegger, Martin. 1996. *Being and time* [*Sein und Zeit,* 1927]. Albany, NY: State University of New York Press.

Huhtamo, Erkki. 2005. Slots of fun, slots of trouble: An archaeology of arcade gaming. In *Handbook of computer game studies,* eds. Joost Raessens and Jeffrey Goldstein, 3-21. Cambridge, MA: The MIT Press.

Huizinga, Johan. 1950. *Homo ludens. Proeve eener bepaling van het spel-element der cultuur* [1938]. *Verzamelde Werken,* Volume 5. Haarlem: H.D. Tjeenk Willink & Zoon N.V.

—. 1955. *Homo ludens: A study of the play-element in culture* [*Homo ludens. Proeve eener bepaling van het spel-element der cultuur,* 1938]. Boston, MA: Beacon Press.

Hume, David. 1956. *A treatise of human nature* [1740]. London: Everyman's Library.

Jarkievich, Petra, My Frankhammar, and Ylva Fernaeus. 2008. In the hands of children: Exploring the use of mobile phone functionality in casual play settings. In *Proceedings of the 10th international conference on human computer interaction with mobile devices and services.* Amsterdam, the Netherlands: ACM.

Jenkins, Henry. 2006. *Convergence culture. Where old and new media collide.* New York: New York University Press.

Jin, Dal Yong. 2012. *Hallyu 2.0*: The new Korean wave in the creative industry. *International Institute Journal* 2(1): 3-6.

Juul, Jesper. 2008. The magic circle and the puzzle piece. 2008. Conference proceedings of the philosophy of computer games, eds. Stephan Grünzel, Michael Liebe, and Dieter Mersch, 56-67. Potsdam: Universität Potsdam.

Kerr, Aphra, Julian Kücklich, and Pat Brereton. 2006. New media – new pleasures? *International Journal of Cultural Studies* 9(1): 63-82.

Kücklich, Julian. 2004. Play and playability as key concepts in new media studies. www.playability.de/Play.pdf.

Lammes, Sybille. 2008. Spatial regimes of the digital playground: Cultural functions of spatial practices in computer games. *Space and Culture* 11(3): 260-72.

Lange, Michiel de. 2009. From always on to always there: Locative media as playful technologies. In *Digital cityscapes: Merging digital and urban playspaces*, eds. Adriana de Souza e Silva and Daniel M. Sutko, 55-70. New York: Peter Lang.

—. 2010. *Moving circles: Mobile media and playful identities*. PhD dissertation. Rotterdam: Erasmus University.

Leonard, Robert. 2010. *Von Neumann, Morgenstern, and the creation of game theory: From chess to social science, 1900-1960*. Cambridge University Press Cambridge, MA: Cambridge University Press.

Locke, John. 1975. *An essay concerning human understanding* [1690]. Oxford: Clarendon Press.

Maan, Ajit. 1999. *Internarrative identity*. Lanham, MD: University Press of America.

Maffesoli, Michel. 2000. *L'instant éternel: Le retour du tragique dans les sociétés postmodernes*. Paris: Denoel.

—. 2004. The return of the tragic in postmodern societies. *New Literary History* 35 (1): 133-49.

Mannoni, Octave. 2003. I know well, but all the same... In *Perversion and the social relation*, eds. Molly Rothenberg, Dennis Foster, and Slavoj Žižek. Durham, NC: Duke University Press.

Manovich, Lev. 2008. *Software takes command*. http://softwarestudies.com/softbook/manovich_softbook_11_20_2008.pdf.

Mäyrä, Frans. 2008. *An introduction to game studies. Games in culture*. London: Sage Publications.

Mead, George. 1934. *Mind, self, and society: From the standpoint of a social behaviorist*. Chicago, IL: University of Chicago Press.

Minnema, Lourens. 1998. Play and (post)modern culture. An essay on changes in the scientific interest in the phenomenon of play. *Cultural Dynamics* 10 (1): 21-47.

Mitchell, Elmer and Bernard Mason. 1934. *The theory of play*. New York: A.S. Barnes and Company, Inc.

Montola, Markus. 2005. Exploring the edge of the magic circle. Defining pervasive games. Copenhagen: DAC 2005 Conference.

Motte, Warren. 2009. Playing in earnest. *New Literary History* 40 (1): 25-42.

Mul, Jos de. 1994. *Toeval*. Inaugural address Erasmus University Rotterdam: Rotterdamse Filosofische Studies.

—. 1999. *Romantic desire in (post)modern art and philosophy*. Albany, NY: State University of New York Press.

—. 2003. Digitally mediated (dis)embodiment. Plessner's concept of eccentric positionality explained for cyborgs. *Information, Communication & Society* 6 (2): 247-65.

—. 2004. *The tragedy of finitude: Dilthey's hermeneutics of life*. New Haven, CN: Yale University Press.

—. 2005. The game of life: Narrative and ludic identity formation in computer games. In *Handbook of computer game studies*, eds. Joost Raessens and Jeffrey Goldstein, 251-66. Cambridge, MA: The MIT Press.

—. 2009. Awesome technologies. *Art and social change. International Yearbook of Aesthetics. Volume 13*, ed. Curtis Carter. Milwaukee, WI: Marquette University.

Neitzel, Britta, and Rolf Nohr, eds. 2006. *Das Spiel mit dem Medium. Partizipation-Immersion-Interaktion*. Marburg: Schüren.

Neumann, John von, and Oskar Morgenstern. 1944. *Theory of games and economic behavior*. Princeton: Princeton University Press.

Nieuwdorp, Eva. 2009. The pervasive interface: Tracing the magic circle. In *Digital material: Tracing new media in everyday life and technology*, eds. Marianne van den Boomen, Sybille Lammes, Ann-Sophie Lehmann, Joost Raessens, and Mirko Tobias Schäfer. 199-208. Amsterdam: Amsterdam University Press.

Norman, Donald. 1988. *The psychology of everyday things.* New York: Basic Books.
Oudemans, Theodorus, and André Lardinois.1987. *Tragic ambiguity: Anthropology, philosophy and Sophocles' Antigone.* Leiden: E.J. Brill.
Plant, Sadie. 2003. *On the mobile: The effects of mobile telephones on social and individual life.* http://classes.dma.ucla.edu/Winter03/104/docs/splant.pdf.
Plessner, Helmuth. 1975. *Die Stufen des Organischen und der Mensch. Einleitung in die philosophische Anthropologie.* Frankfurt: Suhrkamp.
Raessens, Joost. 2005. Computer games as participatory media culture. In *Handbook of computer game studies*, eds. Joost Raessens and Jeffrey Goldstein, 373-88. Cambridge, MA: The MIT Press.
—. 2006. Playful identities, or the ludification of culture. *Games and Culture. A Journal of Interactive Media* 1 (1): 52-7.
—. 2009. *Homo ludens 2.0. Metropolis M* 5: 85-8. http://metropolism.com/magazine/2009-no5/homo-ludens-2.0/english.
—. 2012. *Homo ludens 2.0. The ludic turn in media theory.* Inaugural address Utrecht University. http://igitur-archive.library.uu.nl/oratie/2012-0918-200528/1045628_Oratie_Raessens_ENG.pdf.
—. 2014. The ludification of culture. In *Rethinking gamification*, eds. Mathias Fuchs, Sonia Fizek, Paolo Ruffino, and Niklas Schrape, 91-114. Lüneburg: Hybrid Publishing Lab.
—, and Jeffrey Goldstein, eds. 2005. *Handbook of computer game studies.* Cambridge, MA: The MIT Press.
Ricoeur, Paul. 1985. *Temps et récit III: Le temps raconté.* Paris: Editions du Seuil.
—. 1991a. Narrative identity. In *On Paul Ricoeur. Narrative and interpretation*, ed. David Wood, 188-199. London: Routledge.
—. 1991b. Life in the quest of narrative. In *On Paul Ricoeur. Narrative and interpretation*, ed. David Wood, 20-33. London: Routledge.
—. 1992. *Oneself as another* [*Soi-même comme un autre,* 1990] Chicago, IL: University of Chicago Press.
Rideout, Victoria, Ulla Foehr, and Donald Roberts. 2010. *Generation m^2. Media in the lives of 8- to 18-year-olds.* Menlo Park, CA: Kaiser Family Foundation.
Rifkin, Jeremy. 2000. *The age of access: The new culture of hypercapitalism, Where all of life is a paid-for experience.* New York: Jeremy P. Tarcher/Putnam.
Ritterfeld, Ute, Michael Cody, and Peter Vorderer. 2009. *Serious games. Mechanisms and effects.* London: Routledge.
Rodriquez, Hector. 2006. The playful and the serious: An approximation to Huizinga's *Homo ludens. Game Studies. The international journal of computer game research* 6, no. 1.
Ryan, Marie-Laure. 2001. *Narrative as virtual reality. Immersion and interactivity in literature and electronic media.* Baltimore, MD: The Johns Hopkins University Press.
Salen, Katie, and Eric Zimmerman. 2004. *Rules of play. Game design fundamentals.* Cambridge, MA: The MIT Press.
Schäfer, Mirko. 2011. *Bastard culture! How user participation transforms cultural production.* Amsterdam: Amsterdam University Press.
Schiller, Friedrich. 2004. *On the aesthetic education of man* [*Über die ästhetische Erziehung des Menschen*, 1795/1796]. Mineola, NY: Dover Publications.
Sennett, Richard. 1998. *The corrosion of character: The personal consequences of work in the new capitalism.* New York: Norton.
Sigmund, Karl. 1993. *Games of life: Explorations in ecology, evolution, and behaviour.* Oxford: Oxford University Press.

Silverstone, Roger. 1999. *Why study the media?* London/Thousand Oaks, CA: London: Sage Publications.

Spengler, Oswald. 1991. *The decline of the West* [*Der Untergang des Abendlandes*, 1918-1923]. Oxford: Oxford University Press.

Sprague, Rosamond Kent, ed. 2001. *The older Sophists: A complete translation by several hands of the fragments in Die Fragmente der Vorsokratiker, edited by Diels-Kranz. With a new edition of Antiphon and of Euthydemus.* Indianapolis, IN: Hackett Publishers.

Stephenson, Rebecca. 2009. "Doing something that matters": Children's culture video games, and the politics of representation. In *Media/cultural studies: Critical approaches*, eds. Rhonda Hammer and Douglas Kellner. New York: Peter Lang.

Sutton-Smith, Brian. 1997. *The ambiguity of play.* Cambridge, MA: Harvard University Press.

Thimm, Caja, ed. 2010. *Das Spiel: Muster Und Metapher der Mediengeselsschaft.* Wiesbaden: VS Verlag für Sozialwissenschaften.

Timmermans, Jeroen. 2010. *Playing with paradoxes: Identity in the web era.* PhD dissertation. Rotterdam: Erasmus University.

Turner, Victor. 1969. *The ritual process: Structure and anti-structure.* Chicago, IL: Aldine Pub. Co.

—. 1982. *From ritual to theatre: The human seriousness of play.* Performance Studies Series. Volume I. New York City: Performing Arts Journal Publications.

Van Gennep, Arnold. 1960. *The rites of passage.* London: Routledge & Paul.

Vattimo, Gianni. 1992. *The transparent society.* Cambridge, UK: Polity Press.

Vries, Imar de. 2012. *Tantalisingly close. An archaeology of communication desires in discourses of mobile wireless media.* Amsterdam: Amsterdam University Press.

Wittgenstein, Ludwig. 1986. *Philosophical investigations* [*Philosophische Untersuchungen*, 1953]. Oxford: Basil Blackwell.

Part I

Play

Introduction to Part I

Valerie Frissen, Sybille Lammes, Michiel de Lange, Jos de Mul & Joost Raessens

This part of the book sheds light on how play, as it was described in the introductory chapter, actually manifests itself in present-day culture. The authors in this section examine different contemporary expressions of playfulness, varying from people engaging with games, Do-It-Yourself (DIY) computer technologies, or social networks. The contributions in this section substantiate our earlier claims that play is also culturally determined and has different functions in different cultural settings. So we may speak of the current ludification of culture as evidence that play is mutable, and that what this transformation entails is versatile in scope and character. Together these chapters demonstrate that play has become part and parcel of today's media culture. They also underline Huizinga's point that play *is* culture, although this does not mean that play can be defined in universal terms.

Social psychologist Kenneth J. Gergen opens this part of the book with a contribution in which he seeks to define what the ludification of contemporary culture means for our social identities. In *Playland: Technology, self, and cultural transformation,* he argues that play has become omnipresent and far less 'hidden' in specific social spaces. He conceives of our present social landscape as a playland and examines what this playland means for our social identities. According to Gergen, culture has become play. This is an important alteration of Huizinga's adage that play is culture.

Cultural sociologist Stef Aupers is also interested in how the ludic shift has transformed our social identity, but he approaches his investigation from a spiritual angle. As a game scholar and sociologist he is interested in how role-playing games can generate new spaces to perform contemporary spirituality. In *Spiritual play: Encountering the sacred in World of Warcraft,* Aupers argues, based on interviews with players, that Massively Multiplayer Online Role-playing Games (MMORPGs) offer a ritual space (a 'magic circle') for certain players to explore spirituality as part of their identity. The game *World of Warcraft* opens up possibilities for an alternative spiritual playground at a time when Western society is said to be thoroughly secularized. Aupers' chapter thus points to a connection between processes of secularization, re-enchantment, and contemporary play.

In his contribution, entitled *Playful computer interaction,* new media scholar Daniel Cermak-Sassenrath analyzes the connections between ludification and the affordances of digital technologies. He looks at play in contemporary culture as intrinsically related to digital technology and argues that computer technology in itself invites playful interactive conduct.

Menno Deen, Ben Schouten, and Tilde Bekker view games in a similar way in *Playful identity in game design and open-ended play.* They argue that games can have a strong influence on shaping our identities in playful ways because of their interactive qualities. Although some designs have a greater potential for this than others, they maintain that games can trigger people to create their identities in new fluid and playful ways.

Game scholar René Glas takes us to the realm of social network services as a playful platform for identity construction. In *Breaking reality: Exploring pervasive cheating in Foursquare*, he argues that location-based apps like *Foursquare* show how game-like elements are permeating every nook and cranny of today's culture. He pushes the envelope a bit further when he argues that cheating should be included as an important dimension of play to understand contemporary ludic culture and the changeability of play. Cheating points to how the rules of playing are never pre-given and are always bent and broken in an ongoing process of negotiation between different stakeholders. This again supports our claim that play's influence in shaping our identities is far from universal. The practice of cheating demonstrates that meanings, including the rules of the game, are constantly renegotiated and modified.

The last chapter of this section also focuses on the relation between play and modification. In *Playing with bits and bytes: The savage mind in the digital age*, social communication scientist Valerie Frissen considers the relation between DIY culture and play. She asserts that playing with technologies has always been an important driving force for technological transformation, but that this is even more the case in the digital era. She argues that we have witnessed the rise of a bottom-up DIY movement that is crucial to the shaping of digital technologies. The playful mindset that drives this is similar to what Lévi-Strauss called the 'savage mind'. But while structural anthropologist Lévi-Strauss situated the savage mind as a mode of thinking firmly outside of Western culture, Frissen discerns a return to it. Tinkering with digital technologies should be seen as a specific dimension of our playful culture and be understood to drive technological transformation.

2. Playland: Technology, self, and cultural transformation

Kenneth J. Gergen

I opened the morning newspaper and was greeted with a front-page, banner-size headline and photo touting the dramatic win of the city's professional football team. The account of the game bristled with excitement. In smaller print at the top of the page was a report on the winning ways of a local basketball team. It was only in the nether regions of the page that I discovered reports on national and international affairs, all properly phrased in the monochromatic tones of impartial objectivity. Struck by the attention given to matters of sport, I became curious about the general content of the newspaper. Interestingly, the sports section proved to be substantially larger than the first and principal news section. The entertainment section also exceeded the size of the financial section. If I subtracted the advertisements from the pages, the portion of the paper devoted to playful matters was more than twice that of what one might call serious news. A few months later, an editorial in the paper opined that the name of this winning football team "is not only a piece of the town's; it also conjures its essence".

This composition of the news may be commonplace in today's world. But it was not so in the world of my youth, nor it seems in previous history. I have long appreciated the work of Johan Huizinga, whose classic study of play explored its deep historical roots (Huizinga 1938). Yet in making his case for a primordial basis of play, Huizinga primarily focused on somewhat rarefied cultural patterns, such as symbolic rituals, rites, and ceremonies. He also found play elements in battles, legal proceedings, and the arts. Play seemed omnipresent, but secreted into the interstices of cultural life. My curiosity increased. Is a shift in cultural investments now in motion, and if so, is it an important one? Has play truly become the dominant cultural activity? A scanning of statistics on professional sports in the US was provocative. Just in professional baseball, the gross revenues reached a record-breaking $7 billion in 2010. As the Major League Baseball Commissioner Bud Selig announced: "This is the golden era for the sport, and given the (weak) economy this may be the most remarkable year we ever had. We're at numbers nobody ever thought possible". Paid attendance at the baseball games was over 73 million. For professional football, revenue was almost $8 billion, with 26 million paid fans and a television audience of at least 500 times this number. Then there are the basketball and hockey seasons to consider, among others. When we consider the professional sports industry altogether, the gross revenues reached $414 billion in 2010. This figure exceeded the total revenues of the combined governments of Costa Rica, India, Lithuania, Bolivia, Chile, Finland, Morocco, Romania, and Pakistan during the same period.

Yet, I asked, is this interest restricted only to professional sports? Unlikely, since there is also an enormous interest in the US in college football and basketball. And in terms of games, we also find lively interest in golf, tennis, auto racing, and soccer (with independent cable channels exclusively dedicated to sports for continuous viewing), along with skiing, casino gambling, horse racing, gymnastics, skateboarding, online gambling, televised poker, and fantasy sports. Nor do I believe that investments in these activities begin to capture the extent of the gaming activity.

However, the most dramatic developments are surely in the virtual world. A homely example is telling, important as well, in suggesting that the shift toward play is not solely an American phenomenon. When visiting friends in the Netherlands, I was told that they were to entertain their grandchildren for the afternoon. Later, the two boys, three and five, burst into the house, and without more than a nodding acknowledgement of the assembled gathering raced upstairs. Their destination: the two computers in the upstairs office. Within minutes they were both absorbed in online games. They were allowed to remain so for an hour, at which point their cruel grandmother pulled the switch. It was human time again.

Such an event will scarcely be surprising to any young parents. At the present time, there are over 200 million websites related to computer games. One of these sites, chosen at random, offers 1,500 games, and has over 70,000 participants. Another offers games in over 40 languages. Players on the massively multiplayer online games such as those featured on Facebook and other social network sites, cater to over one hundred million participants a year. The participants spend over $1 billion annually. Video games, such as those sold for Xbox, garner far greater income. Revenues of video games now exceed 20 billion dollars internationally. Over 20 million players have spent 17 billion hours on Xbox Live, which is more than 2 hours for every person on the planet. Another 40 million users have registered PlayStation Network accounts.[1]

Among the major characteristics of games, as defined by scholars such as Huizinga (1938) and Caillois (1958), are that they are non-income producing activities, non-obligatory, and circumscribed in space and time. Further, as they see it, there are rules of participation (either explicit or implicit). Participation, in turn, evokes an alternative reality, a reality that has the capacity to enchant or captivate. Defined in this way, it is legitimate to include within the cultural shift toward play, the shared indulgences in TV drama, movies, YouTube, online porn, pop music, romance novels, and social networks. On Facebook alone there are almost 650 million visitors in any given month, twice the size of the US population. As Timmermans (2010) and Pearson (2009) both describe, online activities are essentially playful. To summarize, it is useful to distinguish among three forms of play:

1. *Social play*, which constitutes the vast majority of communication taking place in social networks. Communication in this context not only creates a playful ambience, but it is also a place where people communicate about both spectator and participatory play thereby enhancing their significance.
2. *Spectator play*, which constitutes the vast range of spectator pleasures, as facilitated by television, movies, magazines, newspapers, and radio.
3. *Competitive play*, which consists of an enormous range of participatory competitive games including both electronic and organic games.

Let us characterize the general shift in cultural investments of attention, time, and money in these three spheres in terms of *Playland*, denoting a world in which the dominant cultural activities – along with the meaning these activities give to life – center on participation, either vicarious or active, in the forms of play.[2] If this lens of viewing cultural life carries legitimacy, numerous questions follow. How are we to understand, for one, the historical shift in cultural interests and investments? Further, putting aside the redistribution of time and money, what are the implications for cultural life? What becomes of relationships – with friends, family, community, and the like? Are there implications for the ways in which we come to understand ourselves, and the meaning of our lives? If the cultural implications are unsettling, what then follows in terms of action – both personal and in terms of policy?

In what follows I wish to open discussion on two domains of impact: the self and human relationships. The issues are both complex and profound, and in a circumscribed context such as the present, I can do little more than scan the terrain. My hope is that such a perambulating treatment can invite the kind of dialogue that will facilitate broad illumination and new forms of action.

The emergence of playland

Let us first consider possible reasons for what appears to be a major shift in cultural life. That play should come into such significance could be viewed as highly surprising. In much of Western culture, and in the US in particular, the number of hours devoted to work has steadily increased. Indeed, in the US there is currently an attempt to establish a "Take Back Your Time" day, a day devoted to restoring leisure hours to the American worker. The manifesto of this movement points out, "an epidemic of over-work, over-scheduling and time famine now threatens our health, our families and relationships, our communities and our environment". Clearly, then, there are significant changes in the ways in which leisure hours are filled (and as we shall see, various venues of play have infiltrated the spaces of work). One might also reason that with increments in daily work demands, there might be a compensatory desire for play. By indulging in play – vicarious or active – tedium can be relieved and cares forgotten. I think now of the pivotal place that pachinko parlors play in Japanese life, for many years one of the few forms of escapist entertainment available to compensate for the rigors of a six-day workweek.

One cannot rule out the compensatory explanation for the burgeoning of play in contemporary culture. However, in my view, the chief driver of this cultural shift is the coalition of technology and business. Technological developments open new and highly lucrative business opportunities, and as these businesses profit, they also spawn new developments in technology. The impact of these twin forces must also be seen against a cultural and historical background. On the one hand, following Huizinga, there is a rich history of engagement in forms of play, and most relevant, forms of play that are contentious, in which protagonists are embattled or striving to achieve dominance over the other. As Roland Barthes (1972) has also pointed out, there is a strong tendency in this context to conflate issues of good and evil with winning and losing. One "fights" to achieve some end, and this end is often saturated with moral value. In effect, games possess enormous potential as resources for generating morally saturated drama. As Goldstein (1994) has pointed out, the blueprint for such drama is typically established within the first three years of life when one is developmentally prepared for rapt engagement in forms of play

Now, one may also argue that the number and range of real-life dramas is such that adults have little need for contrived games. In traditional terms, participation in play is considered essential to childhood development. However it is also thought that as one matures, play should be largely replaced by the active responsibilities of adult life. And these responsibilities – succeeding at work, achieving happiness in one's relationships, raising children, attending to issues of public importance, and the like – are loaded with dramatic significance. In each case, there is success and failure, progress and decline, winning and losing, and good vs. evil. Why should these not fill the available space of dramatic engagement? Why should such dramas not demand our full attention? In my view, the answer lies in the ambiguities of the narrative forms that make drama possible.

To expand, in an earlier work (Gergen 1992) I proposed that the communication technologies of today facilitate the development of multiple meaning making clusters, that is, groups of people that co-construct visions of the real and the good. There are increasing numbers of groups – professional, political, religious, and so on – that make claims to "having it right" about the world. Simultaneously, these same technologies – now in the form of everyday media – saturate us with these various visions. For example, the question of how to invest one's savings has dramatic implications. One can win or lose, and the outcomes will make a significant difference to the quality of one's future life. Yet there are now scores of books treating the topic of investment, along with daily radio and television commentators, and stockbrokers and money managers who also provide informed decisions. The problem, however, is that there is substantial disagreement among these sources and opinions shift daily. In effect, there is no rational decision. Almost every choice is wise and unwise, promising and perilous. When life is a random walk, drama dissolves. The same can be said regarding many policy issues from the local to the national level. With the legion of talking heads thriving on contention, there is little clarity on whether we are progressing or regressing at any point. In the crush of disagreement, drama is dissipated.

Given this context, let us return to the twin impact of technology and business on the growth of playland culture. Consider the following: Technologies allow unlimited, low-cost participation in high-drama activities. Because of their relatively low costs, technologies such as television, the Internet, radio, cell phones, and video games are available to large and ever increasing sectors of the population. The most widely televised event in the history of the world was the 2010 World Cup. The Xbox game *Call of Duty: Black Ops*, was issued late in 2010, and now one will encounter at any time of day or night over a million fellow players – from all corners of the earth.

Technologies intensify the dramatic narratives (e.g. video games, professional sports). With the development of microscopic microchip technology, it became possible to increase dramatically the dimensions of electronic communication. The video industry is increasingly capable of generating realistic, life and death, sound-accompanied games. The dramatic engagement is intense. With the increasingly popular Nintendo Wii games, indeed the entire body is engaged in the game.

In terms of narrative meaning, most games offer increased opportunities for heroism. Games are typically about winning or losing, and accolades are reserved for those who win. Even those computer and cell phone games that demand hours of effort to increase one's skill offer the player steady increments in esteem for the self (Gee 2005). Further, even in the case of spectator games, fans take vicarious pleasure in identifying with the star players. Stories of "the stars" are everyday fare in newspapers and magazines, essentially generating the new cultural myths about men and women who are enshrined in the increasingly numerous "halls of fame". In playland, games offer continuous opportunities for homely heroism. Either vicariously or interactively, one becomes the major protagonist in the story.

In the narratives of daily life, play is highly consequential. Marriage and career success may hang in the balance, or on the national sphere, the games of war can bring death to hundreds of thousands. In playland, however, the drama is intense, but the consequences are minimal. In most video and computer games, one is continuously losing, but the loss serves only as an invitation to improve with the next turn. In the *Call of Duty: Black Ops* game, a player may be killed a dozen times within a five-minute period, only to rise each time from his prone position to resume the attack. One plays without the public shame of losing and without bodily risk.

As many commentators have argued, with the growth of modernism, and particularly with the spread of the scientific worldview, our capacities for enchantment have dwindled.[3] The prizing of objectivity – with its value-free approach to the world – demolishes drama. If there is nothing to value – no goals, no ideals, no transcendent virtues – then what is worth doing? The religions of the world continue to be sources of enchantment. However, in comparison to the enchanting power of games in the world today, religions are a poor competitor. There is a further catalyst to incitement in the form of social interchange. As games enchant, so do they invite conversation. And within conversation the game deepens in significance. It is an event about which people care, and thus, for example, the enormous crowds so dramatically engaged in the outcome of the World Cup.

We now turn to the question of cultural impact. Other than the obvious redistribution of time and money, in what ways is cultural life being transformed? How shall we regard these transformations, and are there ways in which we might alter our current behavior, from the forms of daily relations to national or global policy? If, as Huizinga proposes, "culture arises in the form of play," how are we to understand the emerging culture and how best to go on? These are scarcely new issues. For example, there has been considerable discussion about the impact of games on the brain and our capacities for thought,[4] along with discussions of the educational potential of electronic games.[5] More expansively, Dyer-Witheford and de Peuter (2009) have linked the gaming ethos to the development of global capitalism, corporate exploitation, and militarism. These are issues of such complexity that traditional attempts to establish clear answers are no longer relevant. Rather, the desire for certainty must be replaced by reflective and sustained dialogue. And such dialogue itself will alter the complexion of the phenomenon, since the phenomenon is not separate from the dialogue that sustains it. In this spirit, I wish to touch on only two issues: the self and relationships.

The playing self

In earlier writings I have been concerned with what may be viewed as an erosion in the Western conception of the self-contained individual, that is, the agent whose mental resources serve (or *should* serve) as an originary and efficacious source of action.[6] In part, I have traced this erosion to the increasingly dominant technologies of communication and the enormous increments in the relational processes they invite. As one's sense of self is increasingly absorbed into networks of relationships, I proposed, the sense of oneself as inherently social replaces that of self as an independent actor. In effect, the emerging technologies of the 20th century slowly subvert the legacy of the Enlightenment. In large measure I have welcomed this transformation in the conception of the person. Joining in the ongoing critique of individualism, I have argued that the vision of the world as composed of bounded or singular entities is inimical to human and planetary well-being. When relational conceptions of human action are fully extended, they invite consideration and appreciation not only of global interdependency, but environmental care.

It is within this context that I confront the emergence of playland culture. For it seems in this case one might well be inclined to see in this movement an extension and intensification of the agentive "I". After all, don't most games celebrate the individual strategist, who aspires to success, who vanquishes, who trains, plans, schemes, and carries out tactics for the purpose of winning? In the process of playing, personal agency is reified; individualism is refurbished. I am not denying this possibility, and particular gaming structures certainly lend themselves to such a result as opposed to others. Yet, in general, I am not persuaded. To explore further, I distinguished earlier between three forms of cultural play: social play, spectator play, and competitive games. It is at this first level that my case for the erosion of the bounded self and the emergence of the relational being was largely based. E-mail, Facebook, cell phones, Twitter, and the like, all immerse us in the co-constituting process of communication. In each case, our actions are inherently "for the other" and without the other they lose meaning altogether. To abandon all one's interlocutors would eviscerate one's sense of self. Yet as Timmermans (2010) notes, the playful ambience of social network communication also generates a conflict between the impetus toward authenticity on the one hand, and artifice on the other. Paradoxically, one may simultaneously be both sincere and insincere. There is erosion in the obdurate sense of self, but not eradication.[7]

On the level of spectator pleasure, there is also a diminishment of the agentive "I", but the route is different. In this case the dominant pleasure is taken from the process of identification. While the concept of identification may be defined in many ways, I use the term to refer to one's fantasized narrative of self as the other. Because the drama of games is one typically featuring success vs. failure, or good vs. evil, the potential for games to generate heroic figures is great. Movie and television dramas yield a similar panoply of "gods" and "goddesses". As a spectator, the identification process may remain wholly in fantasy, for example, as one excitedly watches a favorite athlete perform on TV. However, such fantasies are also made more concrete in one's activities, such as purchasing apparel fetishizing the hero, or adopting the hero's mannerisms, gestures, or ways of life. The important point here is that when immersed in spectator pleasures, one brackets the sense of authentic being. One lives temporarily as the other.

In both these conditions we find an alteration in consciousness from the traditional sense of "I am the master of my actions" to an "out-of-self' condition. In the former case, "I am an actor for others", and in the latter case, "I experience as the other". Let us view these as subtle movements in terms of the emergence of a *second-order self*, a sense of self as other than self, or a state of para-being. At the more extreme level, the sense of a second-order self may characterize one's condition under the influence of a drug, or when sexually aroused, romantically infatuated, or fully immersed in a stage role. One is fully compelled by activities that might be described as ego-alien. These activities spin out spontaneously, without deliberate thought, and often surprisingly. Now consider the case of competitive games: I watch as my 12-year-old grandson sits in a special chair designed for online gamers. The chair approximates the seat of a jet fighter pilot or a motorcycle driver. His eyes are focused on the television screen, his hands grip precision controls for the events unfolding before him, and the booming sounds of these clamorous events bellow from nearby speakers embedded in the chair. This is not "John, my studious grandson, with polite manners, tidy room, and careful eating habits". That John is absent, now replaced by a rampant killer, emptying bullets into dark figures lurking in shadows or leaping from doorways, casting grenades across barriers to see bodies torn to bits, moving ever forward to slay as many combatants as possible. If uninterrupted, he may remain in that state for hours. He will sometimes come home early from school because he knows he will have the house to himself and can return to the enchantment of the killing fields. This is the intoxication of a second-order self. All the frustrations, ambiguities, complexities – along with the possible emptiness – of daily life are removed. One lives a thrilling life as a hero with a thousand lives, but returns to the dinner table as a dutiful son. To be sure, this is a dramatized account, and it is clearly more relevant to some forms of participatory games than others.[8] But virtually all competitive games invite one – for whatever amount of time – to become a second-order self.

The increased presence of a second-order being might not be so important in itself. To play tennis or golf once or twice a week probably has little impact on the remainder of one's life. One plays, and when play is terminated, one returns to their everyday demands. However, a closer examination is required. There is now substantial literature in the human sciences – from the late 19th century to the present – proposing that one of the major influences on human development is imitative role-playing. In their play, children imitate their parents, for example, and in playing out these roles their personalities and potentials are shaped. In the same way, when entering a profession, one imitates the behavior of other professionals and attempts to play the role of the professional. What is crucial for the present chapter, is that out of these processes one's sense of self emerges. In being the other, one becomes oneself. Play gives way to a sense of obdurate identity. Consider again the emergence of the playland. As we have seen, activities in social networks invite playing with one's identity, while spectator activities invite the imitation of players and with competitive games, one indeed does become a player. With sustained and intense participation in playland, the conditions are in place for the emergence of a genuine *playing self.* The sense of a second-order self gives way to a first order: "I am a player".[9]

As the sense of the playing self gains strength, the states of the authentic being become more suspect. To create a series of avatars or game identities poses little problem; with chameleon-like ease, one can fit congenially into the game at hand. Within the individualist tradition, with its emphasis on authenticity, one might *choose* to play, depending on the outcome; however, as a playing self, one is simply playing without asking questions about the outcome. In the same way, one does not choose to breathe the air; breathing is just the nature of life. For the playing self, one who calculates daily decisions about work and play may seem naïve. To fancy oneself as a rational agent, carefully weighing the outcomes of a decision is foolish: "Don't you know it's all a game?" Richard Rorty's (1989) conception of the *liberal ironist* is apt. For Rorty, propositions about the real and the good are without rational foundations. And yet those realizing this is so may nevertheless commit themselves to the good of relieving suffering in the world. They commit themselves to liberal causes understanding full well that there are no knockdown arguments for doing so and no rational grounds for their commitment. In the same way, in taking issues of life seriously, the playing self understands that they are not serious. Or as Oscar Wilde would put it, "Deep down he is superficial".

As the playing self emerges in cultural life, what are the implications for daily life? What is worth doing? On what kind of narrative journey is one embarked? In order to treat such issues we must obviously broaden the realm of interpretive complexity. As commentators we are immersed in the very processes about which we write; we grapple with understanding a condition that is not, for us, an object of observation. The hope, however, is that by grappling with these ideas we generate resources for collectively navigating our way.

With this said, it is my view that with the playing self, the strong individualist account of human functioning recedes. One does not ask, in the abstract, "What would I like to be?" and look inward for the resources to reach this self-determined end. Rather, one recognizes that one is forever functioning within a relational context, with other players, with rules and expectations, and with offerings of what is possible and what is precluded. One may ask about preferred ends within this context, but there is no meta-contextual place to stand. The playing self is relationally dependent. This does not mean confronting a pre-fixed world, where one can only play within the boundaries of tradition. On the contrary, because one understands that one comes into being through play, and that the games are created by players, then new games are always a possibility. All that is required is another player responding enthusiastically to the invitation, "Let's imagine that...".

The life-course for the playing self is thus indeterminate. As Timmermans (2010) proposes, in the digitalized contexts of the game world the vision of a coherent life narrative is no longer compelling. The latter vision is a by-product of a textual world. In effect, the playing self is ideally adapted to the technologically driven *ethos* in which change is continuous and rapid. Living disjunctively is not, then, unsettling. Rather, the infinite possibility of new and exciting life-games is optimistic and energizing. Does the playing self thus lack moral fiber? Is this just a spineless creature for whom anything goes? I don't think so. Rather, one's existence as a playing self requires the presence of a game, and games require for their existence rules of conduct. These rules, in turn, contain values – what it is to win and lose, to succeed and fail, to play fairly or unfairly. As mentioned earlier, most video games are based on a narrative in which heroes are pitted against villains. Thus a world of virtue is built into both the content and structure of the game. Extrapolating to life outside the game, the playing self would be prone to a *situated ethics*. He or she would be sensitive to local moralities, but would be resistant to transcendent moral principles. This means that because the rules of a game are ultimately arbitrary, and one ultimately plays to win, the situated ethics may run thin. Therefore, bending the rules may be a pervasive temptation.

Relationships in playland

Social history sensitizes us to the shifting character of social relationships across time. In a previous work, for example, I have traced the corrosive effect of 20th century modernism on the romanticist tradition, and explored the new potentials opened by the postmodern cultural turn (Gergen 1992; 2009). What I could not appreciate at the time was the rapid expansion of the ludic mentality. How are we to understand contemporary transformations in relational mores, and how should these be regarded? Again, such questions are without culminating answers, and it is to a sustained dialogue that we must subscribe. To that end, I touch on only two related issues in the present offering: commitment and alienation.

As proposed earlier, the playland ethos does not lend itself to sustaining the individualist tradition of the past, but rather, it sets the context for diffusion and rebirth as a playing self. As also proposed, for the playing self the world is seen through the metaphoric lens of the game. Most important in this context, the vast majority of all games require other players – actual or simulated. In effect, to be a playing self is to exist in a world not as a lone agent, but fundamentally *with* others. And, as players in all competitive games are aware, one does not fully control one's actions. The success or failure of one's behavior is inherently dependent on the behavior of the other (or others). The outcome of any game emerges from the relational process.

At the same time, the relationship between the playing self and others is tenuous. At once, the other is needed (either as a partner in play or a team member), but simultaneously he or she serves as (or can become) an antagonist whose actions can hasten one's defeat (or game death). In business circles – when one's allies in a given field are also one's competitors – one speaks of "frenemies". Thus one may sustain broad regard for one's acquaintances, but they always remain at a distance. Special regard may be expressed toward fellow players – a tennis or golf partner, for example. However, such regard may frequently be context-specific. That is, one may spend many enjoyable hours playing with one's companions, but have little or no interest in seeing them outside these times.[10]

Much the same ambivalence may influence relations that were once defined in terms of depth or commitment: friendships, romantic love, and one's family central among them. Such relations are often viewed as bonding, suggesting that one is no longer a free agent. The playing self may think little of "free agency", but bonded commitment is also alien. To demand a commitment that transcends the boundaries of a particular context would be akin to asking one to serve a tennis ball when seated at the bridge table. In contrast to the modernist, for whom deep relationships smell of an antiquated and saccharine romanticism, the playing self is versatile. He or she can "play at" being the soulmate, a baleful romantic, or the adoring father or mother. And in doing it well, one may achieve great pleasure. However, these are all situated activities – effectively, games of the moment. They are not necessary indicators of cross-time commitments. Ample support for this waning of commitment is found in Zygmunt Bauman's *Liquid love: On the frailty of human bonds* (2003). However, where Bauman sees human bonding as a natural desire, I am more inclined to view bonding as a cultural tradition that is more or less valued and practiced depending on historical conditions. In this case, the playing self may feel little anxiety at the deterioration of bonding. Fragility in this case is not a threat, but an opportunity.

Although I move here into more conjectural territory, there is a second and more menacing movement that demands discussion. Ironically, while the playland *zeitgeist* promotes social engagement, there are also ways in which antagonisms are intensified. This groundwork is laid by the agonistic structure of most games, and the way in which the social landscape can so easily be indexed in terms of friends and enemies. With relationships in a tenuous condition, others may easily be thrust into the latter category. Here I was struck by a recent article in the *New York Times* (5/12/10) reporting on the increasing incidence of digital bullying among young people. They speak of the "cavalier meanness" with which adolescents can treat each other on Facebook or by cell phone texting. Small cliques will gang up on an individual, and bombard him or her with comments like "go cut yourself", "you are sooo ugly", "your pic makes me throw up". Swear words like "bitch", "shit", and "fuck" are also commonplace.[11] What also caught me about this article was the response of a straight-A student to her mother. Her mother had been notified by the school that her daughter had been caught making a MySpace page about her classmate in middle-school calling her a "whore" and pointing to her private parts. The distraught mother rushed to school to find her daughter at the guidance counselor's office, her arms defiantly crossed. The mother pleaded for her daughter to consider the impact of this page on her victim's feelings. "This is a human being… This girl will be destroyed for the rest of her life!" The daughter sullenly replied: "I don't care, It's all true". The weeks following at home were marked by arguments, recriminations, screaming, and slammed doors.

It is this latter schism that particularly concerns me. I find from countless parents that their relationships with their adolescent children are fraught with antagonism. Their admonishments do not yield compliance, or even silent resistance. Rather, a very likely response is a full volley of vituperation, replete with oaths that the parents never once uttered in the company of family. Adolescence in Western culture has long been a difficult period for family relationships. However, we seem to have entered a period of extreme distance and disrespect. In my view, the emergence of playland culture brings with it a broad generational schism. With the early technologies of television, films, radio, and mass publications, the adult population was essentially immersed in spectator pleasure. Competitive play was limited, and the techno-mediated context of play fully absent. However, for two decades now, social and competitive play have radically increased, and the younger generations are the major participants. Electronic games and social networking for pleasure are predominantly activities of the younger generations. As Chatfield (2010) reports, for example, 99% of teenage boys and 94% of teenage girls in the US have played video games. Adolescents are also unlikely to allow their parents access to their Facebook sanctuary (though parents over the age of 30 are not likely to participate in Facebook at all). The result is the emergence of a generation gap in which respect for elders is receding. Not only do the older generations not understand the technology, they have little knowledge or appreciation of the lived worlds of the young. For the older generations, in turn, the young begin to appear both shallow and uncivilized.

Playland and society

These brief explorations into emerging forms of cultural life – focusing on self and relationships – also invite expanded discussion. Again, my concern here is not with the shifts taking place in the way people spend their time and money. More important, in my view, are the broader transformations taking place. In the case of both self-conception and relational patterning, the impact of playland activities is direct. Engagement in play is itself transforming. However, the ripple effects of such activities are of far greater magnitude. Here I call attention to what may be called *metaphoric drift*. By this I mean the way in which the imagery of the game becomes the means by which we understand, enact, and thus transform other forms of life. In the case of games, metaphoric drift is represented, for example, in the way many organizations define their members as a team, or more threateningly, the way in which video games come to resemble war games, and actual war may come to be viewed as play. To illustrate, global combat has now become the basis for the Military Channel on television. The channel features videos on machine guns, special ops, Nazi hunting, snipers, and so on – in effect, reconstituting human slaughter as entertainment. The website for the channel includes, as well, a range of games that parallel the television fare. An iPhone game enables one to "earn a sniper license", another enables one to test their firepower skills. At the same time, over 11 million people worldwide play the video game *World of Warcraft*. The contemporary echoes of "Oh! What a Lovely War" become ominous.

Equally unsettling reverberations accompany the entry of gaming metaphors into economics and politics. In many respects the gaming metaphor has already entered the economic world. Early on, the popular game *Monopoly* sensitized generations to the ludic character of winning and losing money, and economic game theory informed the practices of strategic management. However, in recent years the metaphoric drift has become accentuated. Already by 1994, business executive Jack Stack wrote the popular book *The great game of business*. However, a spate of books has recently emerged showing how the concept and practice of gaming is being instituted within the business world.[12] Games are currently being used, for example, to reach new customers, build brands, recruit and retain employees, and drive innovation. Reeves and Read (2009) propose that game training can provide vital preparation for participating in the contemporary business world. In effect, they wish to use games to change the way people work and do business. Business literally becomes a game.

It is this mentality that many believe informed cultures of finance and banking in their inviting the stock market collapse of 2008-09. Without strict oversight, investment banks such as Goldman Sachs hesitated little to use fraud in rigging the market in their favor. Banks did not hesitate to inflate the housing market, fully understanding that the short-term gains would ultimately lead to disaster. If business is a game for business players, the point is not to benefit the society, but at any cost, to win at business!

The game metaphor had drifted into the political arena long before the emergence of playland. With the establishment of a democracy in which political parties vied for power, the metaphors of the battle and the game were ready at hand. In present times, phrases such as winning and losing the political "race", "playing hardball", "the political game", and "playing politics" have shifted from the domain of metaphor to the literal.[13] Although the play element in American politics was noted in Huizinga's 1938 book, its influence has now become alarming in its proportions. The problem in part is the conflation of the good/evil dichotomy dominating the game tradition with political party differences. Civil debate has been replaced by public acrimony, with the political rhetoric so intensely hostile that it has become associated with deadly assaults. (A recent cover of *The Economist* pictures political debaters with pistols replacing their tongues.) The intense and absorbing contest between mirror images of good and evil also brings about an indifference to the complexities of policy issues. Matters of public good are overlooked and the sole aim becomes defeating one's opponent.

While we are concerned here primarily with cultural deficits, we should not conclude that the playland transformation is altogether negative. Much has been written about the various skills engendered by video and computer game playing, along with the positive uses of games in education and training.[14] However, it is also important to consider the positive potential in terms of broader cultural patterns. For example, games not only generate divisions among people (e.g. my team, political party, my nation vs. your nation), but they can also serve to unite people who would otherwise be apart. People from diverse economic classes, educational backgrounds, and ethnicities unite around a favorite team; players even from the poorest background with sufficient athletic skill can become national idols in a culture; adolescents from around the globe meet together in virtual space to form teams. For every division, there is also inclusion. There is also a way in which the gaming *zeitgeist* can undermine all forms of fundamentalism. As one begins to understand cultural life as made up of gaming sites (e.g. corporate life as a game, law as a game, science as a game), there is a loosening of belief in any tradition of intelligibility. Rather than understanding statements of what is true, real, or rational as foundationally grounded, they all become rhetorics of reality. This is essentially the view taken by James Carse in his 1986 work, *Finite and infinite games: A vision of life as play and possibility.* When life is viewed in terms of playscripts, then one may be liberated from the grasp of any particular playscript and one can play with the forms of play. This mentality is also reflected in the emerging critique within the cyber-community of the work ethic, the privatization and commodification of information, music, and art, and the decline in economic pursuits as the major goal of life. Among the most potent documents is Pat Kane's *The play ethic: A manifesto for a different way of living* (2004). Here he argues for transforming the world of work, education, and spirituality so that play is at its center. Play takes on an ethical dimension.

In conclusion

In this chapter I propose that a major transformation is taking place in Western culture, one in which play is not only becoming a central activity, but in which play increasingly serves as the organizing metaphor for human activity. This ludification of culture results in part from low-cost communication technologies that make dramatically engaging activities available non-stop to increasing sectors of the population. Participation in games is both vicarious and participatory, and is amplified by the play-like ambience of social network activities. Such a transformation invites attention to the broad ramifications for cultural life. My central concern in this chapter is with the implications for self-conception and social relationships. Here I have outlined the emergence of a playing self, the sense that one is fundamentally a performer within a life of game-like activities. This sense of self places a strong value on relationship, but the value of authentic commitment gives way to temporary pleasure. I have also touched on ways in which the metaphor of play increasingly inhabits the major institutions of society, including government, business, and education. While it is tempting to be critical of such a transformation, such a critique largely reflects on investments in the ontologies and values of pre-game cultural life. This is not to discount such a critique, but to invite a continuous dialogue that also takes into account the positive potential of life in playland.

Notes

1. For a detailed account of the burgeoning of game playing and its commercial success, see Chatfield (2010).
2. Social commentators such as Berger (2002) and Kent (2001) have also made a strong case for a major cultural change on the basis of engagements in computer and video games alone. Wark (2007) sees video games as leading to utopian cultural life.
3. See Sayler's (2006) review.
4. See, for example, Healy (1999), Carr (2010), and Winn (2002).
5. Illustrative are Devlin (2011), McGonigal (2011), and Squire (2011).
6. See, for example, Gergen (1992; 2009).
7. See also Wellman (2001) on networked individualism, and de Lange (2010) on mobile media and playful identities.
8. The reader should consult Bissell's (2010) firsthand account of his own hypnotic immersion in video games.
9. In the Freudian sense neither functions on the reality principle, nor on the pleasure principle, but on an imaginary principle, "what if?". It should also be noted that the phrase "playing self" has also been used in the English translation of Melucci's work *Il gioco dell'io* (1991). However, his use of the term has totally different implications.
10. Contemporary retirement communities in the US are typically built around a complex of golf courses, tennis courts, and swimming pools. It is primarily through games that one becomes a neighbor.
11. As Aboujaoude (2011) cogently argues, the Internet allows one to attack others without having to confront their pain. Moreover, one is free to fantasize aggression without ego-controls that might be enhanced by the presence of others.
12. See, for example, Beck and Wade (2004); Connors and Smith (2011); Edery and Mollick (2010); Reeves and Read (2009); Zicherman and Linder (2010).
13. For extended examples of the metaphor in action see Heileman and Halperin (2009) and Mathews (2010).
14. See, for example, Gee (2005) and Griffiths (2002).

References

Aboujaoude, Elias. 2011. *The dangerous powers of the e-personality.* New York: Norton.

Barthes, Roland. 1972. *Mythologies.* New York: Hill and Wang.

Bauman, Zygmunt. 2003. *Liquid love: On the frailty of human bonds.* Cambridge, UK: Polity Press.

Beck, John C., and Mitchell Wade. 2004. *Got game: How the gamer generation is reshaping business forever.* Cambridge, MA: Harvard Business Press.

Berger, Arthur A. 2002. *Video games: A popular culture phenomenon.* New Brunswick, NJ: Transaction Publishers.

Bissell, Tom. 2010. *Extra lives: Why video games matter.* New York: Pantheon.
Caillois, Roger. 2001. *Man, play and games* [1958]. Champaign, IL: University of Illinois Press.
Carr, Nicholas. 2010. *The shallows: What the Internet is doing to our brains.* New York: Norton.
Carse, James P. 1986. *Finite and infinite games: A vision of life as play and possibility.* New York: Ballentine.
Chatfield, Tom. 2010. *Fun inc.: Why gaming will dominate the twenty-first century.* New York: Pegasus.
Connors, Rogers, and Tom Smith. 2011. *Change the culture, change the game: The breakthrough strategy for energizing your organization and creating accountability for results.* New York: Portfolio.
Devlin, Kieth. 2011. *Mathematics education for a new era: Video games as a medium for learning.* Boca Raton: RC Press.
Dyer-Witheford, Nick, and Greg de Peuter. 2009. *Global capitalism and video games.* Minneapolis, MN: University of Minnesota Press.
Edery, David, and Ethan Mollick. 2010. *Changing the game: How games are transforming the future of business.* Upper Saddle River, NJ: FT Press.
Gee, James P. 2005. *Why video games are good for your soul: Pleasure and learning.* Melbourne: Common Ground.
Gergen, Kenneth J. 1992. *The saturated self.* New York: Basic Books.
—. 2009. *Relational being: Beyond self and community.* Oxford: Oxford University Press
Goldstein, Jeffrey. 1994. *Toys, play, and child development.* New York: Cambridge University Press.
Griffiths, Mark. 2002. The educational benefits of video games. *Education and Health*, 20: 47-51.
Healy, Jane M. 1999. *Endangered minds: Why children don't think – and what we can do about it.* New York: Simon and Schuster.
Heilemann John, and Mark Halperin. 2009. *Game change: Obama and the Clintons, McCain and Palin, and the race of a lifetime.* New York: Harper.
Huizinga, Johan. 1955. *Homo ludens: A study of the play-element in culture* [1938]. London: Routledge.
Kane, Pat. 2004. *The play ethic: A manifesto for a different way of living.* New York: Macmillan.
Kent, Steven L. 2001. *The ultimate history of video games: From Pong to Pokémon and beyond - The story behind the craze that touched our lives and changed the world.* New York: Three Rivers Press.
Lange, Michiel de. 2010. *Moving circles: Mobile media and playful identities.* PhD dissertation. Rotterdam: Erasmus University.
Mathews, Chris. 2010. *Hardball: How politics is played by one who knows the game.* New York: Simon & Schuster.
McGonigal, Jane. 2011. *Reality is broken: Why games make us better and how they can change the world.* New York: Penguin Press.
Melucci, Alberto. 1996. *The playing self* [*Il gioco dell'io*, 1991]. Cambridge, MA: Cambridge University Press.
Morozov, Evegeny. 2011. *The net delusion: The dark side of Internet freedom.* New York: Public Affairs Books.
Pearson, Erika. 2009. All the World Wide Web's a stage: The performance of identity in online social networks. *First Monday*, 14(3).
Reeves, Byron, and J. Leighton Read. 2009. *Total engagement: Using games and virtual worlds to change the way people work and business compete.* Cambridge, MA: Harvard University Press.
Rorty, Richard. 1989. *Contingency, irony, and solidarity.* New York, NY: Cambridge University Press.

Sayler, M. 2006. Modernity and enchantment: Historiographic review. *American Historical Review,* June: 692-716.
Squire, Kurt. 2011. *Video games and learning: Teaching and participatory culture in the digital age.* New York: Teachers College Press.
Stack, Jack. 1994. *The great game of business.* New York: Doubleday.
Stahl, Roger. 2009. *Militainment: War, media, and popular culture.* London: Routledge.
Timmermans, Jeroen. 2010. *Playing with paradoxes: Identity in the web era.* PhD dissertation. Rotterdam: Erasmus University.
Wark, McKenzie. 2007. *Gamer theory.* Cambridge, MA: Harvard University Press.
Wellman, Barry. 2001. Physicial place and cyber-place: The rise of networked individualism. *International Journal for Urban and Regional Research,* 25: 227-52.
Winn, Marie. 2002. *The plug-in drug: Television, computers, and family life.* New York: Penguin.
Zicherman, Gabe, and Joselin Linder. 2010. *Game-based marketing: Inspire customer loyalty through rewards, challenges, and contests.* New York: Wiley.

3. Spiritual play: Encountering the sacred in *World of Warcraft*

Stef Aupers

Introduction

The classical work *Homo ludens* (1938) by Dutch historian Johan Huizinga is constantly revisited and generally understood as an indisputable point of departure in the academic debate about modern play (see the introductory chapter of this volume). Huizinga's work is currently used as a standard reference for game designers (e.g. Crawford 2003; Salen and Zimmerman 2004) and in game studies (e.g. Consalvo 2009; Copier 2005; Taylor 2006; Dibbell 2006). It has even been argued that Huizinga is a "pop icon in game studies", while his seventy-five year old theory about play anachronistically functions as a "prehistory" and legitimation of this emergent discipline (Pargman and Jakobsson 2008, 227). At the heart of Huizinga's conceptualization of play lies a rigid distinction between real life and the game – play is an act set apart by hermetically sealed boundaries. Huizinga famously claimed play is a "free activity" standing quite consciously outside "ordinary" life as being "not serious", whereas "it proceeds within its own proper boundaries of time and space" (1955, 13). To emphasize the self-referential *and* the sublime or even sacred nature of play, Huizinga used the concept of a "magic circle". This "magic circle", he argued, protects the freedom of play so as to enable it to bring "a temporary, a limited perfection [...] into an imperfect world and into the confusion of life" (ibid., 10). For Huizinga, the concept of a "magic circle" was not just a loose metaphor. In the opening chapter of *Homo ludens*, he repeatedly emphasizes the affinity between the activity of play and the sacred. For instance, he writes: "[t]he concept of play merges quite naturally with that of holiness", and "[t]he ritual act, or an important part of it, will always remain within the play category, but in this seeming subordination the recognition of its holiness is not lost" (ibid., 25, 27).

Huizinga's assumption about the affinity between play and the sacred is by and large unacknowledged and understudied in academia (Copier 2005). In the social sciences, play and religion are generally understood as different or even mutually exclusive realms. Play in worlds of fiction may invoke, what Coleridge (1817) called, a temporary "willing suspension of disbelief" or "poetic faith" but this does not in any way disturb the "modern divide" between fact and fiction, truth and fantasy, or the secular and the sacred on which a "disenchanted" world is founded (Latour 1993). In the emergent field of game studies Huizinga's conceptualization of the playground as a "magic circle" is increasingly contested. The term is used quite frequently, but generally used as a metaphor to emphasize the self-referential and special nature of games (Salen and Zimmerman 2004). In addition, scholars studying online computer games and massively multiplayer online games (MMOs), such as *Everquest*, *World of Warcraft* (*WoW*), and the like, have made the argument that the strong boundaries between the world of play and the real world are more porous than Huizinga accounts for since "real" cultural values, social capital, and economic transactions are traveling to the "magic circle" and back (Aupers 2007; Castronova 2005; Copier 2005; Dibbell 2006; Harambam et al. 2011; Taylor 2006). From this perspective, Huizinga's "strong-boundary hypothesis" has made way for the "weak-boundary hypothesis" (Pargman and Jakobsson 2008; cf. Lammes 2008) – a hypothesis that implicitly formulates assumptions about the secularization or disenchantment of games. Some authors quite literally conclude that the activity of (online) gaming has become part of the profane activities and routines of everyday life (Pargman and Jakobsson 2008) and ultimately conclude that "there is no magic circle" (Consalvo 2009; Copier 2005).

On the basis of a case study of *World of Warcraft* – probably the most popular MMO, with 12 million accounts at the time of writing – I aim in this chapter to defend and elaborate on Huizinga's thesis of a "magic circle".[1] Notwithstanding the multiple profane meanings of this game and other MMOs, it will be demonstrated that players do in fact experience the online playground as set apart from real life and, more than that, that there is often an affinity between play on the one hand and spirituality on the other. In particular, I argue that online game "play" provides an unacknowledged epistemological avenue to interact with the sacred and to contact the ultimate values that, Max Weber (1919) argued, retreated from modern life.

Mythopoeic spirituality: Constructing the magic circle

It is by now a sociological truism that modern people, especially in Western Europe, are living in a secular, disenchanted world. As Weber famously argued less than a century ago in probably the most cited passage of his essay "Science as a Vocation", "the disenchantment of the world [...] means that principally there are no mysterious incalculable forces that come into play, but rather that one can, in principle, master all things by calculation"

(1948, 139). Contemporary surveys demonstrate over and over again that belief in a transcendent God and the truth of the scriptures is eroding in most Western countries and, consequently, a secular outlook is gaining ground.

And yet things are more complex than this because we are increasingly witnessing the rise of new forms of spirituality outside religious institutions that scrutinize "belief" in a transcendent God and embody alternative epistemological strategies to interact with the sacred (Aupers and Houtman 2010; Houtman and Aupers 2007). One such strategy is, what I will call, "mythopoeic spirituality", which is a manifestation of spirituality that fully acknowledges the constructed, fictitious nature of supernatural claims, but, at the same time, maintains that such claims have real spiritual value. Advocates of secularization, like Richard Dawkins, typically argue that the scientific falsification of truth claims in the Bible have turned it into fiction "as factually dubious as the stories of King Arthur and his Knights of the Round Table" (2007, 122). This development, however, did not lead to the loss of the spiritual significance of such texts. Quite on the contrary, it opened up the possibility to use all kinds of fiction, varying from the Bible and *The Da Vinci Code*, to *Star Trek* or *The Matrix* as meaningful myths or "sacred texts" (Partridge 2004), to construct a spiritual worldview (Possamai 2005). Mythopoeic spirituality, we will see, also plays a prominent role in online games and the formation of its "magic circle".

From Middle Earth to *World of Warcraft*

By far the most important influence on the "mythopoeic" approach is the work of J.J.R. Tolkien. In 1931 he wrote a poem called *Mythopoeia* (myth-making) in which he rejected the common perception of "myth" as being "false", "not true", or an "illusion" – a connotation obviously fed by the secular Enlightenment and the imperative of scientific thinking. Instead Tolkien proposed to understand myth as containing eternal, universal, and spiritual truth and advocated the active construction of such meaningful narratives in a disenchanted modern world. In his famous essay *On fairy stories* (1939), Tolkien elaborated on these themes. He emphasized that mythology, not unlike religion, provides perennial truth and "consolation" vis-à-vis human suffering and believed that the creation of a mythical "secondary world" is not a frivolous matter. Although its content should break with modern reality, its form, structure, and details should be "derived from reality" and reflect "the inner consistency of reality" (Tolkien 1939, 16). A good mythmaker, he argued, "makes a secondary world that your mind can enter. Inside it, what he relates to is 'true': it accords with the laws of that world" (ibid., 12).

Tolkien practiced what he preached. The location of his trilogy *Lord of the rings* that was first published in 1954 is "Middle Earth", which is both fantastic and realistic, both mythical and rational, and is by far the most influential work in the fantasy genre. Its main narrative – featuring creatures like hobbits, elves, and wizards as main protagonists – is mainly based on Norse mythology and embraces a "polytheistic-cum-animist cosmology of 'natural magic'" (Curry 1998, 28). These "premodern" religious worldviews, Tolkien felt, are important since "the 'war' against mystery and magic by modernity urgently requires a re-enchantment of the world, which a sense of Earth-mysteries is much better placed to offer than a single transcendent deity" (ibid., 28-9). In short, Middle Earth was invented to counter modern processes of disenchantment, but ironically became fully embraced by the modern world since the 1960s.

Tolkien's work and his "mythopoeic" approach particularly informed various spiritual groups *and* game designers (although the distinction is analytical, not empirical). *Lord of the rings*, to begin with, was immediately embraced by the spiritual counterculture when it was published as a paperback in 1965. It had an influence in particular on the neopagan movement. Neopagans are "romanticizing the premodern" (Partridge 2004, 77) and are involved in an animistic and polytheistic "nature religion" with an emphasis on magical rituals (e.g. Adler 1986; Berger 1999; Hanegraaff 1996; Luhrmann 1991; York 1995). But neopagans are also mythmakers themselves since it is imperative in the milieu to "reinvent" your own pagan tradition (ibid.). Neopaganism is, first of all, a literary culture and participants ground their worldview in books that claim objectivity *and* fiction to design, legitimate and authenticate their own invented traditions (e.g. Luhrmann 1991; Possamai 2005). *Lord of the rings* is a prime example but even *Witchcraft today* (1954) written by Gerald Gardner – the founder of Wicca – is known to be a fictional ethnography. Pagans, in short, self-consciously and playfully create their own "mythopoeic history" in what they consider to be "a myth-impoverished world" (Luhrmann 1991, 238, 241).

The literary work and mythopoeic approach of Tolkien also spilled over to the game industry and became, as such, a typical example of a "transmedial" phenomenon (Jenkins 2006). Mythmaking, in the context of computer games, became a matter of technical design. Turkle argues: "The personal computer movement of the 1970s and early 1980s was deeply immersed in Tolkien and translated his fantasy worlds into hugely popular (and enduring) role-playing games" (2002, 18). Indeed, although Tolkien died in 1973, his enchanting world was reproduced in Cyberspace around that same time. In 1976 Stanford hacker Donald Woods and programmer Will Crowther developed *Adventure*, the first text-based role-playing game on the computer. *Adventure* "turned out to be one of the most influential computer games in the medium's early history" (King and Borland 2003, 31). An important shift came in the 1980s when Trubshaw and Bartle developed the "Multi-User Dungeon" (MUDs) that made it possible to collectively explore this textual world. Between the end of the 1970s and the beginning of the 1990s, text-based role-playing games and MUDs were booming. Some examples that are directly derived from the work of Tolkien are *The Shire* (1979), *Ringen* (1979), *Lord of the Rings* (1981), *LORD* (1981), *Ring of Doom* (1983), *Ringmaster* (1984), *The Mines of Moria* (1985), *Bilbo* (1989), *The Balrogian Trilogy* (1989), and *Elendor* (1991). In 1996 and 1997, respectively, *Diablo* and *Ultima Online* were launched on the Internet. These were generally understood as the first 3-dimensional Massively Multiplayer Online Role-Playing Games (MMORPG). In the last decade the MMORPG genre has become immensely popular. Well-known examples are *Everquest* (Sony 1999), *Asherons Call* (Microsoft 1999), *Dark Age of Camelot* (Mythic Entertainment 2001), *World of Warcraft* (Blizzard Entertainment 2004), and *Lord of the Rings Online* (Turbine Inc. 2007).

"A world awaits..."

No less than 95 percent of the contemporary MMO games are based on the "fantasy genre" (Woodcock 2009). The main narratives of these games differ in many respects, of course, but they all hark back to an imaginary medieval society that is yet untouched by the juggernaut of modernity (Aupers 2007). Not unlike neopagans in the spiritual milieu, then, the producers of online worlds construct, or rather, literally design a "mythopoeic history" by cutting and pasting premodern religions, myths, and sagas and by offering them for further consumption. The narratives are often derived from well-known Western legends, but also popular fiction varying from Tolkien's *Lord of the rings* to J.G. Frazer's *Golden bow* and Joseph Campbell's *The hero with a thousand faces* (Bartle 2004). Krzywinska argues that by using such intertextual references to other popular (fantasy) texts, designers constitute an appealing "combination of otherness and familiarity for players" thereby enhancing feelings of immersion and "being in a world" (2008, 138).

In short, in line with the approach set out by Tolkien, MMOs are both extremely realistic and distinctly otherworldly (Castranova 2005, 80). This otherworldliness instigated by premodern, mythical and magical content, supports and even enhances the function of play as a "magic circle". It draws strong boundaries between the real world and the game world and, in doing so, contributes to its appeal. On the cover of *WoW* and *Ultima Online* (UO) one can read:

> A world awaits...Descend into the World of Warcraft and join thousands of mighty heroes in an online world of myth, magic and limitless adventure [...] An infinity of experiences await. So what are you waiting for?

> If you've ever felt like you wanted to step out of yourself, your life, into one that was full of fantasy and adventure – virtual worlds offer you this opportunity. [...] You choose your own virtual life and immerse yourself into the mystical, medieval world of Britannia [...]*Ultima Online* is the place where you can be whatever you want to be.

There are, of course, profound differences between these game worlds. The culture of *UO*, for instance, is rooted in specific Anglo-Saxon legends, whereas the *Dark Age of Camelot* (*DAoC*) is a good example of a game that is exclusively based on Northern European myth and legend. At the beginning of the game, players can choose to be part of one of three territories that each have their own culture, religion, and customs and are at war with each other. These three territories include: Albion (portrayed as medieval England and informed by King Arthur legends), Midgard (portrayed as ancient Scandinavia and informed by Viking mythology), and Hilbernia (portrayed as ancient Ireland and informed by Celtic lore). In the manual of *DAoC*, these three territories try to convince players to join them in their battle against the "Dark forces of evil" by promising more magic and enchantment than the others:

> Others may tempt you with mighty deeds and fine words, but in Hilbernia we keep closest to the oldest of the spirits of the Earth. Ours is the most mystical, imbued with the spirit of ancient days and long forgotten powers. If you desire to fight with us against the encroachment of evil and darkness, come to the most magical land of all, Hilbernia.

So it seems that being "the most magical land of all" is not only an important asset in rivalry in the game, but is also important in the competition between online game worlds in today's market. In recent applications of *DAoC*, new territories are opened up, like the "highly advanced civilization" Atlantis (which is according to legend the pinnacle of spirituality), Stygia ("a searing desert where adventurers will encounter creatures from Egyptian mythology"), and Volcanus ("Here you will encounter [...] the warlike Minotaurs").

Of course there are multiple, more profane features and functions installed in the architecture of the game world, such as the options to socialize in guilds, explore the environment, compete, work, achieve, and gain rewards (Bartle 2004; Salen and Zimmerman 2004). What the prominence of fantasy indicates, however, is that the construction of a mythopoeic setting is pivotal in constituting enchantment and establishing boundaries between profane modern life and the game world. Most MMOs offer, what John Caputo called, "a high-tech religious mythology, a fairly explicit "repetition" or appropriation of elemental religious structures outside the confines of the religious faiths" (2001, 89-90). Unencumbered by historical accuracy, designers cut, paste, and sample various popular legends, myths, and religious archetypes and combine them into new idiosyncratic worlds. Time and place are subordinated to this imperative of enchantment. As far as religion is concerned, the Christian tradition is downplayed in favor of polytheistic and animistic forms of religious worship. As to the former, various gods and deities – both good and bad – are prominent in all the games. As to the latter, players are encouraged – or even obliged if they want to proceed in the game – to perform various "quests" to collect spiritual objects, e.g. "totems" or weapons imbued with "mana". Most relevant for the players, however, is the "art of magic". Before the game starts, the players construct a character and choose between various races, classes, and professions. Abstracted from the differences, it can be concluded that in every game there is the choice to become an explorer, a fighter, *or* a magician. Magicians even come in sub-classes. For instance, without providing a complete list, in *Everquest* (*EQ*) one can become a "sorcerer", "warlock", "wizard", "enchanter", "illusionist", "coercer", "summoner", "necromancer", "conjurer", "druid", "warden", "fury", "shaman", "defiler", or "mystic". In *DAoC* one can, for instance, become a "cabalist", "rune master", "bone dancer", "spirit master", "healer", "bard", "mentalist", or "animist". Again, this is just a small sample of the options available. Each subclass has specific abilities and skills. Take the example of the shaman in *WoW*:

> The shaman is an effective spell caster, but can also fight extremely well with mace and staff. The shaman's line-of spirit spells enables it to perform a variety of useful non-combat actions. It can resurrect allies, turn into a ghost wolf for increased movements, or instantly teleport to town. The shaman's unique power is totems. Totems are spiritual objects that a shaman must earn through questing.

The shaman's abilities include: resurrecting the dead, healing, draining souls, summoning spirits, telekinesis, teleporting, paralysis, creating energy bolts, becoming invisible, shape shifting, and causing earthquakes. The spells and the possibility of performing magic in the games are various. In addition, players can develop their magical skills as they are progressing through the game. In fact, they can have a magical career. As *DAoC* states: "For those who wish to dabble in the arts of magic and mysticism, there are several paths that lead to a mastery of the arcane". In *DAoC*, they can do so by joining magical schools and guilds. They can become part of the Academy ("the school founded by the famous wizard Merlin"), the Guild of Shadows, or the Church of Albion. In *UO*, there are eight levels of magic containing 64 magical spells and rituals. The novice starts at the first level (low-magic) and can advance until the eighth level (high-magic). In this last phase, one can attain great – and almost omnipotent – magical powers.

"Why do so many virtual worlds feature magic?" I raised this question in an interview with Richard Bartle and he turned it into a topic of discussion among game designers on the blog Terranova (http://terranova.blogs.com/terra_nova/). The answers ranged from explanations that magic is a functional trope enhancing the boundaries between the real and the game world (i.e. to construct the "magic circle" in a metaphorical sense) to speculations about the intrinsic value of magic, myth, and mystery and its importance in the modern world. As one designer typically noted:

> Magic is growing in popularity. It's a very compelling way to view the world and can provide more meaning and agency than a viewpoint that is strictly materialist. In a nutshell, we want the magic that was stripped by rational materialism to return back into our lives. Immersive 3D worlds provide a nice playground to this end.

Playing with magic

I want to believe...

The question remains whether players identify with the mythopoeic spirituality in online game worlds and in what ways. Player motivations often differ substantially. Some are more engaged in truly otherworldly immersion, exploration, and role-playing, while others are more interested in online sociality, competition, achievement, or status (Yee 2007).

Underneath such differences, however, one finds a shared fascination for the other-worldliness of the game.

The "disenchantment of the world", Weber argued, generates a nonreligious *and* disillusioned worldview. Under the influence of science and technology, he commented, an otherworldly orientation will be gradually replaced by a worldview that is more objective, but undermines – at the same time – the meaning of life. Modern astronomy, biology, physics or chemistry can describe the world as it is, but can (and should!) not teach anything about the ultimate meaning of the world. In a totally "disenchanted world", Weber argued, "the worlds processes simply are [...] and happen but no longer signify anything" (1978[1921]: 506).

Interestingly enough the majority of players of *World of Warcraft* who were interviewed also subscribe to this existential situation. They are basically nonreligious in a traditional sense and are disillusioned. First of all, they pride themselves on being atheists incapable of believing in "supernatural" or "transcendent" realms and especially traditional forms of religion. One gamer typically argued that "[r]eligions like Christianity and Islam are from the past and no longer relevant for me. They are based on a society from two thousand years ago [...]". Others state that "there's nothing holy about the Bible", that religions are just "fairytales" and that "only fools believe in God". They essentially perceive themselves as too rational and sober to believe and often literally claim that scientific knowledge essentially can solve and demystify all mysteries. As self-proclaimed, "true atheists" they accept many secularizing scientific propositions derived from evolution theory, physics, and computer sciences. One of the gamers provides the most explicit and radical example of this thoroughly rationalized and disenchanted perspective:

> I am completely irreligious. I think a human being is nothing more than an animal – a mechanical organism and you can best compare a human with a computer. The body is like a closet – in this closet you'll find the hardware, everything we learned is written on this hardware, our brains, and our personality is therefore nothing more than software interacting with the world.

Many of the gamers are not only nonreligious, but have also "lost faith" in a more general sense. They share, in the words of Caputo, a "tragic sense of life" (2001, 118) and are overtly complaint about the meaninglessness of contemporary modern society, the "emptiness" of politics, the problem of unchecked modern capitalism, relentless consumption and the unforeseen consequences of science and technology. One gamer argues: "Society is all about power and status. You need a job, you need money [...] And all those technologies. [...] We loose [sic] sight on what is really important. People forget: what are you actually living for?" Another gamer comments: "Motivated by the aim for more profits we develop technologies we do not understand. We can not [sic] see the consequences for humanity but they will be dramatic, I think." And put a bit more bluntly, another gamer asks: "Why should I invest in such a world that is so fucked up?"

The flipside of this critical analysis of modern, disenchanted society as meaningless is quite a romantic picture of the more traditional, premodern society. One gamer noted:

> There's this nostalgic longing for the past when all these things where not there yet. In the old days everything was better. The countryside, sunny summers when everybody was happy. If you walk through the world of *World of Warcraft* this is all there. And you are not constantly confronted with high-tech.

Their affinity with the rural, preindustrial environment of *WoW* can be understood, first of all, as motivated by their disillusionment with living in a disenchanted modern society. Like neopagans, the majority of *WoW* players romanticize the premodern past. They praise the simplicity, moral clarity, and "authenticity" of "their" virtual world and, most ironically, they emphasize the lack of technology.

But how do they relate, more specifically, to the premodern religion, polytheism, animism, and magic that permeate the online world? As noted, gamers proudly present themselves as too "rational" to believe. But there is another side to this story – a feeling of loss and disillusionment. Although gamers do not believe in the supernatural, they reveal that like the FBI agent Fox Mulder in the popular TV series *The X-Files*, they very much "*want to believe*". They have a strongly felt religious longing, in short. As one gamer typically confessed: "I would really like that there was more than we can see in life. Telepathic connections between people, or special super powers that people are born with – forces that are prominent in everyday life". Paradoxically, their disenchanted stance motivates these youngsters to enjoy "superpowers", magic, and spirituality online. In this virtual environment, after all, they can freely *play* with spirituality without believing or without being swallowed up by a belief system. "Within these worlds you accept everything as it is", one gamer typically comments, "it is as it is, because it is made that way". Is this engagement with magic, myth, and spirituality online indeed "just" play then – merely entertainment? Things are more complicated than this. Play can be understood as an alibi to seriously engage oneself with the meaning of magic, myth, and spirituality. Moreover, while playing gamers often *experience* their environment as real, including its supernatural entities and propositions. Such ontological transformations occur, as we will see, especially through the activity of role-playing.

Role-playing: Summoning the powers within

Magic is about turning a let's pretend fantasy of being a witch or a wizard into a serious assertion about the world
Luhrmann 1991, 327

It has been assessed in many studies of modern magic in the neopagan movement that "play" and particularly "role-playing" are at the heart of magical rituals (Adler 1986; Berger 1999; Copier 2005; Luhrmann 1991). In general, magic is used in this milieu to "invoke the powers in nature" but, particularly, to "summon the powers within". Berger emphasizes the primacy of this "magical" or "divine" self in ritual performances (1999, 33). Once the "divine" or "magical self" is awake, neopagans assume, one passes the border from the profane world to the sacred world where everything is possible and interconnected.

Luhrmann (1991) argues on the basis of her extensive fieldwork that the model of "play" – or a context of "let's pretend", "as if", or "make-believe" – forms an intricate part of such magical acts. Magic involves role-playing. In rituals, the participants are often called by another "magical" name, they often wear exotic, arcane clothes (especially in the tradition of "Western mystery"), they speak in hermetic vocabularies, formulate archaic sentences and utter strange words. In doing so, modern magicians often play and mimic magical behavior derived from fiction in the media. Luhrmann notes:

> Magic involves and encourages the imaginative identification in which the practitioner "plays at" being a ritual magician or a witch; the theatrical setting and dramatic invocations are directed at evoking precisely that sort of complete identification with what one imagines the magician to be. Here the role models are taken from fiction: the magician fantasizes about being Gandalf, not about being his coven's high priest (1991, 333).

However, neopagan magic is not "just play", but it is "serious play" since role-playing is constitutive for genuine, out-of-the-ordinary experiences and motivates ontological transformations. In the process of role-playing, fiction becomes real, make-believe instigates belief, and play is gradually experienced as serious magic. Johan Huizinga noted in *Homo ludens*, "The disguised or masked individual 'plays' another part, another being. He is another being" (1955, 13). In the context of neopaganism, a housewife becomes the Greek goddess of hunt Artemis, a teacher becomes Osiris, and yet another participant a powerful priest of an ancient Mayan cult, a Celtic druid, or Siberian shaman.

Role-playing, in short, is a technique to summon the "powers within" and align oneself with an imagined "higher" or "magical" self. This applies to online gaming as well. Players choose an archetypical "character" or "avatar" which functions as a digital representation of the player. According to Kolo and Baur (2004), the role of the magician is the most popular among "all players" (at least in *UO*). By incarnating a role as, for instance, a "sorcerer", "warlock", "wizard", or "shaman", players become active subjects in the enchanting online world. Like neopagans, they are moreover "naming" their characters and in doing so they are often inspired by popular legends, myth, and historical knowledge. As one gamer noted: "I gave it a beautiful name derived from history – my character lived during the Roman Empire. That's what I really like. And that's the way I experience it in the game". And more than that, through the act of role-playing, gamers can paradoxically gain access to dimensions of the self and experiences that are not surfacing in real life. Richard Bartle refers to this process as the "role-playing paradox":

> You're not role-playing as a being, you *are* that being; you're not assuming an identity, you are that identity; you're not projecting a self, you are that self. If you're killed in a fight, you don't feel that your character has died, you feel that you have died. There's no level of indirection, no filtering, no question: you are there [...] When player and character merge to become a persona, that's immersion; that's what people get from virtual worlds that they can't get from anywhere else; that's when they stop playing the world and start living it (2004, 155-6).

My own research validates this point to a large extent. The players of *World of Warcraft* who were interviewed emphasized that they increasingly identify with their avatars – especially since they invested a lot of time, energy, and work in it. One gamer typically notes, "it has become a part of me", whereas another states, "[the character] clearly possesses a fragment of my soul [...]". Once players experience the in-game character as real, they project personal desires and idealized identities onto the avatar. Like neopagans, they unleash and play out their "better selves", "magical selves", or "higher potentials" that cannot be expressed in everyday life. "A hero that follows his own path and does his own thing – that's the way I have designed him. And I like playing with the idea that I am him. He is a part of me, something that I would like to be", one player contends. Another adds, "You can be someone else. I think it is a beautiful world full of fantasy – a world that you encounter only in books. Unlike in real life, you can become a real hero". While, finally, respondent number three acknowledges, "It says something about your dreams. You play the person that you cannot be in real life, but would like to be."

While playing *WoW*, gamers thus immerse themselves in the mythopoeic reality of the game world and unleash, what Berger calls, the "magical self" through the activity of role-playing. As one gamer stated: "The impossible becomes possible. In *City of heroes*, you are a superhero with supernatural powers. You can do there what you cannot do in real life. I can't lift things with my thoughts, but I can do this in *City of heroes*. Just like *Spiderman* and the *X-Men*. And that is really cool!" According to Sigmund Freud, magic is all about the "omnipotence of thought" and magicians use their subjective, infantile, and narcissistic desires to seriously control the natural world with their thoughts and feelings (1913, quoted in Oranje 1999, 19, 204). Online environments provide the opportunity to, literally, play out such magical desires and fantasies.

Conclusion and discussion

In *Homo ludens* Huizinga conceptualized play as a "magic circle" to emphasize its self-referential nature *and* to flesh out the intrinsic connection between play and magic; the ludic and the sacred. In this chapter, I focused mainly on the latter meaning since the spiritual dimension of play is by and large understudied but promises to shed light on the vitality of religion in the modern world.

In the social sciences it is noted quite frequently that Western (especially European) societies are witnessing the end of religious belief. Belief versus disbelief is the binary code underpinning endless academic debates about secularization, disenchantment, and the many empirical studies and surveys that inform (and are informed by) it (Bruce 2002). This bias towards "belief" as *the* prime epistemological strategy in the religious field seems to be a heritage of the longstanding cultural trajectories of Christianity and modern science in the West. From a Christian perspective, belief – supported, legitimated, and verified by the Holy Scriptures – is the sacred road to a transcendent God. From a secular, positivistic, or atheist stance, belief in God or the supernatural is above all something that can and/or should be falsified – ultimately resulting in a position of "disbelief" (Dawkins 2007). The dichotomy of "believing" versus "not believing", however, creates a blind spot for new, often subtle strategies people employ to interact with the sacred. Max Weber argued that religious systems of meaning change under the influence of "cultural rationalization" (1956). Through history, religious systems are gradually reconstructed so as to make them less vulnerable to loss of plausibility caused by changes in society. From this perspective, the erosion of religious belief under the influence of science and technology may not be the end, but the beginning of new epistemological strategies that are more modernity-proof (Aupers and Houtman 2010; Campbell 2007).

"Play" is such a strategy. To begin with, the online play worlds of the MMO genre are generally brimming with premodern religiosity and encourage players to immerse themselves in a deeply enchanted virtual world. As such it is part and parcel of a growing "mythopoeic culture" in the West, "one in which stories about supernatural beings and events are continually being created (or more probably rediscovered) and eagerly consumed" (ibid., 329). In online games, the implementation of mythopoeic culture provides the game a supernatural flavor that confirms and strengthens the boundaries of the "magic circle". This is in itself not enough to understand online computer games as having any spiritual significance. After all, one may argue that the "magic circle" of game play is by definition not real and not serious since it stands "quite consciously outside 'ordinary' life" (Huizinga 1955 [1938], 13). But play is more complex than that. Notwithstanding his overly dualistic perspective on play, Huizinga himself has demonstrated a greater sensitivity towards the ambiguity of play than most academics have given him credit for (see the introductory chapter of this volume). This ambiguous, double, or liminal dimension of play is often even considered pivotal to understanding its character (Bateson 1972; Sutton-Smith 1997). "When we play", the editors of this volume rightly note in the opening chapter, "we can enthusiastically immerse ourselves in the play-world, while at the same time keep an ironic distance towards our playful behavior". It is, I theorize, exactly this fundamentally ambiguous nature of play that explains why it is such a feasible strategy to remain engaged with the sacred in a disenchanted world.

First of all, play with all kinds of myth, magic, and ultimate values in the "magic circle" of the online world cannot simply be understood as "not real" since *the act of play is transgressive*. Huizinga already noted that play instigates ontological transformations and (temporarily) turns fiction into faction, fantasy into reality, and make-believe into belief. As demonstrated, this is particularly what happens during role-play in online environments where "playing" a (magical) character slides into "being" a (magical) character and "playing" the game is frequently experienced as "living" in an otherworldly environment (Castranova 2005).

Secondly, the *concept of play is elusive*. Huizinga already stated that it is both serious and frivolous since "the contrast between play and seriousness proves to be neither conclusive nor fixed" (1955, 5). Gamers tap into both meanings of play but, more important, they structure these meanings in a particular way and do so seemingly with particular intentions. Elaborate talk about the seriousness of play, i.e. the significance of the game world, the magical identities online and the intensity of such experience during the interviews, were often followed by sobering remarks and rationalizations that this is "of course *just* play". After serious confessions, in other words, the gamers hastened to add an aura of playfulness. Given this typical sequence in the discourse of players we may theorize that *play* – in the frivolous meaning of the word – *has become an alibi* to cover up for the serious, ultimately spiritual dimensions of play.

Because of the transgressive and elusive nature of play, then, being in virtual worlds provides the opportunity *par excellence* for "disenchanted" youngsters to experience spirituality without believing in supernatural claims; to fully immerse themselves in a spiritual world without conversion to a predefined set of beliefs; to transcend everyday life without too much personal commitment and, basically, to rhetorically hover safely between the sacred and the secular. Concepts like "deep play" (Geertz 1973) or "serious play" (Luhrmann 1991) are adequate to comprehend such ambiguities, but may be complemented by the notion of "spiritual play". It is sometimes claimed that computer games are "laboratories" in which youngsters can safely experiment not only with their personal identity (Turkle 1995), but also with their emotions and violence (Jansz 2005; Chapter 14 of this volume). A similar point can be made about spirituality. Protected by the boundaries of the "magic circle" and the legitimizing mantra that "it's just play", people experiment in games with magic, myth, and "ultimate values" that have retreated from "real" modern life.

However, this "spiritual play" is not exclusively restricted to the world of computer games, but it is more widespread. It is part and parcel of an epistemological current in the popular spiritual New Age milieu where overly rational, highly educated participants have difficulty in actually believing metaphysical truth claims and therefore adopt a playful, ironic stance that is both engaged and detached, serious and playful at the same time (Luhrmann 1991). Irony and playfulness, in such spiritual contexts, is neither a symptom of disenchantment nor of re-enchantment, but serves, as Zandbergen puts it, as "a secular and an enchanting purpose simultaneously and ultimately negotiates both interpretational frameworks" (2011, 157; Saler 2004). Whether one is immersed in the magic circle of online computer games, the metaphysics of films like *Star Wars*, or the otherworldliness of paganism, occultism, or channeling – spiritual play provides a feasible strategy for all those modern people in a disenchanted world who "want to believe", but consider themselves too secular to do so.

Note

1. The study is primarily based on a qualitative content analysis of the manuals of 4 MMOs (*World of Warcraft*, *Everquest*, *Dark Age of Camelot*, and *Ultima Online*) and in-depth interviews with 20 Dutch players of *World of Warcraft*.

References

Adler, Margot. 1986. *Drawing down the moon: Witches, druids, goddess-worshippers, and other pagans in America today*. Boston, Beacon Press.
Aupers, Stef. 2007. "Better than the real world": On the reality and meaning of online computer games. In *Narratives, roles and beliefs in the New Age era. Homo narrans – Homo ludens – Homo religiosus*, ed. Theo Meder, Volume 48(3/4) Fabula, 250-69. Berlin, New York: De Gruyter.
—. 2012. Enchantment Inc. Online gaming between spiritual experience and commodity fetishism. In *Things: Material religion and the topography of divine spaces*, eds. Dick Houtman and Birgit Meyer, 339-55. New York: Fordham University Press.
—, and Dick Houtman. 2006. Beyond the spiritual supermarket: The social and public significance of New Age spirituality. *Journal of Contemporary Religion* 21(2): 201-22.
—, and Dick Houtman, eds. 2010. *Religions of modernity: Relocating the sacred to the self and the digital*. Leiden: E.J. Brill.
Bartle, Richard. 2004. *Designing virtual worlds*. Berkeley: New Riders Publishers.
Bateson, Gregory. 1972. *Steps to an ecology of mind: Collected essays in anthropology, psychiatry, evolution, and epistemology*. Chicago, IL: University of Chicago Press.
Berger, Helen. 1999. *A community of witches: Contemporary neo-paganism and witchcraft in the United States*. Columbia, SC: University of South Carolina Press.
Blizzard Entertainment. 2004. *World of Warcraft*. PC: Blizzard Entertainment.
—. 1996. *Diablo*. Multiplatform: Blizzard Entertainment.
Bruce, Steve. 2002. *God is dead: Secularisation in the West*. Oxford: Blackwell Publishers.

Campbell, Collin. 2007. *The easternization of the West: A thematic account of cultural change in the modern era*. Boulder, CO: Paradigm Publishers.
Caputo, John. 2001. *On religion*. London: Routledge.
Castranova, Edward. 2005. *Synthetic worlds: The business and culture of online games*. Chicago, IL, The University of Chicago Press.
Coleridge, Samuel Taylor. 1967. *Biographia Literaria*.[1817] Oxford: Oxford University Press.
Consalvo, Mia. 2009. There is no magic circle. *Games and Culture* 4(4): 408-17.
Copier, Marinka. 2005. Connecting worlds: Fantasy role-playing games, ritual acts and the magic circle. In *Changing Views – Worlds in Play: Proceedings of the second international conference of DiGRA*, eds. Suzanne de Castell and Jennifer Jenson. Vancouver, Canada: University of Vancouver. www.digra.org/wp-content/uploads/digital-library/06278.50594.pdf.
Crawford, Chris. 2003. *Chris Crawford on game design*. Boston, Indianapolis: New Riders.
Curry, Patrick. 1998. *Defending middle-earth: Tolkien, myth & modernity* [1997]. London: Harper Collins Publishers.
Dawkins, Richard. 2007. *The God delusion*. London: Transworld Publishers.
Dibbell, Julian. 2006. *Play money: Or, how I quit my day job and made millions trading virtual loot*. New York: Basic Books.
Freud, Sigmund. 1999. Totem en taboe [1913]. In *Beschouwingen over cultuur*, ed. W. Oranje, 19-204. Amsterdam: Boom.
Geertz, Clifford. 1973. *The interpretation of cultures*. New York: Basic Books.
Hanegraaff, Wouter Jan. 1996. *New age religion and Western culture: Esotericism in the mirror of secular thought*. Leiden: E.J. Brill.
Harambam, Jaron, Stef Aupers, and Dick Houtman. 2011. Game over? Negotiating modern capitalism in online game worlds. *European Journal of Cultural Studies* 14(3): 299-320.
Houtman, Dick, and Stef Aupers. 2007. The spiritual turn and the decline of tradition: The spread of post-Christian spirituality in fourteen Western countries (1981-2000). *Journal for the Scientific Study of Religion* 46(3): 305-20.
Huizinga, Johan. 1955. *Homo ludens: A study of the play-element in culture* [*Homo ludens. Proeve eener bepaling van het spel-element der cultuur*, 1938]. Boston, MA: Beacon Press.
Jansz, Jeroen. 2005. The emotional appeal of violent video games for adolescent males. *Communication Theory* 15(3): 219-41.
Jenkins, Henry. 2006. *Convergence culture: When old and new media collide*. New York: New York University Press.
King, Brad, and John Borland. 2003. *Dungeons and dreamers: The rise of computer game culture. From geek to chic*. New York: McGraw-Hill.
Kolo, Castulus, and Timo Baur. 2004. Living a virtual life: Social dynamics of online gaming. *Gamestudies* 4(1). www.gamestudies.org.
Krzywinska, T. 2008. World creation and lore: *World of Warcraft* as rich text. In *Digital culture, play and identity: A World of Warcraft reader*, eds. Hilde G. Corneliussen and Jill W. Rettberg, 123-42. Cambridge, MA: The MIT Press.
Lammes, Sybille. 2008. Spatial regimes of the digital playground: Cultural functions of spatial practices in computer games. *Space and Culture* 11(3): 260-72.
Latour, Bruno. 1993. *We have never been modern* [1991]. London/New York: Prentice Hall.
Luhrmann, Tanya M. 1991. *Persuasions of the witch's craft: Ritual magic in contemporary England* [1989]. Cambridge, MA: Harvard University Press.
Mythic Entertainment. 2001. PC. *Dark Age of Camelot*. PC: Electronic Arts.
Origin Systems. 2006. *Ultima Online*. PC: Electronic Arts

Pargman, Daniel, and Peter Jakobsson. 2008. Do you believe in magic? Computer games in everyday life. *European Journal of Cultural Studies* 11 (2): 225-43.

Partridge, Chris. 2004. *The re-enchantment of the West: Volume 1: Alternative spiritualities, sacralization, popular culture, occulture*. London/New York: T&T Clark International.

Possamai, Adam. 2005. *Religion and popular culture: A hyper-real testament*. Brussels: Peter Lang Publishing Group.

Salen, Katie, and Eric Zimmerman. 2004. *Rules of play: Game design fundamentals*. Cambridge, MA: The MIT Press.

Saler, Michael. 2004. Modernity, disenchantment and the ironic imagination. *Philosophy and Literature* 28(1): 137-49.

Sony Online Entertainment. 2013. *Everquest*. PC: Sony Online Entertainment

Sutton-Smith, Brian. 1997. *The ambiguity of play*. Cambridge, MA: Harvard University Press.

Taylor, T.L. 2006. *Play between worlds: Exploring online game culture*. Cambridge, MA: The MIT Press.

Tolkien, John R.R. 1939. *On fairy stories*. http://brainstorm-services.com/wcu-2004/fairystories-Tolkien.pdf.

Turkle, Sherry. 1995. *Life on the screen: Identity in the age of the Internet*. New York: Simon & Schuster.

—. 2002. Our split screens. *Etnofoor* 15(1&2): 5-19.

Weber, Max. 1956. *The sociology of religion*. Boston, MA: Beacon Press.

—. 1948. Science as a vocation. In *From Max Weber: Essays in sociology* [1919], ed. Hans H. Gerth and C. Wright Mills, 129-56. London: Routledge.

—. 1978 [1921]. *Economy and society: An outline of interpretive sociology*. Berkeley, CA: University of California Press.

Woodcock, Bruce. 2009. *An analysis of MMOG subscription growth. Version 21.0*. www.mmogchart.com.

York, Michael. 1995. *The emerging networks: A sociology of the new age and neopagan movements*. London: Rowmann and Littlefield Publishers.

Yee, Nicholas. 2007. Motivations of play in online games. *Journal of CyberPsychology and Behavior* (9): 772-75.

Zandbergen, Dorien. 2011. *New edge: Technology and spirituality in the San Francisco Bay Area*. Leiden: F&N Boekservice.

4. Playful computer interaction

Daniel Cermak-Sassenrath

For a long time the computer was a tool for experts, inaccessible and also prohibitively expensive for private users. This changed in the mid-1980s. The increasingly widespread use of the computer and the growing experience of its users have since led to a new kind of interaction. In many cases the computer is no longer seen as a machine with which well-planned, methodical, or repetitive tasks are conducted. The interaction[1] with it is now perceived as an open-ended process characterized by creative, explorative, goal-oriented, and challenging activities. Connected with this process is self-directed learning, experimental tinkering around, and the self-gambling of the user; and clearly the medial character of the computer invites these types of use. Often, this approach defies a purposeful aim or necessary duty or pushes it in the background. In recent years a number of paradigms have been proposed and discussed that address this change of perspective, but play appears not to figure prominently among them. Some treat it with more sympathy, but others dismiss it entirely. Play is widely understood as a means to an end, e.g. to support the motivation of the user, to make tasks more effective, as a simulation of reality, in an educational game or as an area in which technical improvements can be demonstrated, which is opposed to fooling around, wasting time and energy, and the trivialization of media use. In this chapter, a substantial relation between interactive computer use and play is recognized, and play is proposed as a possible perspective for everyday computer interaction. It is demonstrated how Huizinga's well-known characteristics of play can be applied to everyday computer use, and how the "play spirit" of the player can be identified in the attitude of the user.

The possibility of playful interactions with the computer are explored in this chapter, and some aspects of general media use are also touched upon. This discussion is based on the notion of play proposed by Huizinga. Play is seen as an attitude of the player that expresses itself in a process that is characterized by certain features. Huizinga describes play as "an activity which proceeds within certain limits of time and space, in a visible order, according to rules freely accepted, and outside the sphere of necessity or material utility. The play-mood is one of rapture and enthusiasm, and is sacred or festive in accordance with the occasion. A feeling of exaltation and tension accompanies the action, mirth and relaxation follow" (1955, 132). The perspective and the process interact and complement each other.

In computer interaction, effects of play appear at a lower level in explorative learning, and at a higher level in creative processes. The interaction with the computer also poses a challenge for the user, which promotes internal gambling. The computer is a special machine in inviting play while also following purposes. While the (technical) creation of a perfect medium is an old dream, media become part of reality by limiting and focusing themselves. They do not copy the world, but create it. Designing the interactive computer means designing for action. New media always introduce new conflicts; the computer user fights for control over the digital medium.

Play

Play means taking on a certain perspective. This perspective is the play spirit, a mood that the player willingly takes on and which simultaneously captivates him. It is a perspective that all players share. Play is hovering above ordinary life (Fischer 1925 in Scheuerl 1965), and to enter the world of play means to "dwell in the realms of chivalry and heroism, where illustrious names and coats of arms and splendid lineages bulk large. This is not the ordinary world of toil and care, the calculation of advantage or the acquisition of useful goods. Aspiration here turns to the esteem of the group, a higher rank, marks of superiority" (Huizinga 1955, 60). Players "dare", "take risks", "bear uncertainty" and "endure tension"; "these are the essence of the play spirit", Huizinga writes (1955, 51). Bernard Suit's "lusory attitude" is a "state of mind whereby game players consciously take on the challenges and obstacles of a game in order to experience the play of the game itself. Accepting the artificial authority of the magic circle, submitting behavior to the constraints of rules in order to experience the free movement of play, is a paradoxical state of mind" (Salen and Zimmerman 2004, 574). For Bateson, the play attitude is a "delimited psychological frame, a special and temporal bounding of a set of interactive messages" (1972, 191). Play is an idea, not only an activity. The activity does not create play, but expresses the play spirit. The attitude of the players turns something into play. The playfulness of a game depends on a specific attitude of the players (Scheuerl 1965). Activities are always informed by the perspectives of those who perform them. "[T]he idea of practice is concerned not just with what people do, but with what they mean by what they do, and with how what they do is meaningful to them" (Dourish 2001, 204). Pure activity is not interesting for play and is not even play, because "for whatever [...] play is, it is not matter" (Huizinga 1955, 3). Play is only interested in the "ideal fact that the game is a success or has been successfully concluded" and not in the concrete representation or in "the material result of the play, not the mere fact that the ball is in the hole" (ibid., 49). The play action in itself appears trivial and useless. Only seen from inside, play acquires meaning, value, and sense: "The act of play is the act of interpretation" (Salen and Zimmerman 2004, 372). Play is only play when it is experienced by somebody (Scheuerl 1965). People perceive play in different activities, and play is not limited to certain activities. "The Japanese samurai held the view that what was serious for the common man was but a game for the valiant" (Huizinga 1955, 102). It is a conscious decision to play. It is not entering a tennis court, wearing a jersey or holding a golf club that makes somebody a player, but the mental change from everyday life into the play world. This "*stepping out of* common reality into a higher order" is the precondition and the effect of play (ibid., 13).

According to Huizinga, the process of play is identified by multiple features. Only the convergence of these defines play. They interact, build, and depend on each other and together form an integrated unit. For Scheuerl, the characteristics of play appear as only different ways in which the same phenomenon is represented" (1965, 79, my translation).

Play is free, without end, can be repeated, requires, and produces order, is marked by a certain tension, and distances itself from the everyday world and from the sphere of need, compulsion, and purpose. The player becomes intensely absorbed by play.

Scheuerl defines play with very similar characteristics, but adds the *Scheinhaftigkeit*. Play oscillates between the poles of everyday life and illusion without ever reaching one of them (Scheuerl 1965). He draws on Schiller's notion of the aesthetic appearance [*Schein*] in discrimination from the logical appearance: the appearance "that we love because it is appearance" (ibid., 84, my translation), and not because we are fooled. If and as long as these features of play characterize an activity, it can be play for a player. He verifies their continued existence, and "is constantly noticing if the conditions for playing the game are still being met, continuously monitoring the 'frame', the circumstances surrounding play, to determine that the game is still in progress, always aware (if only unconsciously) that the other participants are acting as if the game is 'on'" (Sniderman n.d., quoted in Salen and Zimmerman 2004, 94). But there is no automatism; the player decides individually if he will keep on playing, and the question of whether someone is playing can only be answered by himself. Play is a very powerful perspective, but at the same time unstable, and "[a]t any moment 'ordinary life' may reassert its rights either by an impact from without, which interrupts the game, or by an offence against the rules, or else from within, by a collapse of the play spirit, a sobering, a disenchantment" (Huizinga 1955, 21).

Learning

Scheuerl (1965) considers learning as a process to appropriate skills that are not realized through normal development. It appears most rewarding when somebody learns what he is interested in, what is relevant for him and what benefits him. "Learning occurs best when there is a desire to attain specific knowledge" (Maeda 2006, 34). It is hardly possible to keep somebody from learning when he wants to learn something. Learning happens only through the learner's activity, and he learns what he is doing: "It's hard to explain this one, but if you were one of us and did it, then you would understand" (Williams 1988, quoted in Winter 1995, 104). Play and learning are connected to each other, but the relationship is not as direct as is sometimes assumed. Like other media, (computer) games offer no guarantee or automatism for substantial learning (cf. Linderoth 2010), but potential. The only thing that can be called educational play, with some justification, is experiential play (Scheuerl 1965, 54) or rather playful exploration, such as with construction kits, which let the player, driven only by his curiosity, try things out and make errors. For Piaget and Papert, "knowledge and the world are both constructed and constantly reconstructed through personal experience. [...] Knowledge is not merely a commodity to be transmitted, encoded, retained, and re-applied, but a personal experience to be constructed" (Ackermann 2001, 7). Giambattista Vico asserts "that we can only understand what we have created ourselves" (Grau 2003, 214). Many computer users learn by trial and error, tinkering around and exploring. This can be realized safely and is quite effective. Home computer use "has continued to be characterized by a kind of exploratory play with computer or software systems" (Lister et al. 2003, quoted in Kücklich 2004). Not only known actions are repeated or replayed, but new functions and processes are tried out and tested. It is a cyclical process in which we see that "through uninhibited play, new avenues of discovery could be found and that, through uninhibited exploration, new avenues of play were discovered" (Stapleton 1998, 432). But play always requires a certain minimal level of ability (Scheuerl 1965), and arguably all or "[m]ost games are about [...] acting skillfully" (Glassner 2001, 58).

Play often demands even considerable skills that are already learned. The necessary practice and training occurs outside of play. There can be no significant amount of play without skill, effort, and tension of the player. In this case, play becomes fooling around which cannot succeed (ibid.). For playful computer interaction, matters are similar. "[S]tress tends to reduce playfulness, while experience with computers increases playfulness in the interaction with computers" (Hackbarth et al. in Kücklich 2004, 23). Play can only happen when it is (practically) mastered, and the higher the skills of the players, the more play can occur and the more free it becomes. "[T]he play-function is especially operative where mind and hand move most freely" (Huizinga 1955, 201). And this relates to play and art to the same degree.

Creative processes

At least since the Industrial Revolution, aesthetics and technics have often been depicted and perceived as opposites. Freedom stood against necessity, art and play against work and technology (Richard and Bruns 2004). But the division of life into work and free time is increasingly challenging (Noelle-Neumann and Strümpel 1984). The aesthetic dimension is always part of the technology (Martin 2003). Adamowsky describes play as the aesthetic center of creativity and experiment without which any relevant technical development is inconceivable (Richard and Bruns 2004). For Flusser, the future human will completely enter the creative process, and play with technology. But he will not get lost in play, but find himself (Flusser 1990 in Keller 1998, 94). Creative processes share characteristics with play: freedom, a certain tension and relaxation, movement and mental associations, variation, initiative, openness, a joy of discovery that focuses on clearly defined goals, the emergence of something new, as well as success and failure. Creativity occurs in a situation of freedom, security, and competence. It demands playful exploration and is sustained by it. Play and creativity rely and build on each other. Stapleton describes play as an "ideal frame of mind in which to experiment interactively" (1998, 437). For Kay (1972), the child who explores the world becomes a potential computer user; children of all ages could use it, led by play and their creativity. Computer interaction departs from the perspective of pre-planned production and adopts cultural and creative applications (cf. Lunenfeld 1999). A low level of formalization may contribute to playful interaction with the computer: "My programmers are typically too lazy to make up any sort of a flow chart. In most cases they don't even know where they're going when they start a program. They try to get a routine working to put in a background, and from that move toward some game" (Ken Williams quoted in Levy 1994, 329). Even in a "totally manufactured environment" there is room for "danger, adventure and transgression" (Dunne and Raby 2001, 6). This kind of interaction has a clear affinity to play: "If it's not fun, if it's not creative or new, it's not worth it" (Levy 1994, 332).

Internal gambling

The interaction with the computer might appear to a user as a competition, "internal drama", or "self-gambling" (Dombrower 1998). When he accepts the challenge, he competes against his own goals. He plays against the computer, as a photographer plays against his camera (Flusser 1983). "You can tell the computer what to do, *and it fights with you*, but it finally does what you tell it to" (Levy 1994, 47, emphasis added).

The high level of interactivity the computer offers and its complex reactions support the perception of a competition: "Insofar as the machine is somewhat predictable, in sum, and yet is also both internally opaque and liable to unanticipated behavior, we are more likely to view ourselves as engaged in interaction with it than just performing operations upon it, or using it as a tool to perform operations upon the world" (Suchman 1987, 42). The course of action is uncertain and the outcome is unknown as "the possibilities [for interaction] multiply as the user's choices call forth different visual or textual responses from the computer" (Bolter and Gromala 2003, 24). As in play, this struggle can go beyond the necessary, and not always aims at a finished product, but on keeping the process going: "To celebrate the unfinished in this era of digital ubiquity is to laud process rather than goal – to open up a third thing that is not a resolution, but rather a state of suspension" (Lunenfeld 1999, 8).

Everybody is equal before the medium, and this applies to play and the computer alike. Media users cannot bring their previous or everyday achievements into the medium. Players "are doing more than just shuffling signs drawn from the domain of the real world", they "are shifting to another domain of meaning entirely" (Salen and Zimmerman 2004, 369). The roles in a game have "nothing to do with the existing departmental, spatial, economic, or authoritative relationships among players" in ordinary life (ibid., 583). In other words, the only way to increase one's reputation is to play for it.

Purpose

The purpose that is often connected to computer use opposes play. If play is to inform the perspective of the user, it needs to overcome the purpose at least temporarily: "It's time to play the work" because of the digital medium (Amerika 2005, n.p.).

Play is extremely effective and strives for the optimization of all processes. While "games are in many cases highly structured and goal-driven activities" (Kücklich 2004, 4), play is concerned only with its own success and not interested in any consequences beyond itself. It aims at a process and not at a product. For instance, it appears that play fails to be utilized or exploited to make work more effective, Of course, a player is motivated, creative, and can be productive while he is playing. *But he does not care.* For him, any material results or outcomes of play are unintentional, incidental, or additional at best; if they become relevant to his play then it will stop. When computer interaction turns into play, it changes its perspective. A process which is carried out to serve an external purpose is then done for its own sake. Somebody who experiences this "is not paying any attention to profit, gain and wage. What he is doing is his duty and reward at the same time. His only point of reference is the activity, is play itself" (Scheuerl 1965, 226, my translation). The purpose is sidelined in this process. The activity of the player might effectively fulfill the work objective along the way, produce something completely different or nothing at all. Play does not share the player with the purpose, it demands exclusiveness. When play occurs in computer use, it is *despite the fact* that the computer is used instrumentally. "Certain activities whose whole *raison d'être* lies in the field of material interest, and which had nothing of play about them in their initial stages, develop what we can only call play-forms as a secondary characteristic" (Huizinga 1955, 199). Or, in Mark Amerika's words: "Let's play, although there is some instrumental purpose connected to what we are doing [...]." (Personal communication, May 27, 2005).

The perfect medium

A perfect medium with a complete and naturalistic representation is an old dream, which was "to occupy Western art throughout much of its history" (Manovich 2000, 172). Examples of "[t]his curious development" (Arnheim 1957, 157) are numerous and include "wall paintings, human size sculpture[s], diorama[s]", "magic lantern shows, phantasmagoria, [the E]idophusikon [...], zoopraxiscope shows", "[b]aroque Jesuit churches" (Manovich 2000, 113, 101, 41), as well as the *Panorama*, Heilig's *Sensorama*, and 3D cinemas (Grau 2004). "[I]n each epoch, extraordinary efforts were made to produce maximum illusion with the technical means at hand" (Grau 2003, 5).

But, as in ordinary life, being perfect is boring. For Arnheim, the "sensory replication of reality" (Salen and Zimmerman 2004, 452) is not an artistic aim. "It is the wish of people who do not know that artistic effect is bound up with the limitations of the medium and who want quantity rather than quality" (Arnheim 1957, 75). But contrary to popular thought, an illusion is not "strong only if it is complete in every detail. [...] in real life we are satisfied to take in essentials; they give us all we need to know. Hence if these essentials are reproduced we are content and obtain a complete impression that is all the more artistic for being so strongly concentrated" (Arnheim 1957, 29). After art explored "the goal of illusionism" (Manovich 2000, 162) and largely and finally rejected it in the twentieth century (Manovich 2000, 162), the pursuit of illusory perfection was indeed taken up by mass media and mass technologies. They pursue it "with mechanical accuracy" (Arnheim 1957, 162). TV, and even more so cinema, remain committed to this aim. "The complete [color, sound, 3D, etc.] film is the fulfillment of the age-old striving for the complete illusion" (ibid., 158). For Bazin, cinema aims for a "total and complete representation of reality" (Bazin 1969, 71, quoted in Manovich 2001, 185). Today, viewers again sit in movie theaters wearing 3D glasses, as in the 1950s, enjoying "films that create a total illusion of reality" (Morton Heilig quoted in Rheingold 1992, 55).

The more the computer turns out to be a mass medium, the greater the danger that it uncritically takes up this tendency. In 1965 Sutherland coined the motto that was to accompany the development of the computer: "The screen is a window through which one sees a virtual world. The challenge is to make that world look real, act real, sound real, feel real" (quoted in ibid., 298). With the advancement of technology the computer developed an increasingly naturalistic way of representation, and "it is certain that virtual image culture will be pushed strongly in the direction of illusion" (Grau 2003, 308). Grau identifies the "field of illusion and immersion" as "the paradigm of this medium" (2003, 9). In the computer game industry it "has always been a popular pursuit" to make "game content look as real as possible" (Price 2006, n.p.). The insatiable hunger of the gamers for "more realism, more interactivity, more action and more exciting gameplay" (Ageia 2006, 66) is only answered with games that are as "photo-real as possible" (Frank Vitz in Krell 2006, 58).

The challenge of design

The design of media is a creative process of choice and selection. The "striving after likeness to nature" (Arnheim 1957) is a popular aim, yet it does not touch on the subject of design. A perfect medium would not solve all design problems, but prevent all design. "The creative power of the artist can only come into play where reality and the medium of representation do not coincide" (ibid.).

It is not the function of media to duplicate reality or nature, and "we mustn't fall prey to the notion that more is always better, or that our task is the seemingly impossible one of emulating the sensory and experiential bandwidth of the real world" (Laurel 1993, 118). Medial limitations or restrictions "which engineers are doing their best to 'overcome' actually form the tools of the creative artist" (Arnheim 1957). The technical possibilities of digital media "do indeed hold enormous promise, but they will not make the central challenge go away – that is, designing and orchestrating[2] action in virtual worlds" (Laurel 1993, 188, emphasis removed).

Knowledge about media informs their use. The experience of participation is always connected to mediation. While media show content, they also emphasize their medial form or character, which is determined by and which determines the possibilities of participation. Participants acknowledge this and are aware of the constraints, but act and immerse themselves in the limited space the medium offers. This can be readily observed in digital media. Computer users are not waiting for the day when "virtual reality is perfected and home computers are as powerful as today's supercomputers" and when output devices can be built "that allow a player to feel as if he's really down on the field" (Rollings and Adams 2003, 503). The computer users are already there and take part, through their mindsets and own actions.

The further development of naturalistic media will nonetheless continue. It will remain a popular challenge, and the thrill of media appears to increase the closer it comes to the edge of the real world.

Focus

Media need to limit their means to be perceived as media and to be used at all.[3] They are aware of their limitations and communicate them towards their users. "As designers, we want the interface to disappear for the user for part of the time, but not completely and not irrevocably. At some subliminal level, the user must be aware of the interface at all times" (Bolter and Gromala 2003, 53). If art does not limit itself and select its means, it only imitates life and nature instead of creating them (Hans Arp quoted in Thomas 1971, 101). There is no music you can play on a piano with millions and billions of keys (Baricco 2005, 74ff.). Games work by substantially limiting their action spaces.

The characteristics of media that distinguish them from the ordinary world and from other media are not deficits or defects that need to be fixed. All media have their own specific form and relationship to the ordinary world. This is their achievement and contribution, and this is what makes them interesting. A medial representation "brings a temporary, a limited perfection" into the "imperfect world and into the confusion of life" (Huizinga 1955, 10). It is more articulate, pure, distinct, and concentrated than the ordinary world: "[A]s far as lovers of art are concerned, they do not look at the movies for imitations of nature but for art. They know that artistic representation is always explaining, refining, making clear the object depicted. Things that in real life are imperfectly realized, merely hinted at, and entangled with other things appear in a work of art complete, entire and clearly, free from extraneous matters" (Arnheim 1957, 136-7).

Media limit their forms and exchange their contents. Their modes of participation differentiate them from each other, while their contents are arbitrary: "[Game] mechanics trump meaning" (Aarseth 2007). It appears that "it takes a long time to discover what is new about what is new" (Alan Kay, in Book & Computer Online Symposium 2003), because "new media, in their aesthetic content, always draw from their precursors, a perennial constituent" (Grau 2003, 350). In the same way, the computer takes content from other media. "[I]n typical McLuhanesque fashion, much of [the computers'] content has been adopted from previous media, and their own attributes are just beginning to be discovered" (Kay 1972, 3). But "[t]he ostensible program content" is only a way to invite participation and a "lulling distraction needed to enable the structural form to get through the barriers of conscious attention" (McLuhan 2002, 263). It is indeed "the *pattern* of a game that gives it relevance to our inner lives, and not who is playing nor the outcome of the game" (ibid., 263). A formal similarity between play and computer interaction is all that can be discovered; playful computer interaction is not about content. Computer games are only an expression and consequence of the possibilities that the computer offers.

Consistency

The notion of consistency describes the relative relation between systems; something is consistent only with regard to something else. "The basic purpose of consistency is to allow the user to generalize knowledge about one aspect of the system to other aspects. Consistency also helps to avoid the frustration induced when a system does not behave in an understandable and logical way" (Foley et al. 1996, 404). In designing, computer interaction, consistency with the natural world, with other media, or self-consistency can be targeted. For novice users, a consistent representation might be the most helpful; the greater the experience of a computer user and the more confidence he acquires, the less important consistency becomes. At least two situations can be identified in which it is given up in favor of other design principles. One is different expectations of the user, the other is greater efficiency of another solution.

Obviously, a medial representation that is consistent with the external world or with other media does no justice to the specific properties of the (new) medium: *QuickTime* still looks like a 1950s tape recorder (Borchers 2004), and "[i]n this way, they make new media simulate old media, hiding its new properties" (Manovich 2000, 116). Nor can it be, in fact, consistent. Consistency does not hang on the conformity with the ordinary world; realism and consistency are, indeed, completely independent categories. However, media usually aim to be self-consistent. In games, there is "no law, written or unwritten, that says that [they] have to conform to reality. They just have to be self-consistent" (Rollings and Adams 2003, 95).

Media enable, invite and, encourage certain forms of participation, and at the same time limit, focus, and control it. "As it is the case with all cultural representations, new media representations are also always biased. They represent/construct some features of physical reality at the expenses of others, one world view among many, one possible system of categories among numerous others possible" (Manovich 2000, 40). Designing interaction with the computer filters and shapes its applications and the understanding of the users "of what new media is" (ibid., 116). Reducing the interaction with the computer to the forms of interaction with other media is wasting its special capabilities, and "if we simply mimic the existing conventions of older cultural forms such as the printed word and cinema, we will not take advantage of all the new capacities offered by a computer: its flexibility in displaying and manipulating data, interactive control by the user, the ability to run simulations, etc." (ibid., 97).

Real media

Media do not copy reality, but construct it. For Krämer (2000, 85), the essence of media technologies lies in the creation of worlds. In the computer, there are no false real objects, but true virtual ones (Grau n.d.). "Synthetic computer-generated image[ry] is not an inferior representation of our reality, but a realistic representation of a different reality" (Manovich 2000, 183, emphasis removed). According to Svanæs (1999, 180), the Apple Macintosh desktop metaphor does not work by referencing the everyday world but by creating its own meanings, nearly completely independent of it (cf. Bolter and Gromala 2003, 43ff.).

While games freely use actions, objects, settings, and situations from the ordinary world, "[r]ealism doesn't matter" (Rollings and Adams 2003, 122). "Simulating reality is an approach that may or may not be useful in creating a believable experience" (Swartout and van Lent 2003, 37). The question of reality is not relevant for media because all media are real. "From the beginning, I cautioned about the 'trap of realism' which would limit virtual reality to merely imitating life when it offered the possibility of something completely new. We should celebrate these new realities, explore them, and be confident that the worlds that we create are every bit as valid as the one we started in. Ultimately, reality is whatever we say it is" (Myron Krueger in Turner 2002, n.p.).

Media create internal meaning and emancipate themselves from the ordinary world. Obviously, all kinds of intended and unintended connections and transfers exist in both directions between the computer and the ordinary world. But, as all media, the computer preserves itself a degree of independence: "Rather than being a neutral medium of presenting information, the screen is aggressive. It functions to filter, to screen out, to take over, rendering nonexistent whatever is outside its frame" (Manovich 2000, 100). Simply put, if something is not seen on the screen, it is not in the computer.

Media are not a copy, simulation, or substitute, but part of the world and of reality. Although the actions of the computer user are real, their effects are limited initially to the *scheinhafte* world of the computer. As in play, these actions cannot be denied, but as in play, they are not happening in the ordinary world. This hiatus does not compromise the reality of the medium, but causes it.

Design for action

The computer is a multimedium with a high level of interactivity. This makes it "a very powerful machine" (Norton Starr, personal communication

July 17, 2008), a new medium for action and a "truly revolutionary tool" (Levy 1994, n.p.).

The computer depends on an active, initiative and decisive participation of its users, as play depends on its players: "interactivity and computer games are defined by the player's possibility of influencing the game *now*" (Juul 1998, n.p.). Play *is* not (in the sense of an artifact or finished product) but is *being made to happen* (in the sense of an ongoing process). It is always close to those who create it. By acting in the special world of play it is established. It exists only as long as its players can maintain, validate, and extend its existence by their own actions. The end of their activity marks the end of their play: "During the game, the magic circle persists until the game concludes. Then the magic circle dissolves and players return to the ordinary world" (Salen and Zimmerman 2004, 333).

The experiences of the computer user and of the player are defined by their possibilities for participation. The computer and play are media for action. The gameplay remains the essential quality of computer games. Stories or realistic representations are no preconditions or substitutions for play. Examples include the computer games of the 1980s, in which technical limitations forced the developers to concentrate on gameplay, the voluminous CD-ROM games of the 1990s, in which graphical extravagance could not hide the missing gameplay, as well as the current First-person shooters in which cinematic elements are disabled by players who focus on the gameplay. While graphics are "of great importance in screen-dominated interaction [...] the aesthetics of disciplines dominated by design-by-drawing tells us very little about the computational aspects of this new material we are working with" (Hallnäs and Redström 2002, 107). The new quality of the computer is not to display content. Games are about the action of the players and the reaction of the system; players immerse themselves through and in their activity. "We've all had the experience of playing an action game really well, getting into a sort of 'groove' in which your eyes and hands seem to meld with the machine. The best user interfaces allow you to immerse yourself in the game so deeply that you are no longer aware of the user interface at all – the infamous Tetris Trance. That's what well-designed interactivity does for a game" (Rollings and Adams 2003, 13).

The computer is not a *better* medium than other media, but a different one: "The degree of interactivity is the well-recognized key difference between computation and all previous media" (DiSessa 1986, 126) The user is not interested in watching the computer (Dombrower 1998), he wants to take part, and this is what computer interaction is about (Crawford 2003).

"The authority of the computer experience is not based on its realism, but on its interactivity" (Krueger 1993, 303, my translation). Compared with other technical media the computer invites play because it is highly interactive. Creating this interactivity means designing for action.

Conflicts

New media introduce new conflicts. Every medial development appears to take the dichotomist form of movement and counter-movement; the first euphoric reaction is followed rapidly by disenchantment and critical review. This process is not a new phenomenon, and it existed before the computer. McLuhan asserts a medial *reversal*: "Every technology creates new stresses and needs in the human beings who have engendered it. The new need and the new technological response are born of our embrace of the already existing technology – a ceaseless process" (2002, 249). Grau (2004) points out the cyclical contest between including and excluding forces in media, between new sensory stimuli and gradual adaption.

Since the 1970s, it has been obvious that the computer is not only improving the world, but also redistributing power (Seeßlen and Rost 1984, 17). The computer has turned out to be a "great organizer", as well as "a clandestine anarchist" (ibid., 14, my translation); it transcends the borders between inner and outer reality, material and illusion, toy and tool, working world and leisure time, incapacitation and autonomy, the private and the public (Keller 1998). The computer is at the same time inviting play and trying to restrict it. But the interaction places the control over the new medium in the hands of its users, arguably more so than with previous media. Levy notes that "[b]y manipulating a world inside a computer, people realized that they were capable of making things happen by their own creativity. Once you had that power, you could do anything" (1994, 291). This conflict shows in the area of commercial software with pirated copies, software registrations, and Digital Rights Management. Playful computer interaction can draw on a certain anarchic potential (Rauterberg and Paul 1990), and it is not surprising that the perceived irrationality of play is always answered with forms of rationalization and control (Seeßlen and Rost 1984, 39). Play can be seen as resistance against external control because players decide to follow only the rules of play, and put aside the order and customs of the ordinary world (ibid., 215s).

Conclusion

Play is not a new perspective in computer interaction. Computers have always been used in playful ways, although only by a small number of computer experts and freaks. But since the number of professional and private computer users began to expand substantially in the 1980s, the experience, competence, and confidence of these users have grown so much so that the computer is now perceived as a medium, a cultural object, and a part of everyday life. Playful interaction appears plausible and possible, and is also tolerated by people who have already experienced for themselves that play is not contradicting "art, information, education, science or work" (Rötzer 1993, quoted in Richard and Bruns 2004, 3, my translation). It becomes increasingly clear that the interaction with digital media invites play and cannot succeed without it.

Notes

1. The notion is taken to mean everyday, explorative, and creative "productivity application[s]", not computer games (Bolter and Gromala 2003).
2. Rather: inviting, enabling.
3. Cf. Pierre Bourdieu's notion of *illusio* (1996).

References

Aarseth, Espen J. Dec 5, 2007. Semiotics vs. mechanics, or fiction/simulation/reality? Two game-ontological models. Lecture, Informatik-Kolloquium, Univ. Bremen. My notes.

Ackermann, Edith. 2001. Piaget's constructivism, Papert's constructionism: What's the difference? http://learning.media.mit.edu/content/publications/EA.Piaget%20_%20Papert.pdf.

Ageia (Double Forte). 2006. Ageia phys x technology. *Game Face* (17): 64-6.

Amerika, Mark. May 25, 2005. Cyberpsychogeography: An aimless drift. Lecture, Informatik-Kolloquium, Univ. Bremen. My notes.

Arnheim, Rudolf. 1957. *Film as art* (18th ed.). Berkeley, CA: University of California Press.

Baricco, Alessandro. 2005. *Novecento. Die Legende vom Ozeanpianisten*. München: Piper.

Bateson, Gregory. 1972. A theory of play and fantasy. In *Steps to an ecology of mind*, ed. Gregory Bateson, 177-93. Chicago, IL: University of Chicago Press.

Bazin, André. 1969-71. *What is cinema?* Volume 1. English trans. Hugh Gray. Berkeley, CA: University of California Press.

Bolter, Jay David, and Diane Gromala. 2003. *Windows and mirrors. Interaction design, digital art, and the myth of transparency*. Cambridge, MA: The MIT Press.

Book & Computer Online Symposium. 2003. The dynabook revisited. A conversation with Alan Kay. www.honco.net/os/kay.html.

Borchers, Jan. 2004. Personal Orchestra: Dirigieren als Interaktionsmodalität für zeitbasierte Medien. Invitation to his lecture in the Informatik-Kolloquium, Universät Bremen.

Bourdieu, Pierre. 1996. *The rules of art. Genesis and structure of the literary field.* English trans. Susan Emanuel. Stanford, CA: Stanford University Press.

Crawford, Chris. 2003, Sep-Oct. Understanding interactivity. Course, Medieninformatik, Universät Bremen. My notes.

DiSessa, Andrea A. 1986. Notes on the future of programming: Breaking the utility barrier. In *User centered system design, new perspectives on human-computer interaction*, eds. Donald A. Norman and Stephen W. Draper, 125-52. Hillsdale: Lawrence Erlbaum.

Dombrower, Eddie. 1998. *Dombrower's g.* New York: McGraw-Hill.

Dourish, Paul. 2001. *Where the action is: The foundations of embodied interaction.* Cambridge, MA: The MIT Press.

Dunne, Anthony, and Fiona Raby. 2001. *Design noir: The secret life of electronic objects.* Basel/ Boston/Berlin: Birkhäuser.

Fischer, Aloys. 1925. Psychologie der Arbeit. *Die Arbeitsschule*, 65-76.

Flusser, Vilém. 1983. *Für eine Philosophie der Fotografie.* Göttingen: European Photography.

—. 1990. *Ins Universum der technischen Bilder.* Göttingen: European Photography.

Foley, James D., Andries van Dam, Steven K. Feiner, and John F. Hughes. 1996. *Computer graphics: Principles and practice* (2nd ed.). The Systems Programming Series. Reading: Addison-Wesley.

Glassner, Andrew. 2001. Interactive storytelling: People, stories, and games. In *Virtual storytelling. Using virtual reality technologies for storytelling. Proceedings international conference ICVS 2001, Avignon, France,* eds. Olivier Balet, Gérard Subsol, and Patrice Torguet. Volume 2197 of *Lecture Notes in Computer Science*, 51-60. Berlin: Springer.

Grau, Oliver. 2003. *Virtual art. From illusion to immersion.* English trans. Gloria Custance. Cambridge, MA: The MIT Press.

—. Jan 21, 2004. Immersive Bilder & ihre Betrachter: Suggestionspotential vs. Distanzierungskraft. Lecture, Informatik-Kolloquium, Universät Bremen. My notes.

—. n.d. Telepräsenz. Zur Genealogie und Epistemologie. www.arthist.hu-berlin.de/arthistd/mitarbli/og/texttelepraesenz.html.

Hackbarth, Gary, Varun Grover, and Mun Y. Yi. 2003. Computer playfulness and anxiety: Positive and negative mediators of the system experience effect on perceived ease of use. *Information & Management* (40): 221-32.

Hallnäs, Lars and Johan Redström. 2002. Abstract information appliances: Methodological exercises in conceptual design of computational things. In *Symposium on designing interactive systems*, 105-16. New York: ACM Press.

Huizinga, Johan. 1955. *Homo ludens: A study of the play-element in culture* [1938]. Boston, MA: Beacon Press.

Juul, Jesper. 1998. A clash between game and narrative (why computer games do not tell good stories and why this is not a problem). *Proceedings digital arts and culture conference.* Bergen, Norway.

Kay, Alan C. 1972. A personal computer for children of all ages. In *Proceedings of the ACM national conference.* Palo Alto, CA.

Keller, Paula E. 1998. *Arbeiten und Spielen am Arbeitsplatz: Eine Untersuchung am Beispiel von Software-Entwicklung.* Frankfurt a. M.: Campus. Also: Univ. Bremen, PhD dissertation, 1997.

Krämer, Sybille. 2000. Das Medium als Spur und Apparat. In *Medien, Computer, Realität: Wirklichkeitsvorstellungen und Neue Medien* (2nd ed.), ed. Sybille Krämer, 73–94. Frankfurt a. M.: Suhrkamp.

Krell, Peter C. 2006, April. Interview with Frank Vitz. *Game Face* (17): 58-61.

Krueger, Myron W. 1993. Die Kunstgeschichte der Künstlichen Realität. In *Cyberspace. Zum medialen Gesamtkunstwerk*, eds. Florian Rötzer and Peter Weibel, 289-304. München: Boer.

Kücklich, Julian R. 2004. Play and playability as key concepts in new media studies. STeM Centre, Dublin City Univ. www.playability.de/Play.pdf.

Laurel, Brenda K. 1993. *Computers as theatre*. Reading: Addison-Wesley.

Levy, Steven. 1994. *Hackers: Heroes of the computer revolution*. http://mitya.pp.ru/chamberlen/hackers/cover.html.

Linderoth, Jonas. 2010. Why gamers don't learn more: An ecological approach to games as learning environments. *Nordic DiGRA 2012 proceedings*. Stockholm.

Lister, Martin, Jon Dovey, Seth Giddings, Iain Grant, and Kieran Kelly. 2003. *New media. A critical introduction*. London: Routledge.

Lunenfeld, Peter. 1999. Unfinished business. In *The digital dialectic: new essays on new media*, ed. Peter Lunenfeld, 6-22. Cambridge, MA: The MIT Press.

Maeda, John. 2006. *The laws of simplicity: Design, technology, business, life*. Cambridge, MA: The MIT Press.

Manovich, Lev. 2000. The language of new media. www.manovich.net/LNM/Manovich.pdf.

—. 2001. *The language of new media* (paperback, 2002, first ed.). Cambridge, MA: The MIT Press.

Martin, Fred. Nov 11, 2003. Engaging computing. Lecture, Univ. Bremen. My notes.

McLuhan, Marshall. 2002. *Understanding media. The extensions of man*. London: Routledge.

Noelle-Neumann, Elisabeth, and Burkhard Strümpel. 1984. *Macht Arbeit krank? Macht Arbeit glücklich?* München: Piper.

Price, Jeremy. 2006. Is photorealism in games the right direction? *Gamasutra*. www.gamasutra.com/php-bin/news_index.php?story=11489.

Rauterberg, Matthias, and Hansjürgen Paul. 1990. Computerspiele – Computerarbeit: Spielerische Momente in der Arbeit. Abschlussbericht der Arbeitsgruppe 1. In *Ergebnisse der 9. Arbeitstagung "Mensch-Maschine-Kommunikation"*, ed. Frieder Nake. Number 8 in Informatik Report, 13-49. Bremen: Univ. Bremen.

Rheingold, Howard. 1992. *Virtual reality*. New York: Simon & Schuster.

Richard, Jörg, and F. Wilhelm Bruns. 2004. Mensch und Maschine im Spielraum. Technische Praxis und ästhetische Erfahrung. artec Arbeitspapier 111, Univ. Bremen.

Rollings, Andrew, and Ernest W. Adams. 2003. *Andrew Rollings and Ernest Adams on game design*. Indianapolis: New Riders.

Rötzer, Florian. 1993. Kunst Spiel Zeug. Einige unsystematische Anmerkungen. In *Künstliche Spiele*, eds. Georg Hartwagner, Stefan Iglhaut, and Florian Rötzer, 15-38. München: Boer.

Salen, Katie, and Eric Zimmerman. 2004. *Rules of play. Game design fundamentals*. Cambridge, MA: The MIT Press.

Scheuerl, Hans. 1965. *Das Spiel. Untersuchungen über sein Wesen, seine pädagogischen Möglichkeiten und Grenzen* (4th/5th ed.). Weinheim: Julius Beltz.

Seeßlen, Georg, and Christian Rost. 1984. *Pac-Man & Co. Die Welt der Computerspiele*. Reinbek bei Hamburg: Rowohlt.

Sniderman, Stephen. n.d. The life of games. www.gamepuzzles.com/tlog/tlog2.htm.

Stapleton, Christopher. 1998. Theme parks: Laboratories for digital entertainment. In *Digital illusion. Entertaining the future with high technology*, ed. Clark Dodsworth, Jr., 425-37. Reading: Addision-Wesley.

Suchman, Lucy A. 1987. *Plans and situated actions: The problem of human-machine communication*. Cambridge, MA: Cambridge Univ. Press.

Svanæs, Dag. 1999. *Understanding interactivity*. http://dag.idi.ntnu.no/interactivity.pdf.

Swartout, William, and Michael van Lent. 2003. Making a game of system design. *Communications of the ACM* 46(7): 32-9.

Thomas, Karin. 1971. *Bis Heute: Stilgeschichte der bildenden Kunst im 20. Jahrhundert.* Schauberg: M. DuMont.

Turner, Jeremy. 2002. Myron Krueger live. www.ctheory.net/printer.asp?id=328.

Williams, Brett. 1988. *Upscaling downtown: Stalled gentrification in Washington D.C.* Ithaca, NY: Cornell Univ. Press.

Winter, Rainer. 1995. *Der produktive Zuschauer: Medienaneignung als kultureller und ästhetischer Prozess.* München: Quintessenz, MMV Medizin Verlag.

5. Playful identity in game design and open-ended play

Menno Deen, Ben Schouten & Tilde Bekker

Introduction

At the end of the 1980s, a thorough analysis of Go games played by Hiroshi Yamauchi conducted by a specialist enabled the latter to draw Yamauchi's psychological profile: the former president of Nintendo was thus described as an unusual nonconformist, a visionary endowed with acute intuition, great (sometimes excessive) self-confidence and nimble-mindedness which enabled him to accept and amend his mistakes straight away.

Gorges and Yamazaki 2010

Gamers are, like Yamauchi, described as nonconformist, creative, and self-confident persons, who seem unafraid to make mistakes (Beck and Wade 2004). Is it true that games present us with an opportunity to develop a particular identity, or are specific people attracted to games that create these opportunities? In the last decade, research has been conducted into the (playful) organizational style of gamers, and into the leadership qualities that may be developed in a game (DeMarco, Lesser, and O'Driscoll 2007; Reeves and Malone 2007). The search for an answer to the above question is the aim of this chapter. To be more specific, we would like to better understand identity construction and representation. For this reason we would like to further elaborate on the notion of *playful identity* as discussed in the introductory chapter of this volume. In contrast to other identity constructs, a playful identity characterizes someone's ludic activities without immediately discussing the valuing and moralizing practices arising from these activities.

According to Goffman (1959), identity is based on interaction: a fluid, active process, depending on the context of the actions and individual differences (gender, class, ethnicity, etc.). It consists of independent and partial sub-identities, which are constructed anew in everyday life. Identity and interests are not, as Habermas (1992) supposed, settled within the private world, and consequently brought fully formed into the public sphere. Today's blurring of the "private" and "public sphere" has an influence on this. In many cases, identity is constituted through experiences, conflicts, and other interactions. In this way, information and communication technologies (ICT) can be seen as tools that support these actions. Today's individuals build and maintain social networks through which they "negotiate" their identities (Lamb and Davidson 2002).

In the last decade, identity information shifts from being published (self-presentation) to being negotiated, interacted, co-created, and played upon. The latter is of most interest to us as designers and new media researchers, since it signifies the most crucial change in today's interactions. To understand this process better, we will adopt Varnelis' (2008) concept of "networked publics". In a networked public space, people interact with their identity information, and the identity of others. According to Varnelis, these public spaces are restructured by networked technologies. Networked publics serve many of the same functions as other types of publics. The term "publics" foregrounds a more engaged and interactive stance (Ito 2008). It is an alternative for terms such as consumers and audiences. Networked publics allow people to gather for social, cultural, and civic purposes and they help people connect with a world beyond their close friends and family.

We will focus mainly on (game) mediated and networked identities, which we define as multilayered identity relations established through a network and interacted through new media like games, social networks, new media, etc. Within these environments, identity relations are in many cases a mix of strong and weak ties. Strong and weak ties are distinguished by a "combination of the amount of time, the emotional intensity, the intimacy (mutual confiding), and the reciprocal services which characterize the tie" (Granovetter 1983, 1361).

In more historical notions of identity, accountability and reliability, among others – carefully constructed over time – play an important role. In modern identity construction, (instant) meaningfulness is of increased significance. This (instant) meaningfulness can, for example, be established by playing the same games in social networks including *Mafia Wars* (Zynga 2008), *Pet Society* (Playfish 2009), or *Restaurant City* (Electronic Arts 2009), or by participating in other activities like chat, MSN, Skype, etc., or by belonging to the same interest groups. In social games like *FarmVille* (Zynga 2009), identities are reshaped through collaborations around certain thematic activities. Within these online games a friend's value corresponds to his or her instant meaningfulness in the game. To be a friend in *FarmVille*, means to be of value. A friend transforms into a sort of commodity, friends become assets to play the game. This directly ties in with the social rules on social networks, in which someone's popularity, or "value", is qualified by his/her number of friends.

This chapter is organized as follows. In the next section we will consider identity construction with respect to young people and discuss the notion of self-esteem. Then we will define the notion of a playful identity, while in the following section we discuss this in the framework of gaming and open-ended play, respectively. We will then look at some design challenges before presenting our conclusion.

Identity construction among children

Almost all of today's children play computer games (Haan and Pijpers 2010), and they are becoming engaged in online social networks like Hyves and Facebook at an increasingly earlier age. To better understand the actions within these social networks and games, we will take a look at one of the most well-known theories about identity development by psychosocial theorist Erik Erickson.

Erickson argues that people's identities are developed and formed by their experiences in life (Berk 2009). People go through phases, and have to resolve a conflict in each phase. How the crisis is resolved influences how their identity is shaped. Individuals' sense of self is closely related to their sense of self-esteem.

According to Erickson, this is especially true for children that are seven to eleven years old and attending elementary school. These children are in the *industry* versus *inferiority* phase. Children in this phase are developing their sense of *self-esteem*. When children have positive experiences working and collaborating with others they build up a sense of self-efficacy (Bandura 1997) and become industrious while they are performing tasks. However, if children have negative experiences, are presented with negative feedback, and feel they are unable to meet people's demands, then they are more likely to develop a sense of inferiority.

Around the age of twelve, according to Erickson, children gradually shift from childhood to adulthood. This phase is called *identity* versus *confusion* (12-19 years old). Here children start exploring their future role in the world, and what they deem as personally valuable. They explore different variations that can result in commitment to a particular identity.

Then between the age of seventeen and twenty-two they go through the *intimacy* versus *isolation* phase. This is related to the ability of early adults to make a permanent commitment to an intimate partner

(Berk 2009). Such commitments require them to give up some of their independent self and redefine their identity to adjust it partly to the values and interests of their partner. They explore relationships leading toward longer-term commitments with someone other than, for example, family members. A successful completion of this phase can contribute to comfortable relationships and a sense of commitment, safety, and care within a relationship.

As children grow up, they are better able to examine more complex problems and to understand the world from other peoples' perspectives (Selman 1980). They also start examining their role in a wider sense in relation to the world. Young children (3-6 years old) understand that other people can have different thoughts and feelings than they do themselves, but they can easily confuse the two.

When they become older they gradually develop an understanding that people may have a different perspective of the world because they have access to various information sources. Around the age of ten to fifteen they develop the ability to look at the world from a three-way perspective. In other words, they can imagine in a sense how a third person might look at the situation where the child itself and a second person play a role.

Selman's theory describes how children of fourteen years and older develop the ability to understand that a third-party perspective can be influenced by larger societal values. They become aware of their individuality and of being an autonomous agent in an increasingly networked world of other autonomous actors (Castells 2002). This self-determined behavior is closely related to a sense of self-esteem. People's sense of self-esteem and sense of self are influenced by the feedback from others. As children grow older, they slowly develop a more nuanced view about their own self-esteem. Furthermore, they develop a hierarchically structured sense of self-esteem, which integrates aspects of academic competence, social competence, athletic competence, and physical appearances (Berk 2009). Children and adults can be in different stages of how fixed they are in their identity development.

One's identity is a constant state of flux. The aforementioned phases are therefore not as rigid and formalized as this section might have suggested. James Marcia's (1980) research about different identity statuses amongst adolescents confirms that some adolescents are still exploring diverse values and goals for their lives, whereas others are already very committed to their developed identity. Thus people can be in different phases of identity development that might influence how open they are for exploring alternative identities with related value sets.

Narratologists versus ludologists: A definition of a playful identity

We recognize similar phases in the way people can play with their identity in games. In the literature, the identity construct that caught our attention was the concept of "narrative identity". According to Ricoeur, a narrative structure (story) is not only a metaphor to describe the personal identity, it is also a way for human beings to construct their identity (Rasmussen 1995). Using stories we can quell the heterogeneity in our lives or, to put it differently, a narrative can help us unifying ourselves.

The construction of something new, by restructuring the existing, seems inherent to play (Deen and Schouten 2010). A playful identity has the quality to restructure itself according to the experiences one encounters.

In *Life on the screen: Identity in the age of the Internet*, Sherry Turkle writes, "If there is no underlying meaning, or a meaning we shall never know the privileged way of knowing can only be through an exploration of surfaces" (1997, 47). For Turkle, players discover that the idea of a unified self (identity) is not always valid. By engaging in role-playing, for example, one can see that multiple characters (or identities) can be explored and played out. In this sense, the ludic identity has a divergent nature, unlike a narrative identity.

Although one's playful (ludic) identity can be consistent with one's values, emotional state, or moral code, a playful identity does not necessarily have to be consistently defined. For example, an aggressive posture will supposedly confirm to high-paced (i.e. aggressive) activity. However, many playful activities can be conducted within a contradicting posture, happiness or eagerness, as well. A playful identity differs from narrative identity, as it does not necessarily include moral codes of behavior; instead it stipulates the way a person approaches and negotiates with a particular procedure or set of objects and rules.

The question arises, then, how games stimulate the identification within the gameplay, if playful activities in games mainly concern the restructuring of game objects, goals, and environments? Gameplay remains enclosed in a system of rules and regulations that are difficult to breach. Players interact not only with the game, but actively negotiate with game designers, other players, and its connected discourse. Copier (2007) describes this negotiation as a system of communication: a continuous negotiation of (role) players with a socio-cultural network of human and inhuman actors. Clearly, if players are able to (partly) internalize the game experiences that are embedded in the negotiation with the game and its community, the internalization may influence the players' identity. Even more, if players can restructure actors and negotiate with personal values then the influence on their identity may be even more eminent.

In the following section, we will elaborate on these issues and discuss some of the elements that allow the internalization of values in gaming and open-ended play. Play seems more open to the continuous negotiation of rules and communication practices than any other activity. It is therefore a well-suited activity to influence today's flexible identity.

Games and self-esteem

Cognitive psychologists Przybylski, Rigby, and Ryan (2009; 2010) allocate the satisfaction of a need for "competence" to video games. As such, self-esteem seems inherently connected to video games through feedback systems that signify players' progression and failure. As Przybylski et al. point out: "[G] ames have become more sophisticated in how they provide performance feedback and acknowledge the prowess of players" (2010, 156). What is more, the increasing difficulty of a game is similar to a learning curve. Games educate gamers to overcome the game's obstacles, building gradually to increase a player's sense of self-esteem in relation to the activity at hand.

The visual feedback, however, is more easily recognized and discussed. This becomes clear in recent debates about positive and negative reinforcements in game design (Hecker 2010). These discussions especially concern visual (or textual) feedback like the achievement system of the Xbox Live. Although some gamers identity themselves as "achievement addicts" the system seems capricious in granting rewards compared to the work done to accomplish them. Many players who at first identify themselves as Xbox Live achievement addicts seem later to abandon their addict-identity.

Initially people can identify themselves with the Xbox Live achievement system. However, the individual players' inadequacy when compared to their overstated qualifications to accomplish specific objectives can result in the abandonment of the game, which influences the player's sense of self-esteem. In a way Xbox 360 gamers are at the mercy of a capricious system since players are rewarded equally for watching their first cinematic game or for having Superman fly 10,000 miles (which is a serious accomplishment). The capricious nature of Xbox Live achievements seems to make it hard to retrieve a sense of self-esteem from the game's feedback. Consequently, the system complicates the identification with the gameplay.

As mentioned above, games do not only facilitate a sense of self-esteem through the use of feedback. The way a game is designed to create an optimal flow offers players gameplay that is, presumably, always within the reach of their ability. Recent breakthroughs in adaptive gameplay affect self-esteem as well. Most notable in this regard is the horror surviving game *Left 4 Dead* (Certain Affinity and Valve Corporation 2008), where the artificial intelligence, dubbed *the Director*, adapts the level of difficulty in accordance with the player's skill and position in the field.

Another example are fighting games. In games like *Mortal Kombat* (Midway 1993), gamers need to perform specific button patterns to succeed in the game. *Mortal Kombat* stands out from other fighting games, as the game does not reward the act of randomly and vigorously hitting buttons ("button mashing"). Within the genre of fighting games, players identify themselves by their ability to execute difficult button combinations. *Sub-Zero*'s fatality illustrates the difficult button combinations well: Hold Low Punch, Back, Back, Down, Forward, Release Low Punch. *ButtonMashers* are considered inexperienced players or *noobs*, as a quote from the UrbanDictionary illustrates: "WTF N3WBI3!!! U R 5UCH A BUTToN MA5H3R!! I M SOOOO MoR3 L33T THAN U!!!!!!!!"(n3rdma5t3r5oooand1 2009). The quote translates as: "What the fuck newbie! You are such a ButtonMasher! I am so more leet (better) than you are!" Clearly, ButtonMashers are not only perceived as inexperienced players, but they are also considered to spoil the play experience of more experienced players as well. Winning by randomly hitting buttons curtails the value of the experienced player's dexterity in hitting complex button combinations. ButtonMashing devaluates the gameplay. Consequently, experienced players may have difficulty in retrieving a sense of self-esteem from the match. Players are clearly identifying themselves here with their gameplay.

Gameplay and identity

To transcend the debates on feedback systems and discuss players' identification with gameplay, an analysis of the game genre seems an appropriate start. Gamers often identify themselves with a specific genre like "sports games" or "shooters". However, the identification seems to be still stronger when it relates to a specific style of play, like the aforementioned ButtonMashing. A genre relates to what Hunicke, LeBlanc, and Zubek (2004) dubbed aesthetics (emotional responses to gameplay, moral values, cultural expressions etc.) and possible dynamics (possibilities and actual play emerging from the negotiation with games' rules and regulations) of the game. The style of play concerns the underlying mechanics[1] and the *actual* dynamics.

We argue that it would be more interesting to research dynamics and to some extent aesthetics in order to discuss identity constructs. Players can identify with gameplay and represent their identity in various ways. We will elaborate on some of them. First, the concept of high scoring and play recordings will be discussed. Second, we look at how gamers tend to name their character in accordance with the dynamics of the play, thereby presenting an ambiguity concerning the discussion of dynamics. The aesthetics and dynamics seem interrelated and intertwined in a complex way. Nevertheless, in light of understanding playful identity it seems fruitful to discuss various playing styles. We suggest that to understand a playful identity better, we need more appropriate names for playing styles, names that transcend the moralizing and valuing tones of most game research.

High scores and play recordings

In early game design, the concept of High Score Lists often describes the end goals met by a gamer. This is especially true for pinball machines, which can be considered the first arcade games to adopt high-scoring lists (DeMaria and Wilson 2003). Ever since Exidy (1979) launched *Star Fire*, the first arcade game with a personalized high score list, high-scoring lists have become an even greater part of one's identity. Posting one's high scores was slowly gaining popularity in game magazines in the early 1990s. To prove one's high score, gamers where asked to videotape their game session. Gamers then started to negotiate the game's dynamics by sharing each other's play sessions.

Game designers quickly seemed to recognize this and created software to record complete play sessions for the benefit of play-training. Especially racing games are known for their ability to record play sessions. For example, *Super Mario Kart* (Nintendo EAD 1992) offers gamers the opportunity to race their "ghost" in a time trial. Consequently, other genres like *action-adventures* (*TombRaider* [N-Gage edition] Core Design 1995) offered players the possibility to share their speed run.

The game *Demon's Souls* (From Software 2009) extends the developments of speed run communities. Players can leave *bloodstains* that can be activated by others to show a ghost playing out the player's final moments. Reviewing the player's death may help others to avoid the same fate in advance. *Demon's Souls'* bloodstains strengthen the game's educational system by incorporating the successful strategies of other players. By analyzing the ghost of another, or leaving their bloodstain behind, players both develop and represent a gamer's sense of self-esteem without relying on end goals, but specifically negotiating about the game's dynamics.

Lastly, the user-generated gaming platform *Little Big Planet 2* (Media Molecule 2010) elevates social negotiations about dynamics even further. Not only can players enjoy the dynamics designed by other players, they can actually construct their *own*. This results in heated debates about the gameplay of user-generated games, but more importantly, in an intense amount of appraisal of other players' designed dynamics.

Here we signify a transcendence from the *industry* versus *inferiority* phase to the *identity* versus *confusion* phase. Players explore various variations on existing games by (re)creating them. This can result in the commitment of a player to a particular playing style, or the exploration of new and unknown playful identities. Furthermore, players are able to review the work of others, and gradually develop an awareness that other gamers may have a different understanding of the game. They develop the ability to look at games from a three-way perspective; in line with Selman's (1980) theory, players can imagine how a third person enjoys a game and how a third-party perspective can be influenced by the larger game community.

As this becomes more clear, gamers retrieve their sense of self-esteem not only from audio-visual feedback (achievements) and social negotiations (high score lists), but also from actual gameplay (the dynamics) as well. This is an important aspect of the playful identity, as a playful identity can represent itself through dynamics in very various ways.

Naming and playing styles

The aforementioned identity signifiers, including high scores, play recordings, and the ability to play together (competitive or cooperative), offer players a way to develop and represent their identity. However, how this playful identity is represented has not yet been discussed. One signifier of the playful identity is one's *name*. Although we do not know how naming practices originally transpired, it is safe to assume that names often have a meaning.

Many nicknames in games relate to the game's narrative and theme (i.e. the aesthetics). This partly explains identifying processes. However, a *World of Warcraft* (Blizzard Entertainment 2004) character/player name like *BritneySpear* does not relate to the *World of Warcraft* lore whatsoever.

Instead, it brings the identification process (the identification with a pop star), happening outside the game's magic circle, into the game itself.

When names do relate to the in-game theme they can also express one's game role. In *HalfLife: Counter-Strike* (Le and Cliffe 1999), a player named *Lt. Sniper* will probably camp on strategic places in the game world to shoot passersby with a sniper rifle, instead of running around shooting others with a shotgun.

Lastly, naming practices seem related to the quality of the gameplay itself. Names in the fast-paced game *Counter-Strike* are surprisingly shorter than names in the time-consuming game *Ikariam* (GameForge 2006). This suggests that gamers identify with both the (slow/fast) gameplay and the narrative. In turn, players may develop and represent themselves accordingly.

One's playing style seems an important identifier of one's personality. Notable in this regard is the work of Allesandro Canossa (2005; 2007; 2008). Canossa deduces various *playing styles* from *Hitman* (IO Interactive 2007) playing sessions, and has named each playing style in accordance with a culturally fitting persona. A *Dirty Harry*, for example, will not take appropriate precautions before heading into a building to kill its target (like *Lt. Sniper* would). Instead, the person will expect to enter a building "head on – guns blazing".

Linguistic research into game player/character naming may prove to be a useful approach for better understanding playful identity, as it is an exploration of "surfaces" (Turkle 1997). However, the analysis of play recordings seems a more logical and direct approach to research dynamics and their associated playful identity, as deducing playing styles from actual gameplay seems closer to the actual style of play than naming does. What is profound in these examples is that naming and playing styles do not refer to the player's proficiency in gaming, but to the way the game is explored and how this playful identity is expressed to the public.

Open-ended play

Constructs such as self-expression, exploration of one's favored playing style, and commitment to a particular playful identity may present game designers with new principles for design. Developmental psychologists Jarvis, Brock, and Brown describe how play "emphasizes the restructuring, enrichment and discovery [by players, such that they can build] on personal experiences and knowledge to create new concepts and experiences"

(2008, 25). It is through this restructuring that new forms of meaning are constructed.

We already signified a change in game design, like *Little Big Planet 2* and *Minecraft*. In these open-ended game environments players explore various facets of their playful identity. In this section, we will elaborate more on open-ended play environments where no predefined rules of play are provided and which present more opportunities for self-expression and exploration.

The idea of computer aided open-ended play is inspired by theories about situated action (Lave 1988; Nardi 1996; Suchman 1987). Instead of designing for goal-directed behavior, as is assumed by Norman's (1990) action cycle, the situated action model assumes that players do not structure their activity beforehand, but that the activity grows as the interaction in the context of use occurs. People are opportunistic as they interact with the world.

One research prototype that was designed according to the open-ended play philosophy is the *ColorFlare* (Bekker, Sturm, and Eggen 2010; Bekker and Sturm 2009; see Figure 1). These objects can detect whether they are shaken or rolled. They provide feedback to players by changing color. Children can explore how the *ColorFlare* responds to their own movements. Furthermore, children can allocate meaning to the different types of feedback, thus creating their own game rules and goals. The *ColorFlare* emits one of six colors at a time, chosen in random order. When it is rolled, its light changes to a different color. When it is shaken, the light starts blinking for five seconds. While the *ColorFlare* is blinking, it is able to transmit its color to another *ColorFlare* in the vicinity using infrared technology. The other *ColorFlare* then takes on the same color.

Another project that shows other opportunities in relation to exploring identity by examining social roles, was conducted by industrial design students at Eindhoven University of Technology on the *Ennea project* (Frens 2008). *Enneas* are little portable devices that measure and visualize social interactions between high school freshmen (12-13 year olds). Animal icons are used to visualize social roles. The icons visualize a representation of each pupil's social behavior and place them within a group, based on the diversity and intensity of their social interactions. There are no good or bad roles, there is no goal. The roles are there to provide a handle for reflection and discussion about differences between people and roles within a group. This allows pupils and teachers to collaboratively reflect on and discuss actual, real-life information. In this manner, they provide open-ended opportunities for children to search for other children with different social roles.

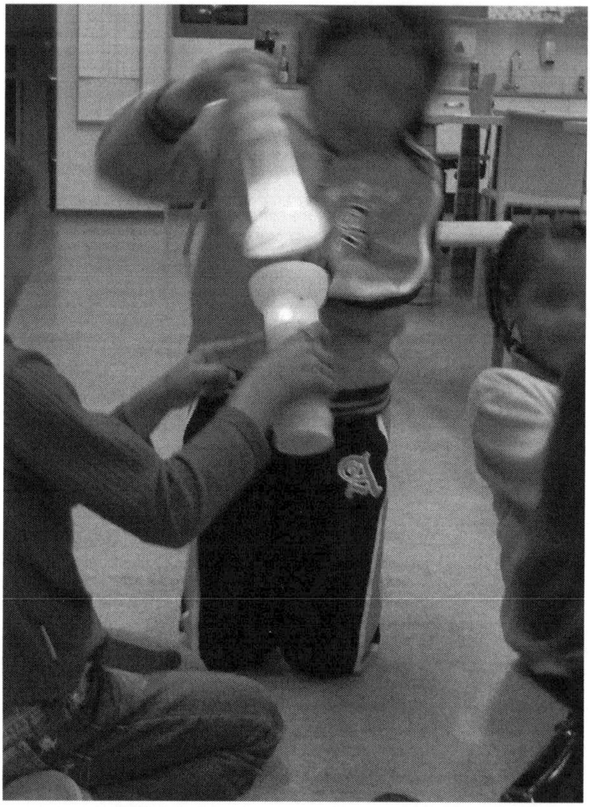

Fig. 1: Children who are trying to send the color of their *ColorFlares*.

What these examples have in common is that these intelligent open-ended play objects can provide children with opportunities to create their own game goals and game rules and in this way stimulate a more social play behavior since rules need to be negotiated. Players can adapt the meaning they allocate to input and output behaviors to the context in which they play. They can adapt the rules as they play to adjust to the challenge, or they can shift the whole game focus to another play script altogether. Therefore, the objects should have a level of abstraction to allow children to imagine them to be different real-world objects.

In the current design practice, no specific suggestions are provided to children to choose different role-playing games when they play with objects such as the *ColorFlares*. We have seen children come up with role-playing games when playing with open-ended objects, such as using the color feedback, to show how much power a child had playing a bear that was catching other children (Bekker, Sturm, and Eggen 2010). In the context of most open-ended play objects, the meaning of the feedback in itself is undefined. We have seen various examples of children introducing scores to play scenarios in order to create a game that has a winner, which contributed to their sense of accomplishment.

An advantage is the fact that open-ended play objects offer a diversity of play activities and stimulate less compliant behavior. Children can practice different types of behavior through this emergent gameplay and thus develop different components of their sense of self-esteem, including their social, physical, and intellectual development.

To summarize we could say that in intelligent play objects players receive feedback about their behavior, either by technology (mediated) or directly from their playmates, which in many cases influences their sense of self-esteem allowing them to construct an understanding of how they are perceived by others.

Design requirements supporting a playful identity

We are witnessing a transition in the game industry, game research and within the gamers' community that corresponds with Erickson's mature growth from childhood to early adulthood. Initially, games were a stage to "show-off" one's playing capabilities and, by doing so, develop a playful identity that is mainly based on a sense of self-esteem (what Erickson refers to as the industry – inferiority phase) that is derived from predescribed rules and goals, high-scoring lists, level completions, and the discovery of game secrets (Easter eggs, warp-zones, other short cuts). Now, the in-game development of these hard skills is slowly transforming into the practice and development of social skills. Whereas games where traditionally designed around combative strategies and dexterity skills (button combination, hand-eye coordinative tasks, etc.), socio-cultural values and norms are increasingly used in game design to enrich the playful activities. The design of gameplay for the development and practice of soft skills (communicating with the user base, connectedness, integrated in other activities and game culture, maintaining one's reputation and expressing oneself through other means than high scores alone) is in line with the development of other media, which are becoming increasingly social. In a way, we are witnessing a transition from the "industry versus inferiority phase" to the "identity versus confusion" phase. Games increasingly offer environments in which players explore their role in the (hybrid) game world. Moreover, open-ended play with innovative toys (like the *ColorFlare*) also offer players the opportunity to individually decide what is of personal value and what is not.

This transition to a more mature game design is supported by facilitating more autonomous actions for gamers. For example, for games like *Tetris* (Pajitnov and Gerasimov 1984) or *Boom Blox Bash Party* (EA Los Angeles 2009) playing with boxes is traditionally facilitated through the design of predefined structures and attainable goals. In contrast, games like *Minecraft* (Persson 2009) offer many more ways for gamers to express and share their game environment with others and negotiate the restructuring of (in-game) practices. Moreover, in more user-oriented games, such as *Minecraft* or *Little Big Planet*, game designers pay more attention to self-expression, which is of increased interest to researchers.

Another important aspect of design is the relevancy of topics subject to gaming. Mature activities, like playing with intimacy, become of increasing interest in MMORPGs like *World of Warcraft*. Intimate role-playing communities are developing in virtual worlds such as *Second Life* (Linden Lab 2003) and *IMVU* (IMVU Inc. 2009). In *World of Warcraft*, people play with the notions of marriage, role-played love, and sexuality (gender bending, online gay prides, etc.) In *Second Life* and *IMVU*, we find various communities that explore different facets of intimacy through diverse fetishisms (furries, Gorge, etc.). As such, games gradually become a mature medium, offering diversity in play behavior (playing styles) to elicit the exploration of different identities and related values (identity states), which could facilitate alternative identities with related value sets, according to the theory of Marcia (1980).

Moreover stimulating different types of cognitive, social, and physical play opportunities in game design could consequently facilitate various playing styles that elicit insights about different components of self-esteem and self-concept, which, in accordance with Selman, help individuals to see the world from different perspectives. It seems that game culture, as a whole, pays more attention to the individual qualities of the gamer, an autonomous discipline in an increasingly networked world of autonomous actors.

Game designers can use several constructs to facilitate the development of what we call a playful identity. Designers can (1) provide reactive feedback opportunities that may influence the player's sense of self-esteem. Although today's (direct) achievement systems are rather capricious and therefore difficult to relate to, we see that the incorporation of developmental psychology constructs, such as scaffolding, the zone of proximal development, and the search for optimal flow, indirectly teaches players to become proficient gamers, and as a result changes their sense of self-esteem. This is what Johnson (2005) dubbed the "sleeping curve": the unconscious construction of (game) knowledge that might be applicable to other domains. We think it would be interesting to explore possibilities to transform this indirect knowledge construction to a more direct approach, and thereby facilitate active reflection and transfer from game knowledge to meta-knowledge.

What is more, the impact of a game on one's self-esteem seems strengthened by (2) the design of an environment in which social negotiations between players, game designers, and the connected discourse are stimulated. Within this community, the practice of conflict resolution is facilitated by presenting players with (online) high scores, play recordings, forums, in-game chat-channels, and various multiplayer modes. This can be illustrated by the MMORPG EVE-Online (CCP Games 2003). The game developers created an election process to democratize the design of rules and regulations in the game. Furthermore, players themselves depict what are valuable spaces and goods in the game through active negotiations and discussion about in-game norms and values.

Additionally, games should (3) offer diversity in types of play. Since players can approach and resolve game-related issues in their own personal way, games increasingly offer various playing styles. This transforms the experience to a more personal one. Canossa's research is notable in this regard. By offering players various styles of play, players can experiment and develop various strategies and personal styles, enhancing their individuality in accordance with their personality. The player's personal style is often revealed to the community by naming a player's character, or by creative-playful outlets (in for example *Little Big Planet* and *Minecraft*). The latter seems enhanced by open-ended games, which we discussed earlier.

Lastly (4), by offering players the opportunity for a more open-ended gameplay or focusing on a more emergent gameplay, games can facilitate the exploration of different identities through role-play. The tension between prestructured and unstructured gameplay relates to the strictness of the gameplay and the rule set. It consequently determines the extent to which certain playful activities (and identity constructive practices) emerge. This emergent gameplay is also determined by the open or closed nature of the game (e.g. to play a game amongst friends or anonymously). A social environment forces players into a specific role that suits their tabilities in accordance with the negotiated theme or gameplay. Designers may ask themselves if they want the goals of the game to be fixed or multi-interpretable. They may also want to consider if the goals should suggest a (measured) identity status or whether the players themselves should negotiate the value of games, goals, rules, or activities.

The above-mentioned constructs range from targeting self-esteem to autonomous activities. Their impact may be enhanced through active negotiation about presented feedback, various playing styles, and the interpretation of game units, such as rules, goals, environments, and play objects. All contribute to the development of an individual's playing style, which in turn corresponds to one's personality.

Conclusion

In this chapter we studied the influence of modern gameplay on identity. We have seen that in modern society, identity is constructed through an instant reiterative process. Social media like Facebook and Twitter mainly provide opportunities for social interaction, and some games focus on solving cognitive skills. Although games do not allow for the construction of personal information directly (besides naming and creating small profiles), they enable identity expression and development through other means such as gameplay, role-play, interactive attributes, measures, and other (non-verbal) forms of communication.

Insights taken from psychology, social studies, and media theory can enrich game designs. However, we find more research is needed to provide a grounded theory and design practice. Finally, in this paper we examined whether open-ended play can stimulate a wider diversity of play activities and influence the development of a more playful identity. We found that in open-ended play children do seem to practice different types of behavior and thus develop different components of their sense of self-esteem, including their social, physical, and intellectual abilities.

Notes

1. Mechanics are a synonym for the "rules" of the game (Hunicke, LeBlanc, and Zubek 2004). These are the constraints under which the game operates. How is the game set up? What actions can players take, and what effects do those actions have on the game state? When does the game end, and how is a resolution determined? These are defined by the mechanics.

References

Bandura, Albert. 1997. *Self-efficacy in changing societies.* Cambridge, MA: Cambridge University Press.

Beck, John C., and Mitchell Wade. 2004. *Got game: How a new generation of gamers is reshaping business forever.* Harvard: Harvard Business School Press.

Bekker, Tilde, and Janienke Sturm. 2009. Stimulating physical and social activity through open-ended play. *Proceedings of the 8th international conference on interaction design and children,* 309–12. New York: ACM.

—, Janienke Sturm, and Berry Eggen. 2010. Designing playful interactions for social interaction and physical play. *Personal Ubiquitous Computing.* 14(5): 385–96.

Berk, Laura E. 2009. *Development through the lifespan* (4th ed.). Boston, MA: Pearson, Allyn & Bacon Publishers.

Blizzard Entertainment. 2004. *World of Warcraft.* PC: Blizzard Entertainment.

Brock, Avril, Sylvia Dodds, Pam Jarvis, and Yinka Olusoga. 2008. *Perspectives on play: Learning for life.* Harlow: Pearson and Longman.

Canossa, Alessandro. 2005. Designing levels for enhanced player experience: Cognitive tools for gameworld designers. *IO Interactive / Denmark's School of Design and Technology.* www.itu.dk.

—. 2007. Weaving experiences values modes styles and personas. *IO Interactive / Denmark's School of Design and Technology.* www.itu.dk.

—. 2008. Towards a theory of player: Designing for experience. *IO Interactive / Denmark's School of Design and Technology.* www.itu.dk.

Castells, Manuel. 2002. *The Internet galaxy: Reflections on the Internet, business, and society.* Oxford: Oxford University Press.

CCP Games. 2003. *Eve Online.* PC: CCP Games.

Certain Affinity, and Valve Corporation. 2008. *Left 4 Dead.* Valve Corporation.

Copier, Marinka. 2007. *Beyond the magic circle: A network perspective on role-play in online games.* PhD dissertation. Utrecht: Utrecht University.

Core Design. 1995. *Tomb Raider.* PC: Eidos Interactive.

Deen, Menno, and Ben A.M. Schouten. 2010. *Let's start playing games! How games can become more about playing and less about complying.* Unpublished paper. www.academia.edu/336403/Lets_Start_Playing_Games_2010_.

DeMarco, Michael, Eric Lesser, and Tony O'Driscoll. 2007. *Leadership in a distributed world.* IBM Global Business Services, Institute for Business Value. www.ibm.com/ibm/gio/media/pdf/ibm_gio_ibv_gaming_and_leadership.pdf.

DeMaria, Rusel, and Johnny L. Wilson. 2003. *High score! The illustrated history of electronic games.* Second Edition. San Francisco: McGraw-Hill Osborne Media.

EA Los Angeles. 2009. *Boom Blox Bash Party.* Wii: Electronic Arts.

Electronic Arts. 2009. *Restaurant City.* Facebook: Electronic Arts.

Exidy. 1979. *Star Fire.* Arcade: Exidy.

Frens, Joep. 2008. *Ennea.* Catalogue Dutch Design Week, TU Eindhoven.

From Software. 2009. *Demon's Souls.* PS3: Sony Computer Entertainment.

GameForge. 2006. *Ikariam.* PC: GameForge.

Goffman, Erving. 1959. *The presentation of self in everyday life.* New York: Anchor Double Day.

Gorges, Florent, and Isao Yamazaki. 2010. *The history of Nintendo: 1989-1980. From playing-cards to game & watch.* Paris: Les Editions Pix'N Love.

Granovetter, Mark. 1983. The strength of weak ties: A network theory revisited. *Sociological Theory,* 1: 201-33.

Haan, Jos de, and Remco Pijpers. 2010. *Contact! Kinderen en nieuwe media*. Houten: Bohn Stafleu Van Loghum.

Habermas, Jürgen. 1992. *The structural transformation of the public sphere: An inquiry into a category of bourgeois society*. New edition. Cambridge, UK: Polity Press

Hecker, Chris. 2010. Achievements considered harmful? Paper presented at the GDC2010, San Francisco. www.gdcvault.com.

Heinla, Ahti, Priit Kasesalu, and Jaan Tallinn. 2003. *Skype*. Skype Limited. www.skype.com.

Hunicke, Robin, Marc LeBlanc, and Robert Zubek. 2004. MDA: A formal approach to game design and game research. www.cs.northwestern.edu/~hunicke/MDA.pdf.

IMVU Inc. 2009. *IMVU*. PC: IMVU.

IO Interactive. 2007. *Hitman (Series)*. Eidos Interactive.

Ito, Mizuko. 2008. Introduction. In *Networked publics*, ed. Kazys Varnelis, 1-14. Cambridge, MA: The MIT Press.

Jarvis, Pam, Avril Brock, and Fraser Brown. 2008. Three perspectives on play. In *Perspectives on play: Learning for life*, 9-39. Harlow: Pearson Longman.

Johnson, Steven. 2005. *Everything bad is good for you: How today's popular culture is actually making us smarter*. New York: Riverhead Books.

Lamb, Roberta, and Elizabeth Davidson. 2002. Social scientists: Managing identity in socio-technical networks. *System sciences. HICSS. Proceedings of the 35th annual Hawaii international conference on system sciences*, 1132–1141.

Lave, Jean. 1988. *Cognition in practice: Mind, mathematics and culture in everyday life*. Cambridge, MA: Cambridge University Press.

Le, Minh, and Jess Cliffe. 1999. *Half-Life: Counter-Strike*. PC: Vivendi Universal.

Linden Lab. 2003. *Second Life*. PC: Linden Lab.

Marcia, James E. 1980. Identity in adolescence. In *Handbook of adolescent psychology 1*, ed. Joseph Adelson, 159–87. New York: Wiley.

Media Molecule. 2010. *LittleBigPlanet 2*. PlayStation 3: Sony Computer Entertainment Europe.

Microsoft. 1999. *MSN Messenger*. PC: Microsoft.

Nardi, Bonnie A., ed. 1996. *Context and consciousness: Activity theory and human-computer interaction*. Cambridge, MA: The MIT Press.

Nintendo EAD. 1992. *Super Mario Kart*. SNES: Nintendo.

Norman, Donald A. 1990. *The design of everyday things*. New York: Basic Books.

Pajitnov, Alexey, and Vadim Gerasimov. 1984. *Tetris*. GameBoy: Nintendo.

Persson, Markus. 2009. *Minecraft [Beta]*. PC: Mojang Specifications.

Playfish. 2009. *Pet Society*. Facebook: Playfish.

Przybylski, Andrew K., C. Scott Rigby, and Richard M. Ryan. 2010. A motivational model of video game engagement. *Review of General Psychology* 14(2): 154-66.

—, Richard M. Ryan, and C. Scott Rigby. 2009. The motivating role of violence in video games. *Personality and Social Psychology Bulletin* 35(2): 243-59.

Rasmussen, David. 1995. Rethinking subjectivity: Narrative identity and the self. *Philosophy and Social Criticism* 21(5): 159-72.

Reeves, Byron and Thomas W. Malone. 2007. *Leadership in games and at work: Implications for the enterprise of massively multiplayer online role-playing games*. Palo Alto, CA: Seriosity.

Ryan, Richard M., C. Scott Rigby, and Andrew Przybylski. 2006. The motivational pull of video games: A self-determination theory approach. *Motivation and Emotion* 30 (4): 344-60.

Selman, Robert L. 1980. *The growth of interpersonal understanding: Developmental and clinical analyses*. New York: Academic Press.

Suchman, Lucy A. 1987. *Plans and situated actions: The problem of human-machine communication*. 2nd ed. Cambridge, MA: Cambridge University Press.

Turkle, Sherry. 1997. *Life on the screen: Identity in the age of the Internet.* New York: Simon & Schuster.

Varnelis, Kazys. 2008. *Networked publics*. Cambridge, MA: The MIT Press.

Zynga. 2008. *Mafia Wars*. PC: Zynga.

—. 2009. *FarmVille*. PC: Zynga.

6. Breaking reality: Exploring pervasive cheating in *Foursquare*[1]

René Glas

Introduction

♫ *This ain't Seaworld, this is as real as it gets / I'm on a boat, MF'er, don't you ever forget!* ♫

'I'm on a Boat!' The Lonely Island, 2009

These song lyric lines accompanied a badge I earned in February 2010 while using *Foursquare* on my mobile phone. This location-based social network service, created by Dennis Crowley and Naveen Selvadurai and launched in 2009, offers its users the opportunity to check in at real-world venues, earning rewards (like badges) in the process. The badge I was rewarded, appropriately called "I'm on a Boat!", is the reward for the first time you actually check in on a boat in real life.

The problem, however, is that I never actually was on a boat. I checked in at Amsterdam Central Station to take the train to work. *Foursquare*'s virtual venues are supposed to be linked directly to real physical venues, but Central Station had virtually changed into something else. Amsterdam Central Station "ain't Seaworld", to use The Lonely Island's lyrics, but for *Foursquare* users, it suddenly was also no longer "as real as it gets". And in case I would "ever forget", *Foursquare* had automatically posted the fact that I earned the badge on my Facebook wall, triggering friends to not only question my real location, but also my sincerity: "Have you started cheating?"

After a short investigation, I found out what happened. As a service depending on user participation, *Foursquare* invites its users not only to add new venues to the database, but also to describe what these venues are, or what you can find there, through a system of tags. Many different tags are possible, but only some of them are linked to badge rewards. The person responsible for the "I'm on a Boat!" badge had to know; he or she apparently added the "boat" tag to the station. By doing so, this person not only cheated the system, but also included me – and everyone else checking in before the tag was removed – in his or her devious act.

This chapter deals with the notion of cheating in the location-based mobile social networking application *Foursquare*. It addresses the question if and how devious practices, like the one described above, impact the boundaries between play and reality as a negotiated space of interaction. Having actively participated in using *Foursquare*, and observed its developments for over a year, the application will act as my main case study. *Foursquare*, with its millions of users, is furthermore exemplary for what has become known as "gamification", a phenomenon which stretches the notion of what constitutes a game. To investigate the conceptual boundaries of play, I will start by elucidating what the gamification phenomenon entails. I will then move on to frame *Foursquare* as a pervasive game and, subsequently, cheating in *Foursquare* as *pervasive cheating*. Finally, an investigation of the various stakeholders involved in and around *Foursquare* will show how pervasive cheating impacts both play and the use of the application. This enables me to focus on the pervasive nature of *Foursquare*, which is central to my argument that cheating in these types of location-based mobile media results in shifts in control and agency over play, as well as shifts in identity of both players and users.

The matter of gamification

The term "gamification" is a true industry buzzword, often used to describe applications with game-like characteristics. As game designer Jesse Schell put it during one of the many gamification conference panels, gamification is "taking things that aren't games and trying to make them feel more like games" (quoted in Graft 2011, n.p.). In an effort to show that gamification does, however, demarcate a distinct group of phenomena, Sebastian Deterding, Dan Dixon, Rilla Khaled, and Lennart Necke describe it as:

- *the use* (rather than the extension) *of*
- *design* (rather than game-based technology or other game-related practices)
- *elements* (rather than full-fledged games)
- *characteristic for games* (rather than play or playfulness)
- *in non-game contexts* (regardless of specific usage intentions, contexts, or media of implementation) (Deterding et al. 2011, 5, emphasis in original).

Or, as a short definition, gamification is the "use of game design elements in non-game contexts" (ibid., 2). While Deterding et al. do not explicitly link gamification to specific usages or purposes, in many cases the goal of gamification is to make applications and online services more like games and therefore more engaging for the user, i.e. the consumer.

As an industry term, gamification is in danger of following the path of "interactivity", which, as game scholar Espen Aarseth has noted, became a form of industry rhetoric implying that "the role of the consumer had (or would very soon) change for the better" (1997, 48). The way gamification in media use is sometimes put forward as a revolutionary force is similar in terms of rhetoric. Take, for instance, this quote about *Foursquare* from game designer Jane McGonigal's prominent book *Reality is broken*:

> [W]hat makes a *Foursquare* social life better than your regular social life is the simple fact that to do well in *Foursquare*, you have to enjoy yourself more. You have to frequent your favorite places more often, try things you've never tried before, go places you've never been, and meet up more often with friends whom you might not ordinarily make time to see in person. In other words, it's not a game that rewards you for what you're already doing. It's a game that rewards you for doing new things, and making a better effort to be social (2011, 166).

While McGonigal calls *Foursquare* a "good game" (2011, 167), gamification's detractors would argue that an app like *Foursquare* is hardly a game at all. It is a borderline case at best when viewed through standard game definitions (cf. Salen and Zimmerman 2004; Juul 2005), and some argue that apps like *Foursquare* consist mostly (or only) of feedback systems, not any game mechanics (Deterding 2010; Bogost 2011). Feedback systems, like points or badges, are seldom part of gameplay; they usually communicate the results *of* gameplay. As game designer and critic Margaret Robertson argues, "what we're currently terming gamification is in fact the process of taking *the thing that is least essential to games* and representing it as the core of the experience" (Robertson 2010, n.p.; emphasis in original). She proposes the alternative term "pointsification" to describe the phenomenon, adding that while the implementation of game-like reward systems in media are not bad *per se*, it has the potential to strip the sense of agency and competence so important for gameplay (Robertson 2010). It should also be said that the team behind *Foursquare* does not consider it to be a game – on the official website it is referred to as a location-based mobile platform. That the company sometimes has trouble addressing the exact nature of this platform, becomes clear in a statement by Alex Rainert, head of production at *Foursquare*'s. In an interview he stated that they "don't consider *Foursquare* a game", adding that they do "recognize the value of using game mechanics to change behaviors" (Van Buskirk 2011, n.p.), seemingly disagreeing with both supporters (it is not a game) and critics (it *does* have game mechanics) of gamification at the same time.

While the discussion above is certainly interesting, it is not my goal in this chapter to untangle the different, sometimes conflicting views on gamification, or argue for or against the phenomenon. Rather, I want to explore play practices that emerge from the increased implementation of game-like characteristics in location-based mobile media. In their overview of current uses of the term, Deterding et al. point to another industry use of gamification which refers to the "increasing adoption, institutionalization and ubiquity of (video) games in everyday life" (2011, 1-2). This use of the term gamification can be seen as part of a larger process of "ludification" of culture, which can be traced back to the 1960s (Stenros et al. 2009; see also the introductory chapter of this book). With games and play increasingly pervading mainstream culture, the gamification phenomenon only adds to the articulation of the playful dimensions of our individual and cultural identity.

While some critics might lament gamification's exchange of gameplay for feedback-systems, as the core experience of play, for other players playing the feedback system *is* the core of their experience. For these players, the "new things" they undertake through *Foursquare* might not involve getting out more or being more social, as McGonigal attests in her work. Instead, these new things could involve finding out new ways to actually not leave the house at all, or being rather anti-social, while still receiving the same rewards as those who play "by the rules". Such players, who do not play *by* but rather *against* the rules, are usually referred to as cheaters.

According to the *Foursquare* FAQ, cheating is "not a widespread phenomenon" within the service (Foursquare 2010). Many instances of cheating are subtle and often indirect, creating at most annoyance with other users. I will, however, point out that such instances of cheating not only raise new considerations for thinking about identities which I consider to be playful (as is also explained in the introductory chapter of this volume), but that cheating practices can also impact the relationship between play and non-play (i.e. regular use) in location-based mobile applications like *Foursquare*. If we want to explore the notion of cheating in these media, we need to first acknowledge that cheating, both as a practice and as a term describing such practices, is rather hard to define. To understand the volatile nature of cheating, one should first look at the boundaries of play.

Framing the *Foursquare* experience

Cheating describes a host of deviant, devious, anti-social, and/or unsportsmanlike practices which break the metaphorical "magic circle" that separates the activity of play from the outside world. This magic circle supposedly defines the boundaries of play. The concept is that breaking the magic circle, which some forms of cheating can do, results in play being suspended momentarily or indefinitely by the players and/or referee. The term originates from Johan Huizinga's *Homo ludens* (1955) and has been subject of much discussion within Game Studies since the early 2000s (see also the chapters by Aupers and Calleja in this volume).

The consensus seems to be that the magic circle, even if such a boundary actually exists, never really excludes the outside world. It is framed as an imperfect separation that players negotiate and uphold (Juul 2008); a ritualistic contract based on implicit agreements (Montola 2009); or as non-existent, since ordinary life always pervades play (Pargman and Jakobsson 2008; Consalvo 2009). Goffman's discussion of "frame analysis", as embraced by sociologist Gary Alan Fine in his classic ethnographic study of tabletop fantasy gaming (Goffman 1974; Fine 1983), has become a popular alternative for the magic circle concept (e.g. Glas et al. 2011). Rather than dealing with a somewhat formalist notion of boundaries between the play world and the real world, frame analysis looks at different levels of engrossment players experience when engaging in a game. Players organize these experiences through frames of meaning. While the types of frame which can form during play are endless, Fine focuses on three main frames: the primary frame of the real world grounding all activities; the game context with its rules and structures; and the fictional world presented within the game in which players are present as characters (1983, 183-6).

The concept of frames is helpful when dealing with gamified media like *Foursquare*, as it leaves more room for games which, like the role-playing games Fine studied, deviate from classic game models. As a location-based social network application, *Foursquare* can be considered a "pervasive game": a type of game with one or more salient features which expand the spatial, temporal, or social boundaries of play (Montola 2009, 12). *Foursquare* exhibits all three forms of boundary expansion. First, it uses the real world as its playground and as such does not feature a fictional game world in which players create characters. While the explicit link with the real world does not prevent players from creating fictional characters[2], in theory, players "play" with themselves. Second, while there are weekly rankings of top users, the game is continual rather than divided into separate play sessions. Third, *Foursquare* features a large amount of nonparticipants among its users, expanding the game beyond the core players.

The argument that *Foursquare* includes nonparticipants among its users might need some elaboration. Playing *Foursquare* does not seem to involve any bystanders, at least not in the way many pervasive games use them as audience, challenge, or obstacle (Montola et al. 2009). There are, however, nonparticipants active within *Foursquare* itself. While it might be considered a pervasive game due to its gamified nature, for many users it is mainly a location-based social network application. As pointed out in the introductory chapter of this book, "a playful affordance is [...] 'virtual' (in the sense of a potentiality) until it is actualized by the playful attitude of the user and experienced as such". Not all *Foursquare* users engage with the service with such an attitude, and for them it might never feel like a game. Due to the fact that these users are aware of the playful affordance of *Foursquare* (they too receive points and badges when checking in), they are not "unaware participants" (Montola 2009, 6), but rather *aware nonparticipants* in play.

The line between being a player and user is, of course, thin. As Deterding et al. point out, it is a boundary that is "empirical, subjective and social: whether you and your friends 'play' or 'use' *Foursquare* depends on your (negotiated) focus, perceptions and enactments", adding that "the addition of one informal rule or shared goal by a group of users may turn a 'merely' 'gamified' application into a 'full' game" (2011, 3). From a frame analysis perspective, however, players and users approach *Foursquare* from a noticeably different frame. As Fine points out, every frame has meanings associated with it, and "these meanings are not necessarily shared with figures (persons, players, characters) operating in other frames" (1983, 187). The regular user's experience of *Foursquare*, for the most part, remains in the primary frame of the real world, which makes them less sensitive to issues which matter for players who are engaged in the game from a ludic frame.

Pervasive cheating

The dual experience of *Foursquare* as a game and as a location-based social app – manifested through the presence or absence of a playful attitude – is usually not thought of as problematic by either players or other users. Players, for instance, benefit from other users' involvement in adding and editing locations to the game when expanding their playground. Conversely, users can see their experience enhanced by players who never miss a check-in anywhere they go, making *Foursquare* feel alive as a social service. The exposure to each other's attitudes and practices mostly remains indirect. Players who cheat, however, do not only potentially break the metaphorical magic circle of other players, they also directly expose non-players to their antics, potentially breaking or at least influencing their user experience as well. Montola states: "[P]ervasive games can take the pleasure of the game to ordinary life" (2009, 21). Cheating in pervasive games, or *pervasive cheating*, can, as I will show below, pull ordinary life into a game – whether non-players want to or not.

As an application heavily dependent on user-generated content and honest behavior when it comes to check-ins, *Foursquare* offers ample opportunity for cheating practices. As a result, cheating practices vary greatly in form and (perceived) severity. Cheating practices are not limited to breaking the boundaries of play that result from the social negotiation processes discussed above. The socially negotiated rules could be called "soft rules". In digital games, however, there are also "hard rules", which are presented through the actual game code (Consalvo 2007, 87). Additionally, everyone using a service like *Foursquare* agrees to obey certain contractual rules put forward in the Terms of Service documents. Cheating in digital games therefore is socio-technical in nature, with the rules and boundaries of play both set and contested at the levels of play, game design, game contracts, and game culture (Kücklich 2008; De Paoli and Kerr 2009; Glas 2010). With pervasive cheating, the act and effect of cheating is further complicated due to the different frames of engrossment through which players and users approach *Foursquare*. While I will forego an effort to categorize cheating practices, I will explore different forms of cheating to show how they affect the various parties involved in creating, playing, and using *Foursquare*, as well as how these parties all have different stakes in pursuing and contesting pervasive cheating.

The stakes of *Foursquare*

All parties with certain interests in a game can be considered stakeholders. In the case of *Foursquare*, these parties include the aforementioned players and users, but also its makers and other companies and businesses associated with the game. Whether their interests are commercial or affective in nature, stakeholders usually strive to achieve what they think is in the game's or their own best interest (cf. Glas 2013). Cheaters are no exception.

While their practices might be deemed deviant or even devious, many of them see their activities as highly pleasurable. They too can be seen as stakeholders. In the following sections, I will seek to describe how *Foursquare*'s stakeholders are affected and subsequently deal with cheating differently, exposing various negotiations between these stakeholders about the rules of play which provide valuable insight in the ways cheating influences the pervasive nature of the play in gamified media.

The players

According to Salen and Zimmerman, there is a hypothetical "standard" and honest game player who plays a game as it was designed to be played. This player type forms the "test case against which all other types of players are contrasted" as he is the most "law-abiding citizen" when it comes to following the (hard) rules (2004, 268-9). The other types they mention (the dedicated player, the unsportsmanlike player, the cheat, and the spoilsport) all deviate in various ways from the rules of play, by finding ways around them, breaking them, or ignoring them altogether (ibid., 268-9). The standard player, however, is an idealized player, at least from the viewpoint of most game designers. While Salen and Zimmerman rightfully point out that such an ideal player might not exist, the idea itself provides a "backdrop against which less rule-governed styles of play can be understood" (ibid., 269).

And indeed, while most *Foursquare* players would probably consider themselves standard players, many do bend the rules. The idea behind checking in at venues, for instance, is that you only do so when you are actually there. Many players, however, check in beforehand (to show friends they are on their way) and/or retroactively (in case they forgot to check in). One reason is that the app tracks and keeps all your check-in data, making it available on the website for yourself and, if desired, for others. Many players (and regular users) like this list to be as complete as possible. While not complying with the basic check-in rules, these practices are generally considered acceptable behavior, showing that what defines a standard player does not just rely on the way a game is designed, but also on the rules created and negotiated socially. In a blog post on cheating practices, the *Foursquare* design team shows it is well aware of these socially accepted rules: "We're fine with pre-check-ins and post-check-ins [...] (Trust us, we do it too to fill out our history pages!)" (Team Foursquare 2010).

While check-in etiquette might be lenient toward pre- and post-check-in practices, for standard players, honesty about checking in is nevertheless seen as key to the *Foursquare* play experience. According to disgruntled players, the first year after *Foursquare*'s launch in March 2009 saw rampant dishonest check-ins. During this period, it was easy to check in at any location from anywhere. This situation forced *Foursquare* to implement a "cheater code" (discussed below), but also triggered players to vent their dissatisfaction through social media like Twitter and blogs.

The players' ire was particularly provoked by people using dishonest check-ins to become mayor of venues. Becoming mayor through standard play requires consecutive visits to places, and only the person who has visited such places the most is crowned mayor. Places like train stations and coffeehouses are therefore hotspots for *Foursquare* players trying to oust each other as mayor. In terms of time investment, being a mayor of such a hotspot has high value for players and one can imagine the frustration if someone who has never been there suddenly grabs the mayorship.[3] When the stakes are high for players to abide by the rules of play in gamified media, cheating can feel just as destructive as in classic games.

The cheaters

Why players cheat or in other ways deviate from the rules (social and/or coded) is difficult to address. As game scholar Mia Consalvo points out after having conducted countless interviews on why players cheat, "perhaps the only constant is the lack of a constant factor" (2007, 94). In the case of the "I'm on a Boat!" badge, the person responsible might just have wanted the badge without going to the trouble of actually going to a boat. Maybe adding the #boat tag was a joke, as right behind the station area is enough water with enough boats on it. Maybe he or she wanted to annoy (or please) other *Foursquare* users by forcing the badge upon them. Maybe he or she just wanted to show how easy it is to trick the system.

While the reasons behind deviant behavior might differ, an overarching concern among players about cheating in games is that it provides an unfair advantage over those who play by the rules (ibid., 87). In a game like *Foursquare*, which hardly has any quantifiable outcomes which could be deemed a winning scenario, this advantage might sound superfluous. With the exception of deviously achieving a mayorship, which might directly affect players striving for this position the standard way, in most cases cheating in *Foursquare* only affects other players indirectly, lessening the impact of cheating considerably. This suggests cheating in a game like *Foursquare* functions mostly to annoy other players. Some cheaters have, however, invested larger stakes in the way they play – and cheat – the game.

An interesting case to illustrate this point is the phenomenon of Indonesian cheaters. In 2010, many player complaints were heard about this group. These users, whose online profile made it clear they were in fact located in Indonesia, managed to amass almost all badges with thousands of check-ins all over the world. The badges include those tied to very specific locations and/or very specific moments in time. Examples are a badge for having voted on US Mid-term election day, having participated in political comedian Stephen Colbert's "March to Keep Fear Alive" event in Washington DC, or a Banksy Badge which could only be achieved by checking in at select movie theaters playing the Banksy documentary *Exit Through the Gift Shop* and, while being there, mentioning Banksy in a "shoutout" (one of the ways *Foursquare* allows you to alert others of your presence). To achieve their large amount of badges and other rewards they managed to check in from one place to another (including locations in different countries) faster than realistically possible, a deviant practice called "jumping". Many of these Indonesian cheaters were to be found at the top of *Foursquare* user lists.

According to one Indonesian blogger, this trend among Indonesian *Foursquare* users can be seen as a continuation of their use of social network sites as a form of popularity contests, where getting as many friends in their network as possible, through whatever means possible and regardless of whether they actually know these people (mia1984 2010). In her eyes – and those of many other players – these users just don't understand how services like Facebook and *Foursquare* work (i.e. what the rules of play are). However, as cultural anthropologist Michiel de Lange points out in his study of mobile media practices in Indonesia, cultural context is important. "Being able to play with, and subvert pre-programmed rules is considered a valuable asset" in Indonesia due to people having lived under the strict rules of Suharto's regime (2010, 193). It is not only seen as fun, but as a source of prestige among peers. In other words, for these cheaters, the stakes are such that they do not consider their behavior as deviant, but as status-enhancing.

Other users

As indicated, the distinction in *Foursquare* between players and other users, or aware nonparticipants, can be difficult to make. When users are the direct or indirect victim of cheating practices, however, one could argue that the effect is different from players. Cheating for players means that the metaphorical magic circle of play becomes unstable, which transports them back from the playworld to the real world. To use Goffmanian terms (1974), the game is temporally downkeyed from the ludic frame to the primary frame. For a user normally not really concerned with the ludic frame, cheating practices can cause a reverse frame switch, where the game is not downkeyed, but instead reality is upkeyed to a ludic level.

To explain this process of frame switching, I will use the "I'm on a Boat!" anecdote as an example. The fact that Amsterdam Central Station was turned into a boat within *Foursquare*'s venue database confronts users with the ludic frame, shattering the service's supposed link to the real world. Furthermore, the unfair advantage gained by the cheater to get the badge was distributed to both players and users without their consent, making them involuntary and potentially unwilling "accomplices". While I consider myself someone who engages *Foursquare* with a playful attitude – engaging it from a ludic frame – many non-players were also affected by the devious action taking place. When they suddenly got the badge that day during their routine check-in, they were turned into cheaters, an identity which is largely linked to the ludic frame of the game, rather than the primary frame of the real world.

Cheaters therefore do not just focus non-players' attention on various deviant uses of *Foursquare*, but can actually pull aware nonparticipants into reluctant (or willing) participation in play. As frames are shifted as a result of cheating practices, we could therefore say that while cheating may break a game for players, it can simultaneously break reality for all others.

While the argument can be made that a playful attitude is always voluntary and can therefore not be forced upon a user by a cheater, the same cannot be said about his or her identity. Even when people using *Foursquare* consider themselves non-players, their user profile still shows the points, badges, and mayorships they have earned by using the service. If maintaining social network profiles function as a way to write one's (virtual) identity into being (Boyd 2007, 13-5), we could say that if we follow the notion of a ludification of culture, we can argue that maintaining profiles like *Foursquare*'s attributes to what can be considered *playing* one's identity into being. If cheaters mess with these profiles, identity construction and/ or proliferation of players and users alike can be at stake.

The designers

The design team behind *Foursquare* is well aware of cheating practices and the grievances it can cause to both players and non-players. They have implemented barriers against practices they deem cheating. At the level of game contract, for instance, they warn users against taking any action, or contributing any content that "you know is false, misleading, untruthful or inaccurate" (from the Terms of Use, Foursquare 2011). These game contracts, which all users agree to when they create their account, allow the design team to block or even cancel accounts. At the technical level there is the aforementioned "cheater code" to prevent location cheating. While *Foursquare*'s design team keep details about their anti-cheating techniques deliberately sketchy, an investigative study shows that it involves using a phone's GPS for location verification, monitoring check-in frequency at single venues, distance between different check-in venues, and rapid-fire check-ins in multiple venues in one location (He et al. 2011).

While the measures mentioned above sound tough, checking in while not actually being physically at a venue remains possible. The catch is that the potential to unlock rewards (mayorships, points, badges) is blocked during false check-ins. Technical loopholes to reach these rewards still exist, as shown by the Indonesian cheaters who mostly check in through mobile web browsers (an option developed as an alternative for users without GPS-enabled phones). While checking in through mobile web browsers does allow users the chance to earn badges and to use many of *Foursquare*'s other social networking functionalities, it does not count check-ins for mayorships. This design prevents users without access to modern smartphone hardware and data plans from becoming mayor but, at the same time, it does not stop those willing to cheat from exploiting the chance to earn badges deviously.[4]

Foursquare's design team makes no secret of balancing issues like these. Commenting on a well-known cheater's blog post, the company's co-founder Dennis Crowley asks:

> What's more valuable – a system in which everyone can play & participate? Or a system that places emphasis on the validity of each check-in/post at the expense of all-inclusiveness? I think the thing that makes foursquare so interesting – and yet so difficult – is that it wants to be both things at the same time. And if you survey users, just as many use it for finding their friends as they do for trying to get points / badges / mayorships (Crowley in a comment on Krazydad 2010).

What these remarks show is that *Foursquare* is designed to appease both players and users existing on different frames of engrossment. Cheaters, on the other hand, constantly raise the stakes for the designers, prompting them to act against them to keep the playful spirit of *Foursquare* alive, while preventing other users from leaving in frustration due to the overly strict check-in system. Keeping both players and other users on board is important as the service's business model depends on it, which brings us to the final stakeholder group discussed in this chapter.

Businesses

As *Foursquare* is a free-to-use service for users, its business model depends on other means of income. Primary sources of income are marketing partnerships, with brands using the service to reach the social media crowd. The *Foursquare* reward system is comparable to loyalty programs like airlines' frequent flyer systems, rewarding repeat customers in a similar fashion (Bogost 2010). Interested parties can tap into this loyalty by offering promotional, brand-unique badges. For venue owners, a free set of tools is available to set up *Specials* for regular customers or mayors. These types of in-game marketing, in which both *Foursquare* and the participating businesses do not have affective but commercial stakes, can be derailed by cheating practices.

Specials are especially sensitive to exploitation. Promoting a *Special*, e.g. free drinks in a bar for the mayor, invites potentially dishonest check-in behavior. This in turn might put off honest players – potential customers for a business. To protect *their* customers against situations like this, in late 2010, *Foursquare* began offering businesses the possibility to oust mayors from their venues if they have reason to believe the mayorship was not gained through legitimate means.[5] Understandable from a commercial perspective, decisions like these make businesses, rather than game makers or players, into arbiters of the rules of play.

While the experience of players and non-player users, as well as the content they generate, matters greatly to the design team, we should not underestimate external business partners, whether they are big brands buying their own badges or small companies using the free *Specials* tool. They are increasingly becoming key stakeholders, forming a source of (potential) revenue and fuelling growth of gamified media like *Foursquare*, but they are also acting as participants in the realm of play. If and how these commercial parties use (and potentially misuse) their agency over the rules of play, is beyond the scope of this chapter, but unquestionably shines new light on how the boundaries of play are negotiated in gamified media and culture.

Conclusion

In their discussion of pervasive games in media culture, game researchers Jaakko Stenros, Markus Montola, and Frans Mäyrä have pointed out that a clear distinction between serious and playful mindsets and contexts is not sufficient to cover all pervasive play forms. They argue that it "omits the constantly growing phenomena of fabrication and pretense, which exist in the gray borders of playfulness" (2009, 271). Both fabrication and pretense result in situations where one party is oblivious of a playful situation while the other is not. This chapter has been an effort to address another such gray area of pervasive games, cheating, where all parties are aware of the presence of a playful situation, but deviant practices challenge the boundaries between play and ordinary life. To be able to do so, I first engaged in a discussion about the status of these boundaries in gamified media and pervasive games, concluding that cheating adds further complexity to the already blurred distinction between play and non-play inherent to these types of games. By exploring various forms of cheating as well as how different stakeholders influence and are influenced by these practices, I have shown that cheating can be much more than just a nuisance. Similarly to fabrication and pretense, where an "asymmetry in information also creates an asymmetry in power and control" (Stenros, Montola, and Mäyrä 2009, 273), cheaters can create situations where another stakeholder's agency over gamified media like *Foursquare* – and, as a consequence, their own identity – is at stake.

Game scholar Julian Kücklich reminds us that the study of cheating "foregrounds the fact that games are embedded into a larger social and cultural context with undeniable links to the world we inhabit" (2008, 69). With the phenomenon of gamification on the rise in our culture, we will most certainly see an increase in the amount and variety of pervasive cheating practices. As such, further research is needed to explore the concept of cheating in relation to the increasingly prominent role of playful identity in our culture.

There are, however, other venues for research that result from the notion of pervasive cheating. Kücklich for instance points out that cheating in massively multiplayer online role-playing games (or MMORPGs) is of special interest:

> as these [games] are novel participatory media forms that are infused with cultural codes from the real world such as the flow of currency and commodities. Insofar as the characters themselves become a commodity in MMORPGs, cheats that address this commodification can be said to possess critical potential (2008, 69).

Like MMORPGs, gamified media such as *Foursquare* are novel participatory media forms also, and here cheating has critical potentials as well. Take, for instance, Bogost's argument that gamification, or "exploitationware" as he prefers to call it, perverts the traditional two-way relationship between institutions and customers. In his view, "organizations ask for loyalty, but they reciprocate that loyalty with shams, counterfeit incentives that neither provide value nor require investment" (2011, 4). From this perspective, we should explore to what extent pervasive cheating practices that highlight the futility of gamification's reward systems have the potential to confront players with this asymmetrical relationship.

The link between cheating and critique is not limited, however, to exposing the business models behind the gamification phenomenon. Players themselves find other creative uses for manipulating the rules of play. I have, for instance, come across a *Foursquare* venue which, translated from Dutch, was named "Hangout for idlers, potential criminals and people who've lost their way" and was tagged with terms like #freeloaders, #homeless, and #dangerous. Additionally, someone used *Foursquare*'s "tips" option (usually reserved for positive feedback about a venue) pointing out how the local government had failed to stop impoverishment of the building in question – as it turned out, an old high school turned squat. Entries like these suggest that bending the rules of a playful platform like *Foursquare* can be used for political activism.

Although it can be argued whether actions like these can still be considered a form of cheating, the link between pervasive cheating and critique is nevertheless intriguing. It again shows that, as a practice pervading the spatial, temporal, and social boundaries of play, pervasive cheating has the potential to affect the real world in unexpected ways.

Notes

1. This chapter was previously published as René Glas. 2013. Breaking Reality: Exploring Pervasive Cheating in Foursquare. *Transactions of the Digital Games Research Association Journal*, 1(1). http://todigra.org/index.php/todigra/article/view/4.
2. Some *Foursquare* users do create fictional characters, often meant for humorous purposes. One cheater admitted having created, among others, a fake Martha Stewart checking into dollar stores and pawnshops, a fake Tommy Chong who he made mayor of 120 cannabis clinics and a "random nerd" who likes to check in at large Silicon Valley campuses (Krazydad 2010).
3. As *Foursquare* was one of the first big gamification phenomena in early 2010, the frustration about cheating practices during battles for mayorships even entered pop culture. Popular webcomic *Player vs. Player*, for instance,

dedicated a story arc to it (Kurtz 2010), and it even spawned an online video series called *Foursquare Cops* (Tondorf 2010).

4. This situation has furthermore prompted the design team to implement a system in which players suspected of cheating practices are flagged. When deemed guilty, they will have their accounts blocked from earning any rewards.
5. Additionally, businesses can assign employees and managers for their venues (in effect preventing these users from collecting rewards) and display check-in codes on screens that players need to type in for validation.

References

Aarseth, Espen J. 1997. *Cybertext, perspectives on ergodic literature*. Baltimore, MD: The Johns Hopkins University Press.

Bogost, Ian. 2010. Persuasive games: Check-ins check out. *Gamasutra*. www.gamasutra.com/view/feature/4269/persuasive_games_checkins_check_.php.

—. 2011. Persuasive games: Exploitationware. *Gamasutra*. www.gamasutra.com/view/feature/6366/persuasive_games_exploitationware.php.

Boyd, Danah. 2007. Why youth (heart) social network sites: The role of networked publics in teenage social life. In *MacArthur foundation series on digital learning – Youth, identity, and digital media volume*, ed. David Buckingham, 119-142. Cambridge, MA: The MIT Press.

Consalvo, Mia. 2007. *Cheating: Gaining advantage in videogames*. Cambridge, MA: The MIT Press.

Consalvo, Mia. 2009. There is no magic circle. *Games and Culture*. 4(4): 408-17.

Crowley, Dennis, and Selvadurai, Naveen. 2009. *Foursquare*. Foursquare Labs, Inc.

De Paoli, Stefano, and Aphra Kerr. 2009. The cheating assemblage in MMORPGs: Towards a sociotechnical description of cheating. In *Changing views – Worlds in play: Proceedings of the second international conference of DiGRA*, eds. Suzanne de Castell and Jennifer Jenson, Vancouver, Canada: University of Vancouver. www.digra.org/dl/db/09287.23190.pdf.

Deterding, Sebastian. 2010. Pawned. Gamification and its discontents. Paper presented at *Playful 2010*, London. www.slideshare.net/dings/pawned-gamification-and-its-discontents.

Deterding, Sebastian, Dan Dixon, Rilla Khaled, and Lennart Nacke. 2011. From game design elements to gamefulness: Defining "gamification". Paper presented at *MindTrek '11*, Tampere. http://dl.dropbox.com/u/220532/MindTrek_Gamification_PrinterReady_110806_SDE_accepted_LEN_changes_1.pdf

Fine, Gary Alan. 1983. *Shared fantasy: Role-playing games as social worlds*. Chicago, IL: University of Chicago Press.

Foursquare. 2010. Foursquare FAQ: How do you prevent people from cheating? http://support.foursquare.com/entries/195341-how-do-you-prevent-people-from-cheating/.

—. 2011. Foursquare Labs, Inc. Terms of Use. https://foursquare.com/legal/terms.

Glas, René. 2013. *Battlefields of negotiation: Control, agency and ownership in World of Warcraft*. Amsterdam: Amsterdam University Press.

—, Kristine Jørgensen, Torill Mortensen, and Luca Rossi. 2011. Framing the game: Four game-related approaches to Goffman's frames. In *Online gaming in context: The social and cultural significance of online games*, eds. Garry Crawford, Victoria K. Gosling, and Ben Light, 141-58. London: Routledge.

Goffman, Erving. 1974. *Frame analysis: An essay on the organization of experience*. Cambridge, MA: Harvard University Press.

Graft, Kris. 2011. GDC 2011: Time to ditch the term "gamification"? *Gamasutra*. http://gamasutra.com/view/news/33315/GDC_2011_Time_To_Ditch_The_Term_Gamification.php.

He, Wenbo, Xue Liu, and Mai Ren. 2011. Location cheating: A security challenge to location-based social network services. http://arxiv.org/abs/1102.4135.

Huizinga, Johan. 1955. *Homo ludens: A study of the play-element in culture* [1938]. Boston, MA: Beacon Press.

Juul, Jesper. 2005. *Half-real: Video games between real rules and fictional worlds*. Cambridge, MA: The MIT Press.

—. The magic circle and the puzzle piece. 2008. *Conference proceedings of the philosophy of computer games*, eds. Stephan Grünzel, Michael Liebe, and Dieter Mersch, 56-67. Potsdam: Universität Potsdam.

Krazydad. 2010. Mayor of the North Pole. www.krazydad.com/blog/2010/02/mayor-of-the-north-pole/.

Kücklich, Julian. 2008. Forbidden pleasures: Cheating in computer games. In *The pleasures of computer gaming: Essays on cultural history, theory and aesthetics*, eds. Melanie Swalwell, and Jason Wilson, 52-71. Jefferson: McFarland.

Kurtz, Scott R. 2010. Hopscotch. *PvPonline.com*. www.pvponline.com/2010/02/03/hopscotch/.

Lange, Michiel de. 2010. *Moving circles: Mobile media and playful identities*. PhD dissertation. Rotterdam: Erasmus University.

McGonigal, Jane. 2011. *Reality is broken: Why games make us better and how they can change the world*. London: Jonathan Cape.

mia1984. 2010. Indonesians on the social network. http://mia1984.wordpress.com/2010/10/29/indonesians-on-the-social-network/.

Montola, Markus. 2009. Games and pervasive games. In *Pervasive games: theory and design*, eds. Markus Montola, Jaakko Stenros, and Annika Waern, 7-24. Burlington: Morgan Kaufman.

—, Jaakko Stenros, and Annika Waern (eds.). 2009. *Pervasive games: Theory and design*. Burlington: Morgan Kaufman.

Pargman, Daniel, and Peter Jakobsson. 2008. Do you believe in magic? Computer games in everyday life. In *European Journal of Cultural Studies* 11(2): 225-43.

Robertson, Margaret. 2010. Can't play, won't play. *Hide & Seek*. Available at www.hideandseek.net/cant-play-wont-play/.

Salen, Katie, and Eric Zimmerman. 2004. *Rules of play: Game design fundamentals*. Cambridge, MA: The MIT Press.

Stenros, Jaakko, Markus Montola, and Frans Mäyrä. 2009. Pervasive games in media culture. In *Pervasive games: theory and design*, eds. Markus Montola, Jaakko Stenros, and Annika Waern, 257-76. Burlington: Morgan Kaufman.

Team Foursquare. 2010. On Foursquare, cheating, and claiming mayorships from your couch... http://blog.foursquare.com/2010/04/07/503822143/.

Tondorf, Woody. 2010. Foursquare cops. HubSpot Blog. http://blog.hubspot.com/foursquare-cops/tabid/76228/Default.aspx.

Van Buskirk, Eliot. 2011. Foursquare: the SXSW interview. *Wired.com – Underwire*. www.wired.com/underwire/2011/03/foursquare-the-sxsw-interview/.

7. Playing with bits and bytes: The savage mind in the digital age

Valerie Frissen

Introduction

This chapter focuses on the relation between play and the practices of technological modification and innovation.[1] Playing with technologies has always been an important driving force behind technological transformation. This is even more the case in the digital era, which has given rise to a lively Do-It-Yourself (DIY) culture, in which amateurs and ordinary users have become prominent players in the technological game. It is argued that play offers an interesting angle to understand the characteristics of this DIY culture. In the digital DIY culture technology is used and tinkered with in an open-ended way. In the process of playing around, new connections, ideas, and applications spring up. Improvisation, trial and error, and playing with the rules characterize these practices. Digital DIY practices are highly socially driven: collaboration and communication with others is a crucial element. The motivation of a digital DIY enthusiast is not so much to produce serious, intentional innovations, but is more intrinsically shaped by the fun and enjoyment of tinkering itself, which can be quite an absorbing pastime. Innovations are often just the accidental results of such processes.

This reminds us of how Johan Huizinga – the great source of inspiration for this book – has described play (1955). He considers play as a free activity standing outside "ordinary" life, in the sense of having no serious purpose (be it "holy" serious in how it may absorb us completely). Play does not serve any material interest or profit, but is intrinsically motivated. Huizinga considers the social aspect of play very important.[2] Although Huizinga actually saw the technologies of his time and play as complete opposites, in this chapter it is argued that digital technologies are essentially *playful technologies*, not only as apt *tools for play*, but also as being the *result of playful practices*. In this chapter we focus particularly on the second aspect: how playfulness shapes technological innovation. Furthermore, we argue that the playful mindset that characterizes the digital era, is similar to what anthropologist Lévi-Strauss has called "the savage mind".

On amateurs, DIY enthusiasts and ordinary users

Ask anyone how important innovations occur and most will tend to think of clever engineers in a high-tech lab rather than of tinkering amateurs working together in a playful, open, and social atmosphere. Yet it is often these communities of amateurs, with all their improvisation and fiddling with anything that comes to hand, that have stood at the cradle of striking inventions and technological breakthroughs. If it had not been for the efforts of enthusiastic radio amateurs, the radio might not have become such a successful mass medium (cf. Moores 2000). The invention of the radio telegraph by Marconi at the start of the 20th century led to all kinds of experiments with this new technology. Amateur wireless operators – also referred to as "radio hams" – played a prominent role in disseminating and improving the new technology. In Dutch broadcast history these radio hams have a special place even now: the name of the current broadcaster VARA – "Vereniging van Arbeiders Radio Amateurs" (Workers' Association of Amateur Radio Operators) – harks back to the construction kits of the thirties that enabled VARA members to easily assemble a simple radio, the so-called Varadyne. These self-assembled and operated radios with manuals included can still be found for sale on digital marketplaces, many still in perfect working condition.

Von Hippel (2005) proposes another example of the power of amateur innovation when he describes how the tinkering of a group of fanatical surfers in Hawaii gave professional windsurfing a huge boost. The surfers were all experimenting with acrobatic leaps, which caused many injuries and damage to the equipment. Keeping the board with you on the waves was a true art. So the surfers came up with an experimental design for a surfboard with foot straps. These enabled all kinds of new surfing techniques that have changed the sport considerably. Von Hippel cites one of these surfers:

> That's when I first started jumping with foot straps and discovering controlled flight. I could go so much faster than I ever thought and when you hit a wave it was like a motorcycle rider hitting a ramp; you just flew into the air. All of a sudden not only could you fly into the air, but you could land the thing, and not only that, but you could change direction in the air! The whole sport of high-performance windsurfing really started from that. As soon as I did it, there were about ten of us who sailed all the time together and within one or two days there were various boards out there that had foot straps of various kinds on them, and we were all

going fast and jumping waves and stuff. It just kind of snowballed from there (2005, 1-2).

According to Von Hippel, by 1998 more than a million people engaged in windsurfing, and a large fraction of the boards sold incorporated these user-developed innovations for the high-performance sport (ibid, 2).

A third and final example comes from the history of music. In the late 1970s hip-hop and rap emerged in the subculture of African-American kids in large cities.[3] Rapping, American slang for talking, builds on an old black American tradition of storytelling accompanied by music. In West Africa, the *griots* were traveling singers and storytellers who went from village to village. Today's rappers are, as it were, the inheritors of this tradition. Rappers started using beats taken from other music (samples) to back their lyrics. This was done by "scratching": DJs moving the record back and forth as it was playing, thus creating a rhythmical pattern. Various musical traditions and styles were used, from the inspiring sounds of the Jamaican music scene to the high-tech sound of European bands like Kraftwerk. Computers enabled all kinds of samples to be connected or mixed by DJs during live performances in the way that is now popular in dance music. Hip-hop, rap, and dance have not only become a mature commercial product, but the fun "cut and paste" technique of sampling and scratching has also generated various kinds of new techno music in which beats are at the core. Dick Hebdige (1979) has described a similar process of remixing and recombining in his analysis of the punk subculture of the 1970s. At this time, familiar symbolic elements of ordinary consumerism were mixed into a new subversive style, which was then in turn absorbed back into mainstream consumer culture.

These examples make it clear that experimenting amateurs can be a driving force behind innovation processes. In their pamphlet *The pro-am revolution* (2004), Charles Leadbeater and Paul Miller argue that recent innovation history is characterized in particular by the advance of the professional amateur, or the *pro-am*. The twentieth century was largely shaped by professionals who worked in large, hierarchically structured organizations. The production of knowledge also came about mainly within a strongly regulated and streamlined environment in closed R&D laboratories where "amateurism" had no place. But according to these authors, in the last two decades of the last century exciting innovations were more frequently emerging from informal networks of amateurs. These amateurs often playfully experimented with the things that were happening in their own field of practice. In an open-ended process of improvisation and trial and error, whereby they challenged each other and made smart use of the latent knowledge in their networks, they – often more or less accidentally – invented, improved existing processes, and developed new ideas.

This rise of the pro-am (or "lead users", as Von Hippel would call them) is particularly manifest in the ICT domain. A famous example of a pro-am ICT innovation is Linux (Bretthauer 2001), which came about when the student Linus Torvalds shared the source code of the kernel he was working on with other amateur software developers. He asked them for comments and suggestions for improvements and invited them to tinker with the software themselves. The outcome is well-known: the famous operating system GNU/Linux. According to Linuxcounter.net some 66 million people worldwide are currently using Linux.[4] Since its birth many communities of users have been helping to improve the system, and Linux has now acquired the reputation for being one of most reliable operating systems in the world. In many ways, Linux has shaped other systems not only in pushing open source code, but also in showing that teamwork and imagination in the community of users can be a driving force behind innovation.

The open source approach of which Linux is probably the most prominent example, originates in the hacker culture, historically associated with the renowned Massachusetts Institute of Technology (MIT).[5] The blogger Tristan Louis claims that hacking and gaming have a common history at MIT, and this can be traced back to MIT's Tech Model Railroad Club (TMRC) where playing and experimenting with model trains in turn led to all kinds of new technological experiments like hacking and gaming.[6] The underlying driver was a subculture where pleasure and value in experimenting and exploring were highly esteemed. The value of this experimental hacker culture has since become much more broadly recognized. A sign of this is that government institutions and major companies are increasingly employing computer hackers and crackers to help develop high-tech, secure software.

In the ICT world we find many illustrations of the striking role played by enthusiastic amateurs, such as in the development and use of P2P technology in which amateurs were very influential. This innovation, and especially its unintended use, saw users take over a large part of the distribution of digital content. Now file sharing, along with downloading and sharing music and films, has become a standard practice, with quite a disruptive impact. It probably will not be long before physical picture and sound carriers (CDs and DVDs) are consigned to the past for good. This has had serious implications for the music and film industry. Although these implications are quite disruptive, they are not necessarily all negative, as they have also spawned successful new inventions like the MP3 player and the iPod as well as new services like iTunes and Spotify. The development of text messaging is also often cited as an illustration of how ordinary users can contribute to getting an unexpected technological and economic innovation off the ground (cf. Taylor and Vincent 2005). Since texting was increasingly used as a key tool for everyday interaction, a relatively marginal business application became the cash cow for the telecom industry, contrary to all expectations (cf. Rheingold 2003). And finally, in the explosive emergence and growth of what has been labeled WEB 2.0, we are now witnessing many examples of the innovative potential of the ordinary user. The current Internet can be seen as a large playground for users, where many loose building blocks are available which invite them to use their imagination, to contribute actively, and to build up the web by interacting and cooperating with others. WEB 2.0 generates a constant flow of new services and applications that come out of the social networks of users and everything they do and share in those networks. Through what is now more commonly being referred to as social media, the everyday trivial contributions of ordinary users suddenly became a fascinating source of innovation and value creation. Because of this trend even the pro-am, the professional amateur, is now being passed left and right by the full-blooded amateur, or the ordinary user. The emergence of social media gave ordinary users not only a joyful playground, but also an exciting innovation lab where they can tinker and experiment to their heart's content. Although we have to keep in mind that to a certain degree this playground is a "walled garden" where the boundaries of play are determined by others, including big companies which define the rules of the game.

In 1982, *Time* magazine chose the personal computer as its "person of the year", but now, more than 30 years later, the user has taken over the mantle from technology.[7] In 2006, *Time* magazine voted us ("You!") person of the year.[8] In the accompanying *laudatio*, we read that the "user has taken over the power of the global media and established a new digital democracy". Not everyone considers this development with the same degree of positive value. The emergence of social media has also prompted various pessimistic views about the homogenization, trivialization, and loss of the professional culture.[9] One of the most well-known pessimists is Andrew Keen (2008). The title of his book says it all, as he mercilessly slates the social media trend in *The cult of the amateur: How today's internet is killing our culture*. But whether you belong to the optimist or pessimist camp, it is an irrefutable fact that a remarkable development has taken place in recent years: bottom up, user-driven innovation is now strongly (co)defining further development of the web.

Digital tinkering

In the current phase of development, ICT innovation is increasingly shaped by DIY practices: tinkering with the digital building blocks that every user can access from the abundant web arsenal. The current state of the technology has brought those building blocks within the reach of everyone.[10] Today's web is extremely user-friendly: it invites play, improvisation, and experimentation and tempts the user to keep discovering new things. Ordinary users have a better infrastructure and more sophisticated resources at their disposal at home these days than the average employee in a professional organization. Facebook for instance gives ordinary users a nearly professional multimedia platform, enabling them to present themselves in a slick and positive way to the network they belong to and to the outside world, using photos, videos, a permanent news line and real-time interaction possibilities. ICT has enabled 21st century users "to beat the pros at their own game", as *Time* magazine put it, in "a story about community and collaboration on a scale never seen before".[11]

The breakthrough of this tinkering amateur, joyfully playing around with all the bits and pieces that the web offers him, may be regarded as a symptom of what Johan Huizinga (1955) has labelled the *ludification* of our modern culture. A thoroughly *playful* attitude and style is becoming more and more common in almost every domain of our everyday life, including those domains previously regarded as serious. Andrew Keen considers the emergence of the amateur as a loss of seriousness, e.g. of "serious media" and "serious culture". In his view, the cult of the amateur leads to the homogenization, trivialization, and marginalization of the "true" experts. Expert knowledge, according to Keen, increasingly has to give way to a "childish game of Trivial Pursuit" (2008, 6). However, if we take Huizinga's perspective, ludification is not so much a sign of the demise of the serious, but a key constituent element of culture, a real and powerful element of human civilization. The characteristics of digital media, as described in the introductory chapter of this volume, reinforce this play element because they allow the user to give rein to his creativity more than ever before: digital media affords users new opportunities to play. The play concept thus offers useful points of reference to better understand the increasing importance of the amateur as described above.

In her famous study of identity construction on the Internet, Sherry Turkle (1995) shows how computer technology in the 1980s and 90s grew into an "expressive" medium *par excellence*. The rise of the personal computer and the Internet offered more scope for a style of programming that she referred to as “soft programming”: an associative style, bottom-up, unplanned, not based on rules, but much more on “playing with the code” (which is very important in the hacker culture described above). Even more programming scope has been created by the enhanced possibilities to visualize, simulate, and manipulate virtual objects – specifically in computer games – which gives users more possibilities to usefully exploit the web and themselves on the web. According to Turkle, this style of programming is reminiscent of the concrete kind of thinking and learning that is quite normal for children as described by Jean Piaget. Concrete elements from daily life are playfully used to gain abstract insights like playing marbles and learning to count. Turkle also links this development to the concept of *bricolage* as used by the anthropologist Claude Lévi-Strauss (1966). This involves a way of thinking whereby the concrete experience is prominent and abstractions derive from intuitive, playful improvisations and associations. Lévi-Strauss terms this kind of thinking the “savage mind”. The rise of the amateur in the digital world can be seen in that light as a breakthrough or, perhaps better, the revival of the savage mind.

The savage mind

Recent ICT history and the emergence of the digital amateur reveal striking parallels with what the anthropologist Claude Lévi-Strauss (1966) describes as the “savage mind” or the “science of the concrete”. In his analysis a central role is assigned to the *bricoleur*, the tinkerer, or DIY enthusiast, as the perfect representative of the savage mind. The *bricoleur* – as opposed to the engineer – uses everything in his vicinity that comes to hand, creating something new from previously used materials, things with a history of use. Lévi-Strauss also uses the image of the kaleidoscope as a metaphor for the savage mind: in a kaleidoscope the shards of glass that have already been used elsewhere, time and again display surprising combinations of color and shape along with the natural environment (the light). The current user-driven development of the Internet and the coincidental, kaleidoscopic innovations that continue to spring out of it, can in our view also be regarded as the breakthrough of the savage mind in our modern era.

Lévi-Strauss describes the savage mind as a way of mental organization that is characteristic of “primitive” cultures. The savage mind, or the science of the concrete, is in some sense the counterbalance to modern science. But despite the differences in approach and implementation, both emanate from the same human need for structure. According to Lévi-Strauss, it is a fallacy to see the savage mind as a not yet mature stage in the evolution of thought. It is a *different* way of mentally organizing what we perceive around us. By systematically labeling and classifying what we perceive in our everyday environment, we structure our thinking. By organizing we see the coherence, cause and effect, and possibilities to combine and recombine. This process generates explanatory concepts, like myths of creation or technological discoveries and innovations.[12] Such explanations and discoveries are not a matter of coincidence, but the fruits of thorough, systematic perception and of many experiments.

So-called primitive peoples often have very detailed knowledge of their natural surroundings, which is expressed in a rich and differentiated vocabulary along with an extensive arsenal of technology to cope with those surroundings. Lévi-Strauss cites, for instance, a biologist who was very impressed by the inexhaustible knowledge that a hunter-gatherer community in the Philippines seemed to have of the flora and fauna in their surroundings. Not only did they have names for all the animals and plants, they knew all about the animal behavior, all kinds of special properties of the plants, and revealed an amazing insight into the ecological balance between all the species. For example, they had detailed knowledge about fifteen different kinds of bats, twenty species of ants, and forty-five sorts of edible fungi. In terms of technology, they had fifty different kinds of darts. They constantly studied their surroundings through smell and taste and taking everything apart. They knew exactly what they could and could not use by experimenting with what they encountered. The knowledge of medicine men and women was particularly impressive.

According to Lévi-Strauss, the need for order that is evident here translates into practical applications as well as in more magical forms of thinking. Magical thinking and its elaboration in rituals and invocations in his view derive as much from the basic and fundamental human need for order as from the more pragmatic and rational use of plants for curing disease. This relates to a comparable way of understanding the world around us in which immediate perception and imagination play a major role. Magical imagination is important for instance when there is a concrete transition or rupture (birth, death, marriage) in our daily lives. Such transitions stir up insecurity that we try to exorcise by ritual: it is then that we appeal to what we know and trust, a fixed and repeated series of actions, which at first sight appear not to be founded on anything rational.

Now we turn to the definition of play as presented by Johan Huizinga as

> a free activity standing quite consciously outside "ordinary" life as being "not serious", but at the same time absorbing the player intensely and

> utterly. It is an activity connected with no material interest, and no profit can be gained by it. It proceeds within its own proper boundaries of time and space according to fixed rules and in an orderly manner. It promotes the formation of social groupings which tend to surround themselves with secrecy and to stress their difference from the common world by disguise or other means (1955, 13).

If we compare Huizinga's play concept of and the way Lévi-Strauss approaches ritual, we see a striking correspondence. Lévi-Strauss describes these forms of mental organization as "intellectual tinkering". Therefore, the objects in our surroundings, including technology, form a key tool because they are objects "to help us to think".[13] The notion of tinkering, *bricolage*, is important for Lévi-Strauss to illustrate the savage mind. He differentiates between the *bricoleur* and the engineer, indicative of two styles of mental organization: the science of the concrete and modern science. The engineer works with a preconceived plan or design, generally with new materials and concepts, and focuses on an abstraction as his target. The tinkerer, by contrast, makes optimum use of the things that he more or less chances across in everyday life. The way he uses the used materials around him – material history – depends more or less on what he wants to do with them. In the words of anthropologist Igor Kopytoff (1986), the things around us have a "cultural biography". That biography restricts us in one sense but, at the same time, any material that is available can be reused for something else, and what was once a resource can now also become a goal in itself. The tinkerer sees his surroundings as a *trésor* or a treasure chest of experiences that contain opportunities.

Improvisation, coincidence and experiment in this type of thinking are much more important than in the engineer's largely programmatic way of thinking. The savage mind thinks more in terms of possibilities than solutions. The *bricoleur* weighs the possibilities against the history of use and on this basis makes his choices that may subsequently lead to new experimental combinations. From a *bricoleur*'s perspective this gives innovation a more incremental and even, in some respects, conservative character as the tinkerer remains organically and contingently bound to the past to a certain degree. An engineer's perspective of innovation is more likely to make the limitations of the concrete evident. He will endeavor to leap from the past and focus on the development of something new. The modern engineer's thinking is, moreover, abstract while the savage mind is a "science of the concrete", in the words of Lévi-Strauss, who also suggests that the contrast between tinkerers and engineers is not so absolute. The engineer also always has to form a picture of what is concretely at hand. Yet he then still has to try to overcome those limitations and attempt to abstract from them, while the *bricoleur* stays within the realms of the possibilities of the concrete world of experiences.

Thus the *bricoleur* also stays close to himself, "giving an account of his personality and life by the choices he makes between the limited possibilities" (Lévi-Strauss 1966, 21). In the savage mind the biography of things more or less coincides with the personal biography of the *bricoleur*. Sherry Turkle (2007) therefore also speaks of "evocative objects". Inspired by Lévi-Strauss she describes the things around us as things that help us to "think-with", objects that enable us to order our thinking as well as things that help us to think about ourselves, since they are also an evocation of ourselves and therefore help us reflect on ourselves and help us shape ourselves as creative beings.

Looking now at recent ICT developments, we see not only the emergence of professional amateurs and ordinary users in the digital domain, but in a more radical sense we see a breakthrough in a different way of thinking. In line with Lévi-Strauss' analysis we might postulate that at the beginning of the twenty-first century the instrumental and rationalist way of thinking of the engineer, which was emblematic for most of the twentieth century, has been surpassed by the savage mind and the logic of the tinkerer. That savage mind in turn reveals striking parallels with the concept of play or playfulness as a constituent element of modern culture. The *bricoleur* is as it were the game leader in the process of ludification in the modern digital culture. This argument is elaborated below.

The breakthrough of the savage mind in the digital domain

Digital technology has become interwoven with all we do at the beginning of the twenty-first century. Network society is no longer a vision of the future, but a reality. As Barry Wellman and Carolyn Haythornthwaite conclude in *The Internet in everyday life* (2002), networks have become the dominant principle of social organization. We no longer live *with* networks, but *in* networks (Deuze 2012). Digital media have become the main tools we use to get a grip of the world around us. At the same time, a life *in* networks forces us to continuously reflect on ourselves. The world around us is extensive, complex, and dynamic and pushes us towards constant rebalancing and reinterpretation. Digital media are our observation hole of the kaleidoscope: opening a new window leads to yet more new combinations of loose impressions and impels us to constantly improvise and imagine so that we can bring order to what we see. In doing this, we use our earlier online and offline experiences. By playfully ordering and reordering the individual experiences and elements, like the marbles in Jean Piaget's game, new rules and structures emerge and we get a grip on the world around us. The savage mind enables us to continually modify the rules of the game and to act as if the digital world is "sacrosanct", as Huizinga put it (1955, 77).

Digital technology has given us easy access to the networks of others. We are part of familiar networks and of new networks that we come into contact with by accident, thanks to technology. We not only meet many other people, but we also gain access to a much more extensive treasury of concrete experiences than we could ever access before and to the tacit knowledge of many others. The biography of technology is interwoven with the history of our personal use and, on top of that, that of all those many others. A characteristic of the WEB 2.0 phenomenon is, as described above, the exploitation of the value created by the users themselves – the experiences, insights, and products of others that are made manifest by the technology and can be shared. The modern DIY enthusiast, with his social media toolbox, has access to an almost inexhaustible quantity of *débris*, as Levi-Strauss calls it. It is the *débris* of aged material that he can and must use to shape his own world (again and again). In that sense, he resembles the modern gamer who is able to simulate and reshape real life with virtual objects.

The huge quantity of "raw material" that we as Internet users constantly and incidentally come across, urges the *concrete*, the immediately perceptible, the irrevocable on us. A nice example of this is a social network like Facebook. Once you are a member, have created your own profile and invited friends to connect with you, the network begins, as it were, to live a life of its own and constantly urges you to do something. And so you continually have to improvise. On Facebook it is very difficult to rationally and systematically promise to yourself how you intend to behave on this site and what you want to get out of it. You have to dare to experiment and give your imagination a chance as well as have a sense of the rules of the game that make Facebook a temporary kind of "magic circle" in which time and space are organized in their own particular way. On a fairly regular basis you receive requests from relatively unknown people to become friends. And if you consent, you do not really know in advance what this may involve. You can only build on your own experiences from the past and those of other Facebook visitors to find your way around. And in doing this you come across other new things time and time again. On each new page of your fellow Facebookers a new microcosm unfolds in which the technology more or less coincides with the personal biography of its user. Everyday, trivial and intimate experiences alternate with serious reflections, discussions with others, or calls to action. The next time you drop in the picture has changed again; your new friend has added YouTube clips, shared his holiday snaps with his network, via a link to Flickr, has started up a blog and has given the site yet another new look. And he has another twenty-five friends/connections, all of whom have their own profiles and circles of friends.

In such a hyper-dynamic environment the *concrete* experience, the immediately perceptible, and that which anthropologist Thomas Hylland Eriksen (2001) calls the "tyranny of the moment" all reign. The science of the concrete may be the only way to deal with this overdose of impressions, experiences, and concrete perceptions. In this light, Jos de Mul (2008) asks whether we should see a typically modern information disease like ADD as a disorder or rather as a symptom of the human condition of the modern web-dweller. Paradoxically enough, the web itself offers the tools to get a hold on all these confusing experiences and impressions and mentally arrange them. In the digital world, we tinker to our heart's content with all the building blocks provided there. The result of our home industry determines the current face of the Internet and is an odd amalgam of wondrous novelties in a familiar old jacket. Take blogs, for instance. There is nothing new under the sun about blogs when we remember that the diary is a time-honored phenomenon, but still it is different and innovative due to the shameless publication of what we previously considered private. Here, too, an aspect typical of the savage mind is evident: namely repetition with a difference, or "discontinuous continuity" (de Mul 2014, 166ff). The recombination of familiar elements ultimately generates something new again. Take the example of the *avatar* as a virtual representation of ourselves in a game. Research indicates that people who are active in a virtual world such as *Second Life* do not so much use the technical possibilities to create a dream world or to slip into an entirely different body, but actually stay very close to themselves and their familiar concrete life in the First Life so that they more or less take this life into the *Second Life*.[14] Our second life in the digital world is different to our "normal", first life, and yet again it is not: it is both reality and appearance, deadly serious, because it concerns us, and then again it is anything but serious. Our daily movement in and out of the magic circle of the Internet profoundly reveals this ambivalence that we also see in the descriptions of Huizinga's *Homo ludens*. An avatar is in that sense also a nice example of a "thing to think with", as an evocative object, or an object that enables self-reflection.

In conclusion

Living in digital networks is certainly no sinecure. The constant confrontation with new impressions and experiences, and the embedding of this in what we already know, also brings with it great insecurity. We can see a parallel in this with the savage mind described by Lévi-Strauss. Just like the hunter-gatherers of the Philippines, we use our magical powers of imagination in the confrontation of old and new and develop our own differentiated frame of reference and rich and colorful language and imagery to organize our impressions and exorcize them to a certain degree. The creativity we show in this has an almost magical nature. As Jos de Mul suggests in *Cyberspace odyssee* in the chapter dealing with the relationship between religion and technology: "Where technology aims at controlling reality it is related to magic rather than religion, as a successful continuation of the latter" (2010, 213). Without much insight into the actual operation of the technology, users know how to make very good use of the magical potential of ICT. Which is why imagination is more powerful than ever on the today's Internet.

If we briefly define digital technology, as Lévi-Strauss probably would have done if he were alive today, as a way of mentally organizing, or "intellectually tinkering", then we might conclude that the savage mind and the logic of the tinkerer will shape the face of our present information society. The engineers that sculpted the original information era will have only a modest role at the beginning of the twenty-first century. And while the logic of the *bricoleur* may not be primarily geared to discovering the new, paradoxically we see in the current development of the Internet how these "primitive", "untamed", and playful ways of thinking can actually lead to many surprising and radical innovations. Our imagination holds sway more than ever.

Notes

1. The term "innovation" is used here in a broad and sensitizing sense and refers to the implementation and realization of new ideas, products, or processes.
2. See also the introductory chapter of this book for a more extensive description of Huizinga's play concept.
3. http://en.wikipedia.org/wiki/Hip_hop_music.
4. www.linuxcounter.net.

5. See for instance Eric Raymond's famous essay, *A brief history of hackerdom*, www.catb.org/esr/writings/homesteading/hacker-history/ and Levy's *Hackers: Heroes of the computer revolution* (2010).
6. www.tnl.net/blog/2012/04/01/hackers-and-players/.
7. www.time.com/time/covers/0,16641,19830103,00.html.
8. www.time.com/time/magazine/article/0,9171,1570810,00.html#ixzz2580CDipA.
9. Recent examples are Carr 2010; Pariser 2011; Turkle 2011.
10. However, we must not overestimate the creative scope of users, because the number of building blocks offered by social network sites like Facebook is often limited and the platforms have of course not been created by the users themselves. Nevertheless, these kinds of sites often use open standards that enable users themselves to write software that works as a plug-in. So they can relatively easily shape a site as they wish by using the added applications of other sites or applications they have made themselves. However, most users remain within the confines provided. The influence of users is also evident in the various cases of successful resistance to user-unfriendly action by providers, such as Facebook.
11. www.time.com/time/magazine/article/0,9171,1570810,00.html#ixzz2580CDipA.
12. In the work of Lévi-Strauss, the analysis of myths as an illustration of the structures of human thinking is a focal point. "It is in the field of mythology that the spirit appears to be most free; if the human spirit is controlled by the laws even in this field, then this will apply even more so in other fields" (de Ruyter 1979, 7). According to Lévi-Strauss, we specifically see a number of universal patterns of human thinking in the creation of myths from all different kinds of cultures.
13. Turkle uses this phrase to describe the role of ICT in the construction of identity.
14. www.sciencedaily.com/releases/2010/07/100726094905.htm.

References

Bretthauer, David. 2001. *Open source software: A history*. UConn Libraries Published Works. Paper 7. http://digitalcommons.uconn.edu/libr_pubs/7.

Carr, Nicolas. 2010. *The shallows: What the Internet is doing to our brains*. New York: W.W. Norton & Company.

Deuze, Mark. 2012. *Media life*. Cambridge, UK: Polity Press.

Eriksen, Thomas. 2001. *Tyranny of the moment: Fast and slow time in the information age*. London: Pluto Press.

Hebdige, Dick. 1979. *Subculture: The meaning of style*. London: Methuen & Co.

Hippel, Eric von. 2005. *Democratizing innovation*. Cambridge, MA: The MIT Press.

Huizinga, Johan. 1955. *Homo ludens: A study of the play-element in culture* [1938]. Boston, MA: Beacon Press.

Keen, Andrew. 2008. *The cult of the amateur.* London/Boston: Nicholas Brealey Publishing.
Kopytoff, Igor. 1986. The cultural biography of things: Commoditization as process. In *The social life of things: Commodities in cultural perspective*, ed. Arjun Appadurai, 64-91. Cambridge, MA: Cambridge University Press.
Leadbeater, Charles, and Paul Miller. 2004. *The pro-am revolution: How enthusiasts are changing our society and economy.* Demos. www.demos.co.uk/publications/proameconomy.
Lévi-Strauss, Claude. 1966. *The savage mind* [1962]. Chicago, IL: University of Chicago Press.
Levy, Steven. 2010. *Hackers: Heroes of the computer revolution*, 25th Anniversary Edition. Sebastopol: O'Reilly Media.
Moores, Shaun. 2000. *Media and everyday life in modern society.* Edinburgh: Edinburgh University Press.
Mul, Jos de. 2008. Overlast en overleven. Kleine psychopathologie van Homo Zappens Junior. In *De draagbare lichtheid van het bestaan. Het alledaagse gezicht van de informatiesamenleving*, eds. Valerie Frissen and Jos de Mul, 166-83. Kampen: Klement.
—. 2010. *Cyberspace odyssey: Towards a virtual ontology and anthropology*
—. 2014. *Destiny domesticated. The rebirth of tragedy out of the spirit of technology.* Albany, NY: State University of New York Press.
Newcastle upon Tyne: Cambridge Scholars Publishing.
—. 2014. *Destiny domesticated. The rebirth of tragedy out of the spirit of technology* [*De domesticatie van het noodlot: de wedergeboorte van de tragedie uit de geest van de technologie* 2006]. Albany, NY: State University of New York Press.
Pariser, Eli. 2011. *The filter bubble. What the Internet is hiding from you.* New York: The Penguin Press.
Raymond, Eric. 2000. *A brief history of hackerdom.* www.catb.org/esr/writings/homesteading/hacker-history/.
Rheingold, Howard. 2003. *Smart mobs. The next social revolution.* Cambridge MA: Perseus Publishing.
Ruyter, Arie de. 1979. *Een speurtocht naar het denken. Een inleiding tot het structuralisme van Claude Lévi-Strauss.* Assen: Van Gorcum.
Taylor, Alex, and Jane Vincent. 2005. An SMS history. In *Mobile world: Past, present and future*, eds. Lynne Hamill and Amparo Lasen, 75-91. London: Springer.
Turkle, Sherry. 1995, *Life on the screen: Identity in the age of the Internet.* New York: Simon & Schuster.
—. 2007. *Evocative objects: Things we think with.* Cambridge, MA: The MIT Press.
—. 2011. *Alone together: Why we expect more from technology and less from each other.* New York: Basic Books.
Wellman, Barry, and Caroline Haythornthwaite, eds. *The Internet in everyday life.* Malden, MA: Blackwell Publishers.

Part II

Media

Introduction to Part II

Valerie Frissen, Sybille Lammes, Michiel de Lange, Jos de Mul & Joost Raessens

The authors in this part of the book all look at how contemporary media technologies afford playful interactions. Underpinning all chapters are questions pertaining to power and agency. Do digital media mark a shift in how the user as player engages with and has agency in everyday life, and if so, do we need a new vocabulary to understand this engagement properly? The authors in this section of the book share a special interest in how specific digital technologies and genres can be approached as playful media. They interrogate how play can be defined in contemporary media cultures, be it from a cultural, philosophical, ideological, or theoretical perspective. Through this lens they want to come to a better understanding of how play and identity "work" in contemporary media cultures.

Some of authors tackle this question by looking at mobile playful media that are embedded in daily life. Media scholars Adriana de Souza e Silva and Jordan Frith concentrate on mobile interfaces as platforms for networked play in daily life. In their contribution *Location-based mobile games: Interfaces to urban spaces*, they discuss how mobile apps such as *Foursquare* and *Gowalla* invite "players" to make their location public via the mobile interface. They examine how such playful locative conduct pushes players to make aspects of their daily life public by checking in via their mobile interface, and what consequences this has for notions of privacy and power. Hence, as playful media technologies they change our conception of our visibility in urban spaces and our involvement in how we shape them as networks.

Similarly, sociologist Rich Ling approaches mobile phones as network technologies for ludic and networked interaction. In *The playful use of mobile phones and its link to social cohesion*, he shows how mobile telephones have become multipurpose media technologies and have gone far beyond sheer practical tools for communication. Instead they engage users in various playful activities. While de Souza e Silva and Frith look at mobile devices from an ethnographic and qualitative perspective, Ling uses empirical and quantitative data to support his claim that mobile phones have become playful media technologies. Together these chapters make a convincing argument that mobile interfaces are ludic tools that offer new possibilities for engaging with everyday life.

Mobility takes a different turn in the chapter *Digital cartographies as playful practices* by new media scholar Sybille Lammes. She discusses the relation between play, maps, and spatial stories. Using Google Maps, Google Street View, *Foursquare*, and *Layar* as her main cases, she shows how digital mapping interfaces enable users to construct stories about their movements in playful ways. "Who am I" has become "where am I" in contemporary media culture, so she suggests. Lammes maintains that interfaces enable us to construct ludic identities through navigation, but like de Souza e Silva and Frith, she stresses that what we can construct is still influenced by ideological values.

If these authors focus on mobility and its ludic affordances for the user, other authors in this part of the book focus more on the specificity of computer games in relation to play, power, and agency. In the chapter *Ludic identities and the magic circle* game scholar Gordon Calleja argues that the bounded nature of play as theorized by Huizinga needs reconsideration when we want to understand the contemporary player's identity. This theoretical question is also pertinent to mobile media. Can we nowadays (and could we indeed ever) speak of a delineated arena where the player's identity takes shape? Calleja questions this and argues that Huizinga's modernist conception of the ludic is dated and does not suffice to understand the position of current computer game players. Situating himself in a current and important debate about the value of Huizinga's magic circle for understanding digital play, he instead proposes a "logic of incorporation" to account for how players relate to the (game) world and shape their identity through this engagement.

While all contributions in this part are concerned with questions of power and agency of the media user as player, the last two contributions explicitly deal with the ideological-philosophical dimensions of play. In *Play (for) time*, media theorist Patrick Crogan argues that computer games are the most recent examples of Stieglerian "industrial temporal objects" and he shows how they, as postindustrial objects, differ from non-digital temporal objects. He argues that as examples of "transindividual culture" they show that we live in an era that permanently asks us to be involved in consumerist play, eroding a sense of reality and indeed the very conception that Huizinga had of play and identity.

The last chapter in this part of the book takes a different stance on the way that computer games involve us in reality by examining how games can be used in political ways to engage the player not so much as consumers, but more as critical citizens. In *Playful identity politics: How refugee games affect the player's identity*, media theorist Joost Raessens analyzes refugee games to show that games can affect how players identify with others and the extent to which people become more politically involved.

8. Location-based mobile games: Interfaces to urban spaces

Adriana de Souza e Silva & Jordan Frith

Location-aware mobile technologies produce different forms of control. Parents give their children "chaperone" phones equipped with GPS to control where they might go. Parole officers remotely control parolees' mobility patterns to restrict the places they can visit (Shklovski et al. 2009; Troshynski, Lee, and Dourish 2008). People use their GPS-phone mapping capabilities to feel familiar with their surrounding environment, leading to the belief they are able to "control" the chaos of urban spaces. Other location-aware applications, such as location-based mobile games (LBMGs)[1], allow players to "filter" their environment by selecting the people and things they want to see. By simultaneously helping users control their interactions with other people and with their surrounding environment while also enabling new ways for individuals to be controlled, location-aware technologies have become interfaces[2] to public spaces.[3]

This chapter explores the tension between different forms of control afforded by LBMGs. On the one hand, these location-aware interfaces allow users to increasingly control public spaces and filter the people with whom they interact in these spaces. On the other hand, they mediate complex power relationships between people and raise important issues of surveillance. LBMGs are the perfect example to address issues of play in urban space. By adding physical mobility to the typically sedentary experience of video game play, these applications merge online and physical experiences so that issues of sociability, power, and control in playful spaces are enacted in the public spaces of ordinary life (de Souza e Silva and Sutko 2008).

Earlier mobile technologies such as the book and the Walkman also helped users feel familiar with their environment by allowing them to manage interactions with their surroundings (de Souza e Silva and Frith 2010), but LBMGs are different, because they enable different forms of control by allowing people to personalize urban spaces via the manipulation of location-based information. For example, applications such as *Foursquare* and *Gowalla* allow users to visualize the location of nearby players on a map on their cell phone screen. They allow users to "browse" public spaces in order to find information and people with desirable characteristics. This personalized public space, filtered through the game interface, shows only other people nearby and information that matches the users' interests, leading to possibly exclusionary practices and complex power relationships in public spaces. However, as we will see later in this chapter, there is an equally strong counter-argument by which sameness can pull one into difference. For example, players can choose to visit unfamiliar parts of the city in order to play an LBMG, and as a consequence serendipitously meet other, previously unknown players whom they would not get to know otherwise.

In this chapter, we examine the power and control issues that emerge from the use of LBMGs in public spaces. We also explore how LBMGs might lead to new forms of sociability while simultaneously leading to social exclusion and filtered perceptions of public spaces. We finish by discussing how these new forms of location-based control may change how we understand public spaces.

Controlling personal location

In the late 1980s and early 90s, Mark Weiser and his colleagues at the Xerox Palo Alto Research Center (PARC) envisioned a new paradigm for interacting with computers which they called ubiquitous computing (Weiser, Gold, and Brown 1999). At a time when connecting to the Internet required a desktop computer interfaced via a screen, a keyboard, and a mouse, the idea of networked interactions via "computers" spread throughout the office environment, in the form of sensors, RFID tags and location-aware devices seemed unlikely. But most importantly, it seemed scary. Weiser, Gold, and Brown noted that as soon as their first prototypes started being tested at their lab, fears of invasion of privacy through unwanted top-down surveillance began popping up in newspapers that featured headlines like "Big Brother Comes to the Office". However, as Weiser, Gold, and Brown wisely noted, the perceived problem with context-aware technologies, "often couched in terms of privacy, is really one of control". That is, if users felt they had control over their location information, these technologies, instead of being perceived as a threat to privacy, actually become means of controlling peoples' surrounding space and offering them safety and security.

Initially Weiser and his colleagues developed prototypes that tracked the location of users in their offices to deliver context-based information. For example, the ParcTab communicated users' location to a central server and identified them "to receivers placed throughout a building, thus making it possible to keep track of the people or objects with which they interacted" (Weiser 1999, 694). As computing has moved out into the spaces of the city, so have the forms of control and power people exert through location-based applications.

Headlines such as "Big Brother Comes to the Office" might be misleading, but they do influence how people make decisions and formulate opinions about technology use and its effects. In this sense, media frames are also forms of exerting power and control (Entman, Matthes, and Pellicano 2009). In order to explore the initial framework through which location-aware technologies were portrayed in the media, we analyzed the discourses of major world publications on location-based services and social networks from February 2009 to May 2009 (de Souza e Silva and Frith 2010). While some articles echoed the articles Weiser had discussed warning readers about the fears of co-lateral and top-down surveillance, the majority actually emphasized how users could benefit from being able to control their surrounding space and the information they disclose about their location. For example, *CBC News* (Feb. 4, 2009) praised *Google Latitude* users' ability to control the location information they disclosed by adjusting the accuracy of their location, or even setting their location to a fake place. So, although it is common to read in popular press outlets about the dangers of being located, the very same outlets praise users' ability to control their own location information (which includes the ability to lie about their location). In other words, controlling their own location information is framed as empowering users. Entman, Matthes, and Pellicano suggest that media framing "can have a significant effect on how people make decisions and formulate opinions on any given issue or event" (2009, 183). Popular press discourses about location-based application are also likely to influence the degree to which users adopt and interact with these technologies. Specifically, users might tend to try out new applications if they are framed as "positive" by the media – or get scared if they are framed as "negative".

Frequently, the media warn readers about the dangers of the government or corporations having access to one's location, primarily when users do not know that their location information is being disclosed to third parties. These fears are generally framed as invasions of locational privacy. However, participation in LBMGs does not often trigger complaints about invasions of privacy. Conversely, having one's location checked or monitored is often framed as acceptable and even welcome.

Users of LBMGs opt-in to use these applications, so it is generally assumed that they want to disclose their location to their group of peers – and often to other game players they do not know. They might also be aware that their location is shared with advertising companies because a common feature of games like *Foursquare* and *Gowalla* is that their users receive coupons and discounts at the places where they frequently check in. This is in line with previous research, which states that users are willing to give out location information depending on their perceptions of the usefulness of the application offered to them (Barkhuus and Dey 2003; Ackerman, Kempf, and Miki 2003; Ackerman, Cranor, and Reagle 1999). In fact, most Human-Computer Interaction (HCI) research sees the privacy problem as a cost-benefit issue (Hong et al. 2003), that is, if individuals feel the information they submit is worth the benefits of the service, they will often use the service.[4] According to this logic, if users feel they have control over their personal settings, privacy issues tend to disappear. But the issue is obviously not that simple. LBMGs mediate complex power relationships between users and users and spaces. In some cases, asymmetrical power relations arise even though the player has attempted to control how his/her locational information is shared.

This situation is discussed in Licoppe and Inada's (2006) ethnographic work on the Japanese LBMG *Mogi*. They explain how power asymmetries can arise by sharing one's location. In two separate instances, two different *Mogi* players reported feeling vulnerable. The vulnerability occurred when the player was contacted by another player who could observe her location. But the player doing the contacting refused to divulge his/her location, leading to a distinct power asymmetry. In the second example, the female player felt so vulnerable she immediately called two other male players to help with the situation (Licoppe and Inada 2006). They perceived the situation as a case of stalking. While users may be more selective about who they include on their social network on LBMGs, they can still easily run into a similar situation when they check into a place and an acquaintance not currently checked in anywhere finds them through the game map.

Because of the possibilities of asymmetrical power relations, LBMGs provide ways for players to manage their locational information through the interface of the mobile device. For example, users can check into false locations, hiding their true location from acquaintances. Or, on *Foursquare*, they can check in "off the grid", meaning they still get the points for checking in but they do not broadcast their location to friends. However, users are tacitly agreeing that their location becomes public by using LBMGs. Some location-based social networking sites, such as *Whrll*, even publish users' check-ins in real time on their home page.

While it is important to note that people are forced to negotiate issues of power and privacy when using these games, it is also important to understand that disclosing location information does not necessarily represent a loss of privacy. In the right situation, disclosing one's location may actually increase one's feelings of control over people and things in their environment. For example, checking into *Foursquare* might disclose other *Foursquare* players in the surroundings, and therefore make players feel more familiar with their environment. As Solove (2008) argues, issues of privacy need to be understood contextually – and so do the interrelated issues of control and power.

Controlling public spaces

Issues of control and power do not only apply to interpersonal relationships in public spaces, but are also related to personalizing and managing public spaces themselves. In our media discourse study, we found that the ability to control and personalize public spaces was generally portrayed as empowering individuals to manage their own surrounding space. The scenarios portrayed by media outlets mostly describe the benefits of location-based services when users are able to get contextual information in the form of restaurant recommendations, location-aware coupons, and people in their surroundings.

While the main goal of LBMGs is to identify other people's and objects' locations, they also provide contextual information in the form of reviews and specialized advertisements and coupons. For example, *Foursquare* and *Gowalla* include elements of gameplay where people can compete by scoring points for checking into different places. While the ability to filter the information present in a space through LBMGs does grant individuals increased control over their surrounding space, some of these applications hope to commodify locations through location-based advertising (LBA).

The idea of LBA is not new. It can be traced back at least to the early 2000s (Kolmel and Alexakis 2002). In the LBA model, location becomes a valuable commodity. The idea that location can be commodified through LBA has led to the current LBS market, in which many prominent LBSs are offered to the user for free. The classic example of LBA imagines the user walking by Starbucks receiving a coupon for a free coffee (Greenfield 2006). More recently, however, LBMGs (and more generally location-based social networks) are including advertising in their software as ways to both monetize theirs apps and to retain existing players. For example, *Foursquare* offers coupons and free goods to players depending on how many times they check into specific places. Mayors of locations (people who frequently "check in" at the same place) have special privileges, and may have additional offers.

With LBMGs, not only goods and services become commodified, but also location. Shklovski et al. (2009) suggest that the "commodification of location" happens when locations (represented via a GPS trace) become a tradable entity. In their study of the relationship between parolees, location-tracking technology, and parole officers, they argue that location "begins to have power and meaning in itself" (Shklovski et al. 2009, 8). Their perspective also applies to LBMGs and location-based services (LBS) in general. The ability to attach ads, coupons, and offers to specific locations changes these locations' meaning and transforms them into places of consumption. This does not mean that before the emergence of location-based services urban spaces were not spaces of consumption. Since the development of metropolises and the rise of capitalism, urban spaces have primarily been spaces of consumption, embedded with advertisements in the forms of billboards and street signs. However, LBMGs like *Foursquare* and *Gowalla* make the relationship among people, location, and advertisements even more complex in three fundamental ways. First, these ads are only seen by the small subset of the population playing the game; second it is as if players carry those ads with them; and finally, ads become not only embedded in a location, but also personalized, which means that different individuals receive different information as they move through public space, as we discuss in the next section. These personalized offers and coupons not only create an individual experience of space for each user, but they also shape their users' experiences of public spaces. Advertising has always shaped how people experience public spaces, but with location-based information, the control exerted by companies who target advertising is increased, since ads are contextualized, and therefore much more likely to influence users consumption habits.

The link between digital information and physical space is key to differentiating location-based media from earlier forms of mobile media. Unlike technologies such as the Walkman, the iPod, and the mobile phone which have often been described as isolating individuals from their surroundings (Bull 2000; 2007; du Gay et al. 1997; Habuchi 2005), LBMGs are built around the idea that people want to connect to others in public spaces. The focus on physical space differentiates these services from traditional online games and social networks like Facebook and MySpace, as most of the marketing promoting these services focuses on their ability to facilitate actual encounters in physical spaces.

However, as Humphreys (2007; 2010) found in her ethnographic study of *Dodgeball*,[5] mobile social network users do not necessarily meet more (new) people, but rather tend to use them to socialize with existing friends. This finding is not very different from already existing tendencies with mobile phone use. The terms "tele-cocooning" (Habuchi 2005) and "selective sociality" (Matsuda 2005) described how Japanese teenagers maintained a small group of close friends through mobile phone calls and text messages, often at the expense of building new weak ties with unknown people.

But sociability in urban environments also depends on trust (Sutko and de Souza e Silva 2011; Gordon and de Souza e Silva 2011). People feel comfortable knowing that others around are like them and will likely behave like they would. That is what Lehtonen and Mänpää (1997) called "street sociability" – a particular form of sociality that allows us to remain anonymous in city spaces, trusting that events in the streets will fall within certain familiar schemata. LBMGs, by helping users find other players, can also contribute to people's feelings of familiarity with their environment. In other words, if people can access information about what kind of people are around, they might be able to trust those locations and feel more comfortable in them (Sutko and de Souza e Silva 2011; Hide and seek game causes Aukland bomb scare 2008).

This phenomenon has been observed in early LBMGs such as *Botfighters*. In an article about the game, the *Herald Sun* (Mobile Killers 2001) reported that a player gained motivation to go to unknown parts of the city because he knew there were other players like him in those locations. The knowledge about other players in an unknown (and perhaps untrusted) part of the city contributed to his feelings of familiarity with that location. The visualization of other players' locations on the game map made him feel some control over that space, although he had never been there before. In doing that, the game motivated players to go to parts of the city to which they had never been and "trust" these places more.

Issues of trust are closely linked to issues of control, particularly in how these games allow individuals to "sort" the information about a space. Graham (2005) argues that "software-sorted geographies" increasingly influence how we encounter places, identifying the important links between emerging software-sorting technologies and the production of spaces. He addresses how the ways people move and maintain social relationships are embedded into systems of power. For example, these technologies might be used to dictate patterns of mobility through the city, or to allow some people to connect to each other while excluding others. Furthermore, they might give some people access to information while others are deprived of such access. Although Graham is mostly addressing urban infrastructural technologies, such as CCTV cameras, airport biometric systems, and real-time highway pricing, his logic can also be applied to LBMGs.

LBMGs frame users' perspectives of their environments in a particular way. They allow users to increasingly control the spaces they occupy, but only as far as the design of these systems allows. And because these systems are also designed with profits in mind, Dourish et al. claim that "location-based systems fail to acknowledge the lived practice of urban life, and in particular its diversity and the different urban experiences of different groups" (2007, 2). In doing that, they might contribute to new and different forms of exclusion in urban spaces.

Differential spaces

Wood and Graham (2005) identify a type of exclusion in their discussion of "differential mobility", defined as the exclusion of the population that does not have access to technology, and therefore cannot move freely. They distinguish between high mobility, pertaining to those few with easy access, and slow mobility, which includes the majority with difficult, blocked access. In this sense, mobility is directly related to power. LBMGs employ mobile technologies as interfaces and will likely contribute to Wood and Graham's "differential mobility". But as we have discussed elsewhere (de Souza e Silva and Frith 2010), it is likely that location-based technologies will not only contribute to differential forms of mobility, but also to what we call "differential space". Because LBMGs enable users to select people, things, and information from their surroundings with which they would like to interact, those who use these services might have a radically different experience of public spaces than those who do not. Even among those who use LBMGs, if they are able to filter their environment in different ways, they will also experience spaces in individualized ways. For example, a *Foursquare* player uses the application to find other *Foursquare* players nearby, and then ignores other people who literally do not show up on her radar. Frequent *Foursquare* players repeatedly "check in" at the same places to maintain mayorships, and receive coupons and discounts that other people who are not *Foursquare* players are not being offered. Therefore, these technologies lead to the exclusion of some while helping others to select people and things from one's interactions with public space.

But the consequences of exclusionary practices in the context of LBMGs go beyond the dichotomy of access vs. no access. Their use and the way they mediate relationships directly influence our perception of public spaces. In their book *Net Locality*, Gordon and de Souza e Silva (2011) suggest that we are experiencing a shift in the way we connect to the Internet in which location has become the organizing logic of networked interactions. Our physical location increasingly determines the types of information we access online (e.g. search results on Google Maps, ability to stream films, types of *Wikipedia* articles), and as a consequence it is no longer possible to address digital and physical spaces as separated and disconnected from each other. In fact, our public urban spaces are more and more embedded with networked connections. One no longer "enters" the web – it is all around us. This is what Gordon and de Souza e Silva (2011) call "net localities".

Net localities are not only comprised of all people and things that are physically nearby, but also people and things that are remotely connected to that space. They include not only physical people and things, but also information attached to that space. According to this perspective, our social spaces are no longer spaces where only face-to-face communication happens. It was frequently believed that mobile technologies and remote connections would disconnect people from the interactions with their surrounding environment. But it is no longer possible to ignore that any contemporary conceptualization of public social spaces needs to take into consideration networked connections, location-based information, and remote communication.

LBMGs are an important part of net localities. They are the interfaces that allow us to attach information to places and retrieve place-specific information. As a consequence, not only the web, but public spaces become browsable and searchable. Public spaces then become filtered and manipulable in ways that were not possible before. Although issues of power, control, and exclusion have always been present in social spaces, the emergence of LBMGs presents new configurations and challenges.

As sociologist Georg Simmel (1950) already realized more than a century ago, the metropolitan man cannot go back to the small city. The shift that happened with the increasing size of metropolises, like Paris or Berlin, along with the new challenges it posed its citizens, such as the over-stimulation of senses, was a reality and not something that could be reverted. The same is true for the shift in the meaning of public spaces we are experiencing right now. What we need, however, is to understand the shift, in order to not only design new applications that address the current population that is excluded, but also to understand how social interactions (including perceptions of privacy and surveillance) will likely change and be changed by these technologies.

Notes

1. LBMGs are types of location-based social networks (LBSNs). Some of the most prominent LBSNs (such as *Foursquare* and *Gowalla*), are not games per se, but they include gaming elements, such as points and rewards. For the purpose of this chapter, we consider these also LBMGs, and distinctions will be made when necessary.
2. Interfaces are defined as communication mediators, representing information between two parts, making them meaningful to one another (Johnson 1997; Lévy 2004). However, more than translators or communication mediators, they are symbolic systems that filter and represent information to users. From this perspective, interfaces not only reshape communication relationships, but they also reshape the space in which this interaction takes place (de Souza e Silva 2006).
3. There are many different definitions of public space in academic literature. We are drawing from the definition most commonly identified with Jane Jacobs (1961) and Richard Sennett (1977), which views public space as spaces where strangers congregate.
4. However, often individuals are not aware of the cost (i.e., what types of information are shared with third parties) and therefore cannot make a proper cost-benefit analysis (Consolvo et al. 2010).
5. *Dodgeball* is not a game; it is a mobile social network. However, we use it as an example because we believe Humphreys' findings about communication and coordination also apply to the analysis of LBSNs and LBMGs.

References

Ackerman, Linda, James Kempf, and Toshio Miki. 2003. *Wireless location privacy: A report on law and policy in the United States, the European Union, and Japan*. NTT DoCoMo USA Labs.

Ackerman, Mark S., Lorrie Faith Cranor, and Joseph Reagle. 1999. Privacy in e-commerce: Examining user scenarios and privacy preferences. *Proceedings of the 1st ACM conference on electronic commerce*. Denver, CO: ACM.

Barkhuus, Louise, and Anind Dey. 2003. Location-based services for mobile telephony: A study of users' privacy concerns. *Proceedings of the INTERACT 2003, 9TH IFIP TC13 international conference on human-computer interaction*. Berkeley: Intel Research.

Bull, Michael. 2000. *Sounding out the city: Personal stereos and the management of everyday life*. Oxford: Berg.

—. 2007. *Sound moves: iPod culture and urban experience*. London: Routledge.

Consolvo, Sunny, Jaeyon Jung, Ben Greenstein, Pauline Powledge, Gabriel Maganis, and Daniel Avrahami. 2010. The Wi-Fi privacy ticker: Improving awareness & control of personal information exposure on Wi-Fi. *UbiComp '10*. Copenhagen, Denmark: ACM.

de Souza e Silva, Adriana. 2006. From cyber to hybrid: Mobile technologies as interfaces of hybrid spaces. *Space and Culture* 3: 261-78.

—, and Jordan Frith. 2010. Locational privacy in public spaces: Media discourses on location-aware mobile technologies. *Communication, Culture & Critique* 3(4): 503-25.
—, and Jordan Frith. 2010. Locative mobile social networks: Mapping communication and location in urban spaces. *Mobilities* 5(4): 485-506.
—, and Daniel M. Sutko. 2008. Playing life and living play: How hybrid reality games reframe space, play, and the ordinary. *Critical Studies in Media Communication* 25(5): 447-65.
Dourish, Paul, Ken Anderson, and Dawn Nafus. 2007. Cultural mobilities: Diversity and agency in urban computing. *Proceedings of the IFIP conference human-computer interaction.* Rio de Janeiro, Brazil: INTERACT 2007.
du Gay, Paul, Stuart Hall, Linda Janes, Hugh Mackay, and Keith Negus. 1997. *Doing cultural studies: The story of the Sony Walkman.* London: Sage Publications.
Entman, Robert, Jürg Matthes, and Lynn Pellicano. 2009. Nature, Sources and effects of news framing. In *The handbook of journalism studies*, eds. Karin Wahl-Jorgensen and Thomas Hanitzsch. London: Routledge.
Gordon, Eric, and Adriana de Souza e Silva. 2011. *Net Locality: Why location matters in a networked world.* Malden, MA: Wiley-Blackwell.
Graham, Stephen. 2005. Software-sorted geographies. *Progress in Human Geography* 29(5): 562-80.
Greenfield, Adam. 2006. *Everyware: The dawning age of ubiquitous computing.* London: New Riders.
Habuchi, Ichiyo. 2005. Accelerating reflexivity. In *Personal, portable, pedestrian: mobile phones in Japanese life*, eds. M. Ito, D. Okabe, and M. Matsuda. Cambridge, MA: The MIT Press.
Hide and seek game causes Auckland bomb scare. 2008. *Stuff.co.nz*, February 13, 2008.
Hong, Jason I., Gaetano Borriello, James A. Landay, David W. McDonald, Bill N. Schilit, and J.D. Tygar. 2003. Privacy and security in the location-enhanced World Wide Web. In *Proceedings of the workshop on privacy at Ubicomp.* Seattle, WA: Springer.
Humphreys, Lee. 2007. Mobile social networks and social practice: A case study of Dodgeball. *Journal of Computer-Mediated Communication* 13(1): 341-60.
—. 2010. Mobile social networks and urban public space. *New Media & Society* 12(5): 763-78.
Jacobs, Jane. 1961. *The death of life of great American cities.* New York: Random House.
Johnson, Steven. 1997. *Interface culture: How new technology transforms the way we create and communicate.* San Francisco, CA: Harper Edge.
Kölmel, Bernhard, and Spiros Alexakis. 2002. Location based advertising. *Proceedings of the 2002 first international conference on mobile business*, Athens, Greece.
Lehtonen, Turo-Kimo, and Pasi Mänpää. 1997. Shopping in the East centre mall. In *The shopping experience*, eds. Pasi Falk and Colin Campbell. London: Sage Publications.
Lévy, Pierre. 2004. *As tecnologias da inteligência: O futuro do pensamento na era da informática.* São Paulo: Editora 34.
Licoppe, Christian, and Yoriko Inada. 2006. Emergent uses of a multiplayer location-aware mobile game: The interactional consequences of mediated encounters. *Mobilities* 1(1): 39-61.
—, and Yoriko Inada. 2009. Mediated co-proximity and its dangers in a location-aware community: A case of stalking. In *Digital cityscapes: Merging digital and urban playspaces*, eds. Adriana de Souza e Silva and Daniel M. Sutko. New York: Peter Lang.
Matsuda, Misa 2005. Mobile communication and selective sociality. In *Personal, portable, pedestrian: Mobile phones in Japanese life*, eds. Mizuko Ito, Daisuke Okabe and Misa Matsuda, 19-39. Cambridge, MA: The MIT Press.
Mobile Killers. 2001. *Sunday Herald Sun*, 89. 15 July.
Sennett, Richard. 1977. *The fall of public man.* New York: Knopf.

Shklovski, Irina, Janet Vertesi, Emily Troshynski, and Paul Dourish. 2009. The commodification of location: Dynamics of power in location-based systems. *Proceedings of the 11th international conference on ubiquitous computing*. Orlando, Florida, USA: ACM.

Simmel, Georg. 1950. *The sociology of Georg Simmel*. Translated by K. Wolff. New York: Free Press.

Solove, Daniel. 2008. *Understanding privacy*. Cambridge, MA: Harvard University Press.

Sutko, Daniel M., and Adriana de Souza e Silva. 2011. Location aware mobile media and urban sociability. *New Media & Society* 13: 807-823.

Troshynski, Emily, Charlotte Lee, and Paul Dourish. 2008. Accountabilities of presence: reframing location-based systems. *Proceeding of the twenty-sixth annual SIGCHI conference on human factors in computing systems*. Florence, Italy: ACM.

Weiser, Mark. 1999. The computer for the 21st century. *SIGMOBILE Mob. Comput. Commun. Rev.* 3(3): 3-11.

—, Rich Gold, and John Seely Brown. 1999. The origins of ubiquitous computing research at PARC in the late 1980s. *IBM Systems Journal* 38(4): 693-6.

Wood, David, and Stephen Graham. 2005. Permeable boundaries in the software-sorted society: Surveillance and the differentiation of mobility. In *Mobile technologies of the city*, eds. Mimi Sheller and John Urry, 177–91. London: Routledge.

9. The playful use of mobile phones and its link to social cohesion

Rich Ling

Introduction

This chapter will examine how people's playful use of the mobile phone supports social cohesion. It is true that there are a variety of ways that we use mobile telephones. We can use them to tell time, take pictures, listen to music, keep our appointment calendar, and note down memos. On advanced phones we can surf the web, sign up to play commercial multiplayer games, find directions, and sign in on social network sites. Among all these flashy applications it is important to remember that we can also talk to and text one another. Indeed it is these last functions that are the most critical when thinking of how mobile communication affects social cohesion. The use of the mobile phone to develop and maintain social cohesion is one of the interesting social consequences of the device (Ling 2008). It has been shown by many researchers that talking and texting via the mobile phone supports bounded solidarity in the intimate sphere (Hampton and Ling 2013; Ishii 2006; Kim et al. 2006; Reid and Reid 2004; Smoreda and Thomas 2001; Wei and Lo 2006). These findings suggest that there is indeed social cohesion being produced, but not how it is being done. Influenced by work of Durkheim (1995), Goffman (1967), and Collins (2004), we maintain that it is important to look at the role of ritual interaction, i.e. a mutually focused activity that engenders a common mood, in order to understand the generation of social cohesion. There are several types of socially mediated rituals that we can examine. They include gossip, flirting, and the use of in-group slang in texts. Playful banter and simple joking with one another via the phone is also a form of ritual interaction. These exchanges are banal and mundane. This does not mean, however, that they are not important. It is through these seemingly prosaic exchanges, which are most likely only entertaining to the immediate participants, that we weave the threads of social cohesion. It is how we develop a sense of our interlocutors and how "our gang of friends" develops the bonds that tie them together.

It is often beguiling to look to the flashy and technically advanced applications in mobile phones and on the Internet. Surfing the net via mobile phones is exciting. Using commercially scripted gaming applications can be exciting and personally engrossing and there are important lessons to be learned by observing these activities. However, these activities are relatively rare when compared with the ubiquity of common social interaction via the phone. When thinking of how the mobile phone ties us to our friends and family, it is our talking and texting that is most central.

Commercially scripted vs. mediated interpersonal play

In general I am suspicious of the idea that commercially based gaming – what I am calling commercially scripted play – is having nearly the impact of mundane interaction via the mobile phone. Although the players of *World of Warcraft* will undoubtedly muster their guilds for an all-out attack on this position, when we take a broad look at computer-based gaming it is still a very small-scale affair. Data from Norway shows that only about one person in 20 (4.5%) plays a computer/console-based game on a daily basis (Vaage 2010). The most intense use was by young people in their mid-teen years. If we look globally, commercial gaming is even smaller, particularly when compared to the social impact of mobile telephony. This is not to say that computer-based games are not an arena in which important social interaction takes place (Sicart 2009; Williams et al. 2006). Commercially scripted gaming touches the lives of some, but it is not nearly as widespread or central as is simple social interaction via the mobile phone. If we move outside of the commercial gaming arena, and look instead at mediated interpersonal playfulness (in other words simply joking around with one another over the phone), then the numbers are much larger. We are talking of billions and not millions of people.

For those people who play computer- and net-based games there are important social dimensions that are being exercised. However, computer and console-based gaming is not an arena for the vast majority of sociation. It is not a place where we chat with friends. We do not meet and work out the details of daily life, etc. By contrast about 70% of Norwegians sent a text message and 75% have a mobile phone conversation on a normal day.[1] On a worldwide basis, the sheer number of mobile phones overwhelms access to PCs, gaming devices, and the Internet. It is true that there are some games on mobile phones, but as we will see, these are not the main attraction of mobile phones.

Not all interaction via the phone is playful, but people all over the world are increasingly expected to be available to one another via the mobile phone. To not be available to friends and family represents a serious breach

(Ling 2009). Indeed in some cases it can lead to suspicion and marital rifts (Lasen 2011). It is simple mundane interaction (joking, gossiping, or telling jokes) that is central to understanding the role of mobile telephony as a tool with which to build social cohesion.

Access and forms of mobile phone use

In order to analyze the use of mobile phones for the purpose of play, it is important to understand how many people engaged in this behavior and to examine the role of play vis-à-vis other activities. One way to do this is to look at the ratio of the different types of traffic that pass through the mobile network.[2] Mobile-based commercial games largely employ the net-based functionality of the mobile phone. By contrast, mobile mediated interpersonal play is mostly carried out when we are using the voice and the texting functionality of the mobile phone. I argue that it is the latter of these two that has the greater social consequence since it is through this type of interaction that we are in touch with close friends and family and it is through these types of interactions that we create and maintain social cohesion.

Mobile telephony originated as a tool for interpersonal mediation. Its designers were concerned with the ability to talk and eventually text other individuals using a mobile device (Goggin 2006; Hillebrand et al. 2010). In this phase, the mobile phone was often used almost exclusively for interpersonal interaction. While we were adapting to the system, the design and capabilities of these devices took off. Mobile phones are now multidimensional personal access and information terminals. These terminals assist us in a variety of tasks (calendars, telephone lists, access to weather reports, note taking, etc.) (Ling and Donner 2009). However, even as these possibilities have developed, the main use of the mobile phone has remained the mediation of interpersonal interaction. Of all the actions taken on a mobile phone (i.e. sending text messages, making calls, or clicking on links), less than 10% are related to Internet use. That is, over 90% of what is done on a mobile phone is interpersonal interaction (see Figure 1). Moreover, half of our calls and texts go to less than five persons (Ling, Bertil, and Sundsøy 2010). These are the statistics for Norway where mobile Internet is relatively well developed. In other parts of the world, where mobile Internet capabilities are less well developed, that percentage is even lower. The clear preponderance of use of the mobile phone, i.e. the number of events, were talking and texting. This finding supports the notion suggested above that

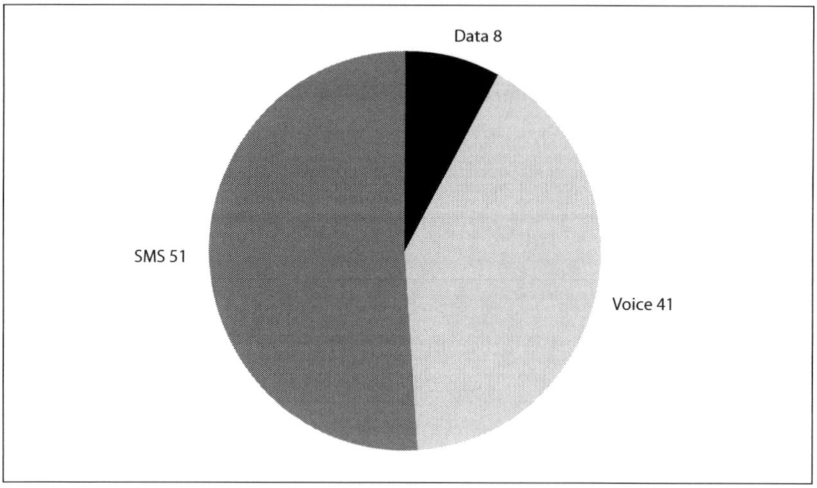

Fig. 1: Percent distribution of mobile-phone-based events for a sample of all users in the Telenor net (regardless of telephone type), Norway 2009.

it is the mundane use of mobile telephony, including our playful and our ritual interactions, that is central to this form of mediation.

It is possible to argue that with the rise of so-called smartphones, this development is moving in yet new directions and this is true to some degree. Mobile phones are increasingly providing access to the Internet. Applications (or apps) allow us to download small programs that can have innumerable functions. There are apps that let us write notes (some with little effort) and do lists. There are applications that help us carry out tasks and there are those that help us entertain ourselves. There are even applications for weather reports and stock prices, among many others. There are things we can use to waste time or to budget it. There are fanciful applications and those that are useful. In the context of this paper, this development might augur towards the use of commercial mobile games, and it no doubt does to the degree that this is a general trend. However, I argue that this trend is marginal when compared with mediated interpersonal playfulness.

This development changes, in some ways, the profile of the mobile phone. Where it has been an arena for social interaction, there has been a turn towards more solitary use. The mobile phone is not only for talking with friends, but it is also a device for cloistered use. The functionality of the system is moving away from being more or less exclusively for person-to-person mediation to including other applications, some of which draw us in from potential social interaction.

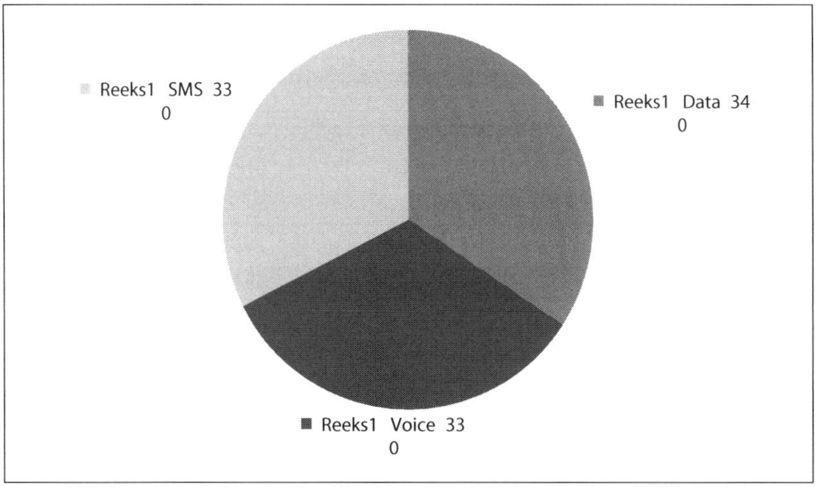

Fig. 2: Percent distribution of mobile-phone-based events for a sample of iPhone users, Norway 2009.

The rise of smartphones has seemingly taken our attention away from the idea of the simpler connections that are supported by the mobile phone. Smartphones, and in particular the iPhone, add some new dimensions and complexity to the situation. There is the sense that this will be "the Eldorado" moment for mobile Internet, and in some ways this may be true. In the case of the iPhone the numbers of events are about equally divided between talking, texting, and data (see Figure 2). Much of the data may be intentional use of the device to look up things. However, the nature of some apps can generate events even when we are not aware of it. For example, weather applications or stock market applications might continually download information.

Figure 2 shows the relative distribution of events for a sample of iPhone users in the Telenor net. It is clear that the iPhone users are far more active in their use of the mobile net. This can be for a wide variety of instrumental, as well as expressive activities. While about one third of the events[3] are IP traffic for iPhone users,[4] only about 8% of the events are IP for the standard user. This means that iPhone users are far more likely to use their phones to access the Internet. It does not tell us what they are doing on the net, only that they are far more likely to be accessing it.

It is perhaps encouraging for those who see the future as dominated by smartphones to read these numbers. However, it is perhaps a bit more sobering to understand that iPhone users are only a small part of the total mobile phone population. Indeed they made up only about 5% of the total number of users in the entire Norwegian sample as late as 2010. To put it differently, if the total population on the telephone network were the size of an apple (a piece of fruit, not the computer) the iPhone users would be a little larger than the o on this page. If we were to add in Android devices and other devices in this category, the number doubles, and this is still a relatively small portion of all phones that are in use (Nielsen and Fjuk 2010). While this group of users has a lot of good press, they are in reality very small. It is clear that this is a dynamic situation and that this ratio can change. Still, if we compare this with all the mobile phones in use in the world (estimated to be around 5.3 billion),[5] the comparison becomes even more lopsided (ITU-D 2010). While there have been very healthy sales of iPhones, Android-based devices, and other smartphones; they are still a very small actor on the broader stage. Drawing on the previous form of comparison, if all the phones in the world were the size of an apple, the iPhones would be about the size of the period at the end of this sentence. It is fair to say that the iPhone is not the only smartphone.[6] If we were to say that on a world basis there are twice as many or five times as many when considering all different types of smartphones, however that is defined, there are still not that many around. The message is that there are extraordinarily few smartphones when compared to the more traditional handsets. Thus while these devices clearly encourage people to use the Internet more, and by extension, are likely to be encouraged to engage more commercially based gaming, this is still for only a small minority. The vast majority of people in the world have far more basic phones and use them far more cautiously. For example, about 75% of the 50 million or so telephones in Bangladesh are Nokia 1000 series phones. Many of these have a simple black and white screen and basic voice/text functionality.

Play as ritual

To bring our discussion back to the work of Durkheim, Goffman, and Collins and the importance of play in social life, it is perhaps best to think of play, to the degree that it is done using the mobile phone, as being non-commercial[7] ritual interaction, i.e. it is a mutually focused activity, engendering a common mood. When thought of in this way, it is a ritual that supports the development of social cohesion. It is perhaps more important to focus on the mundane use of the device as opposed to the flashier uses of the device for commercially scripted gaming.[8]

The link between play and the mobile phone is specifically that the former can be carried out via the latter and result in a socially binding ritual. When I use the word ritual, I understand it to mean mutually focused activity that engenders a common mood in a bounded group. It is through this intense interaction that we, in effect, let down our barriers to others and are open to establishing and maintaining social bonds (Ling 2008). This understanding of ritual has been developed in the work of Durkheim, Goffman, and Collins. It is clear that play is a type of ritual and therefore it fits into this general framework. Mobile-based joking with one another has a ritual dimension. Indeed these interactions help us to account for how the mobile phone is so extremely important for the most immediate sphere of family and friends (Ishii 2006). In the words of Christian Licoppe, it gives us "connected presence" (2004). Among other things, we use the mobile phone to interact in a playful way with our closest friends and family. The way we greet a spouse when they call on the phone often includes special phrases and cadences with which we mark the relationship and further cultivate our intimate connection. We can share an inside joke that, in its telling, reconfirms our tight bond. This mundane form of playfulness is a far more profound and widespread, but far less flashy, than the commercial mobile (or net-based) multiplayer games.

The playfulness of missed calls

When considering socially integrative playful rituals via the mobile phone, what perhaps comes to mind are talking and texting. However, our proclivity for sociation and the use of ritual interaction means that we can engage in social integration using the simplest forms of mediated interaction. Indeed there is not even the need to use words in order to cultivate relationships when using the mobile phone. It is possible to see playfulness in the simple use of missed calls (Geirbo, Helmersen, and Engø-Monsen 2007). Missed calls are widely used in developing countries as a way to signal to one another without it incurring the cost of a call or a text. It uses only the ringing sound of the mobile phone and the caller ID function. One of the interlocutors calls the other, lets the phone ring once or twice and then hangs up. The person receiving the call sees who has called and, provided that they have agreed on the meaning of the call, they act accordingly. For example, if a husband is supposed to pick up his wife after work, they will agree that when she sends him a missed call, he will come to pick her up. This is an exceedingly common form of interaction in some countries

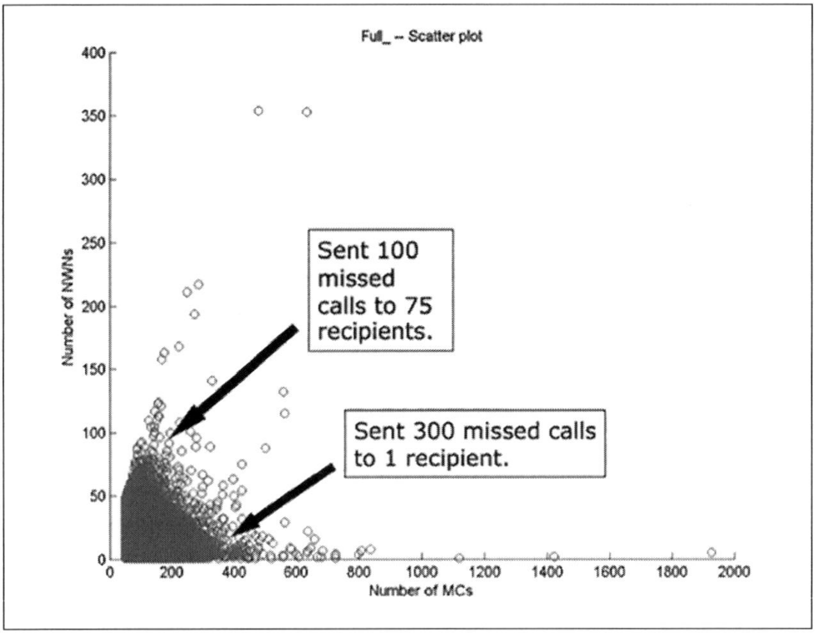

Fig. 3: Number of missed calls (x axis) and number of different phone numbers (y axis) for missed calls, Bangladesh 2007. Source: Geirbo, Helmersen, and Engø-Monsen 2007).

(Donner 2007). While they are often related to functional interaction they can also be used more playfully. To use the words of Asma, an 18-year-old Bangladeshi woman, who confided that: "My friend has a very charming welcome tone that I often want to hear. So I give him three miss-calls to say that I just want to listen to his welcome tone so not to receive my call."

Missed calls are not an isolated phenomena. Indeed in some countries the large majority of calls that are dialed are not answered, that is, they are missed calls. It is also clear from the data that it is not just a functional thing. As noted by Tasmia, a 19-year-old Bangladeshi woman, "I have a special friend but I have not met him. [...] I gave him a missed call. He called me and asked me who I am. [...] Then I told him so that he can talk to me." Thus, this practice can take on flirtatious dimensions. The material in Figure 3 shows that one individual sent 300 missed calls to a single recipient. There are also cases of people sending hundreds and even thousands of missed calls to the same number. There may be an element of control in these cases, but there can also be an element of flirting or play. It could simply be the desire to hear the ringtone, or it could just be the desire to give the object of one's adoration what Ito and Okabe (2005) call a virtual tap on the shoulder many times over. It is easy to see that the playful exchange of missed calls fits the notion of a ritual, i.e. the engendering of a common mood through a focused activity in a bounded group. It is through these types of interactions that social cohesion is developed.

Ricoeur: The tension between individual and group identity

We will now move our discussion to the other intellectual guidepost of the project, Paul Ricoeur, in order to pursue the question of individual as opposed to group identity. The Playful Identities project maintains that there are several different moments to the ludic self-construction of identity. Quoting somewhat loosely from the project outline, these include:

- Lived experience;
- Expression of this implicitly experienced ludic nexus in the player;
- The individual understands her/himself from the perspective of this space of possible actions;
- The space is reflectively applied to the self and internalized.

Each of these points is important in understanding the individual identity, but the progression is individualistic. We are constructing our own identities. There is the sense that social identities are also a part of the picture, but this portion of the discussion has not been elaborated on. The focus is on the individual.

Narrative identity

I argue that when examining identity construction it is worth considering the social dimension of ICT since mediated communication is inherently social. Considering the mobile phone that has been largely a mediation device, it is important that we look beyond individual identity construction to more group-based dynamics. Ricoeur believed we construct a narrative history out of memories in our past. By the same token, the group constructs its sense of identity out of similar materials. Indeed it is these collective events that result in group identity. We remember the time we had a beer with the gang after the game. We remember the family's summer holiday. We reflect on our Grandmother's 85th birthday party and recall how nice (or how tedious) it was to gather the entire family together for the evening. In each case, the specific event represents both a new episode, a new opportunity to gather memories, and a chance to cultivate and rearrange our past memories.

It is these collective times that provide the raw material for group identity development. As these situations move into the past we start to set them into a broader narrative line. We abstract the essence of them and come to some type of agreement within the group that, for example, Aunt Marge always needs to be at the center of attention by telling awkward jokes or that just like last year Tom bet Frank that the New York Yankees would beat the Boston Red Sox but it always seems like Boston chokes in the last inning. In other words, the specific events of the group are collected, arranged into a mosaic that is again used to characterize expectations for the current and future interactions.[9] Indeed, for married couples the actual facts are often bent and formed into a narration that supports a collectively founded sense of "who we are" (Berger and Kellner 1964).

It is also the responsibility of members – however they are defined – to maintain the lore of the group. Tom and Frank need to keep track (in some vague way) of how many times Boston has choked. Uncle George (Marge's brother) knows that when she starts to wind up for a story, he can usually move her onto another track by telling stories of their youth. Another dimension of this is that access to the narrative history of the group has boundary issues associated with it. People have varying access to this narration. Some people only get the superficial version while others are steeped in the details. Access depends to a large degree on the level of trust that group members are willing to afford the newbie. Access to the narration is accumulated and eventually a new member has participated in enough of the interactions so that they also build a reservoir of insight. In a like way, a new person's participation will, over time, become an element in the narration of the group. Obviously, there can be received elements in the narration of the group. Drawing on the work of Burger and Luckmann there can be the sense that the group does particular things, "because that is the way we do that" (Berger and Luckmann 1967). This legitimation is developed at some point in the history of the group and it becomes institutionalized. To the degree that it is orthodoxy, there is an ethics associated with the decision to respect the narration.

The mobile phone is involved in this to the degree that we use it to engage in social interaction. Just as the trip to the bar with the gang, the instrumental but more likely the expressive and phatic messages that are exchanged between individuals can become the raw material for group identity. We might remember the joke sent by a good friend, the nice chat we had with our Aunt Marge, some juicy gossip, or the text message from our now ex-boy/girlfriend that told us they need "more space" and that they would like to stop meeting.

And analogously, there are the sets of memories that individuals share with other members of their group. Through this "collective memory", a group of people has access to past events and deeds that have been reconstructed and recounted to them. Indeed, from one perspective, this collective memory antedates individual memories.

This ties us to Ricoeur's notion of narrative identity. With this concept, he makes the abstract idea of time into a way of understanding individual identity. This notion of identity pulls together our understanding of different events and dealings in our individual past into a single, more or less unified account. It takes the raw history of different incidents and gives us a broader sense of who we are and how we are positioned in society. There is the sense that "I have always liked pizza," that blue is my color, or the idea that our latest adventure was just like all the times before. At a personal level, we match the emerging situation with our sense of who we are with the various exigencies that need to be dealt with (what shirt to buy, which bar to choose, whether to spend the day reading or practicing our backhand shot, etc.).

If left at the level of individual identity, the notion of narrative identity would perhaps be of interest to psychologists. However, there is also a reciprocal social dimension to this. It is here that the communicative dimension of the mobile phone becomes interesting. The design or the type of mobile phone we consume might be an element in the integration of our personal identity. We can, for example, be a person who always has a Nokia, or insists on having a red mobile phone, etc. We can be the type of person who always wants to have a technically advanced device, one with a touch screen or we may take pride in having an old scratched up phone that is held together with tape and where the "#" key does not work. Our insistence on having a specific device can be a way for us to make sense of ourselves. We might not feel comfortable having a particular type of mobile phone and may have the sense that it is out of kilter with who we are. In this way, this decision has resonance with Ricoeur's individual notion of identity construction.

I suggest that it is also important to examine this at the group level. We construct an individual identity, but just as importantly we construct group identities. We have a notion of our family or circle of friends, our bowling team or our work colleagues. We have episodes in our past that we collectively work into a narrative of how the group came together and how it functions. If these narratives are abused too much, then the group has a reduced reservoir of cohesion. We develop these narratives by collectively experiencing things such as playfulness. More importantly we develop the group cohesion by discussing and elaborating these elements into a single narrative. It is here that the communicative practices of the group become important. The mobile phone, along with many other forms of mediation, provides us with a channel through which we construct these narrative identities. Mobile telephony has the advantages of being able to do this more or less immediately and it also allows for us to reach one another regardless of where we might be. Thus it can make the events of the group more intense and vibrant. We can get the call that Susie has been in a car crash and that our wife is on the way to the hospital and that we need to pick up another child, almost as the events unfold. Cohen, Lemish, and Schejter (2007) describe this type of drama mediated through the phone. The fact that dramatic events, or for that matter indescribably happy events ("Hi Dad, I just got engaged!"), can be mediated so quickly and so directly to the relevant individuals, means that there is a real vibrancy to the use of the device.

Thus, at the level of both personal integration and also the cohesion of the group, the mobile phone gives us both a physical object and a communication channel through which these messages can be mediated. At both the level of the individual and the level of the group, the mobile phone provides us with a way to work out our narrative identity.

Metaphoricity

Another notion that contributes to group cohesion suggested by Ricoeur is the notion of metaphoricity. He starts by noting that we use leaps of imagination and literary flourishes to underscore the meaning of certain events. These metaphoric assemblages are important since they underscore the importance of the event and give it a memorable character. The metaphors, however, have a limited shelf life. To use them too often means that they become worn and they lose their ability to describe the special nature of the instance. This is reminiscent of Simmel's notion of fashion. Simmel (1904) described fashion along two dimensions. The first is quite similar to the notion of metaphoricity in that our use can be described as being on a continuum between either being progressive or dated, or being avant-garde or dowdy. He also used another dimension, namely the degree to which a particular fashion can be seen as being a sign of inclusion. Our adoption or rejection of a particular fashion item marks our interest and indeed our ability to be a member of a particular social group.

Mobile phone practices can be seen using these dimensions (Fortunati 2005; Ling 2003). There are waves of popularity associated with them and our ability to adroitly deal with these dynamic phenomena. Our stylized orthography, newly popular smiley, cool new phone, or even our app *de jure* all place us in a particular place in the fashion terrain. We will be at some point on the continuum between being unrecognizably ahead of the coming fashion or laughably behind. In addition, our use of these symbolic devices will allow others to determine our status vis-à-vis membership in the broader group. It is also possible to think of how language in texting is used. Quite often, text message language is simple and it is mundane, i.e. messages such as "Hi. Can you call me?" sent by a 35-year-old male or "What time are you coming home" sent by a 45-year-old woman.[10] These all reflect simple interactions that are of importance at the moment, but do not really draw on any literary flourishes. However, in the same corpus a 17-year-old Norwegian male reported sending the text "Cy la8ter".[11] This is in itself an interesting text. It plays on the more common CUL8R that again is a rendition of the phrase "see you later". In the teen's version the exact phrasing is off. He used y instead of a u, he used a space between the Cy and the la8ter and he also reported actually spelling out the whole word "later" in addition to inserting the 8. Some of this may have been because he was not operating in his mother tongue and some of it may have simply been typing mistakes. Regardless he was using non-standard language on the mobile phone. His use of the phrase was not particularly early in the life cycle of such abbreviations, but it is still interesting that he chose to use it. This type of mediated "playing" with the language can also elicit special responses from his friends who in turn play on his text.

Although we do not have the total context of this interaction, the exchange that included the phrase was likely a way to underscore the group membership and develop a social bond based on a slight, though recognizable literary flourish. The use of this literary device was likely simply a closing to a series of text messages that covered another topic. However, it was also, in a small way, a recognition that both interaction partners shared the facility to use text messages and that they were both hip enough to use this phrase. Thus it fits into the landscape described by Simmel and also Ricoeur.

At the time of its use in Norway, it had a slightly dulled but still cutting-edge tone to it, and it was a marker of common membership in some social grouping. It has since lost that edginess. Middle-aged cubicle occupants along with the parents of 17-year-olds can even imagine using such a phrase with suitable ironic distance. Thus there has been a career associated with the phrase CUL8TR where it has gone from being a hip way of binding together teen interlocutors to being a more staid or even a time-bound antiquated phrase such as "23 skidoo" from the 1920s or "hot rod" from the 1950s or "groovy" in the 1960s and 1970s. At the time of their vogue, their correct use signified that the user was knowledgeable of the current lingo. In another work, I have described how Norwegian teens use purposely misspelled Swedish phrases in their texting as a way to mark social cohesion (Ling 2008). Indeed, early in their popularity curve, these terms often signify those persons who are *avant-garde*. As it becomes popular its ability to identify the cutting edge is blunted and eventually it can even become *kitsch*. Thus the mobile phone has been, and in many ways still is, an arena where metaphors are used to help define ourselves and our social sphere.

Conclusion

Mobile telephony helps us to maintain social cohesion. One of the ways that this is done is through playful interaction. While the mobile phone allows for both commercially scripted forms of play, it more importantly allows for non-commercial and unscripted forms of interaction. It is the latter that has the most profound social consequences. Commercial gaming via the Internet and increasingly on mobile platforms is often the focus of our attention. While this receives much of the current attention, there are still relatively few people on a global basis that use these. By comparison, there are many more mobile phones. Mobile gamers number in the millions while mobile phone users number in the billions. Thus, when looking at mobile telephony as an arena for playfulness and as an arena for the construction of social cohesion, it is more fruitful to look at mundane interpersonal interaction. It is when people are informally joking with one another, or when they are purposely constructing misspelled texts that play with inner group understandings, that the work of social cohesion is being done. To be sure, there is a social dimension to commercial gaming and it has many of the same outcomes. However, looking broadly, it is legacy of everyday social interactions via the mobile phone that helps the group to build a narrative identity.

The mediated artifacts, i.e. the in-group phrases and the forms of address used by interlocutors play on commonly held elements of the group lore. The way of telling a joke, announcing a party, or saying good bye serves to generate social cohesion, albeit in small increments. There is a phatic element to these interactions which extend beyond their communicative purpose expressing also a meta-message to show that the relationship of the two partners is still as it should be.

By looking at the use of mobile telephony, play, and social cohesion, we have seen that playful practices, such as purposefully misspelling words in texts, are a type of ritual interaction where there is a mutually focused activity engendering a common mood among the participants. It is in this way that the mobile phone helps us to maintain friends and to keep the lines of communication open within our social sphere.

Notes

1. These numbers come from Statistics Norway and their nationally representative sample of 1700 persons who were asked about their media use in 2009.
2. This is as opposed to the open Internet. When a person is connected to the mobile network, the Internet (or Internet protocol) traffic goes through the mobile telephone network before it moves into the more traditional Internet.
3. An event in the case of voice is a call, in the case of SMS it is a text message and in the case of IP it is a link being activated.
4. Other smartphone users were not as active on this front as iPhone users were.
5. By way of comparison there are about 2 billion Internet users on all platforms.
6. The definition of smartphones is contested. Often there are categories for 1) "high-end" smartphones such as HTCs and iPhones, 2) Smartphones that are somewhat more downscale, 3) feature phones, 4) high-end entry phones, and 5) entry phones.
7. Obviously there is a commercial dimension in our relationship with the mobile phone operator. However, they have a much different role than a commercial game provider.
8. It is clear that this kind of play can also take place in the context of commercial games, such as *World of Warcraft* and *Second Life*, despite the commercial aspects of the software.
9. This is quite close to the idea of group cohesion associated with ritual (Collins 2004; Ling 2008).
10. These text messages have been translated from Norwegian.
11. This is a verbatim rendition with no translation.

References

Berger, Peter, and Hansfried Kellner. 1964. Marriage and the construction of reality. *Diogenes* 46: 1-24.

Berger, Peter, and Thomas Luckmann. 1967. *The social construction of reality: A treatise in the sociology of knowledge*. New York: Anchor.

Cohen, Akiba A., Dafna Lemish, and Amit M. Schejter. 2007. *The wonder phone in the land of miracles: Mobile telephony in Israel.* Cresskill, NJ: Hampton Press.

Collins, Randall. 2004. *Interaction ritual chains.* Princeton, NJ: Princeton University Press.

Donner, Jonathan. 2007. The Rules of beeping: Exchanging messages using missed calls on mobile phones in Sub-Saharan Africa. *Journal of Computer Mediated Communication* 13: 1-22.

Durkheim, Emile. 1995. *The elementary forms of religious life* [1912], trans. K.E. Fields. Glencoe, IL: The Free Press.

Fortunati, Leopoldina. 2005. Mobile phones and fashion in post-modernity. *Telektronikk* 3: 35-48.

Geirbo, Hanne C., Per Helmersen, and Kenth Engø-Monsen. 2007. *Missed call: Messaging for the masses. A study of missed call signaling behavior in Dhaka* (Internal Telenor R & I Publication). Telenor R & I, Fornebu.

Goffman, Erving. 1967. *Interaction ritual: Essays on face-to-face behavior.* New York: Pantheon.

Goggin, Gerard. 2006. *Cell phone culture: Mobile technology in everyday life.* London: Routledge.

Habuchi, Ichiyo. 2005. Accelerating reflexivity. In *Personal, portable, pedestrian: Mobile phones in Japanese life*, eds. Mizuko Ito, Daisuke Okabe and Misa Matsuda, 165-82. Cambridge, MA: The MIT Press.

Hampton, Keith N., and Richard Ling. 2013. Explaining communication displacement and large-scale social change in core networks. *Information, Communication & Society*, 16(4), 561-89.

Hillebrand, Friedhelm, Finn Trosby, Kevin Holley, and Ian Harris. 2010. *Short message service: The creation of personal global text messaging.* New York: Wiley.

Ishii, Kenichi. 2006. Implications of mobility: The uses of personal communication media in everyday life. *Journal of Communications* 56: 346-65.

Ito, Mizuko, and Daishuke Okabe. 2005. Intimate connections: contextualizing Japanese youth and mobile messaging. In *The inside text: Social, cultural an design perspectives on SMS*, eds. Richard Harper, Leysia Ann Palen, and Alex Taylor, 127-45. Dordrecht: Springer.

ITU-D. 2010. *The world in 2010: The rise of 3G.* International Telecommunications Union.

Kim, Hyo, Gwang Jae Kim, Han Woo Park, Ronald E. Rice. 2006. The configurations of social relationships in communication channels: F2f, email, messenger, mobile phone, and SMS. *ICA Pre-conference on mobile communication*, ed. Maren Hartmann. Erfurt/Dresden, Germany: The International Communications Association.

Lasen, Amparo. 2011. Mobiles are not that personal: The unattended consequences of the accountability, accessibility and transparency afforded by mobile telephony. In *Mobile communication: Bringing us together or tearing us apart? Mobile Communication Research Series*, eds. Rich Ling and Scott Campbell, 83-105.. New Brunswick: Transaction.

Licoppe, Christian. 2004. Connected presence: The emergence of a new repertoire for managing social relationships in a changing communications technoscape. *Environment and Planning D: Society and Space* 22: 135-56.

Ling, Rich. 2003. Fashion and vulgarity in the adoption of the mobile telephone among teens in Norway. in *Mediating the human body: Technology, communication and fashion*, eds. Leopoldina Fortunati, James E. Katz, and Raimonda Riccini, 93-102. Mahwah, NJ: Lawrence Erlbaum Assoc.

—. 2008. *New tech, new ties: How mobile communication is reshaping social cohesion.* Cambridge, MA: The MIT Press.

—. 2009. The "taken for granted" nature of mobile phones. *Telektronikk* 2: n.p.

—, Troels Bertil, and Pål Roe Sundsøy. 2010. Texting among same-aged individuals: An analysis of traffic data. *International Communication Association Pre-conference on mobile communication,* Singapore, Singapore.

—, and Jonathan Donner. 2009. *Mobile communication*. Cambridge, UK: Polity Press.

Matsuda, Misa. 2005. Mobile communication and selective sociality. In *Personal, portable, pedestrian: Mobile phones in Japanese life*, eds. M. Ito, D. Okabe, and M. Mastuda, 123-42. Cambridge, MA: The MIT Press.

Nielsen, Petter, and Annita Fjuk. 2010. The reality beyond the hype: Mobile Internet is primarily an extension of PC-based Internet. *The Information Society:* 26: 375-82.

Reid, Donna, and Fraser Reid. 2004. Insights into the social and psychological effects of SMS text messaging in *160 characters*, http://educ.ubc.ca/courses/etec540/May08/suz/assests/SocialEffectsOfTextMessaging.pdf.

Sicart, Miguel. 2009. *The ethics of computer games*. Cambridge, MA: The MIT Press.

Simmel, Georg. 1904. Fashion. *International Quarterly* 10: 130-55.

Smoreda, Zbigniew, and Frank Thomas. 2001. Social networks and residential ICT adoption and use. *EURESCOM Summit 2001 3G technologies and applications*. Heidelberg: EURESCOM.

Vaage, Kjetil O. 2010. *Mediebruksundersøkelsen 2009*. Statistics Norway, Oslo.

Wei, Ran, and Ven-Hwei Lo. 2006. Staying connected while on the move: Cell phone use and social connectedness. *New Media and Society* 8: 53-72.

Williams, Dmitri, Nicolas Ducheneaut, Li Xiong, Yuanyan Zhang, Nick Yee, and Eric Nickell. 2006. From tree house to barracks: The social life of guilds in *World of Warcraft*. *Games and Culture* 1(4): 338-61

10. Digital cartographies as playful practices

Sybille Lammes

Where was I?

My neighbor recently looked up a Google Street View image of his tattoo parlor in Amsterdam. He noticed that his bicycle was parked in front of his shop, so he gathered that the specially equipped cars that made the panoramic photographs were traversing the city on one of his working days. Becoming intrigued he returned to the map and looked up the school of his children, whom he always picks up after school on his non-working days. On the Google Street View image a crowd of parents were gathering outside the school building. So he figured that the picture must have been shot at the end of the school day. His bicycle was nowhere to be seen and therefore his presumption that the cars drove through the city on one of his working days must have been right. He then looked up his home address on the map and saw that his car was not parked in front of the building. Had his wife gone somewhere that day? On the square in front of the house he noticed a huge billboard with posters for the European elections. So now he knew that the Google cars must have been driving around Amsterdam around June 2009.

The story that my neighbor told me provides a good illustration of what I want to discuss in this chapter. What my neighbor was doing here was constructing a spatial story through the use of digital maps. He actually tried to reconstruct two spatial stories at once: that of his own movements (and of his wife and children) and that of the movement of the Google cars. That his stories may hinge on the arguably wrong presumption that the Google Maps Street View cars covered Amsterdam in one single day is of less importance here. More important is that he became intrigued with the possibilities of digital cartographical technologies to construct *spatial stories*, a term cultural philosopher Michel de Certeau coined to describe how people understand their everyday whereabouts by weaving spatial narratives (1984, 122-35). However, my neighbor didn't just create any spatial story, but a story about the whereabouts of himself and his family. So his endeavors to create a spatial story were closely bound to his (social) identity. He actually asked himself the question *where am I* instead of *who am I*. Moreover he described the whole project as something he did for fun, as a playful activity that was worthwhile sharing in a light conversation.

This chapter is about the triad relation between digital mapping practices, spatial stories, and playful identities that can be distilled from my neighbor's story. Contrary to what media scholars have argued before about new media and contemporary cultures (Augé 2008; Eberle 2004; Kunstler 1994; Kupfer 2007; Meyrowitz 1985), digital mapping practices have actually brought us new senses of place and a strong urge to locate ourselves and to come to terms with our identities through story-like constructions of our whereabouts.[1] Central to my argument is the notion that digital cartographies allow a greater degree of two-way interaction between map and user than analogue maps (cf. November et al. 2010). Digital map users are not just reading maps, but are also to a far greater extent constantly influencing the shape and look of the map itself. At home, at work, or while traveling: maps have become more personal, transforming while we navigate with and through them. Digital maps have thus altered our conception of maps as "objectified" representations of space which have been a touchstone for centuries (de Certeau 1984; Anderson 1991; Crampton 2002; Harley 1989; Wood 2003). Instead digital maps have become more personal sources for constructing stories of one's whereabouts (Lammes 2008).

As this book illustrates, contemporary culture is also becoming increasingly ludic. Although play has always been a key element of many cultural practices, since the 1960s a tendency can be discerned in which daily cultural practices have become far more imbued with play. Some have called this an infantilization (Bauman 2007) and others a gamification (McGonigal 2011) of postcapitalist culture (Dibbel 2006). In this book we refer to it as the "ludification of culture" (cf. Raessens 2006; 2014). Pivotal to this change is that playing has become less separate from other, more serious, daily activities. These shifts in our experience of play and cartography are synergized in a myriad of playful mapping practices that people currently engage with. Whether it is with games, social networks, fantasy maps on the Internet, locative artworks, or location-based augmented reality applications, all these experiences ask users to actively play with maps.

The advent of digital maps and a simultaneous ludification of culture has thus opened up new possibilities for maps to function as "play equipment" that allow users to engage in what play-theorist Brian Sutton-Smith has called "informal social play" and "performance play" (1997, 4-5). Perhaps they are even an incarnation of what geographer John Kirkland Wright had in mind in 1947 when he called for an open acknowledgment and incorporation of the emotional and imaginative connection between people, places, and maps (Wright 1947).

Mobile mapping

My neighbor was using Google Maps on his desktop computer. So although the two spatial stories he constructed where all about mobility, he made his quest from a more-or-less stationary position. Here I will actually take his story a step further and discuss the playful use of digital maps on smartphones like the iPhone and Android phones. The mobility of the user and technology adds yet another layer to the dynamics between map, spatial story, and playful identity than is prevalent in my neighbor's account because such phones "house" mapping technologies that enable the user to use maps and locate their own position on the map while being on the move (Lammes 2013).

Smartphones are increasingly becoming prime loci for digital mapping practices.[2] One of the reasons that the use of maps has been so successful on smartphones is of course the mobility of the user and phone. Just as you could take an old paper map with you to check your route, you now have your phone with you, yet with the crucial difference that your whereabouts are now rendered on the map which adapts itself to your mobility and wishes. But besides the sheer convenience of having it all in your pocket, I believe that the fascination with cartographical technologies on phones should also be seen as a counterbalance to the act of mobile phoning itself which is very much about displacement. The availability of location data attaches a sense of physical location to mobile telephony by visualizing your whereabouts on the map.

Making things visible

With the emergence of Android phones, the iPhone, and other types of smartphones a myriad of highly popular applications and mash-ups have been developed in which digital maps are used for more purposes than just solely finding your way (Verhoeff 2012). I will discuss two such applications: *Foursquare* and *Layar*. *Foursquare* is a social networking game in which "players" gather points by checking in at various locations they visit. *Layar* is an augmented reality browser that allows users (as the name implies) to put a layer over their direct environment (camera view or map), which shows, for example, local restaurants, houses for sale, people who are on Twitter,

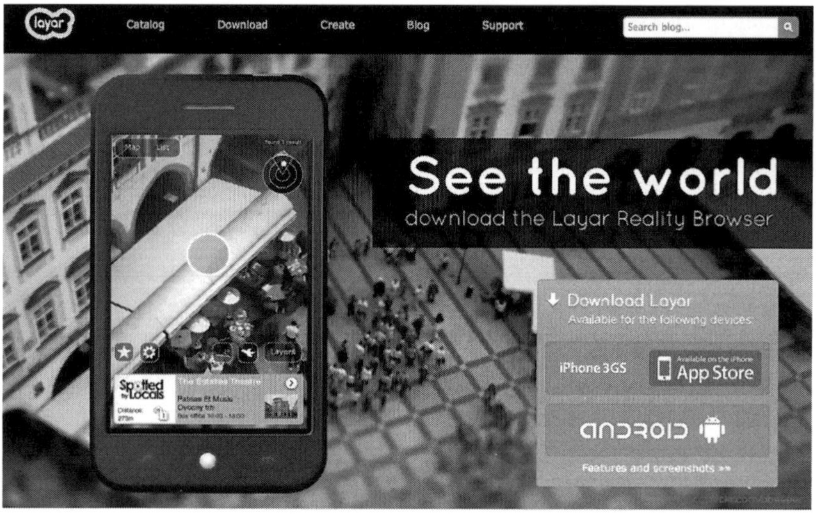

Fig. 1 Screenshot *Layar.*

campaigns for music artists[3] or games that have your own environment as the battleground. As the company describes *Layar* on its website: "a beautiful fun augmented reality app that shows you the things you can't see".

In this catchphrase a feature of *Layar* is highlighted which actually holds for many digital mapping practices on mobile phones: the possibility of rendering visible locations in your direct vicinity that otherwise would stay obscure or unknown. Locative social networks such as iPling, Plazes, or Citysense, games like *Assassin* or Google Maps mash-ups (e.g. *Panoramia*), all share this playful fascination with finding and creating spatial connections that would otherwise not be visible (or be there at all).[4] Take for example the *Layar* applications *Tweeps Around*.[5] In Twitter it often remains unclear *where* tweets are sent from, let alone that you can situate them in relation to your own location.[6] *Tweeps Around* shows you geo-tagged tweets (e.g. "@P: shopping list on the table", "having a shower") of people in your vicinity and enables you to locate in detail where they have been sent from on the linked Google map. Thus your daily life is augmented with a layer of spatial information that otherwise would have been unknown to you.

Spatial stories

According to Michel de Certeau, creating spatial stories is a means of coping with and experiencing spatial relations in daily life. As in the above examples they are a personal exploration of spatial surroundings, performative acts in which the traveler becomes the story-maker. De Certeau claims that spatial stories are the main way in which we make sense of everyday life: they are the essential organizing principle of all human activity (1984, 115). In order to understand how such spatial stories are created, he makes a distinction between space and place. Place refers to the "proper" ideologically informed order and to the way spatial positions are related in objective representations, such as maps. Space relates to how we deal with spatiality in daily life. He gives the example of walking in a city to explain what he means by this. The geometrical configuration of the streets he equates with place, while the act of traversing these streets on foot changes them into space. So, as place is set and univocal, the notion of space has as many meanings as there are walkers (ibid., 117). De Certeau speaks of both terms as constantly influencing each other. He identifies place as having the purpose to create unchanging and lifeless objects. While space, on the other hand, presupposes a subjective goal and implies movement and change. In stories, these two determinations should be understood as reciprocal since an abstract place can become a lively changeable, tangible space and vice versa (ibid., 117-21).

As I have argued elsewhere, digital cartographical interfaces actually upset the distinction between maps as abstract and objectified, and the practice of going somewhere as a personal and subjective experience of space (Lammes 2008). De Certeau's distinction of map and tour becomes problematic since maps are points of contact that change appearances according to where we wish to go and, as the example of *Tweeps Around* so clearly demonstrates, what others wish us to see. Indeed, the map and the tour can no longer be easily distinguished. Digital maps are in this respect reminiscent of maps in pre-Renaissance Western cultures when traces of touring were still visible on the map. Yet they also share similarities with certain "gestural and performative" mapping practices in non-Western cultures, such as the aboriginal songlines (Kitchin and Dodge 2007, 337). The main shift is that users of digital maps are no longer mere readers of maps, but have become cartographers on tour.

However, to what extent, and how, users are being invited to make maps through a personal exploration of space depends on the precise digital tools involved. In *Layar* you can choose which information is superimposed on the map or photographic image of your environment, such as reviews of restaurants near to where you are. Still the question remains how much this is about creating spatial stories. Certain applications, such as *Tweeps Around*, do trigger curiosity about other people's spatial stories that may be woven into a grander spatial story about the user's movements, similar to what my neighbor did. Others, such as the Rolling Stones application, may prompt you to add landmarks like posters and flyers to your direct environment, thus encouraging you to be more directly involved in the creation of a spatial story. Nevertheless, I would say that most layers are not so much about your own local movements, but more about other people and "things" (buildings, monuments, etc.) that surround you and could prompt you to move in a particular way (e.g. going to see a film). Similar to Google Earth, creating your own spatial story is thus largely determined by the landmarks of others. Furthermore, how you create such stories remains largely out of focus. In this way, *Layar* may be open to adding personal traces and conduct, such as tweets or reviews, but it is still an old-fashioned map in the sense that it offers a pretext for your personal journey and is not primarily about the subjective journey itself.

So although your own location is always the center point of the chosen radius that you see in *Layar*, and (to paraphrase Michel de Certeau) personal traces have reappeared on the map, the emphasis is mostly put on "local attractions" that others have put on the map. Needless to say, what is being put on the map is often commercially driven, and thus as much an ideological product as maps are in de Certeau explanation. It actually adheres to a definition of augmented reality in which "real life" is very much defined by (post)capitalist interests. In relation to identity, one can say that *Layar* changes your socio-spatial identity by offering you playful tools for selecting locations in your vicinity that are considered of social interest to you by others.

Where am I headed?

It is true that social network games like *Foursquare* (Fig. 2) or – the less competitive – *Gowalla* also offer you a selection of locales that are not entirely of your own making. Companies make money from localized advertisements and you can earn points if you check in at certain companies. If you, for example, check in three times at an Apple store you earn a so-called Job-Badge which you can trade in and if you check in at enough Starbucks locations "you become the envy of your friends with the Barista Badge".[7] In this way, you are lured in by commercial companies to consume goods and services. Moreover, reviews of such companies left by players on the *Foursquare* network often look like advertisements for such companies since the spirit of fun seems to dictate an upbeat display of their daily life. Play, identity, and branding are thus in close collusion when players are invited to engage in mapping. The map may have become more flexible and personal yet is very much part of a prosumer culture where ideological motivations are still far from vanished (see also Crogan's chapter in this book).

So (postcapitalist) ideological motivations have not disappeared, although the distinction between map and tour may have become muddled. Yet a crucial difference with *Layar* is that the emphasis shifts to putting yourself on the map and showing others your spatial movements and whereabouts. While *Layar* invites you to develop spatial stories, for the most part it does not show them, since such games are far more about showing the creation of your own spatial stories through playing, or cheating, as René Glas writes in this book. Furthermore, they encourage you to share your stories, whether or not fabulated, with other players while others in their turn are triggered to share their stories with you. The central objective is to travel, gather points by visiting places, and share (albeit competitively) your whereabouts with others. Your social identity is actually created by putting yourself on the map for others to measure themselves with and to connect to.

On a typical working day, I always use *Foursquare* while on my way to work. After a short bike ride, I first check in on my phone at the main railway station in Amsterdam. I open the *Foursquare* application and choose the option "places" at the bottom of the screen to look at all identified "locales" in the vicinity. Besides the railway station, the list includes shops in the vicinity and platform numbers that can be selected for check-in. By clicking on a place, I can read more detailed information about it (e.g. "great coffee, good service") or I can open a link to a Google map that pinpoints where I am exactly. I can also add locations and information myself. When I have checked in at the railway station, *Foursquare* gives me the option to share this information with friends on Facebook and Twitter. It also shows me all other people who have been checking in at the station that morning. The person who has checked in the most in the last two months is identified as the mayor of the railway station. After the train has departed, I usually check in at the next train stop before reaching my destination. During the trip I may get notifications from the *Foursquare* team about earned badges, such as "Hey there – Congrats! Your check-in to Utrecht Central Station just unlocked Photogenic – You found 3 places with a photo booth!" When I reach the office, I always check in again to see if I have lost my mayorship to one of my colleagues who also plays the game and to see if he has already checked into the premises as well. On my way back I repeat the procedure in the reverse order. When I enter my apartment I conclude my day by checking in there. Since I am the only one in the house who plays the game I remain the unchallenged mayor.

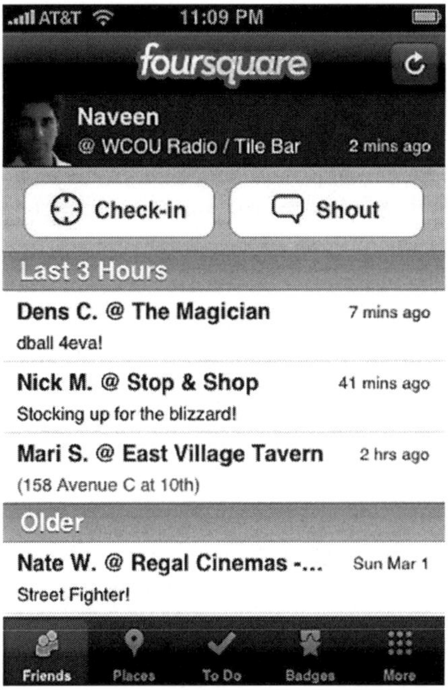

Fig. 2: Screenshot *Foursquare*.

By playing *Foursquare* I have become far more aware of my routine itinerary as I travel to work than I would normally be. I am more conscious of my spatial whereabouts by playfully being encouraged to weave a spatial story with myself as the main protagonist. Furthermore, I am telling my story to others, including the *Foursquare* team, other *Foursquare* players, and (if I wish) my friends on Facebook. Conversely, other players can tell me their spatial stories and if these players are friends of mine and we find ourselves in the same place, our stories may merge by for instance having a drink together. So *Foursquare* makes places (as they are called on the graphic interface) more like spaces: personal and social landmarks that are hybrids of objective mapping and subjective touring. Without doubt *Foursquare* still depends on conventional mapping techniques in the sense that it uses the classical cartographical representation of a Google map, yet as a player I heavily inscribe this "navigational interface" (Lammes 2011) with layers of my personal "adventures". As a matter of fact, I can even change the location of a landmark on the map, as René Glas points out in his contribution to this book, or for example I can fabricate an even more successful and exciting story in which I become the mayor of the North Pole. All of which is made visible to others.

In his contribution to this book media anthropologist Michiel de Lange identifies how mobile phone users in Jakarta, Indonesia create their social identity by using their phone as a material item that is put on display for others to see. Having and showing your phone as a material good gives you social prestige and is a playful way to create a social and modern identity. Location-based games like *Foursquare* – judging by the messages shown on *Foursquare*'s website which are also rather popular in Jakarta – adds another dimension to the level of material status that comes with mobile phones. Now one's *physical location* becomes part of the equation since mobile phone users can tell others where they are and thus create spatial stories as a way of mediating identity. Undoubtedly a spatial account that contains more trendy and prestigious places, more sought-after mayorships, and more signs of hooking up with friends earns you more social prestige than I obtained on my trip to work. As such location-based social network games add a material and locative dimension to smartphones to show and create social identities.

In applications like Google Earth or *Layar* the emphasis is placed on what others want to promote as important locations to shape your social identity. To refer back to the *Layar*'s slogan: they mainly show you things that others want you to see and go to. Although this component has not vanished from social network games, here the accent is put on how you make yourself spatially visible and powerful in a social network in order to gain social prestige. What both cases have in common is that as applications they open up possibilities for users/players to employ the visualization of locations to shape their identities. As has been shown to us throughout this book, there are indeed fine examples of the ludification of our culture that can demonstrate how digital technologies open spaces for shaping and displaying our spatial identities.

Acknowledgement

The research leading to these results has received funding from the European Research Council under the European Community's Seventh Framework Programme (FP7/2007-2013) / ERC Grant agreement No. 283464.

Notes

1. Discussions about digital media used to frequently focus on how new media, such as the Internet, generated new virtual experiences of space

that were distant from everyday material realities (Fuller 2005). In relation to space, scholars even argued that new media deprived us of a sense of place. Through their global and ubiquitous use and representations they would create "geographies of nowhere" instead (Augé 2008; Eberle 2004; Kunstler 1994; Kupfer 2007; Meyrowitz 1985). Lately a "material turn" can be discerned in which the conception of new media as immaterial, global, and placeless is contested as being naïve. It has recently become more common to assert that digital media re-mediate existing spaces (Bolter and Grusin 1999), that they are site-specific (McCarthy 2001), local as well as global (Appuradai 1996; Bakardjieva 2005; Lammes et al. 2009; Poster 2004; Schwartz 2006), and that virtuality is not opposed to material or physical practices (Fuller 2005; Hayles 2002; Kalaga 2003; Lievrouw and Livingstone 2002; Nunes 2006; Poster 2004; Shield 2003).

2. Satnav companies like TomTom are losing a lot of profit due to the popularity of these mapping applications because people are turning to these other devices or apps on their phones instead. See, for example: "TomTom vestigt hoop op autofabrikanten" [TomTom puts its hope in automobile manufacturers], *NRC Handelsblad*, July 21, 2010.
3. In 2010, the Rolling Stones created a layer that allowed fans to "fly-post their streets, homes or offices with virtual interactive posters of the rock icons" http://site.layar.com/company/blog/layer-of-the-week-rolling-stones/.
4. www.ipling.com; http://plazes.com; www.citysense.com; http://iphoneassassin.com; www.panoramio.com.
5. www.tweepsaround.com.
6. www.twitter.com.
7. https://foursquare.com/starbucks.

References

Anderson, Benedict R. 1999. *Imagined communities: Reflections on the origin and spread of nationalism*, rev. and extended edition. London: Verso.

Augé, Marc. 2008. *Non-places: Introduction to an anthropology of supermodernity*. London; Verso.

Bakardjieva, Maria. 2005. *Internet society: The Internet in everyday life*. London: Sage Publications.

Bauman, Zygmunt. 2007. *Consuming life*. Cambridge, UK: Polity Press.

Bolter, J. David, and Richard Grusin. 2000. *Remediation: Understanding new media*. Cambridge, MA: The MIT Press.

Crampton, Jeremy W. 2001. Maps as social constructions: Power, communication and visualization. *Progress in Human Geography* 25(2): 235-52.

Certeau, Michel de. 1984. *The practice of everyday life*. Berkeley: University of California Press.

Dibbell, Julian. 2006. *Play money: Or, how I quit my day job and made millions trading virtual loot*. New York: Basic Books.

Eberle, Gary. 1994. *The geography of nowhere: Finding one's self in the postmodern world*. Kansas City, MO: Sheed and Ward.

Fuller, Matthew. 2005. *Media ecologies: Materialist energies in art and technoculture*. Cambridge, MA: The MIT Press.
Foursquare Labs, Inc. 2011. *Foursquare*.
Gowalla. 2012. *Gowalla*.
Harley, J. Brian. 1988. Maps, knowledge, and power. In *The iconography of landscape: Essays on the symbolic representation, design and use of past environments*, eds. Denis Cosgrove and Stephen Daniels, 277–312. Cambridge Studies in Historical Geography 9. Cambridge, UK: Cambridge University Press.
Hayles, Katherine N. 2002. Flesh and metal: Reconfiguring the mindbody in virtual environments. *Configurations* 10(2): 297-320.
Kalaga, Wojciech. 2003. The trouble with the virtual. *Symploke* 11(1-2): 96-103.
Kitchin, Rob, and Martin Dodge. 2007. Rethinking maps. *Progress in Human Geography* 31(3): 331-44.
Kupfer, Joseph H. 2007. Mobility, portability, and placelessness. *Journal of Aesthetic Education* 41 (1): 38-50.
Kunstler, James Howard. 1994. *The geography of nowhere: The rise and decline of America's man-made landscape*. New York: Simon and Schuster.
Lammes, Sybille. 2007. Approaching game-studies: Towards a reflexive methodology of games as situated cultures. *Situated play: DIGRA 2007 proceedings*, ed. Baba Akira, 25-30. Tokyo: The University of Tokyo.
—. 2009. Terra incognita: Computer games, cartography and spatial stories. In *Digital material: Tracing new media in everyday life and technology*, eds. Marianne van den Boomen, Sybille Lammes, Ann-Sophie Lehmann, Joost Raessens, and Mirko Tobias Schäfer, 223-35. Amsterdam: Amsterdam University Press.
—. 2011. The map as playground: Location-based games as cartographical practices. *Think, design, play: DIGRA 2011 proceedings*. Hilversum, www.digra.org/dl/db/11310.35282.pdf.
Lievrouw, Leah A.A., and Sonia M. Livingstone, eds. 2002. *Handbook of new media: Social shaping and consequences of ICTs*. London: Sage Publications.
McCarthy, Anna. 2001. From screen to site: Television's material culture, and its place. *October* 98: 93-111.
McGonigal, Jane. 2011. *Reality is broken: Why games make us better and how they can change the world*. London: Jonathan Cape.
Merriman, Peter. 2004. Driving places: Marc Augé, non-places, and the geographies of England's M1 motorway. *Theory, Culture & Society* 21(4/5): 145-67.
Meyrowitz, Joshua. 1985. *No sense of place: The impact of electronic media on social behavior*. Oxford: Oxford University Press.
November, Valerie, Eduardo Camacho-Hübner, and Bruno Latour. 2010. Entering a risky territory: Space in the age of digital navigation. *Environment and Planning D: Society and Space* 28: 581-99.
Nunes, Mark. 2006. *Cyberspaces of everyday life*. Minneapolis, MN: University of Minnesota Press.
Poster, Mark. 2004. Digitally local communications: Technologies and space. Conference paper *The global and the local in mobile communication: Places, images, people, connections*. Budapest, Hungary.
Raessens, Joost. 2006. Playful identities, or the ludification of culture. *Games and Culture* 1(1): 52-57.
—. 2014. The ludification of culture. In: *Rethinking gamification*, eds. Mathias Fuchs, Sonia Fizek, Paolo Ruffino, Niklas Schrape, 91-114. Lüneburg: Hybrid Publishing Lab.

Schwartz, Leigh. 2006. Fantasy, realism, and the other in recent video games. *Space and Culture* 9(3): 313-25.

Shields, Rob. 1996. *Cultures of Internet: Virtual spaces, real histories, living bodies.* London: Sage Publications.

Shields, Rob. 2003. *The virtual.* London: Routledge.

Sutton-Smith, Brian. 1997. *The ambiguity of play.* Cambridge, MA: Harvard University Press.

Verhoeff, Nanna. 2012. *Mobile Screens: The visual regime of navigation.* Amsterdam: Amsterdam University Press.

Wood, Dennis. 2003. Cartography is dead (thank God!). *Cartographic Perspectives* 45: 4-7.

Wright, John K. 1947. Terrae incognitae: The place of the imagination in geography. *Annals of the association of American geographers* 37(1): 1-15.

11. Ludic identities and the magic circle

Gordon Calleja

Introduction

Johan Huizinga's work has received renewed attention with the emergence and expansion of Game Studies. An important aspect of Huizinga's explication of play is its bounded nature. Like other cultural artefacts Huizinga describes in *Homo ludens* (1955), the act of game playing requires the crossing of a boundary that marks the game from the ordinary world. The crossing of this boundary into game-space implies a shift in the players' identity that takes them from their everyday, "ordinary" selves, into their ludic selves. Suits has described this as the "lusory attitude" (1978, 52); a disposition one enters into when interacting with the bounded space of the game.

This chapter examines the conception of digital games as separate from the everyday real, which has, in contemporary Game Studies, become labelled as the "magic circle", and considers the ways in which its adoption impacts upon the player's experience and identity. It draws on the work of theorists like Anchor, Ehrmann, Fink, and Gombrich who have adopted a critical stance towards Huizinga's notion of play as separate from everyday life/reality. The inadequacy of this notion becomes more apparent when we consider contemporary efforts to stretch Huizinga's work and apply it to engagement with contemporary digital games.

This chapter will thus argue against the often taken-for-granted applicability of Huizinga's conception of play as an act apart from a supposed external, ordinary reality. As this apartness of play is central to Huizinga's conception of play, it calls into question the actual utility of Huizinga's theory of play, especially when contemporary digital games are the focus of one's work. Digital games are particularly problematic because, as I have argued elsewhere (Calleja 2007b; 2011), digital games have radically expanded the landscape of possible types of games and merged games with other forms of media objects such as film, literature, and virtual environments. The chapter will end with two practical examples of the problems one encounters if taking Huizinga's conception of play as the foundation of its work by focusing on the clash between the claim that play is a bounded activity and the situated realities of immersion and identity in contemporary digital gameplay.

An act apart

Huizinga's conception of play as an act apart is most evident in the concept of the magic circle. Initially used by Huizinga (1955) in *Homo ludens*, the metaphor of the magic circle has been widely adopted by Game Studies theorists (Juul 2005; Salen and Zimmerman 2004) to articulate the spatial, temporal, and psychological boundary between games and the real world:

> All play moves and has its being within a play-ground marked off beforehand either materially or ideally, deliberately or as a matter of course. [...] The arena, the card-table, the magic circle, the temple, the stage, the screen, the tennis court, the court of justice, etc., are all in form and function play-grounds, i.e. forbidden spots, isolated hedged round, hallowed within which special rules obtain. All are temporary worlds within the ordinary world, dedicated to the performance of an act apart (Huizinga 1955, 12).

The compartmentalization of the play-space from the "ordinary world" is a defining element of play, to which Huizinga returned frequently in his work. For Huizinga, play is a "stepping out of real life into a temporary sphere of activity with a disposition all of its own" (ibid., 9). Additionally, all forms of play, whether engaged in by humans or animals, have some form of rules and it is the adherence to and upholding of these rules that structures and sustains the magic circle (ibid., 12).

The space internal to the magic circle is defined by the rules enacted therein, creating "an absolute and peculiar order" (ibid., 10) within its boundary. The relationship between order and play is necessary for Huizinga's vision of play as *the* ideal of organized human social structures. Once the importance of play as epitome of a perfectly ordered social world is established, Huizinga goes on to use play as an epiphenomenon with which other aspects of human society and culture can be compared and measured. His interest in play can be traced back to his 1919 book *The waning of the Middle Ages* (1954). In this early work Huizinga argued that despite the unattainable nature of chivalric ideals, chivalry survived long after the socio-cultural contexts that engendered it died. He attributed the survival of chivalry to its play-like qualities. Later, in *In the shadow of tomorrow* (Huizinga and Huizinga 1936), Huizinga argued that the crisis in which the world found itself at the time of writing was symptomatic of a culture that had perverted the ideals of play. So it is no surprise that in his final work we find such a definitive statement about the ordered nature of play:

> Here we come across another, very positive, feature of play: it creates order, *is* order. Into an imperfect world and into the confusion of life it brings a temporary, a limited perfection. Play demands order absolute and supreme (Huizinga 1955, 10).

The magic circle thus inscribes the boundary between order and chaos, between the idealized ritual of play and the mess of ordinary life. As Anchor (1978) points out, the notion of a distinct boundary between play and the real world becomes the cornerstone of a model of play against which higher forms of culture are measured. Once the play model is established in the first chapter of *Homo ludens*, Huizinga takes us on a tour of certain facets of culture, such as language, law, war, and ritual; discussing how each expresses the play concept.

The separation of play from the everyday that Huizinga proposes has not escaped criticism. Ehrmann (1968) criticized Huizinga for conceiving "ordinary life" or "reality" as a stable entity that can be compared, contrasted, and measured against play. Huizinga took for granted the existence of a "reality", perpetually escorted by the hesitant presence of quotation marks, that can, in some non-specified manner, be divorced from culture and/or play. But as Ehrmann rightly argued, there is no reality outside of the culture that constructs it:

> The problem of play is therefore not *linked* to the problem of "reality", itself linked to the problem of culture. It is one and the same problem. In seeking a solution it would be methodologically unsound to proceed as if play were a variation, a commentary *on*, an interpretation, or a reproduction *of* reality. To pretend that play is mimesis would suppose the problem solved before it had even been formulated (1968, 33-4).

Reality does not *contain* play; like any other socio-cultural construction, play is an intractable manifestation of reality. A consideration of games, whether it be from the perspective of the game as object, game as activity, or the game's role in the wider community, *is* a consideration of reality. As Taylor (2006) has rightly argued, such a perspective ignores the grounded analysis of these objects and activities while side-lining the fact that they are very much part and parcel of our mundane, everyday reality.

Theorists like Anchor (1978), Ehrmann (1968), Fink (1968), and later Copier (2007), Lammes (2008), Malaby (2007), Pargmann and Jakobsson (2008), and Taylor (2006) have argued that a dichotomous view on the relationship between play/games and the real world does not survive close analyses, whether this is derived from the critical humanities or the applied social sciences.

The magic circle and player experience

The concept of the magic circle has also been applied to the experiential dimension of gameplay. Within Game Studies it is often taken as a given that gameplay involves entering a particular experiential mode that was described by Bernard Suits as the "lusory attitude" (1978, 52). The lusory attitude is closely tied to the notion of the magic circle because it is similarly built on the assumption that players voluntarily adopt an attitude that is apart from ordinary life; an experiential mode that occurs only during game playing:

> The attitude of the game player must be an element in game playing because there has to be an explanation of that curious state of affairs wherein one adopts rules which require one to employ worse rather than better means to reach an end (ibid., 52).

Although Suits was not considering digital games in his writing, the adoption of his theory by contemporary researchers such as Salen and Zimmerman (2004) requires some attention. Like Huizinga, the applicability of Suits' work to digital games is often taken as a given fact by Game Studies researchers, but on closer inspection aspects of his definition of games do not apply to digital games without stretching the text to uncomfortable limits. The voluntary decision to follow an inefficient course of action in order to play by the rules only applies to the socially negotiated aspect of digital games, yet the majority of actions possible in digital games are programmed into the game system and cannot be changed. One cannot decide to ignore the rules written into a game like *Fable II* (Lionhead Studios 2008) and, for example, drag a chair found in one's house to the town square and decide to sit there. The game does not allow for this to take place because the actions are not programmed into it. Similarly the player cannot jump off a low ledge onto the ground instead of running around the prescribed path simply because it would be more efficient, because *this* particular game does not allow that. More efficient ways of doing things outside of the rule structure imposed by the game are simply not available to the players of digital games, so we should be very careful in applying Suits' work to digital games without considering their specific qualities.

But aside from the problem of using Suits' notion of the lusory attitude for digital games, there is also a problematic dimension of his concept when presented as a defining element of all games, digital and otherwise. This creates a problematically circular argument that essentially claims that games are activities that require a lusory attitude and that the lusory attitude is an experience that occurs when playing a game. If we had to follow Suits' logic, the inability in a number of digital games, particularly single-player ones, to voluntarily adopt inefficient means in playing them means that we cannot enter into a lusory attitude, and thus such activities are not games.

It is illogical to claim that play refers simultaneously to a mode of human experience *and* a form of activity. As Malaby (2007) argued, this makes a problematically deterministic claim which presupposes that a specific experiential mode (the lusory attitude, for example) is part of any engagement with a game. We can either assign play to refer to an activity (engaging with a game) or a particular mode of experiencing that game – not both at once!

Opposition to the magic circle as a form of experiential bracketing has been particularly strong from researchers conducting qualitative studies with players. Ethnographic work by Taylor (2006), Malaby (2007), Copier (2007), and Pargman and Jakobsson (2008) indicates that such a separation is not found in the situated study of gamers:

> The idea of a magic circle is alluring, as is the idea of a clear limit between play and non-play. Reality is messier. Problems with using the concept of a magic circle as an analytical tool have been identified repeatedly. These problems become especially clear when the researcher in question has actual empirical material at hand which they try to understand (without much success) by applying the dominant paradigm of the separateness of play (Pargman and Jakobsson 2008, 227).

Any attempt to create a clean demarcation between the game experience and the experience of the world (supposedly) external to it will find it difficult to explain how the players' personal and social histories can be excluded from the game activity. It is hardly possible for the game-space to block out the complexity of social and personal relations. The lived experience of the players invariably informs, to different degrees depending on the circumstances, the experience of the game and vice versa.

Any attempt to separate the experience of gameplay from the experience of the surrounding social and physical contexts is prone to failure. A game's formal properties cannot fully determine the experience a player has when engaging with them. It would be incredibly misleading to label all forms of interactions in virtual environments with ludic properties as having a specific experiential disposition by the very virtue of engagement therein. We are better served by furthering our understanding of game engagement unburdened by such normative assumptions.

The second boundary: Virtual as unreal

If the magic circle formulates all games as separate due to their ludic nature, digital games encounter a second boundary of separation from the "real" of everyday life: the virtuality attached to their digital nature. This is not a division suffered by digital games only, but all digital media ranging from the Internet to any form of virtual environment. These have been characterized from their earliest days by their separation from the real world. Barlow and Kapor (1990) were two of the earliest writers to adopt the rhetoric of the frontier to describe the Internet:

> Over the last 50 years, the people of the developed world have begun to cross into a landscape unlike any which humanity has experienced before. It is a region without physical shape or form. It exists, like a standing wave, in the vast web of our electronic communication systems. It consists of electron states, microwaves, magnetic fields, light pulses and thought itself. In its present condition, Cyberspace is a frontier region, populated by the few hardy technologists who can tolerate the austerity of its savage computer interfaces, incompatible communications protocols, proprietary barricades, cultural and legal ambiguities, and general lack of useful maps or metaphors (1990, n.p.).

The frontier metaphor, taken directly and uncritically from cyberpunk fiction, fostered the idea that virtual worlds lie on the other side of a geographical boundary that separates them from the real world on the other side of the screen. The image of the "hardy technologists" venturing into an austere and savage "landscape" clearly appealed to the imagination fuelled by Gibson's *Neuromancer* that was published in 1984. There is an uncanny resemblance between the register used here and that used by Gibson in his fiction. The fictional image of cyberspace presented in *Neuromancer* became a fact looming on the foreseeable technological horizon. The frontier rhetoric did not stop at Barlow and Kapor. It became a common trope of writers describing new technologies like Rushkoff (1994), Rheingold (1993), Mitchell (1995), and others in the 1990s. However, the rhetoric of the frontier is problematic because it creates the notion of a boundary between the real and the virtual rather than seeing the latter as a constituent of the former. Fundamental concepts like the relationship between the real and the virtual underpin any discussion of digital media and it is thus crucial to consider carefully the assumptions they entail (for this more contemporary stance see Nunes 2006).

Although theorists like Mary-Laure Ryan (2001), Pierre Levy (1998), and Rob Shields (2003) have argued against this opposition of the virtual to the real, the drive to separate digital worlds from a supposed real world that exists outside of these bracketed spaces – much as in the discussion of the magic circle – still persists in fields like Game Studies. Edward Castranova in *Synthetic Worlds*, for example, took issue with the modifier "virtual" in the term "virtual worlds", arguing for a replacement of "virtual" with "synthetic". He outlined how the rise and fall of the hype around virtual reality created a negative association with the term virtual:

> Finally, while being conservative in writing is one decision imposed by the nearness of this book to early VR writing, another is the importance of avoiding words like "virtual". That word points a misleading finger from the game worlds back to the earlier VR paradigm. As I have said, no such connection is warranted. And therefore where I use "virtual" in this book, I just mean "rendered by a computer": a virtual world is a world rendered by computer (2005, 294).

Castronova argued that we should move away from the virtual/real binary by replacing "virtual" with "synthetic". Synthetic is useful in highlighting the designed nature of virtual worlds, but in doing so it also creates another binary; between the man-made, crafted synthetic world and a "largely unmodified reality that has been in existence for a while", which he refers to as "the Earth" (ibid., 294). The problem with such an opposition, as is the case with the concept of the magic circle, is that they create either/or relationships that ignore the richer middle ground. As Haraway (1991) has argued, contemporary culture is best expressed in terms of hybridity and dialectic relationships between poles of difference, rather than reductionist dualisms. Castronova (2005) does not manage to escape the binary view of the phenomenon he identifies as problematic.

The "virtual" in digital games can be more productively characterized by the vast landscape of potential configurations of text and its actualization. This potential emerges from the persistent interaction of human subjectivities with each other and the textual world written for their habitation, and, in the case of online game worlds, is constantly being re-inscribed by the readings and practices of its inhabitants. This constant process of actualizing real human relations – love, hate, frustration, competition, and collaboration – is accelerated by what Bolter and Grusin (1999) have called the "hypermediacy" of networked access.

The computer does not constitute the virtual in itself. It is a necessary tool for enabling the manifestation of the actual-virtual dialectic. The applications that run the digital games, MMOGs, hypertexts, and other digital artifacts are fully realized in their coded structure. The clusters of programmed code interact in a predetermined way until the point of contact with the interpreting human subjectivity. It is at this juncture that the virtual comes into force:

> Potential, not virtual, for the digital engram and the software used to read the text predetermine a set of possibles, which, though immense, are numerically finite and logically bound. However, it is not quantity that distinguishes the possible from the virtual. The essential distinction is to be found elsewhere. If we consider the mechanical substrate alone (hardware and software), computer technology provides only a combination of possibles, albeit infinite, and never a problematic domain. Digital storage is a potentialization, display a realization. [...] The virtual begins to flourish with the appearance of human subjectivity in the loop, once the indeterminateness of meaning and the propensity of the text to signify come into play, a tension that actualization or interpretation, will resolve during the act of reading (Lévy 1998, 52-3).

It is the interaction of the player with the complex problematic presented by the game rules, environmental mechanics, representational signs, and the hardware interface that engenders a movement from virtualization to actualization and back again. Virtual environments, as defined above, are unique sites of mediated instantiation of this recursive process of actualization and virtualization. This process accounts for the creation of a challenge, or problem that needs to be solved (virtualization) to the creation of a solution that is acted upon (actualization). Often, an action in a game system will pose new challenges to be solved, and the process starts all over again. The possibility for exerting agency within the environment beckons the question, "what shall I do next?", creating another problematic; a re-virtualization that requires the solution of practice. The player actualizes thought into action, in itself a creation of a further problematic: the inscription of one's actions onto the environment, affecting the clusters of coded data, as well as other users in the environment. The complexity of this recursive process is multiplied by the presence of others and emphasized by the immediacy enabled by networked computing.

Digital games are designed to enable the actualization of desired experience. Stating that this is their principal attractor would ignore the heterogeneity of players and games, but it is at least a key factor that makes them such compelling media. This view of the virtual gives a constructive account of the essential features of virtual environments and worlds.

The utility of the concept of the virtual applied to digital games and other forms of virtual environments lies in emphasizing their creative potential for actualizing a theoretically infinite range of possible experiences. The ontological value of these experiences is very much of the order of the real, not of its opposite.

Crossing the double boundary

The prevalence of the boundary presented by the magic circle has created a tendency of viewing engagement with digital games as a crossing into a realm of the virtual-ludic *other*. This sense of transportation is the foundation upon which metaphors that describe intense forms of engagement with digital games are built. One such prevalent metaphor is *immersion*:

> Immersion is a metaphorical term derived from the physical experience of being submerged in water. We seek the same feeling from a psychologically immersive experience that we do from a plunge in the ocean or swimming pool: the sensation of being surrounded by a completely other reality, as different as water is from air, that takes over all of our attention, our whole perceptual apparatus (Murray 1998, 98).

Virtual environments are an important part of our everyday reality and should be seen as deeply interwoven with our sense of the real. A metaphor of virtual world habitation, therefore, should draw upon the experiential *gestalts* of everyday habitation; that is, a view of consciousness as an internally generated construct based on the organization of external stimuli according to existing experiential *gestalts* (Damasio 2000; Dennett 1991; Lakoff and Johnson 2003).

The metaphors of immersion founded as it is on an exclusionary logic, do not enable such a perspective on the phenomenon. I have therefore argued elsewhere (Calleja 2007b; 2011) that this metaphor should be replaced with that of *incorporation*. Incorporation accounts for the sense of virtual environment habitation on two, simultaneous, levels: in this first sense of the metaphor, the virtual environment is incorporated into the player's mind as part of their immediate surroundings, within which they can navigate and interact. In the second sense, the player is incorporated (in the sense of embodiment) in a single, systemically upheld location in the virtual environment at any single point in time.

Incorporation thus operates on a double axis: the player incorporates, in the sense of internalizing or assimilating, the game environment into consciousness while simultaneously being incorporated through the avatar within that environment. The simultaneous occurrence of these two processes is a necessary condition for the experience of incorporation. To put it another way, incorporation occurs when the game world is present to the player, while the player is simultaneously present via its avatar to the virtual environment.

Identity and incorporation

Issues of identity in virtual environments, and consequently digital games, have been discussed primarily from the perspective of the opportunities for the formation, experimentation, and expression of identity (Turkle 1995; 2005; Castronova 2005; Rheingold 1993). Importantly, these discussions highlight the role that games play in rewriting identity through digital gameplay (Turkle 1995; 2005). The focus here is on the presentation of self to others in a virtual environment. This addresses one aspect of the incorporation being described here: the presence to others made possible by avatarial embodiment. This topic has received much attention, and it would be redundant to revisit such a discussion in the limited space of this chapter. What I will discuss instead is the second, complementary, half of the incorporation equation: the influence on a player's identity of absorbing into one's consciousness a game world and its inhabitants.

When a player experiences incorporation, the game environment is absorbed into consciousness as a place inhabited. The significance of this for a contemporary notion of a digitally mediated identity can only be understood fully if we acknowledge how powerful these experiences of habitation can be. Players have an increasingly varied plethora of simulated experiences within settings of their choosing available to them. Inhabiting virtual environments can have lasting effects on the players' sense of self, by expanding the realm of possible interactions into increasingly more appealing "shared fantasies" (Fine 1983) instantiated through simulation. Rheric, one of the research participants who took part in the research related to this body of work on immersion (Calleja 2011), described a sequence that aptly conveys incorporation and the lasting effect it can have on the player:

> There was a time when I was playing through Guild Wars [...] it was in the war-torn parts of Ascalon. I was working through some ruins and I turned this corner, and came across this massive, ruined cathedral with this gorgeous stained glass window that was mostly intact. I just stopped, and stared at it. I worked my way around it as much as I could to see it from all angles and ended up on a rise a little above it, just watching it. I don't remember the time of day, but it might have been like a sunset and I swore I could practically feel the breeze on my face and hear the wildlife. If I could pay to experience that in real life I would. And I would pay a lot. It was a real moment for me, a real experience that I carry with me (ibid., 173-4).

This account brings to the fore the intensity of emotion felt in such holistic incorporating experiences. If we were to remove the fantasy names from Rheric's account it would not be obvious to the reader that he was describing an experience in a virtual world. Rheric relates the event with strong connotations of inhabiting a place, emphasized by the synaesthesiac addition of stimuli that were not part of the environment ("I could practically feel the breeze on my face and hear the wildlife"). Rheric's concluding sentence emphasizes the experiential significance of this event and the lack of separation between it and a non-mediated equivalent and, most importantly, the effect this has on Rheric's lived experience.

Rheric's identity is not only effected by the role he plays through the construction of his in-game character, or the relationships he forms with the community on his *Guild Wars* (NC Soft 2005) server, but also by the experiences that are incorporated into consciousness, as much as any other significant moment in the physical world. Identity is not effected because of the otherness of the virtual environment, as is too often taken for granted, but because of the internalization of the world as an engaging, and often memorably exciting, place to inhabit.

Ludic identity?

In light of the above it seems challenging to talk about a ludic identity. Once the magic circle, or any such defined boundary between the game and everyday, is destabilized, so is the notion of an identity that is specific to gameplay. What I am arguing here is not that it is impossible to discuss a particular identity that comes to the fore in some (but certainly not all) engagements with games, but that this form of identity is (a) not specific to games and (b) does not occur in every engagement.

Following from the logic of incorporation discussed above and explicated elsewhere (Calleja 2007b; 2011), we come to a more robust understanding of in-game identities by focusing instead on the dimensions of involvement the specific game or genre of games affords (Calleja 2007a; 2007b, 2011). This avoids the normative assumptions carried by play as both a marker of experience and form of activity. That is, by taking the specific form of involvement afforded by the game in question we do not make the normative claim that every engagement with a game creates a specific form of experience and hence a specific form of (ludic) identity. Focusing on the concrete forms of involvement also avoids the ambiguity of the term (Sutton-Smith 1997) which often lumps together a variety of disparate experiential phenomena without acknowledging the composite nature of the term in question. This creates a problematic situation where the experiences being contained in one formulation of play in a certain context can be completely different from the experiences contained by another, essentially talking about completely different experiences and dressing them as equivalent.

I am not here arguing that there is no element of boundary negotiation and interpretation in our engagement with games, but that the notion of games as acts apart, somehow separate from the real or everyday, is not the best formulation of this or any other experiential boundary. More complex models of boundary negotiation and interpretation have been formulated in other fields that would more adequately account for the phenomenon in question. A number of theorists, including Deterding (2009) and Pargman and Jakobsson (2008), for example, make a convincing argument for using Goffman's (1986) *Frame Analysis* to express the boundary negotiation that occurs in game engagements instead of the magic circle. The metaphor or model we use to understand the nature of game engagement forms a foundation for other, more specific discussions about our interaction with games. Such foundational concepts need careful consideration and the clearest and analytically richest of formulations; qualities which the magic circle, as a foundational concept, does not possess.

References

Anchor, Robert. 1978. History and play: Johan Huizinga and his critics. *History and Theory* 17(1): 63-93.

Barlow, John P., and Mitchell Kapor. 1990. *Across the electronic frontier.* http://w2.eff.org/Misc/Publications/John_Perry_Barlow/HTML/eff.html.

Blizzard Entertainment. 2004. *World of Warcraft*. PC: Vivendi Universal.

Bolter, Jay D., and Richard Grusin. 1999. *Remediation: Understanding new media*. Cambridge, MA: The MIT Press.

Calleja, Gordon. 2007a. Digital game involvement. *Games and Culture* 2(3): 236-60.

—. 2007b. *Digital games as designed experience: Reframing the concept of immersion*. PhD dissertation. Victoria University of Wellington, Wellington, New Zealand.

—. 2011. *In-Game: From immersion to incorporation*. Cambridge, MA: The MIT Press.

Castronova, Edward. 2005. *Synthetic worlds: The business and culture of online games*. Chicago, IL: University of Chicago Press.

Copier, Marinka. 2007. *Beyond the magic circle: A network perspective on role-play in online games*. Utrecht: PhD dissertation. Faculty of Humanities, Utrecht University.

Damasio, Antonio R. 2000. *The feeling of what happens: Body, emotion and the making of consciousness* (new ed.). London: Vintage.

Dennett, Daniel C. 1991. *Consciousness explained*. Boston, MA: Little Brown and Co.

Deterding, Sebastian. 2009. The game frame: Systemizing a Goffman approach to video game theory. Paper presented at the *DIGRA 2009: Breaking new ground: Innovation in games, play, practice and theory*, Brunel University, United Kingdom.

Ehrmann, Jacques. 1968. *Homo ludens* revisited. *Yale French Studies* 41: 31-57.

Fink, Eugen. 1968. *The oasis of happiness: Toward an ontology of play*. Yale French Studies (41): 19-30.

Goffman, Erving. 1986. *Frame analysis: An essay on the organization of experience*. Boston, MA: Northeastern University Press.

Huizinga, Johan. 1954. *The waning of the Middle Ages: A study of the forms of life, thought, and art in France and the Netherlands in the XIVth and XVth centuries* [1919]. New York: Garden City.

—. 1955. *Homo ludens: A study of the play-element in culture* [1938]. Boston, MA: Beacon Press.

Huizinga, Johan, and Jan H. Huizinga. 1936. *In the shadow of tomorrow*. New York: W.W. Norton and Company.

Juul, Jesper. 2005. *Half-real: Video games between real rules and fictional worlds*. Cambridge, MA: The MIT Press.

Lakoff, George, and Mark Johnson. 2003. *Metaphors we live by*. Chicago, IL: University of Chicago Press.

Lammes, Sybille. 2008. Spatial regimes of the digital playground: Cultural functions of spatial practices in computer games. *Space and Culture* 11(3): 260-72.

Lévy, Pierre. 1998. *Becoming virtual: Reality in the digital age*. New York: Plenum.

Lionhead Studios. 2008. *Fable II*. Xbox 360: Microsoft Game Studios.

Malaby, Thomas M. 2007. Beyond play: A new approach to games. *Games and Culture* 2(2): 95-113.

Mitchell, William J. 1995. *City of bits: Space, place, and the infobahn*. Cambridge, MA: The MIT Press.

Murray, Janet H. 1998. *Hamlet on the holodeck: The future of narrative in cyberspace*. Cambridge, MA: The MIT Press.

NC Soft. 2005. *Guild Wars*. PC: ArenaNet.

Origin Systems. 1997. *Ultima Online*. PC: Electronic Arts.

Pargman, Daniel, and Peter Jakobsson. 2008. Do you believe in magic? Computer games in everyday life. *European Journal of Cultural Studies* 11(2): 225-44.

Rheingold, Howard. 1993. *The virtual community: Homesteading on the electronic frontier*. Reading, MA: Addison-Wesley.

Rushkoff, Douglas. 1994. *Cyberia: Life in the trenches of hyperspace*. London: Flamingo.

Salen, Kate, and Eric Zimmerman. 2004. *Rules of play: Game design fundamentals*. Cambridge, MA: The MIT Press.

Shields, Rob. 2003. *The virtual.* London: Routledge.

Suits, Bernard H. 1978. *The grasshopper: Games, life, and utopia.* Toronto/Buffalo: University of Toronto Press.

Sutton-Smith, Brian. 1997. *The ambiguity of play.* Cambridge, MA: Harvard University Press.

Taylor, T.L. 2006. *Play between worlds: Exploring online game culture.* Cambridge, MA: The MIT Press

12. Play (for) time

Patrick Crogan

Through their deployment of interactivity, virtualization, and simulation, video games are prime examples of the contemporary form of what philosopher of technology Bernard Stiegler has termed the "industrial temporal object" (2009, 241). This is his term for mass produced media works designed to provide experiences that unfold over time through the user's provision of his/her conscious attention. From the phonograph's replaying of musical performances, to editing together film shots and the compilation of longer sequences of experience in television scheduling, to the design of systems for user-configured perceptions in newer media forms, industrial temporal objects have played an increasingly significant role in the formation of individual and cultural identity since the launch of industrialization in 19th century Europe. In Stiegler's view, "industrial temporal objects" amount to much more than novel forms of entertainment or communication. The experiences produced by these media are constituted in the course of the flux of the interior consciousness of the individuals engaged in following – and in the interactive era, in co-producing – the flux of their unfolding. The very nature of experience, as what is lived by the individual in and as a necessarily shared milieu of mediated, collective experience, is to a significant degree determined today by industrial temporal objects. In this our "postindustrial" moment, the influence of digital industrial temporal objects tends to outweigh that of the other, older forms of mediated experience as they are integrated into the convergent paradigm of the "being digital" of mediation in general.

In an era when concepts such as "experience design" and the "attention economy" define the milieu of commercial digital media production, it is crucial for critical accounts of contemporary audiovisual culture, and of video games in particular, to take account of the nature of these forms as industrial temporal objects. As the first major entertainment media "native" to the digital computer, video games offer a privileged vantage point from which to develop such an account. This paper proceeds from the conviction that the experience of video game play in its conventional, commercially designed form makes readable a major influence digital industrial temporal objects have in shaping contemporary experience. The predominant tendency manifest in "game time" is toward an anticipation, indeed a preemption, of events that are experienced as phenomena requiring a solution or a decision. The user learns to anticipate game challenges, which are designed to arrive as configurable – that is, readable, navigable, decidable, solvable, and treatable – through the instrumentation provided by the interface. A certain temporalization of the future events, that is, a certain way of experiencing what happens in time, in short, a certain experience of time or a certain temporality of experience, is provided in the conventional adoption of the video game industrial temporal object by its player.

I have elsewhere characterized this "preemptive temporalization" with reference to the histories of digital simulation, computerization, and interactive virtualization (Crogan 2003). The task there was to show how these key components of today's digital culture emerged from the logics – or, in Paul Virilio's terms, the logistics – of Cold War techno-science (ibid.). What I will offer in this chapter are some reflections on the challenge to individual and cultural becoming associated with this tendency toward the temporalization of the future as anticipated, configurable eventuality. I say individual and cultural becoming here to signal the importance of approaching this question of game-time as one that bears directly on, precisely, the dynamic that links individuals and collectives. This is what philosopher of technology Gilbert Simondon calls individuation (2007). Individuation as a process, rather than preexisting, individual entities entering into relationships, is the key conceptual shift Simondon produces with this notion. Individual entities must always be understood as elements related to other elements in groupings and, moreover, it is the development of these relations that constitutes the elements rather than the converse. Simondon has been influential in a number of major philosophical and critical projects, including those of Paul Virilio, Gilles Deleuze and Félix Guattari, and Stiegler. The focal point of this influence is Simondon's insistence on the primacy of the dynamic of the reciprocal becoming of the individual and its ensemble. This was elaborated first in his account of technological evolution and subsequently as a general principle for understanding all manner of phenomena natural, technical, and social.[1]

This challenge to individual and cultural becoming, then, is related to – indeed it coincides with – the challenge to critical thinking of and in the coming digital age. Drawing on Bernard Stiegler's activist mobilization of Simondon's account of individuation, I will argue that the ludic industrial temporal object exemplifies a wider digital cultural tendency toward the radical destabilization of the dynamic of individuation constituting contemporary identity and sociality. Being precisely a dynamic relation between individuals and collectives, individuation is always *mediated* by specific techniques, technologies and technological systems. Individuation rolls on at the always technical and prosthetic nexus of the "and" between individual and collective.

From this nexus, however, arises also the potential for critical and creative detourings of this preemptive tendency. I will explore some of these that are being pursued in critical game design, and via other interventions in the routines of gameplay cultures. These detours play out contemporary playtime differently, seeking to lengthen and complicate the circuits of communication, response, reflection, negotiation, translation, and so forth that comprise the interactions between individuals and collectives in and between the virtual digital "spaces" of gameplay and its contemporary techno-cultural context. They serve both to sharpen the apprehension of the ludic industrial temporal object in its mainstream development and to play with/in that developmental trajectory. If, as Johan Huizinga claimed, *homo ludens* remains a constitutive and crucial characteristic of humanity (1955), then today it does so more on the basis of such counter-adoptions of the digital techno-cultural "program" than based on the observation that all computer-mediated activities appear increasingly game-like. What today goes by the neologism of "gamification" – the creation of game-like interfaces and the inclusion of game-like elements in all manner of digitally provided goods and services – may in fact constitute the very antithesis of what Huizinga called the "play-element" of culture.

Second Person Shooter: Dislocative media

The experimental games artist/activist and theorist Julian Oliver has been playing with a variant of a First-person shooter game (FPS). The FPS has been one of the most influential proponents of the commercial video game form of interactive engagement in an illusory three-dimensional space. First exhibited in 2006 at the exhibition organized by Furtherfield entitled "Game/Play", *Second Person Shooter* disturbs the player's routine identification in FPS gameplay with a dynamic perspective of the world provided by the game's scene generation engine (Game/Play 2006).[2] Instead of seeing the virtual space as if one is looking at it from the point of view of one's in-game avatar, the player sees (from) the point of view of the other. Instead of driving the vision of what can be seen and therefore targeted in the conventional mode of situated immersion in the simulated space of play, the player's control input can bring him/her face to face with themselves in the form of their avatar. Their actions are then perceived as both divided from and reunited from their perspective of the virtual space. As Oliver has it, seeing from the "outside looking in", they now no longer embody the "vision machine", but must negotiate and navigate its machinations differently (Selectparks 2010).[3]

Oliver has commented on the occasion of his recent return to the task of developing a downloadable playable demo of *Second Person Shooter* that it amounts to a "displacement of agency and [...] a crisis of control – a Dislocative Media if you like" (Selectparks 2010). The dislocation in virtual spatial orientation is an apparently simple artistic and technical gesture, but it enacts a profound temporal and conceptual dislocation of the FPS industrial temporal object and, more generally, of all the ludic forms adopting the first person view as a mode of interactive gameplay. This mode, aside and often in combination with the third-person view showing the player's avatar in action in the virtual space, comprises the majority of play modes in the majority of commercial video game genres, from adventure to massively multiplayer online games, to flight, vehicle, and sport simulations, and all the FPS variants from classic shooters to survival horror. Agency and control, as Oliver says. These are the constituents of the experience being constructed through the attention given to gameplay by the player. The player learns to make the vision machine show him/her that agency in the virtual space.

The industrial temporal object is an experience generator. Cinema was one of the first global industrial temporal objects. Its most significant predecessor, the phonograph, offered a temporal experience of a musical recording, but it made the technological means of its delivery – recording and playback system – its key commodity. With cinema, the collective experience of its unfolding became the commodity in the form of a ticket to see rather than to own the film. One encountered an experience prosthetically grafted onto one's consciousness; an experience not lived by the viewer except in its "recollection" where its unfolding, as Stiegler argues, coincided exactly with the unfolding of the consciousness who comes to constitute it in and through this coincidence (Stiegler 2011, 23). And this was a collective, indeed a mass phenomenon.

There was nothing new, however, in the fact that one's particular individual experience was prosthetically supplemented by those of others. As Stiegler argues, this is the very condition of human beings as cultural beings, that is, as historical beings that inherit the past experiences of those forbearers who no longer exist. This inheritance comes in the form of the passing down of techniques and the artifacts that go with them. Stiegler's philosophy of technology turns on this apprehension of technical artifactuality as the exterior form of memorization that is co-constitutive of cultural transmission, along with the interior, experiential memory of the psychic individual, itself composed with the genetic memory of the biological organism. In this regard, cinema is a technique and a technology whose lineage stretches way back to the earliest marking and sculpting tools, pigment production techniques, and other forms of recording and making communicable the psychic, interior response to experience (Stiegler 1998, 152). The production, reproduction, and evolution of cultural experience rests on the memorious capacity of these "exteriorizations" which outlive their creators.[4] With the phonograph, and even more the cinema and its progeny – including computer games – what was new was the capacity to industrially design and produce experiences made of the very flux of attentive minds on a massive, indeed, international scale.

In the tradition of modernist artistic gestures such as the Russian Formalists' *ostranenie* ("making strange") and Brecht's *Verfremdung* (alienation-effect), Oliver exposes the norms of the FPS industrial temporal object by displacing their usual taking place. The player has learned to anticipate an engagement in the task of successfully constituting an experience of interactive mastery over the challenging elements in the virtual space. The rewiring of his/her input-output node in the game system frustrates mastery and immediately confronts the player with an uncertainty that industrial temporal objects are designed precisely to avoid: what is this experience I am "having"? Is it entertainment? Will it still be "fun"? What am I paying attention to, paying with my attention, spending my time on?

By expropriating the player's usual point of view and reallocating him/her the position of the virtual other, *Second Person Shooter* disturbs the reigning "worldview" of FPS forms of play. The opponent is no longer just over there, encountered as a challenge, obstacle, or competitor. The confusion of first and second person, of virtual and actual opponent, of self as "director" of the gameplay (a ludic "vision switcher", in the terminology of live television production) and as avatar surprising the player with its appearance on screen, undoes the cybernetic functionality of gameplay. What Peter Galison called the "ontology of the enemy" informing the early development and promotion of cybernetic thought, and faithfully maintained in all the shooter game forms, is deconstructed through Oliver's technical sabotage (Galison 1994).

Hyper-synchronization

The experience of gameplay as an event where the other (and the self) is encountered, is the profound terrain to which Oliver's *Second Person Shooter* quickly relocates one from the habitual expectation of an entertaining experience of interactive control. This is achieved because the FPS form, as a major mode of the video game industrial temporal object, currently conditions experience and eventfulness on a massive scale. In both single-player and multiplayer modes, online and offline, individual and collective interactions are planned and played out in these contemporary technologies and techno-cultural practices. First-person perspective gameplay is a significant component of what Stiegler calls the "relational technologies", which increasingly occupy and supplant the role of older "relational techniques" in the ongoing efforts of industry to design, standardize, and commodify experience of all kinds (Ars Industrialis 2010).[5]

For Stiegler, Simondon's notion of individuation is key to grasping the implications of the passage toward the digital era of real-time, online connectivity where technologies increasingly condition the terms and shape of collectivity. As I outlined in the introduction, Simondon emphasized the dynamic of permanent becoming where what was most important were the relations between elements in an ensemble, and between individual elements and the collective in which they operate. Rather than beginning from a notion of preconstituted, discrete elements that enter into relations with each other, Simondon insisted on the primacy of the relation so that the identity of any individual component only ever emerged as a contingent and at best meta-stable form in what he called the "transductive" becoming of the components in relation to each other.[6] This was fundamental to his theoretical struggle against entrenched notions of technology, which were so many variations on the idea of the tool. From this perspective, the technological object is essentially the instrument of (an equally essential) human user realized in different forms across different histories and cultures.[7] Technology is relegated in this conception to the margins of human being and becoming, playing a purely contingent role as means to human ends. For Simondon, however, the technical object must be understood as a "social organizer", absolutely intrinsic to social and cultural becoming (Simondon in Barthélémy 2010b).

Stiegler's critical adoption of Simondon emphasizes the crucial role of technology in the human socio-historical becoming that Simondon identified as a particular mode of individuation that he called "trans-individuation" (2007). I will venture a brief overview here of Stiegler's reading of trans-individuation because it will enable a key characteristic of video game experience design to be identified from a perspective that properly frames its critical significance in the context of our concerns. This will also occasion a dialogue between Huizinga's work on cultural ritual and play and Simondon's ideas on the individual and collective dynamic. If video game play can be, and has been, approached as a continuation of the centrality of what Huizinga called the "play-element" of culture, we will see that this continuation is techno-culturally conditioned and, as part of trans-individuation, does not proceed from some essential origin in a way that would guarantee its ceaseless re-emergence as the kind of elemental cultural doubling or suspension Huizinga analyzes.

As with individuation more generally, in trans-individuation the individual and the group are theoretically separable, but not in reality. "The psychic individual," Stiegler argues, "is originarily psychosocial, and the social is not an 'intersubjective' aggregate of already-constituted individuals" (2011, 94). Individuation is a process, and incompletion is its key characteristic, indeed, its engine. With human trans-individuation, the questions of agency, decision-making and politics in general immediately arise around the themes of identity and its horizon: who or what should "we" become? For Stiegler, the political must be approached through a critical apprehension of Simondon's notion of trans-individuation because only in this way can contemporary technological dynamics be effectively conjugated with the urgent ecological, economic, and political questions confronting an increasingly global human becoming. The digital mediation of the (experience of) world assumes its full significance in this perspective. This is increasingly the milieu in which people and cultures negotiate a response to their incompletion by individuating themselves.

I and We are two faces of a single process of individuation. What is common to both along with their incompletion is the reservoir of potential that Simondon called "preindividual reality":

> Participation [in the social], for the individual, is the fact of being one element in a much bigger individuation through the intermediary of the charge of preindividual reality that the individual contains, that is, of the potentials it conceals (Simondon in Stiegler 2011, 95).

For Stiegler, this preindividual reality needs to be thought, indeed, equated with the heritage of technical artifacts which amount to an exteriorized memory enabling human cultural transmission. The recollections stored in these artifacts are analyzed in the *Technics and Time* volumes as "tertiary retentions" inasmuch as they form a retentional complex with the two other forms of memory informing human becoming – the primary retention of the conscious perception of events and the secondary retention of events as remembered experiences (Stiegler 1998, 246ff.).[8] Tertiary retentions comprise the "already there" of culture, its language, stories, rituals, techniques, arts, objects utilitarian and sacred, all the norms and prescriptions carried on and passed down in the form of practices and things. All this amounts to an archive of exteriorized memory (ibid., 249).

The constitutively incomplete psychic individual inherits this archive and negotiates with it the emergence of his/her individuality. The individual's own recollected experiences (secondary retentions) and indeed his/her consciousness of and in the living present (primary retention) have the tertiary retentional archive as their structural substrate (Stiegler 2011, 97). There is no "proper" human being that does not individuate on the basis of a specific adoption of particular cultural practices and identifications made possible by tertiary retention. Just what constitutes this propriety, this humanity, is ethically and indeed politically debatable, a debate which would always have to negotiate particular historical and cultural contextualizations. It is precisely the comprehension of this that is on the critical horizon of both Stiegler's project and that of this essay.

In its dynamic response to incompleteness, the psychic individual mobilizes the resources of preindividual reality in generating its "group dynamic" of the negotiation and evolution of identification(s). The stock of tertiary retentions is also, and through this same process, what the collective bears as its potential for change. Each individual member invested in the group repeats this process differently by adopting and actualizing the potentiality stored in tertiary retentions. Stiegler has a neat formula for this elsewhere: techno-cultural artifactuality is the "and" in the phrase "individual *and* collective individuation" (Stiegler 2006c).

Huizinga's "play-element" of culture can be understood, then, in relation to preindividual reality inasmuch as the latter is never a static or idealized ground of identity. Rather, it is lived in individuation. The play-element would seem to characterize a major mode of engagement with the inheritable tradition of techno-cultural forms. For example, Huizinga discusses how the "savages" participating in "archaic rituals" retain an awareness of "only pretending" to incarnate spirits and deities (1955, 22). The suspension of disbelief in the entity invoked by the ceremonial mask is taught by tradition inasmuch as it is reproduced in the execution of all the techniques of preparation for the ritual. Similarly, the "magic circle" is a technique as much as it is an irreducible, "primary" category of life (ibid., 3). The interior mentality of pretending is transmissible precisely because of its exterior, artifactual retention.

From the perspective I am seeking to develop here on video gameplay as a techno-culturally enabled form of contemporary trans-individuation, it is less significant than it appears to be for Huizinga that play is an irreducible, "primary" element humans share in common with the higher mammals. For Stiegler, who draws extensively on André Leroi-Gourhan for his perspective on the emergence of the human being from an animal being, genetic and biological modes of transmission and becoming are no doubt components of human individuation, but they are no longer exclusive or essential. On the contrary, a human being is a becoming based on a non-basis; on a "being-in-default" of essence (Stiegler 1998, 188). What distinguishes (if it does not absolutely oppose) the human from other animals, even tool-using and technology-building species, is that human collective development and differentiation is principally techno-cultural. The phylogenetic becoming of animality is no longer the primary ground of human "evolution". Ethnic, that is, *cultural* becoming has already supplemented and supplanted this with what Stiegler calls an "epiphylogenetic" process (ibid., 177).[9] The recording of individual experience that enables the creation of the artifactual heritage of collective cultural records supplements human development and in the process transforms it from species to ethnocultural evolution. Technicity is the key medium of this transformation through the formation of the artifactual "preindividual reality". We can think of *homo ludens* then as a figure of the human-in-potential at play in the *Spielraum* of individuation afforded them via the stock of tertiary retentions.

To be fair, Huizinga in *Homo ludens* is concerned not with a simplistic essentializing of human beings, but with the developmental trajectory of play from "lower" to "higher" forms across the history of cultures and civilizations. Moreover, he recognizes the potential for this trajectory to end in the transformation of cultural practices into other non-playful modes of living. To cite a famous (and not irrelevant) example, in discussing war as an instance of the play-element, Huizinga proposes that so long as war is made through a system of limitations it remains a form of play, but "the theory of total war" banishes war's cultural function and extinguishes "the last vestige of the play-element" (1955, 90). It is not simply the theory, however, but the techno-cultural "invention" of total war out of the industrial, logistical, and techno-scientific revolutions in the conduct and preparation of war (with wargaming not playing an insignificant role) that must be considered as key to the extinguishing of the play-element. What calls forth the theory's crystallization in the early decades of the 20th century is the dynamic of the mobilization and transformation of the preindividual milieu known as industrial modernization, rationalism, capitalist political economy, the development of techno-science, and so forth.

The collective, then, is not simply a spiritual or ideal projection. No spirit without the artifactual, no interior without the exterior, no individual without a technically facilitated gesturing toward the potential future of the group. The gestures are always techniques, and today, more and more of these are technologically conditioned and prescribed. In a reciprocal fashion, Simondon states that "an individual who is absolutely, perfectly complete and perfect individual can never be part of a group; the individual must be the bearer of tensions, predispositions, potentials" (Simondon in Stiegler 2011, 97). Stiegler adds that individuation "puts the I in motion, which moves the I (emotion). The I has space to project many ideal possibilities of itself as a we," entailing it in the living out of all kinds of "dramaturgies, intrigues and stories; metastability is resolved in movement, structure and transformation" (2011, 98). I would add here to this list the games, rituals, and ceremonies with which Huizinga is concerned. His identification of the play-element in the *droemonon* (action, rite) of ancient Greek culture can be considered as a source form of the long-running Western drama of inadequation (1955, 14).

Stiegler does not have much to say specifically about video games, but his analysis of the tendency of the contemporary expansion and penetration of industrial temporal objects into the spheres of lived experience offers an insight about their contribution to the shifting of the technical conditions of trans-individuation today. For Stiegler all media, as technical components of human becoming, are both necessary supplements and dangerous *pharmaka* – forms that like medicinal compounds can be both poison and cure (Stiegler 2010a, 5).[10] In terms of our discussion of individuation, the principal danger Stiegler identifies today is to be found in industrial media programming trying to overdetermine individuation. As experience generators, industrial temporal objects provide increasingly larger proportions of the material upon which the to and fro of individuation is transacted. This material is the store of experiences available for recollection by the "living-present" of consciousness, having passed through it in the form of lived experiences. The proliferation of digitally mediated experience tends to construct a pathway toward a quasi-"living present" of the psychic individual, a kind of predetermined, quasi-complete individuation.[11]

The danger, then, has resonances with what Heidegger characterized in *Being and time* in his analysis of the "They" (*das Man*, in French, *l'On*, the One; Stiegler 2011, 102). For Stiegler, what is most troubling is that this "synchronization" of the individuation of individuals confuses the I-We dynamic; worse, it tends to annul it. It tends to annul what he calls "diachronization", the movement of individuation in time. This is where the play-element can reside as a potential mode of the replaying of inherited and received experience (ibid., 96). That is, it annuls becoming, which is to say it annuls human time, insofar as it is the timing of the drama of incompletion. At least, this appears as a tendency today, on the horizon of contemporary trans-individuation.

Now, as Stiegler makes clear, synchronization itself is not the danger, but rather it is a necessary, technically enabled component of individuation. Stiegler points out: "A synchronization is always at work in public commemorations, private or public festivals, and other cultural moments, but always as moments of exception" (ibid., 100). The play-element resides as much in the provision of these synchronizing moments as in their playful reinvention through diachronization. Contemporary digital media's extensive expansion of intensive synchronization (tending toward the becoming-mediatized of all work and social instrumentalities), however, floods experience with a continuous flux of "moments of exception" – specials, spectaculars, new technologies of presentation (HD, 3D), communication (mobile devices, pervasive media) and interaction (Kinect), new devices and apps, unmissable new releases, models, sequels, add-ons, plug-ins, among others. A hyper-synchronization arising from the competition to capture and retain the attention of users, to regulate and sustain consumption in the service of the most rapid amortization of investment in production, undoes the meta-stability of individuation, and undermines belief and consequently investment in it. Hyper-synchronization breeds hyper-diachronization: atomization, fragmentation, discrediting of political and cultural values, extremist politics, generalized cynicism, pathologies of civility, de-sublimation of the idealized objects of social identity, order, and morality (ibid., 102). This is the scope of Stiegler's diagnosis of the pharmacological risk of the predominant logics informing the implementation of the global digital techno-cultural medium of trans-individuation. As major forms of the contemporary digital entertainment milieu, video games participate in and might even be thought to exacerbate this problematic hyper-synchronization. The virtualization characteristic of mainstream video game forms is found among so many genres that it is delivered through the modeling of a preemptive *droemenon* encountered in technologically designed and interactively controlled space. "Serious" simulation designer Robert G. Sargent calls this the software model of reality's "problem space" (2005). As a default mode of engagement, one is synchronized with the task of attaining control over the problem through virtual agency. The replaying of experience in this mode tends to squeeze out the *Spielraum* of Huizinga's play-element. Its function is already programmed as an anticipatory preemption of the event.

From this perspective, video games can be approached as industrial temporal objects that tend, paradoxically, to extinguish the play-element in culture rather than inherit and reanimate it. To take up and play a video game in the "designed" manner may not be to "play" in the sense of playful adoption of tradition that we have drawn out as one important element of Huizinga's play-element. More often than not it retains the agonistic component also identified by Huizinga as a core characteristic of play. In its widely recognized cybernetic character, however, perhaps it is best approached – along with much of contemporary digital culture, as a casualty corresponding to the extinguishing of the play-element of war in total war that Huizinga acutely observes – total war amounting in effect to the collapse of any distinction or limit between war(time) and peace(time).[12]

Digital artist and activist Joseph DeLappe's intervention in America's Army provides a telling example of the stakes of hyper-synchronization. Using the ID tag, "dead-in-iraq", DeLappe logs in and joins multiplayer squad-based shooting contests in this successful US military-designed tactical shooter. Rather than participate in the gameplay he uses the in-game chat window to list the name, rank, and death dates of US military personnel killed in Iraq since 2005. Commentators have examined the way *dead-in-iraq* confronts players with the "reality" that their virtual game world both evokes for the purposes and objectives of gameplay and avoids in its virtual, circumscribed modeling of armed conflict (Stahl 2010, 63; Blackmore 2005, 75).

From our perspective, however, the genius of *dead-in-iraq* is the way it confronts the player with the collective dimension of their definitive incompletion. DeLappe's project is an ongoing memorial intervention in this hyper-synchronizing mediatized experience of permanent virtual combat. DeLappe counterposes one synchronizing gesture of recollection against another: the Army is proud to showcase its tradition of professionalism and achievement, as the "Real Heroes" pages on the official America's Army website demonstrates (America's Army 2010). These pages provide profiles and links to media relating to selected personnel who have been decorated as a result of their actions in Iraq and Afghanistan. *Dead-in-iraq* tries to create another kind of pause for an exceptional, suspensive mode of synchronized recollection amidst the permanently respawning, intensive play of virtual combat. It can be read "epistemologically" as an assertion that "this is real while you play a fake game", but it is closer to DeLappe's method to say *dead-in-iraq* gestures towards a time that the players have "lost" in their agonistic, but perhaps, no longer playful simulation.

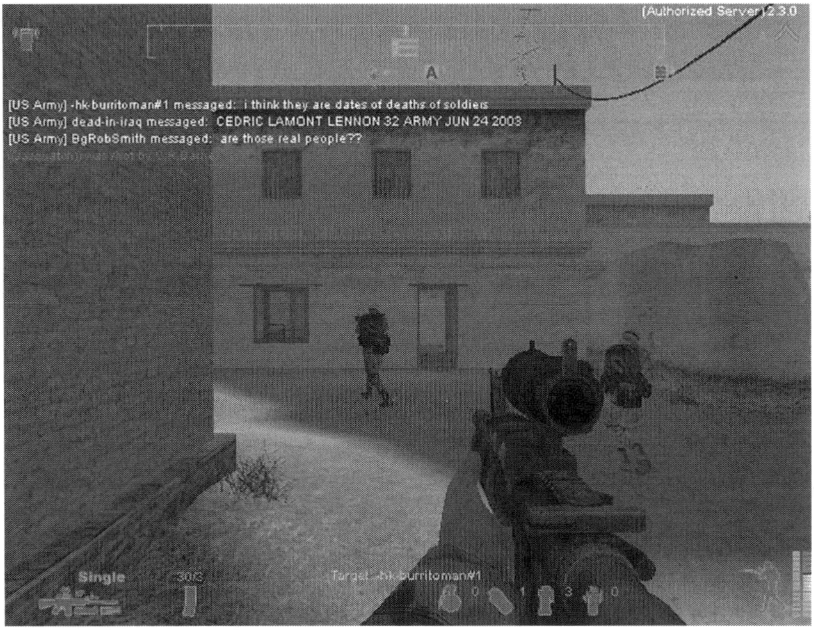

Fig. 1: Joseph DeLappe, *dead-in-iraq* (2006 – ongoing).

Playing (for) time

Hyper-synchronization is, for Stiegler, a tendency of contemporary digital techno-culture, a counterpart and, indeed, a crucial agent of the possible breakdown of the ecological milieu in which humans currently continue to exist – ever more precariously scientists advise us – in their present techno-cultural state of development. As our examples have already shown, along with many other critical and creative adoptions of the simulational and virtual industrial temporal object, the latter may be adopted, lived out, and lived through other than in the predominant logics of commercial experience design. Such alternative works seek to interrupt these logics playfully, and make a crucial gesture toward opening up other potentials in these forms that are now part of the substrate of preindividual reality.

If I have presented a rather gloomy prognosis for contemporary digital techno-culture, it is somewhat to echo and amplify the forebodings about the dominance of a mechanistic, technocratic reorganization of society that Huizinga saw all too clearly from his vantage point in occupied Netherlands during the era of total war. Even if we do not share his conditions of incarceration, and military occupation, we are nonetheless also living during a "wartime" today.[13] We are in a permanent war on terror, in which the "post-war warring" that James Der Derian analyzed as the latest phase of Virilio's "pure war" – the permanent preparation for war has become the organizing principle for "peacetime" lived in the shadow of thermonuclear war – and our experience in post-9/11 in the redefinition in the US and elsewhere of national politics and international relations in terms of "security" (Der Derian 2001, 59).

Roger Stahl argues that America's "militainment" media culture is best understood as a wartime media culture, but one that serves through its reprocessing of war as an entertaining spectacle to keep it at a distance from consumer society in order to avoid any critical reflection on the civil and political responsibility of waging war in the name of "the people". It also exacerbates, however, some of the contradictions of this distancing through its intense and immersive involvement of the spectator-player in the (often) interactive experience of armed conflict (Stahl 2010, 8). Whether one concurs with this reading of militainment, Stahl is right to start from the observation that war is not missing from video games and many of the other industrial temporal objects of mainstream entertainment media. On the contrary.

All the more important, then, are those efforts to question the default settings of these relational technologies through which we live (through) wartime. The British new media artists Langlands and Bell's *The house of Osama Bin Laden* (2003) is an interactive installation that explores the Western world's efforts – military, cultural, and economic – to refashion Afghanistan in the wake of 9/11. A centerpiece of the installation is an interactive virtual recreation of a residence once occupied by Osama Bin Laden in Daruntah in the eastern province of Nangarhar. Among other things, *The house of Osama Bin Laden* re-stages the experience proposed by the shooter video game system. Like the other works I have examined, it interrupts the industrial temporal object's routine adoption.

Executing a commission from the Imperial War Museum in London, Langlands and Bell worked multimodally to interfere with the spatial and temporal orientations to this other sphere – this sphere of others – typically provided by the news and entertainment media of the principal partners of the NATO coalition coordinating this effort at eradicating the terrorist threat. Examining the contradictory position of the plethora of non-government aid organizations operating in Afghanistan, for example, they produced a number of digitally composed still images where a pattern of NGO logos overlay images of bomb-shattered buildings, landscapes of destroyed vehicles, and discarded munitions (Langlands and Bell 2004, 164-77). The ambivalent and often conflictual relations between Western

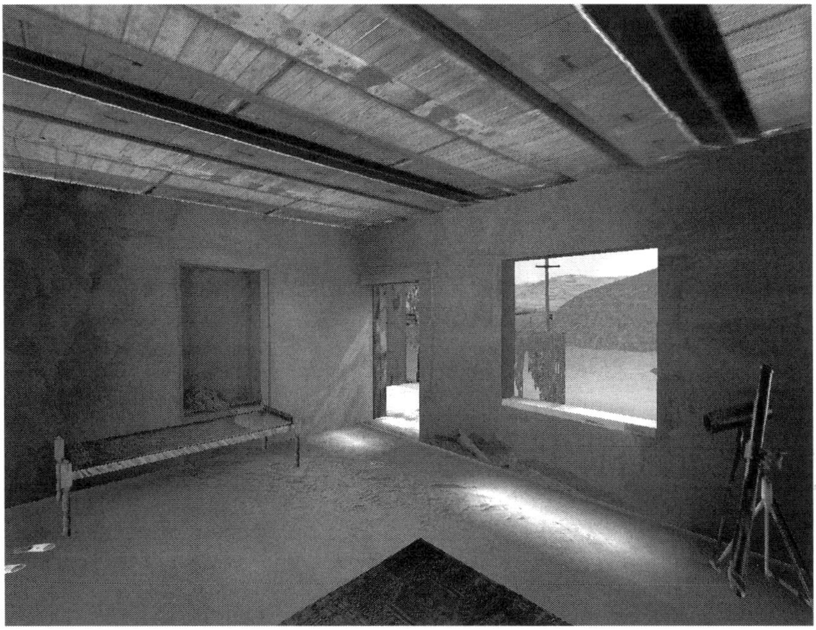

Fig. 2: Langlands and Bell: *The house of Osama Bin Laden* (2003).

aid efforts and development are juxtaposed with military operations so that a paradoxical, structural complicity is posed. The default "narrative" of war followed by the restoration of peacetime is disturbed by the simultaneity of these composited still images.

The centerpiece of the installation was the navigable virtual rendition of the house once occupied by Osama Bin Laden. This was created using the *Quake* engine. Visitors used a joystick to move about in the virtual space, but there was no other interaction afforded by the system. Nor were there any virtual others to encounter. What to do then? There is an obvious metaphor being put in play here: the target has long gone. The "mission critical", most-wanted Ace card (if an Afghanistan theater version of the Iraqi "personality identification playing cards" had been produced), the primary motivation of the US-led Afghanistan invasion, is still at large. The whole Afghanistan military "adventure" can be asked this same question: what to do then?

The technological system of perspectivally produced, virtual interaction is designed to provide a solution: the game engine enables the building of a virtual arena for navigating the challenges of targeting and avoiding becoming the target. It is a technical system reproducing what Sam Weber has called a "certain kind of targeting" predominant today in Western techno-culture:

one in which the ambiguities, uncertainties, and complexities are precluded from the production of the representational and operational media for identifying and dealing with the target (Weber 2005, 12).

Langlands and Bell build such a virtual space, but the experience it generates does not produce the routine synchronization of the player in the meta-game of a certain kind of targeting. Instead of seeing the anticipated, virtual other appear as an identifiable and therefore eradicable enemy other, the target is absent, already gone – no problem in this "problem space". That is its problem: what is this space without its problem? The artists have documented their rigorous efforts to locate, and then record and survey the house and its surrounds with its digital reconstruction as a virtual simulation in the mind (Langlands and Bell 2004, 89-93).[14] In doing so their process faithfully imitates that of military and entertainment simulations in providing sufficient authenticity for the virtual suspension of disbelief. In *The house of Osama Bin Laden's* (non-)video game, the historical, geographical, and techno-cultural links between the place and the virtual space fail to function in this way; they emerge in the form of questions for the one holding the joystick, unaccustomed to such a response to his/her control input.

I suggested above that today video game play is tending to foreclose on the routine of a playful suspension of virtual disbelief rather than perpetuate it, and that it is not so much disbelief in the simulated reality but a discrediting of reality in general (as trans-individual milieu of individuation) that is at stake today. In both their simulation of virtual spaces of interaction and their programming of that action in terms of problems, targets, and decisions in need of anticipatory preempting by the user, mainstream video games are exemplary digital media forms. The recent trend alluded to in the introduction to this essay toward a generalized "gamification" of interface design in other commercial applications assumes its full significance from this perspective – and its most troubling cast. The "consumer", who has already for the most part replaced the citizen in the trans-individual dynamic, is now being further remodeled to play the role of the permanently engaged player. No better instance of the disbelief and discredit in contemporary cultural life that Stiegler examines in the series with that name – a life lived in this sea of digital solicitation of the user-consumer's attention – can be found than in the immediate cynicism inspired by the becoming game-like of what are obviously not games that would offer nurture to anything like Huizinga's play-element (Stiegler 2004-2006).

The house of Osama Bin Laden, in stopping the routine playing out of the techno-logics of targeting, pauses for long enough to at least pose some questions about other kinds of synchronization of and with others, other We's with which "we" are individuating ourselves, other trajectories for "our" *droemonon* of incompletion. Western techno-culture's globalizing trajectory – borne increasingly in the virtualizing spatiality and preemptive temporalization of its increasingly ludic digital media – is in urgent need of this kind of questioning.

Notes

1. Such was the order of publication of Simondon's two major works, whereas in fact the conceptual development was the converse. The work on individuation, *L'individu et sa genèse physico-biologique* [Individuation and its physical-biological genesis], published in 1964, was Simondon's main doctoral dissertation (or, at least, part of it), and followed the publication of what was its complementary thesis, *Du mode d'existence des objets techniques* [On the mode of existence of technical objects].
2. Game/Play was a networked national touring exhibition focusing on the rhetorical constructs of "game" and "play". It was a collaboration between Q Arts in Derby and Furtherfield's HTTP Gallery, London.
3. The "vision machine" is a term used by Paul Virilio for the evolution of visual and weapon technologies and the dissemination of their coupled techno-logics across all fields of human endeavor (Virilio 1994).
4. Exteriorization is a term Stiegler borrows from André Leroi-Gourhan for this process. He insists, however, on an originary complex of interiority and exteriority (that is the very crux of technicity) to avoid the assumption of an already constituted human psyche preceding the development of technics (Stiegler 1998, 152-3).
5. Stiegler's project is constructed in part as a return to and critical revision of the *Kulturindustrie* critique of Adorno and Horkheimer in the *Dialectic of Enlightenment*. See Stiegler 2011 (Chapter 2) and Ars Industrialis 2010.
6. Simondon describes transduction as a developmental process that involves multiple elements in a "domain": "A process – be it physical, biological, mental or social – in which an activity gradually sets itself in motion, propagating within a given domain, by basing this propagation on a structuration carried out in different zones of the domain: each region of the constituted structure serves as a constituting principle for the following one, so much so that a modification progressively extends itself at the same time as this structuring operation" (Simondon cited in Mackenzie 2003, 16).
7. Simondon characterized the predominant conception of technology as "hylemorphic", i.e. as emerging from the classic metaphysical division of form and content so that the ideal notion of the tool as instrument in the hand of the human found expression in the shaping of matter according to the

idea of the tool. Barthélémy shows how Simondon insisted on an approach to technology as a compositional element in an open-ended dynamic not ruled by ideal forms or teleological determinations (2010a). This transductive dynamic leads, at best, to meta-stabilities, which is to say also beyond them.

8. This notion is developed in a critical transformation of Edmund Husserl's notion of "image consciousness" that makes it co-constitutive of human retention along with the primary and secondary retentions manifest in consciousness. For Husserl the interplay of these two, the one enabling the perception of present phenomena as they are experienced and the other the recollection of past experience, constitute the continuity of consciousness that is the focus of his phenomenological project. For Stiegler, tertiary retention is the structural substrate and supplement to consciousness, and ties its development inextricably to that of the collective. It plays an increasingly central role in the second and third volumes of the *Technics and time* series as they elaborate a critique of contemporary industrial temporal objects.
9. "Epiphylogenesis, a recapitulating, dynamic, and morphogenetic (*phylogenetic*) accumulation of individual experience (*epi*), designates the appearance of a new relation between the organism and its environment, which is also a new state of matter. If the individual is organic organized matter, then its relation to its environment (to matter in general, organic or inorganic), when it is a question of a *who*, is mediated by the organized but inorganic matter of the *organon*, the tool with its instructive role (its role *qua* instrument), the *what*. It is in this sense that the what invents the who just as much as it is invented by it" (Stiegler 1998, 177).
10. Stiegler draws on *Plato's Pharmacy*, Derrida's influential and rigorously playful reading of Plato's dialogue, the *Phaedrus*, in mobilizing this concept (Derrida 1981). See Stiegler (2010a, 33-5, and 2010b).
11. This is one that would function for all the I's as a kind of precomposed Kantian synthesis of experience, or a Husserlian "primary retention" able to be technologically disseminated en masse. These are the philosophical conceptualizations through which Stiegler develops this analysis of the "time of malaise" (*mal-être*, which can also be translated as "ill-being" to mark the allusion to Heidegger's *Dasein*) in *Technics and Time 3*, modifying the overly metaphysical framings of both in order to insist on the other potentials of the technical conditions of human becoming.
12. I have developed this position in more detail elsewhere, for instance in Crogan 2003, 2007, and 2008. Furthermore, we are in the terrain here of Roger Caillois' critical response to Huizinga in *Man, Play and Games* (1961). Writing in the Cold War and in the period "after Auschwitz" – to cite Adorno's famous question about the continued possibility of art in Western civilization – Caillois argues stridently for a concept of gameplay that is less *agôn*-centered than Huizinga's, and for the necessity of the maintenance of a

space (or rather, time) for play unsullied by its incorporation in the serious business of military, political or commercial activities. The subsumption of gameplay to these is a sure sign, for Caillois, of the terminal condition of cultural becoming.

13. "We", i.e. the inheritors and adopters of the European, "Western" traditions of humanities and social science scholarship, "we" the adopters and inheritors of the global digital, connected network of "researchers" – recalling Heidegger's prescient portrait (1969) of "research" in "The Age of the World Picture" – "we" with access to the resources and commodities of Western "lifestyles", "we" with the time and resources to investigate questions concerning video games, technology, individuation, hyper-synchronization, and so forth.

14. Richard Stamp, in "'No sense in this situation': targeting animation in *The house of Osama bin Laden*" (Animation Deviation, Bristol, July 2010), discusses the tension between the critical effort of the artists in constructing this reflection of the digital mediation of Afghan territory, and their inevitable complicity with the Western techno-cultural over-mapping and appropriation of the former.

References

America's Army. 2010. *America's Army: The official U.S. Army game.* www.americasarmy.com/aa3.php.

Ars Industrialis. 2010. *Manifesto 2010.* http://arsindustrialis.org/manifesto-2010.

Barthélémy, Jean-Hugues. 2010a. What new humanism today? trans. Chris Turner. *Cultural Politics* 6(2): 237-52.

—. 2010b. Individuation and knowledge. Gilbert Simondon: Transduction, translation, transformation. Conference at American University of Paris (May 2010). www.simondonconference.org/program.

Blackmore, Tim. 2005. *War X: Human extensions in battlespace.* Toronto: University of Toronto Press.

Caillois. Roger. 1961. *Man, play and games.* New York: Free Press.

Cannon, Rebecca. 2006. *2nd Person shooter* by Julian Oliver (2005). http://blog.game-play.org.uk/?q=2ndPersonShooter.

Crogan, Patrick. 2003. Gametime: History, narrative and temporality in Microsoft *Combat Flight Simulator 2*. In *The video game theory reader,* eds. Mark J.P. Wolf and Bernard Perron, 275-301. London: Routledge.

—. 2007. Logistical space: Flight simulation and virtual reality. In *The illusion of life 2: More essays on animation*, ed. Alan Cholodenko, 368-401. Sydney: Power Publications.

—. 2008. Wargaming and computer games: Fun with the future. In *The pleasures of computer gaming: Essays on cultural history, theory, and aesthetics*, eds. Melanie Swalwell and Jason Wilson, 147-66. Jefferson, NC: McFarland and Company.

Der Derian, James. 2001. *Virtuous war: Mapping the military-industrial-media-entertainment network.* Boulder, CO: Westview Press.

Derrida, Jacques. 1981. *Dissemination*, trans. Barbara Johnson. Chicago, IL: University of Chicago Press.

Galison, Peter. 1994. The ontology of the enemy: Norbert Wiener and the cybernetic vision. *Critical Inquiry* 21: 228-66.

Heidegger, Martin. 1969. *The question concerning technology, and other essays*, trans. William Lovitt. New York: Harper.

Horkheimer, Max, and Theodor W. Adorno. 2002. *Dialectic of Enlightenment*, ed. Gunzelin Schmid Noerr, trans. Edmund Jephcott. Stanford, CA: Stanford University Press.

Huizinga, Johan. 1955. *Homo ludens: A study of the play-element in culture* [1938]. Boston, MA: The Beacon Press.

Langlands, Ben, and Nikki Bell. 2004. *The house of Osama Bin Laden*. London: Thames & Hudson.

Mackenzie, Adrian. 2003. *Transductions: Bodies and machines at speed*. London: Continuum.

Oliver, Julian Holland. 2010. Adventures in the second person. www.selectparks.net/modules.php?name=News&file=article&sid=284.

Sargent, Robert G. 2005. Verification and validation of simulation models. *Proceedings of the 2005 winter simulation conference*. Orlando, FL, December 2005, eds. Michael E. Kuhl, Natalie M. Stieger, F. Brad Armstrong, and Jeffrey A. Jones, 130-43. Institute of Electrical and Electronics Engineers, Piscataway, NJ: USA.

Simondon, Gilbert. 1964. *L'individu et sa genèse physico-biologique* [Individuation and its physical-biological genesis]. Paris: Presses Universitaires de France.

—. 1989. *Du mode d'existence des objets techniques* [On the mode of existence of technical objects, 1958]. Paris: Aubier.

—. 2007. *L'individuation psychique et collective: A la lumière des notions de Forme, Information, potentiel et métastabilité* [Psychic and collective individuation: On the concepts of form, information, potential and metastability, 1989]. Paris: Aubier.

Stahl, Roger. 2010. *Militainment, Inc: War, media, and popular culture*. London: Routledge.

Stamp, Richard. 2010. No sense in this situation: Targeting animation in *The house of Osama Bin Laden*. Animation deviation. Conference at University of the West of England, Bristol, UK.

Stiegler, Bernard. 1998. *Technics and time 1: The fault of Epimetheus*, trans. Richard Beardsworth and George Collins. Stanford, CA: Stanford University Press.

—. 2004. *Mécréance et discrédit 1. La décadence des démocraties industrielles*. Paris: Editions Galilée.

—. 2006a. *Mécréance et discrédit 2. Les Sociétés Incontrôlables d'Individus Désaffectés*. Paris: Editions Galilée.

—. 2006b. *Mécréance et discrédit 3. L'esprit perdu du capitalisme*. Paris: Editions Galilée.

—. 2006c. *Nanomutations, hypomnemata and grammatisation*, trans. George Collins. http://arsindustrialis.org/node/2937#_ftnref3.

—. 2009. *Technics and time 2: Disorientation*, trans. Stephen Barker. Stanford, CA: Stanford University Press.

—. 2010a. *For a new critique of political economy*, trans. Dan Ross. Cambridge, UK: Polity Press

—. 2010b. *Ce qui fait que la vie vaut la peine d'être vécue: De la pharmacologie*. Paris: Flammarion.

—. 2011. *Technics and time 3: Cinematic time and the question of malaise*, trans. Stephen Barker. Stanford, CA: Stanford University Press.

Virilio, Paul. 1994. *The vision machine*, trans. Julie Rose. London: British Film Institute.

Weber, Samuel. 2005. *Targets of opportunity: On the militarization of thinking*. Ashland, OH: Fordham University Press.

13. Playful identity politics: How refugee games affect the player's identity

Joost Raessens

Contemporary computer games are increasingly being used both to entertain people as well as to "educate, train, and inform" them (Michael and Chen 2006). Refugee games belong to this so-called genre of "serious games": these games frame refugee issues by letting the player taste life as a refugee. Refugee games have the potential to convince players of the veracity of a certain point of view or the necessity of a behavioral change. But they also help non-profit organizations (such as the United Nations and Free Press Unlimited) and commercial enterprises (such as Reebok, the music channel MTV, Microsoft, and Konami) to reinvent activism and political engagement for the Internet generation. During the last few decades, refugee games have addressed all kinds of political problems. *Against All Odds* (2005), *Food Force* (2005, 2011), *Darfur is Dying* (2006), and *On the Ground Reporter: Darfur* (2010) were used as educational tools to teach people about what it is like to be a refugee, about famine and humanitarian aid, and the hostilities and genocide in Darfur.[1]

In this chapter I examine how serious games frame refugee issues in ways that are specific to the medium. My analysis is primarily theoretical: it aims at a conceptual clarification of how (playing) these kinds of games can affect the player's identity.[2] The starting point of my investigation is the conceptual framework of cognitive scientist and linguist George Lakoff who theorized how issues such as the environment, poverty, education, health care, and social change, which are today addressed in serious games, constitute a politics of identity. Though he provides a productive framework for understanding how those issues are intimately tied to one's identity, both personal and cultural, he does not address the question of how the form of a specific medium embeds itself in the message. Referring to three different modes of participation – reconstruction, deconstruction, and construction – I will further develop Lakoff's framework in order to turn it into an analytical toolkit in the domain of Computer Game Studies.

In the first section of this chapter, I analyze the ways in which the field of serious games defines the "seriousness" of these games and their effect on the forming of identity. In the second section, I will introduce Lakoff's concepts of "metaphor" and "framing" in order to be able to analyze *Food*

Force (2005, 2011) and *Darfur is Dying* (2006) from "a family-value" perspective in Lakoff's sense of the term. I suggest that players "play their identity" on the basis of who they are and how they understand themselves. In the third section, I focus on the medium-specificity of these games, arguing that they not only represent refugee issues, but that they also invite the player to interact with them. Both representations and interactions are designed according to ideologically motivated rules the player has to master in order to win the game. I will evaluate whether the games' potential as educational tools lies in strengthening or changing the basic dimensions of human experience: knowing, feeling, and acting.

The impact of serious games

When we take into account the ways in which the field of serious games – practical as well as theoretical – defines the "seriousness" of these games, we can develop the following provisionary definition: Serious games are games that are designed and used with the intention or purpose to address the most pressing contemporary issues and to have real-life consequences, for the world outside the magic circle of the game as well as for the player of the game, during and after playing. In this definition, five elements play a crucial role: 1. The intention or purpose with which these games are designed; 2. The intention or purpose with which they are used in a specific context; 3. The issues addressed by these games; 4. Their possible real-life effects on the outside world; and 5. Their impact on the player.

The first element is part of Michael and Chen's definition of serious games. Serious games "have an explicit and carefully thought-out educational *purpose* and are not *intended* to be played primarily for amusement [...] there is another purpose, an ulterior motive in a very real sense" (2006, 21; my italics). The Serious Games Initiative (SGI) aims at helping to organize and accelerate the adoption of computer games for a variety of challenges facing the world today. It emphasizes the second element, the serious *use* of games. On their website, SGI writes that they focus on the use of games in education, training, health, and public policy. Not only non-entertainment games especially designed for such a serious use, but also many commercial games are already in use for purposes other than entertainment. Titles such as *SimCity*, *Civilization*, *Hidden Agenda*, and others have been used as learning tools in schools and universities across the globe. The third element – the "seriousness" of the *issues* addressed by these games – can be found on the website of Games for Change (G4C). G4C facilitates the creation and distribution of social impact games that serve as critical tools in humanitarian and educational efforts. These games are worlds constructed from particular viewpoints and expressing particular ideas. The fourth element – a focus on real-life *effects* – can be found on the sites of Games for Health (GfH) and the Serious Games Initiative. GfH's mission is to foster awareness of, education about, and development of games that have a positive impact on the health of communities and health care. SGI wants to solve problems in areas as diverse as education, health care, national defense, homeland security, corporate management, and more. The impact of serious games on the *player* – the fifth element – becomes clear when we have a look at the persuasive power of these games. These games are designed to engage and manipulate the players' identity in specific ways. This is illustrated best in the following description: "[serious games] attempt through their content and social practices to recruit people to think, act, interact, value, and feel in certain specific ways" (Gee 2003, 44).[3]

Both *Darfur is Dying* and *Food Force* adhere to all of these five conditions. They are serious games, because they are designed (element 1) and used (element 2) on their website and in classrooms with the intention and purpose of engaging players and raising their awareness (element 5) in order to have a real-world impact on (element 4) the humanitarian crisis in Darfur and food crises all around the world, respectively (element 3).

One thing needs to be emphasized here. From the perspective of medium-specificity that I advocate in this chapter, both intentionality and purpose have to be related to the ways in which different modes of player participation are designed as part of the game. The three modes of player participation (re/de/construction) that I propose in this chapter add to the "if" and "how" of a game becoming a serious play experience. In other words, it is insufficient, though helpful, to find out what the intentions or purposes behind a game's design are by asking the game director of *Darfur is Dying* (Susana Ruiz, for example) or by studying annual reports of the organization which commissioned the game (the WFP, for example). Intentionality and purpose always (also) have to be analyzed in relation to how these modes of participation are embedded in the game design itself, as we will see in the third section of this chapter.

Refugee games: Playing your identity

Games for Change (G4C) was established in 2004 as a sub-group of the Serious Games Initiative. Two games that perfectly fit the framework of the

G4C-initiative are *Darfur is Dying* (2005) and *Food Force* (2005; 2011). *Food Force* is a social networking game that was released by the United Nations World Food Programme (WFP). It builds on the success of the downloadable PC version that was played by over 10 million users worldwide since its release in 2005.[4] The 2005 original tells the story of a food crisis on the fictitious island of Sheylan. The free downloadable game provides players with information about the outside world: "In the world today hundreds of millions of people suffer from chronic hunger and malnutrition". Furthermore, players can learn about WPF's mission to fight hunger worldwide and learn how they can actively support the WFP activities (cf. WFP 2006, 43). The 2011 sequel takes players online as part of Facebook and connects players with their friends to deliver humanitarian aid across the globe and impact the real world. On the games' website, you can also play two additional educational games *Freerice* and *Hunger IQ* that have real-world consequences. After people play these games, sponsors donate rice and warm meals to the WFP.

Darfur is Dying was the winner of the Darfur Digital Activist Contest launched by the music channel MTV in partnership with the Reebok Human Rights Foundation and the International Crisis Group during the G4C-conference in October 2005. The goal of the student contest was to design a computer game that raises awareness about the humanitarian crisis in the Darfur region of Sudan where civilians run the risk of being killed or raped by militias backed by the Sudanese government. By playing the game the player becomes involved in this world. The game was released in March 2006 at the *Darfur is Dying* website where it can still be played for free. The website describes the game as "a narrative based simulation where the user, from the perspective of a displaced Darfurian, negotiates forces that threaten the survival of his or her refugee camp". On the game's website, the player can play the game ("Help stop the crisis in Darfur. Start your experience") and can receive background information about the crisis in Darfur ("In the Darfur region of western Sudan, a genocide is occurring") and the different ways in which he can try to stop the crisis ("Take action. Do something now to stop the crisis in Darfur"). Players can contribute toward stopping the crisis in Darfur by sending a message to the US President, by asking their representatives to support funding for African Union peacekeepers, and by beginning a divestment movement on their college campus.

Lakoff's concepts of "metaphor" and "framing" allow me to analyze the political rhetoric of these kinds of refugee games. The emerging body of research on framing has signaled the latest paradigm shift in political-communication research (cf. Scheufele and Tewksbury 2007, 10). The most recent stage of research into political effects can be situated in the 1980s and early 90s: "The term 'framing' refers to modes of presentation that journalists and other communicators use to present information in a way that resonates with existing underlying schemas among their audience" (ibid., 12). According to Lakoff, metaphors frame our understanding of the world: "Our ordinary conceptual system, in terms of which we both think and act, is fundamentally metaphorical in nature [...] *The essence of metaphor is understanding and experiencing one kind of thing in terms of another*" (Lakoff and Johnson 2003, 3, 5). According to Lakoff:

> Frames are mental structures that shape the way we see the world. As a result, they shape the goals we seek, the plans we make, the way we act, and what counts as a good or bad outcome of our actions. In politics our frames shape our social policies and the institutions we form to carry out policies. To change our frames is to change all of this. Reframing *is* social change (2004, xv).

In order to increase our understanding of how both these games frame political issues, it may be insightful to approach them from a "family values" perspective. According to Lakoff, "we all have a metaphor for the nation as a family [...] because we usually understand large social groups, like nations, in terms of small ones, like families or communities" (ibid., 5). Contemporary American political discourse is divided into "two different models of the family: a [Republican, conservative] strict father family and a [Democratic, progressive] nurturant parent family model" (ibid., 6). According to the metaphor of the nurturant parent, "in foreign policy the role of the nation should be to promote cooperation and extend these values to the world" and to focus on "international institutions and strong defensive and peacekeeping forces" (ibid., 40, 63). This metaphor differs from the metaphor of the strict father that, in foreign affairs, leads to the following: "The government should maintain its sovereignty and impose its moral authority everywhere it can, while seeking its self-interest (the economic self-interest of corporations and military strength)" (ibid., 41).

An example of a political discussion where these two models collide is the attitude of the United States towards the United Nations. According to Lakoff, "most of the United Nations consists of developing and underdeveloped countries. That means they are metaphorically children" (ibid., 11). Having displayed its aversion to the United Nations time and again, the Bush administration opted for the strict father worldview. Because in *Darfur is Dying* and *Food Force* the United Nations Peace Operations and the United Nations World Food Programme are represented as organizations that are able to – literally – "nurture" their family members, both games express the values of the nurturant parent family model.

The Democrat Lakoff favors a foreign policy based more upon nurturant parent values, such as protection from harm, community building, caring, and responsibility. His descriptions of these values resonates in the goals of both games: protection from harm equals "an effective military for defense and peacekeeping". Building and maintaining a strong community equals "building and maintaining strong alliances and engaging in effective diplomacy". Caring and responsibility equals "caring about and acting responsibility for the world's people; world health, hunger, poverty [...] rights for women, children [...] refugees, and ethnic minorities" (ibid., 92).

Because of their ideological focus, serious games such as *Darfur is Dying* and *Food Force* constitute what Lakoff calls "a politics of identity" (Lakoff 2002, 289). The player of these kind of games generally (as we will see in the next section) accepts the purposes, the goals, and the very mode of life of the game. The actions during the game strengthen the very identity of players, reinforcing the values they have and the values they want to live by. What Lakoff writes about voting, I would argue, also applies to playing serious games. People do not only "vote" for their identity (Lakoff 2004, 19), they also "play" their identity: people play their values, they play the games they identify with, they play on the basis of who they are, how they understand themselves, what values they have, and who and what they admire. *Darfur is Dying* and *Food Force* both reinforce the nurturant parent values from – as Lakoff calls it – a Democratic, progressive point of view.

Before I analyze in more detail how both *Food Force* and *Darfur is Dying* involve players in these nurturant parent values in a medium-specific way, it is important to show that the United Nations strongly adheres to these values. James T. Morris, Executive Director of the World Food Programme, refers to "the United Nations family" and "the whole UN family" (WFP 2006, 5-6). In *The WFP Mission Statement* and in its *Annual Report 2005*, the World Food Programme describes the responsibility the international community has for primary health care, access to clean water, proper hygiene; it emphasizes the fact that food aid is essential for social and humanitarian protection; and it stresses the importance of helping people survive and rebuild their lives. In their *Mission Statement* and their *New Challenges, New horizons. Year in review 2006*, the United Nations Peace Operations also refer to "the United Nations family" (UNPO 2007, 24); to the international community's "duty of care"; to its responsibility to support health care missions; to the protection of community and minority rights; and to the protection of human rights. And on its news blog, the WFP describes how

Food Force (2011) works: "Money spent by players goes to fund WFP school meals projects in the real world. These projects provide daily meals to 20 million children every year, helping to keep them in school while providing them with the energy they need to learn".[5]

The medium-specificity of computer games

Computer games rely on rule-based interactions as their core mode of signification:

> A game is a rule-based formal system with a variable and quantifiable outcome, where different outcomes are assigned different values, the player exerts effort in order to influence the outcome, the player feels attached to the outcome, and the consequences of the activity are optional and negotiable (Juul 2003, 35; see also Juul 2005, 6-7).

In order to answer the question of how both *Darfur is Dying* and *Food Force* frame refugee issues and thereby strengthen or change the basic dimensions of human experience, we will have to focus on the six different game features distinguished by Juul. These features include: 1. What are the rules of these games? 2. What are their possible outcomes (related to the game's goal)? 3. Are the outcomes positive or negative? 4. Does the player influence the outcomes by reconstructing the preprogrammed possibilities of these games while playing according to the rules (reconstruction), by discovering how the software is put together while demystifying the rules (deconstruction), or by modifying these games while playing with the rules themselves (construction)? 5. Is the player happy with a positive outcome (winning the game) and unhappy with a negative outcome (losing the game)? 6. Are there any real-life consequences? Because of the important role of interactivity, or participation as I prefer to call it, as a factor which distinguishes computer games from most other media forms, I will organize my answers around the three modes of participation as mentioned earlier in this chapter: reconstruction, deconstruction, and construction.

Reconstruction

Reconstruction is the dominant mode of participation in *Darfur is Dying* and *Food Force*. Reconstruction consists of "the exploration of the unknown, in the computer game represented worlds" and the selection of "objects and actions from a fixed set of system-internal possibilities" (Raessens 2005, 380). At the beginning of *Darfur is Dying* the player selects one out of eight Darfuri avatars to represent the refugee camp. The game has a simple two-level structure. On the first level, the player has to explore the area outside the refugee camp to forage for water. The avatar has to provide water for the community, but because the well is five kilometers from the refugee camp, he runs the risk of being captured and possibly killed by the militias. The player can move his or her avatar by using the arrow keys of the keyboard and the spacebar to hide from the militias. After having reached the well and returned to the camp, the player can decide to go foraging again (as long as there are avatars left to do so) or to enter the second level inside the refugee camp. Here the player has a *SimCity*-style top-down view of the camp. The player has to explore the camp and select urgent tasks, such as obtaining food, building shelter, and staying healthy.

The basic rule of the game is clearly an ideologically motivated one: players can win the game by supporting Darfuri civilians. The goal of the game is to safeguard the refugee camp, keep it up and running for seven days, and protect as many adults and children from being killed by the Janjaweed militias. At the end of the game, players can put their name on a high score list on the game's website. When the avatar successfully brings water to his family and community, a screen with "Goal Accomplished" pops up. The message of the game is communicated most clearly in its rhetoric of failure. If captured by the militias, the avatar faces "real-life" consequences: "You will likely become one of the hundreds of thousands of people already lost to this humanitarian crisis". When a girl avatar is captured the consequences are heartbreaking: she faces "abuse, rape and kidnapping by the Janjaweed". The game is programmed in such a way that players are not only unhappy with a negative outcome, but also with a positive one. When players succeed in accomplishing the goal of the game, they are informed that this will not end the real conflict: "The men, women, and children of Darfur have been living under harrowing conditions since 2003". Although the game does not have real-life consequences for the players, it does have consequences for the Darfuri avatars of the player. Because players identify with the onscreen avatar, some of them have become engaged in the problems of Darfur through of the game.

In the virtual world of *Food Force* (2005), the player's engagement does not come from identification with an onscreen avatar, but from a first-person perspective. For the player of the game, its protagonist is a young rookie who is briefed on a humanitarian crisis on the fictitious island Sheylan in the Indian Ocean. It is the player's mission to deliver food as quickly as possible to the residents of Sheylan. Guided by a team of experts, in a race against the clock, the player has to accomplish six missions or mini-games in a linear order, all aimed at delivering food to an area in crisis. In the Air Surveillance mission, for example, the player has to explore the crisis area by helicopter and count the number of people who need help by selecting one of the preprogrammed actions: fly to the right, left, up or down. The 2011 sequel of *Food Force* is a kind of *FarmVille* for do-gooders. The game puts players at the head of a virtual humanitarian aid agency with the goal of eliminating hunger in different parts of the world. The game consists of three levels: The game welcomes you first to your WFP farm where you grow crops à la *FarmVille* to fight hunger; in the factory you can then process and package the crops; finally, in the Operations Center you can organize the food distribution (by plane or ship), conduct awareness campaigns, and raise food donations from countries around the world. Here you can invite your Facebook friends to join and help you fight world hunger. Players must interact with each other in order to get ahead, which they can also do by buying crops, equipment and other virtual goods. Money spent by players goes to fund WFP school meals projects in the real world.

The basic rule of *Food Force* is also an ideologically motivated one: players win the 2005 game by completing the six missions and in doing so, they help to fight hunger. The goal of the game is directly conveyed to the player: "You can learn to fight hunger [...] Millions of people are now depending on you for help. This is more than just a game. Good luck!" Players receive positive feedback on their performance from team members if their missions are successful. If the outcome of the mission is less successful, then the player is encouraged to try again. After playing the game, a player can summit his or her final score to a worldwide high score list on the game's website. In the 2011 sequel, players win the game when they grow and process crops and distribute the food around the world to fight hunger. In this case, the goal of the game is also directly conveyed to the player: "Grow food, distribute it around the virtual globe and change the lives of hungry children". Although both versions do not have real-life consequences for the player, players are constantly reminded of the fact that in real life the WFP missions have huge consequences for these hungry people.

Deconstruction

Looking through and exposing the hidden, naturalized, ideologically presupposed rules of a medium is an important aspect of media knowledge and literacy or "media wisdom" (cf. Dutch Council for Culture 2005; mediawijzer.

net). As mentioned above, I call this form of exposing "deconstruction" (Raessens 2005, 376-8). Talking about the process of deconstruction, Friedman, who calls this process "demystification", states:

> Learning and winning [...] or "reaching one's goals at" a computer game is a process of demystification [deconstruction]: One succeeds by discovering how the software is put together. The player molds his or her strategy through trial-and-error experimentation to see "what works" – which actions are rewarded and which are punished (Friedman 1995, 82).

According to Friedman, "computer games reveal their own constructedness to a much greater extent than more traditional texts" (ibid., 82). *Darfur is Dying* rests on the premise that the United Nations Security Council has the right and the duty to authorize military intervention to stop severe abuses of human rights in regions all over the world. *Food Force* rests on the premise that fighting hunger is a responsibility of the international community.[6] The "baseline ideological assumptions that determine which strategies will win and which will lose" (Friedman 1999, 144) become apparent through actually playing the game. That is why Friedman claims that "to win [...] you have to figure out what will work within the rules of the game" (ibid., 136). This is because a computer game, as opposed to, for example, a film, is played over and over again until all of the game's secrets have been discovered.

Friedman's claim is problematic because he overlooks the fact that the effects of computer games are always ambiguous and never just one-way traffic. From a framing perspective, games – like all media texts – are polysemic and, therefore, open to multiple readings or "playings". Game players may activate three interpretative strategies as a reaction to what Turkle calls the "seduction of simulation" (Turkle 1996, 71): players can either surrender to the seduction of *Food Force* and *Darfur is Dying* by interpreting the game more or less according to the encoded UN ideological frames (simulation resignation); they can understand these frames by demystifying them (as Friedman claims) or by deconstructing the assumptions or frames that are built into the simulation (simulation understanding); or they can completely disavow the social and political importance of these kinds of games (simulation denial).

These three strategies do, indeed, determine the reactions to both these games by players and critics. On the Water Cooler Games forum, for example, game critic and forum editor Gonzalo Frasca writes about *Food Force* (2005): "Finally! An educational game that rocks! Informative, well produced and very enjoyable to play with. Go United Nations! [...] Overall,

I am extremely happy for this game, it is an excellent example of the way edutainment should be."[7] Most of the comments on this forum reflect this view: "This was a wonderful game [...] successful at teaching the player about a few things, such as what foods are important, where investment is more valuable, etc. Great stuff!" and "Very nice game indeed". On the Gamezebo website, a critic writes about *Food Force* (2011): "An inspired way to educate Facebook gamers about world hunger. Solid gameplay formula. Attractive presentation."[8] This "simulation resignation" is also the dominant reaction towards *Darfur is Dying*: "Fortunately, this game is refreshingly smart about its subject and effective in its delivery".[9] The game "is perhaps the first true survival-horror game in which players experience life as a Sudanese living in Darfur in 2006, fighting to stay alive not from the threat of Space Invader aliens but from real world bullets and sun-cracked soil" (Parkin 2006). "Having a game about Darfur reaches out to lots of young people out there who are clueless about what's going on" (Vargas 2006). From this "simulation resignation" perspective, playing *Darfur is Dying* and *Food Force* in both cases affects the three basic dimensions of human experience: knowing, feeling, and acting. In other words, these games affect what players know and how they feel about current issues and suggest what they can do to act accordingly both inside and outside the game.

Simulation understanding and denial are clearly less important in the games. On the Water Cooler Games forum, some players deny *Food Force*'s importance by criticizing the UN for spending money on computer game development while thousands are starving.[10] And on BBC News, Ian Bogost "worries that MTV's involvement makes the game seem more like a marketing tool" (Boyd 2006). Others criticize the built-in assumptions of *Food Force* because this game does not refer to forms of misconduct by UN personnel: "How much like the real UN is it?"[11], and raise the question whether the difficult work for the WFP lends itself well to mini-games: "It seems more like a[n] MMO (e.g. *Everquest*). Or a Sim where you control the WFP".[12] On the games.com news blog, a critic wonders "if the game [*Food Force* 2011] is going to get enough people to play to really make a difference". *Darfur is Dying* is criticized for the same reason: "It seems to trivialize the problem" (Vargas 2006), and Bogost "also wonders whether *Darfur is Dying* oversimplifies an incredibly complex conflict" (Boyd 2006).

Construction

The concept of "construction" may be understood as the modification of an existing game. A game modification is "an add-on to an existing game engine that alters the original code or state of a computer game" (Schleiner 1999). Examples are the "customization of graphics, sound, game play, architecture or other attributes of the original computer game" (ibid.). In this sense both *Food Force* and *Darfur is Dying* lack a constructive mode. The gamers' activities are better described as modes of reconstruction.

However, there is another definition of construction that refers to the making of new games as such. What is at stake here is the question who can participate in our culture. Whether we face a top-down culture in which a small number of computer game developers and publishers run the show, or whether we face a multitude of bottom-up cultures in which independent companies can (continue to) participate. We see these bottom-up cultures appear when independent games are developed and distributed. This is exactly G4C's goal:

> Founded in 2004, Games for Change facilitates the creation and distribution of social impact games that serve as critical tools in humanitarian and educational efforts. Unlike the commercial gaming industry, we aim to leverage entertainment and engagement for social good. To further grow the field, Games for Change convenes multiple stakeholders, highlights best practices, incubates games, and helps create and direct investment into new projects.[13]

Darfur is Dying and *Food Force* have a clear political agenda, namely the dissemination of the United Nations' nurturant parent frame through popular culture. In itself this can be considered an emancipating and liberating aspect of the construction of frames. When gamers (such as Susana Ruiz) become game programmers and directors and thus move from game to meta-game, players realize that reality is "open source" and they have "the ability to rethink and redesign our world using entirely new rule sets" (Rushkoff 2005, 421; 2012). Although commercial enterprises such as MTV and Reebok initiated the design of *Darfur is Dying*, profit or the provision of mere entertainment is not their main motive. As with *Food Force*, the goal of the game is to provide an engaging experience, to communicate a political message, and, ultimately, the realization of a certain change of knowing, feeling, and acting on the part of the player. The *Food Force* website asks players to become active outside the game world. Players can help by giving money to the WFP, by teaching others about famine, and by organizing fundraising activities at school or at home. "Joe's blog" on the *Food Force* website links the game world with the outside reality in interesting ways. Joe Zake, the Sheylanese nutritionist character of the game, asks website visitors "to spread the word about hunger using this blog: read, comment and link". As I described earlier in this chapter, the *Darfur is Dying* website is organized in a similar way when it offers players different kinds of possibilities to become involved in the reality outside the game.

Conclusion

In understanding how the design of *Darfur is Dying* and *Food Force* helps to convince players of the veracity of the games' point of view and the necessity of a behavioral change, we have to realize that a mere presentation of factual information about the situation in Darfur and global hunger is simply not good enough. In order "[t]o be accepted, the truth must fit people's frames. If the facts do not fit a frame, the frame stays and the facts bounce off" (Lakoff 2004, 17). It seems effective to frame these facts in multiple ways: within the context of two successful games; within the context of two accompanying websites; as part of the framework of the United Nations; in the context of the nurturant parent model. According to Lakoff, "we all have *both* models [nurturant parent and strict father] – either actively or passively" (ibid., 41). The goal of both games is to activate the nurturant parent values I described earlier in the minds of the players of these computer games, and to frame the issues of hunger and Darfur from their perspective.

Darfur is Dying and *Food Force* frame Darfur and global hunger in ways that are specific to the medium. The players of both games mainly reconstruct the preprogrammed possibilities of these games according to their unambiguously motivated ideological rules. It seems that most of the critics and players surrender to the games' baseline ideological assumptions. It is not easy to determine whether the oversimplification of the Darfur conflict turns the game into a United Nations propaganda vehicle. Or whether "it is an entryway into the crisis" (Boyd 2006) – in the words of game designer Susana Ruiz – which deals with the basic questions young people have. I tend to agree with Scheufele and Tewsbury's definition of framing as "a necessary tool to reduce the complexity of an issue" (2007, 12), given the constraints of the media in question. "Frames, in other words, become invaluable tools for presenting relatively complex issues [...] efficiently and in a way that makes them accessible to lay audiences because they play to existing cognitive schemas" (ibid., 12).

As we have seen, the role that serious games play in the process of identity construction is an ambiguous one. This goes for the possible effects these games might have, as well as for the question who is in control of this process. When we look at the impact these games have, we can, on the one hand, argue that people choose those games to play that are already in line with their identity, that they play their identity on the basis of how they understand themselves. This leaves unimpeded that, on the other hand, the playing of serious games seems to have the potential to strengthen specific mental frames and weaken others. Playing *Darfur is Dying* and *Food Force* has an impact on what players know, feel, and do about the issues addressed. Coming back to the question who is in control, we have seen that players may activate different interpretative strategies: they can either surrender to, try to understand, or deny the importance of these kinds of games (and their ideological frames). The fact that, unlike other media, computer games give players the sense that they are "co-creators" of the game – most of the time a "participatory illusion" – inclines me to see serious games as a forceful discursive space and practice, with real enough power to influence the terms in which people think, feel, and act.

One of the main constraints of refugee games is that the development and distribution of computer games is severely dominated by a few commercial companies who focus on entertainment games. Although organizations like G4C are very helpful in catalyzing social impact, the gaming industry as such lacks funding and business models for projects such as *Darfur is Dying* and *Food Force*. It is a small miracle that these kinds of games exist and succeed in raising issues that the media does not always consider newsworthy, given that they do not aim for or make high profits while still requiring substantial production budgets.

Acknowledgments

Some of my descriptions of *Food Force* and *Darfur is Dying,* and of the activities and ideas of The Serious Games Initiative, Games for Change, and Games for Health are based on their websites.

This chapter draws from Raessens, Joost. 2010. A taste of life as a refugee: How serious games frame refugee issues. In *Changes in museum practice. New media, refugees and participation,* eds. Hanne-Lovise Skartveit and Katherine J. Goodnow, 94-105. New York/Oxford: Berghahn Books.

Notes

1. *Against All Odds*: www.playagainstallodds.com; *Food Force*: apps.facebook.com/foodforce; *Darfur is Dying*: www.darfurisdying.com; *On the Ground Reporter: Darfur*: www.radiodabanga.org/darfurgame.
2. Using games as a tool to encourage civic engagement is generally considered to be a promising avenue of research. To date, however, validation research in this domain is limited. One exception is Neys and Jansz (2010). To fill this gap, three contributors of this book – Jeroen Jansz, Ben Schouten, and Joost Raessens – started the research project "Persuasive gaming. From theory-based design to validation and back" (2013-17), funded by the Netherlands Organization for Scientific Research, see www.persuasivegaming.nl.
3. For more info on SGI, G4C and GfH, see their websites: www.seriousgames.org, www.gamesforchange.org, and www.gamesforhealth.org.
4. The 2005 original could be downloaded on the *Food Force* website (www.food-force.com) until 2011. It is still possible to download the original game from sites such as www.download-free-games.com.
5. See www.wfp.org.
6. Both *Darfur is Dying* and *Food Force* build on the metaphor of the West as the helping parent and support the notion that emergencies in borderland zones have local, internal origins that need to be fixed and solved externally. They fall into what is called within Conflict Studies the *new wars frame*, which gained ground at the beginning of the 21st century and which has become prominent in both the humanitarian intervention and aid industry. For a critique, see Demmers and Raessens (forthcoming).
7. www.bogost.com/watercoolergames/archives/food_force.shtml.
8. www.gamezebo.com/games/food-force/review.
9. www.gameology.org/node/1013.
10. www.bogost.com/watercoolergames/archives/food_force.shtml.
11. See note 10.
12. MMO, or MMORPG, stands for Massively Multiplayer Online Role-Playing Game. A Sim is a Simulation game, like *SimCity*.
13. www.gamesforchange.org/about.

References

Boyd, Clark. 2006. Darfur activism meets video gaming. *BBC-News* (July 6). news.bbc.co.uk/2/hi/technology/5153694.stm.

Butch and Sundance Media. 2010. *On the Ground Reporter: Darfur*. Butch and Sundance Media.

Demmers, Jolle, and Joost Raessens. Forthcoming. Gaming war, framing war: A critical frame analysis of the form and function of representations of war in "serious games".

Dutch Council for Culture [Raad voor Cultuur]. 2005. *Media wisdom. The development of new citizenship* [*Mediawijsheid: De ontwikkeling van nieuw burgerschap*]. The Hague: Raad voor Cultuur.

Friedman, Ted. 1995. Making sense of software. In *Cybersociety: Computer-mediated communication and community*, ed. Steven G. Jones, 73-89. London: Sage Publications.
—. 1999. Civilization and its discontents. In *On a silver platter. CD-roms and the promises of a new technology*, ed. Greg M. Smith, 132-50. New York: New York University Press.
Gee, James-Paul. 2003. *What video games have to teach us about learning and literacy.* New York: Palgrave Macmillan.
Juul, Jesper. 2003. The game, the player, the world: Looking for a heart of gameness. In *Level up. Digital games research conference*, eds. Marinka Copier and Joost Raessens, 30-45. Utrecht: Utrecht University.
—. 2005. *Half-real. Video games between real rules and fictional worlds.* Cambridge, MA: The MIT Press.
Konami Digital Entertainment. 2005, 2011. *Food Force.* PC: United Nations World Food Program.
Lakoff, George. 2002. *Moral politics. How liberals and conservatives think.* Chicago, IL: University of Chicago Press.
—. 2004. *Don't think of an elephant! Know your values and frame the debate.* White River Junction, Vermont: Chelsea Green Publishing.
—, and Mark Johnson. 2003. *Metaphors we live by.* Chicago, IL: University of Chicago Press.
Michael, David, and Sande Chen. 2006. *Serious games: Games that educate, train, and inform.* Boston, MA: Thomson.
MtvU, *Darfur is Dying* 2006. PC: UCS Interactive Media.
Neys, Joyce, and Jeroen Jansz. 2010. Political Internet games: Engaging an audience. *European Journal of Communication*, 25(3): 1-15.
Parkin, Simon. 2006. Interview – *Darfur is Dying.* When videogames discovered ethics. *Eurogamer* (September 4). www.eurogamer.net.
Raessens, Joost. 2005. Computer games as participatory media culture. In *Handbook of computer game studies*, eds. Joost Raessens and Jeffrey Goldstein, 373-88. Cambridge, MA: The MIT Press.
Rushkoff, Douglas. 2005. Renaissance now! The gamers' perspective. In *Handbook of computer game studies*, eds. Joost Raessens and Jeffrey Goldstein, 415-21. Cambridge, MA: The MIT Press.
—. 2012. *Monopoly moneys. The media environment of corporatism and the player's way out.* Utrecht: PhD dissertation. Faculty of Humanities, Utrecht University.
Scheufele, Dietram A., and David Tewksbury. 2007. Framing, agenda setting, and priming: The evolution of three media effects models. *Journal of Communication* 57(1): 9-20.
Schleiner, Anne-Marie. 1999. Parasitic interventions: Game patches and hacker art. www.opensorcery.net/patchnew.html.
Turkle, Sherry. 1996. *Life on the screen: Identity in the age of the Internet.* London: Weidenfeld and Nicolson.
United Nations Peace Operations (UNPO). 2007. *New challenges, new horizons. Year in review 2006* New York: United Nations. www.un.org/en/peacekeeping/publications/yir/2006/YIR2006.pdf.
UNHCR. 2005. *Against All Odds.* PC.
Vargas, Jose A. 2006. Darfur Is Dying, The game that's anything but. *Washingtonpost.com* (May 1). www.washingtonpost.com.
World Food Programme (WFP). 2006. *Annual report 2005.* Rome: World Food Programme. www.wfp.org/sites/default/files/2005_wfp_annual_report_0.pdf.

Part III

Identity

Introduction to Part III

Valerie Frissen, Sybille Lammes, Michiel de Lange, Jos de Mul & Joost Raessens

The contributions in the third part of the book look at how digital media technologies shape human identities in playful ways. A common thread that weaves through these chapters is that media technologies and practices mediate how people identify with others, the world, and themselves. When new media technologies rise to the fore the mediation of identity changes along with it, and play offers a range of fruitful perspectives to understand these changes. Another common thread in these chapters involves questioning the intricate connections between play and everyday life. From being a more or less separate space for experimenting with identities to being tightly integrated into everyday life in social role-playing, the boundaries of play feature as a central topic in these chapters.

Different argumentative strands can be identified in addition to these similarities. First, several authors make a media-theoretical argument by exploring how specific media that are widely used, like computer games, mobile phones, online social networks, and casual games, have playful qualities and therefore shape identities in playful ways. Second, a number of authors make the cultural-philosophical argument that play's conceptual ambiguity captures well the ambivalent attitudes many people have towards identity formation as a constant series of oscillations between engagement and disengagement, between pretense and seriousness, individualism and collectivity, and so on. Third, yet other authors make a socio-historical argument that games and play are no longer confined to a separate sphere but have become part and parcel of today's commodified cultural economy that shapes who we are and who we want to be.

In *Playing out identities and emotions*, professor of communication and media Jeroen Jansz argues from a psychological perspective that digital computer games allow people to experiment with their identities, both inside the game itself and in the social context in which the games are played. He pays particular attention to the gendered nature of identity construction. People explore aspects of themselves by playing, even those aspects that are impossible or forbidden outside of the game, in order to test out the reactions of others. Fantasies about who one is and wants to be are being put into practice yet without entirely the same consequences as in everyday life. Games are identity laboratories, constituting safe spaces for playing with the boundaries of gender and self.

If computer games in Jansz' analysis are designated settings more or less separated from everyday life, media philosopher Jeroen Timmermans in *Playing with others: The identity paradoxes of the web as social network* looks at the playfulness of online social networking sites as intimately connected to everyday life. Timmermans observes that people more than ever are split between personal self-expression and growth, and the yearning for communication and community building. The playful self-presentation that people engage in on social networking sites is a way of coping with the very real and seriousness business of interacting, managing personal status, and forging group identities. According to this perspective, play is an intrinsic aspect of the presentation of self in everyday life.

The contribution *New media, play, and social identities* by sociologist Leopoldina Fortunati breaks away from medium-specific identity practices. Fortunati looks at the motivations behind the current relationship between new media, play, and social identities. Her analysis operates at the intersection of ludic culture, social control, and the construction of what she calls an "ir-responsible" identity. Despite many claims to freedom, contemporary ludic culture may just as well be understood as imposing new types of social control and forms of resistance. Today's playful media culture shapes the political economy of gender relations in this dialectical movement between institutional control and user-driven experiment with counter-powers. This contribution therefore serves as a healthy antidote to overly celebratory views of the liberating potential of play in the construction of identity. Furthermore, Marxist theory has taught us not to take the notion of "everyday life" as self-evident. Fortunati's contribution thus serves as a reminder that any inquiry into the relationship between play and everyday life means questioning how hidden structural forces beneath "the everyday" shape people's identities.

Most contributions in this volume situate their analysis in a Western context. Playful media practices can be observed elsewhere, as urban new media researcher Michiel de Lange shows in his chapter *Playing life in the metropolis: Mobile media and identity in Jakarta*. The mobile phone offers Indonesians many opportunities for identity construction and expression. Young people in particular base their identities on shared but contested ideas about what it means to live a "modern urban life". It is argued that play complements narrative identity by highlighting the conditions under which particular stories are told and how identifications come into being. Play acts as a heuristic lens through which focus is shifted from narrative representations to situation-specific performances of the self, which fits better with the dynamics of city life and media culture.

The chapter *The conflicts within the casual: The culture and identity of casual online play* by game scholar Frans Mäyrä focuses on casual gameplay that takes place on online social networking platforms and location-based mobile phone applications. Casual play is typically characterized by short sessions of playful interaction with games that are not particularly challenging, complex, or extensive. This gives participants the chance to divide their attention among other activities and issues besides gameplay. Casual play is not deeply immersive or transformative of personal or social identities like, for instance, live action role-playing or Massively Multiplayer Online (MMO) games. While the vocal parts of game cultures have mostly articulated the pleasures of highly immersive gameplay, the players of contemporary casual games have started to voice an alternative view of what constitutes "good gameplay" based on a slightly different aesthetics of play. This chapter aims to discuss the significance of casual games and highlight their contribution to game cultures. For Mäyrä casual play is the nexus between the two poles of commitment and non-engagement that is typical of today's identities.

In the closing chapter of the book, *Afterplay*, Jos de Mul revisits some of the stakes and claims laid out in the introductory chapter. The argument is made that technologies have become the locus of contemporary ludification of culture and identity. Narrative and play are not opposites. They do not constitute mutually exclusive lenses for understanding the mediation of identity, but rather must be taken as complementary. Nonetheless the notion of play, with its ambiguities and ambivalences, offers a particularly poignant take on the ubiquity and importance of ludic digital media technologies.

14. Playing out identities and emotions

Jeroen Jansz

Introduction

> "Yes, they all have these huge muscles. I could do with a little more, and that is what you see in the game" (Dirk, male, 16 yrs.).
>
> "In Diablo II you have realistic characters, with an Amazon who is armed with a bow and arrow, and throws a javelin. Then I think, I wish I could do that" (Leontien, female, 28 yrs.).
>
> "It really is cool to take your time to cut off someone's legs, or to find a saw to saw off someone's ear" (Arie, male, 27 yrs.).
>
> "The violence in games is fun, and really pleasant, because you can let off steam. On a computer you can and may do things you won't even think about in real life" (Cor, male, 28 yrs.).

These excerpts, taken from interviews with gamers who were asked why they like to play their favorite game, illustrate that people's attractions to games are manifold.[1] Teenager Dirk seems to identify with the physical appearance of his game character, whereas Leontien fantasizes about being an Amazon. Arie communicates the appeal of violent content, as does Cor who also explains the unique properties of the virtual world.

In this chapter, I will develop a specific answer to the question why people are attracted to playing video games, including ones with a violent, if not atrocious content. Central to my argument is the observation that video games function as a safe, private laboratory where players can engage in a rich diversity of activities including ones that may not be possible or will not be tolerated in daily life. The idea of a safe laboratory is indebted to Huizinga's notion of play as proceeding "within its own proper boundaries of time and space according to fixed rules and in an orderly manner" (Huizinga 1955, 13). Huizinga situates the unfolding of play in a range of contexts, including "the magic circle" (ibid., 10), which has become a famous metaphor. Game designers Salen and Zimmerman incorporate the magic circle into their characterization of gaming: "to play a game means entering into a magic circle or perhaps creating one as a game begins [...] The term magical is appropriate because there is in fact something genuinely magical that happens when a game begins [...] In fact, a new reality is created, defined by the rules of the game and inhabited by its players" (2004, 95-6). However, the attempt to conceptualize gaming as roaming in a magic circle is risky, because it suggests rigid boundaries around play, whereas in actuality these boundaries are fuzzy (see the introductory chapter of this volume). In this chapter, however, my argument concentrates on situations of immersion where players are so absorbed in their gaming that they temporarily leave the world outside play. Stepping into that magic circle enables them to play out virtual identities and emotions.

The interactive nature of playing video games

The days are long gone in which critical media scholars conceptualized media as powerful *stimuli* inciting almost automatically *responses* in media audiences (McLuhan and Fiore 1967). Currently, the common understanding among media and communication theorists is that audiences are active agents (Livingstone 2004). Using media implies that audience members engage themselves actively with the content offered. In the process, the so-called media consumers attribute meaning to what they perceive in order to decode what was encoded by media producers (Hall 1997; Ruggiero 2000). The actual activity of the consumer is dependent as much on the media channel as it is on the content offered. For example, decoding Nolan's movie *Inception* (2010) requires a higher level of user engagement than watching a soap series on television.

Playing a video game is the ultimate case of user activity, because playing requires a constant exchange of messages between the medium and its users. When players refrain from communicating, the game simply ceases to exist, making interactivity a key feature of all electronic games (Kiousis 2002). A second feature, immersion, is more applicable to video games than to the short, casual games that can be played in a web browser. It refers to being drawn into the represented world and experiencing a profound feeling of "being there" that has been conceptualized as "presence" (Lee 2004). Research has shown that gamers are indeed less aware of the mediated quality of the experience when they interact with virtual objects in the game world (Tamborini and Skalski 2006). One study established that an existing narrative relates positively to presence. In other words, participants who played a game with a strong story line (*Half-Life* and *Outlaws*) reported a greater sense of presence than players of non-story-based games (*Doom 2* and *Quake 2*) (Schneider et al. 2004). Immersion is psychologically interesting because it requires an investment of effort and time in order to learn, among other things, the scenery, (sub)plots, and possible tactical moves of the game. The market success of video games, including complicated ones, shows that many people are indeed willing to invest substantially in this leisure activity. It has also been corroborated by research that many video gamers play because they want to satisfy a need to be challenged (Jansz and Tanis 2007; Sherry et al. 2006). The necessary investment of time and effort, as well as the subsequent experience of presence, result in a situation that is far more immersive than the one emerging from the use of non-interactive media. The next section addresses how identification unfolds in this context opening opportunities for playing out (virtual) identities.

Identification and playing out identities

Psychological theories of identity argue that identity is a relational construct, because it is embedded in a network of social relations (Ellemers, Spears, and Doosje 2002; Jansz 1991). Gergen (1994) underlines the relational nature of identity by arguing that we should trade Descartes' famous dictum "I think, therefore I am" with "I communicate, therefore I am". Developing an identity is a dynamic process of borrowing from and lending to sources surrounding the individual. Individuals may borrow identity elements from their parents, peers, and other significant people as well as from a variety of public sources. At every stage of the process, personal identities are acted out in communication with others, which implies that elements may in turn be lent to the interactants. Given their relational embeddedness, identities are always open to change across the lifespan, although adolescence turns out to be the most dynamic period (Bosma and Kunnen 2001; Steinberg and Morris 2001).

Media are an important public source for identity elements. When spectators identify with, for example, a movie star like Johnny Depp, they temporarily incorporate elements from Depp's identity into their own. They may identify with Depp for many different reasons. For example, they aspire Depp's role in the movie, or because of similarities between Depp's character and themselves (Cohen 2001). Obviously, identification can also be inspired by a lack of similarity. In this kind of *wishful identification*, spectators desire to incorporate features of the character precisely because they themselves do not possess these features (Konijn and Hoorn 2005). Games are unique among media because they enable players to identify beyond identification:

gamers can enact, or perform, a particular identity in the most literal sense of the word. Klimmt, Hefner, and Vorderer (2009) have detailed the opportunities video games offer by arguing that games facilitate a specific relation between the user and the character. "Players do not perceive the game's (main) character as a social entity distinct from themselves, but experience a merging of their own self and the game protagonist" (2009, 354). They conceptualize the relationship between user and media character as *monadic* to stress the difference with the dyadic relationship between user and character that is characteristic for non-interactive media. The monadic relationship underlines the immersive nature of play, as well as the unique properties of temporarily roaming in a magic circle.

The actual opportunities for assuming a (playable) identity are of course dependent on the characteristics of specific genres and titles. For example, one could be a fighter pilot for as long as the game lasts, or embrace Niko Bellic's (the protagonist in *Grand Theft Auto 4*) violent performance of masculine identity, or temporarily assume Lionel Messi's professional identity as a striker in *FIFA10*. The examples illustrate that the opportunities for identification and performing identities are manifold, but they also point to the structural constraints of what is possible.

Most video games are "green-brown games" covering stereotypical male interests and are targeted at a (young) male audience (Jansz and Vosmeer 2009). The green and brown colors of their packaging aptly reflect a content that is often about fighting wars in camouflage attire, or playing sports matches on green fields. Female characters are under-represented, and generally appear in submissive positions with an emphasis on their virtual breasts and buttocks (Beasley and Standley 2002). Recently, there has been a move to include competent female protagonists like Lara Croft, but these heroines are still portrayed in a hyper-sexualized fashion (Jansz and Martis 2007). The inherent focus on a male audience is further sustained by games being framed as male-orientated and male-dominated in the general media coverage thereof, as well as in game advertisements and reviews (Ivory 2006).

"Pink games" aim to appeal to a (young) female audience with bright colors and game content relating to traditional female roles, like nursing and caring. Ever since the success of Mattel's *Barbie Fashion Designer* in the 1990s, pink games have been criticized for their traditional, if not stereotypical, portrayal of female gender roles (Jenkins and Cassell 2008; Vosmeer 2009). However, this criticism has not interfered with the popularity of pink games (Krotoski 2004). These games seem to cater to girls' preferences for exploration rather than competitive play and their keenness to solve puzzles and riddles (Schott and Horrell 2000; Sherry et al. 2006). But there are also indications that preferences go beyond the predictions of gender stereotyping. For example, the popularity of *Go SuperModel* can, on the one hand, be understood because it enables players to act as a model. On the other hand, its players enthusiastically embrace the competition that is part and parcel of the virtual modeling world (van Reijmersdal et al. 2010). *The Sims* provides another example because it is very popular indeed among girls and women without relying exclusively on stereotypes (Jansz, Avis, and Vosmeer 2009). Female gamers interviewed by Royse and her colleagues even took pleasure in challenging gender norms. While they acknowledged the hyper-sexualization of female images in games, they deliberately chose to pick (or create) avatars that were feminine, sexy, and strong (Royse et al. 2007).

In conclusion, the relationship between the player and the game character is unique and fundamentally different from other entertainment media. It enables players to develop their identities in interaction with the game content. Since game culture is dominated by stereotypical male interests and values, male players can probably draw more from the game than women. The next step in the present argument is to address the emotions players seek to be confronted with in the game.

Emotions incited and played out

The content of entertainment media can be as powerful in eliciting emotions as real life, despite the obvious differences between the ordinary world and its representation in the media. Research about, for example, novels, films, fairy tales, and television programs has shown that entertainment content can generate emotions such as joy, awe, and compassion, but also fear and anger (Oatley 1994; Tan 1996). The aroused emotions are a fundamental component in the experience of entertainment, which also includes emotions aroused by violent game content (Goldstein 2005; Tan 2008). Emotions that occur in the appreciation of entertainment media (and art) are generally known as *aesthetic emotions* (Frijda 1989).

In recent years, the first steps have been taken in developing a theory on aesthetic emotions in video games (Jansz 2005; Tan and Jansz 2008). The interactive nature of video games makes the emotions triggered by games different from the ones that occur in traditional media. Gamers themselves decide which emotional situations they want to confront and which they would like to stay away from. This leads to the experience of what I have called "participatory emotions" (Jansz 2005). This first-person emotional experience contrasts with the reception of film and other non-interactive media where "witness emotions" are always experienced from a third-person perspective (Tan 1996). Following Frijda's functional theory of emotion (1986), I will argue that participatory emotions are best understood as a process that unfolds step by step.

The first step in the emotion process is appraisal, a very swift cognitive evaluation of a particular event or situation. Something happens, usually unexpected, which the individual immediately recognizes as an event that touches his or her interests, or concerns (ibid.). If the event does not touch a concern, an emotion fails to occur. In the context of playing video games, the interests at stake can be manifold. For example, a situation may be interpreted as seriously threatening one's physical survival in the game, which can elicit fear. An event may also be appraised as endangering one's social status, for example, when one's false moves endanger one's teammates, which elicits shame. Lazarus (1991) pointed out that this first step in the emotion process happens very quickly, so quickly that appraisal is hardly experienced at a conscious level. He coined the term "primary appraisal" to underline its almost automatic nature.

The second step is context evaluation. A deliberate kind of appraising takes place, which is done consciously, and will take more time than primary appraisal. In this phase of "secondary appraisal" (ibid.), the individual reflects on what caused the emotion and the situation in which it appeared, and plans how to cope with that situation. At this point, gamers may, for example, ask themselves why they experienced fear in the first place, or what they can do about this shame. When gamers identify with the protagonist they may understand their emotional reaction as signaling the necessity to reconsider their game character's priorities and plans.

The reflexive activities lead to the third step: the readiness to act. According to Frijda (1986), a change in action readiness is the central core of an emotion, because emotions always come with a sense of urgency that incites people to act. Previous research about real-life situations showed that each emotion can be characterized by a specific tendency to act (Roseman, Wiest, and Swartz 1994). For example, people who experience joy want to move or jump, angry people feel like opposing or assaulting someone, fearful people want to run away, and sadness incites a tendency to do nothing. Whether an action tendency is realized or inhibited is dependent on the social context, both in real life and in a video game. An angry gamer, for example, may decide to postpone killing the object of his anger for strategic reasons.

The fourth and last step in the emotion process is concerned with the actual translation of emotions into actions. It includes the expressive display of emotions in the face, as well as bodily reactions like blushing, accelerated breathing, or clenching fists that accompany many emotions. Step four also includes the actual translation of action readiness into activities, for example, when our angry gamer starts killing despite the undesirable strategic consequences.

The emotions incited by game content may be positive, negative, or a combination of the two. Generally, positive participatory emotions are coupled with action tendencies to remain in the situation, or to continue the action that sparked the emotion (Frijda, Kuipers, and ter Schure 1989). For example, when gamers complete a level, they may experience joy or pride. These positive emotions will motivate them to prolong that situation, resulting in the continuation of play. The action tendency of the negative emotion anger may also extend playing time. Generally, anger motivates individuals to approach the source of anger (Roseman, Wiest, and Swartz 1994). In a "beat 'em up" video game, anger will thus prolong, and probably intensify the fighting episodes. In other words, the action tendencies of positive emotions, as well as those of anger result in a prolongation of gaming.

The relation between emotions and playing time is less straightforward in the case of negative emotions like fear and disgust. They may, for example, experience fear when they are trapped in the labyrinth-like rig of *Metal Gear Solid 2*, or disgust during their battles with the atrocious corpses in *Silent Hill*. The action tendencies of fear and disgust urge individuals to withdraw from the situation. People who are fearful or disgusted tend to avert their eyes from the cause of emotion, or leave the situation altogether (Frijda, Kuipers, and ter Schure 1989). The tendency to withdraw can be realized easily in a game context. Turning off the PC or game console breaks the spell of virtuality, and distances the gamer from the emotional source. Obviously, this radical disruption is not common among gamers. On the contrary, they generally play on, thus prolonging the experience of negative participatory emotions.

There are several reasons why games persist in this situation. The first one is rather straightforward: players play on because they like the feeling of anger, disgust, or fear as much as they may like feeling joy, pride, or other positive emotions. When the devastating action tendencies are put into practice, the negative emotions unfold completely in the virtual world of the game, which is not common in daily life. Consequently, the accompanying feelings can be enjoyed in every detail. Research on horror movies has indeed shown that spectators enjoy the aroused feelings of fear (Tamborini

2003). A second reason is concerned with the gamer's curiosity about what an emotion exactly feels like. This may particularly be applicable to fear and disgust, as these emotions do not occur very frequently in the lives of most people. The third reason links emotion to identity: gamers may persist in situations evoking fear, anger, or disgust because they want to prove to themselves that they can commit atrocious actions, and can endure the resulting feelings. This may be a way to test the darker emotional aspects of their identities.

A laboratory for the construction of identities and the experience of emotions

As we have seen above, gamers' activities unfold in a monadic relationship where gamers experience a merging of their own self and their avatar (Klimmt et al. 2009). In other words, the choices made within the metaphorical chalk lines of the magic circle are experienced as the gamers' own choices. It sustains the enjoyable feeling of control gamers report (Jansz and Martens 2005). It is the gamer/avatar who decides what identities are played out. In the same vein, it is the gamer/avatar who is in charge of the emotional confrontations that are sought or shunned. This deliberate choice to experience participatory emotions is in marked contrast with the incitement of emotion in daily life. There, emotions often come as "a thief in the night", overwhelming the person involved, at least temporarily (Frijda 1986).

In actual play emotions and identity are inextricably linked, as they are both features of the game character. It is, after all, the character who runs into a situation thus inciting a participatory emotion. Being in control over (playable) characters opens rich possibilities for experimenting with virtual identities and participatory emotions. The experimental practices point to a location where experiments are usually done: the laboratory. Conceptualizing a video game as a laboratory to experiment with emotion as much as with identities (Jansz 2005; Kestenbaum and Weinstein 1985) also means incorporating the magic circle metaphor into a context that is predominantly characterized by experimenting. The laboratory provides a safe personal context where players can individually interact with their personal computer or game console. Additionally, the game also provides a safe social context because experimenting is often done with like-minded individuals. The final section of this chapter addresses the social aspects of gaming.

Playing video games as a social activity

Notwithstanding the popularity of game titles that are predominantly played individually, playing video games is a social activity for many players (Durkin 2006). LAN parties are an early example within game culture of social play materializing in an actual event: individual players bring their personal computers to the event and attach it to the local area network (LAN) so that they can play with each other and against each other in the same room (Jansz and Martens 2005). The recent massive growth of online gaming obviously underlines the importance gamers attribute to playing in a social context. For example, millions of players pay their monthly dues to be able to compete and collaborate in *World of Warcraft*. In addition, the success of online options with titles as diverse as *Little Big Planet* and *Call of Duty* reinforces the belief that many gamers play for social reasons.

Research into why people play video games has shown the importance of social motivations across a variety of game genres (Sherry et al. 2006; Yee 2006). Again, an important gender difference must be noted. Lucas and Sherry (2004) found that social interaction was the second most important motive (after challenge) for male participants, whereas female participants rated social interaction as the least important of the six motives. Our own research into *The Sims2* corroborated this result, with male players scoring higher on social interaction than their female counterparts (Jansz, Avis, and Vosmeer 2009). Interviews with female players of *The Sims* also revealed that they enjoyed playing the game to experience individual pleasure and relaxation (Vosmeer 2009). In the same vein, female players interviewed by Royse et al. (2007) reported that games provided a needed distraction from their daily worries. These different studies showed that playing allowed female gamers to refrain from social interaction and to separate themselves from domestic and family duties, in the same way that reading romance novels and women's magazines resulted in temporary, comfortable isolation (Hermes 1995). Boys and young men, in contrast, are attracted to gaming because playing enables them to interact with friends. In this sense it has a lot in common with, for example, playing football. Playing digital games offers ample opportunities for male bonding where social and emotional ties are based on sharing an activity rather than on disclosing oneself in intimate conversation (Durkin 2006; Jansz 2000).

In our own research we have linked social motivations to the manifestations of social identity in the game context (Jansz and Tanis 2007). We studied players of First-person shooter games who often collaborate in teams called "clans". We investigated in particular the relation between identifying with a clan and social motivations. We could differentiate between gamers who were not clan members and gamers who played in one out of three types of clans: amateur clans, professional clans (playing for money, for example in international tournaments), and semiprofessional clans. Members of an amateur or (semi)professional clan scored significantly higher on social interaction than non-clan members. The amateurs expressed a stronger motivation for social interaction than the (semi)professionals. This may be somewhat surprising, but it is probably due to the fact that amateur clans are still "under construction". They generally start as a group of friends playing together. In due course they categorize themselves as a clan, but then it takes time before they gain a position among other clans. In the process they need to affirm their shared identity. (Semi)professionals, by contrast, are already more or less established as a group and do not require a prolonged investment in their social identity.

The social identities of gamers will generally be put in meaningful self-categorizations such as "heavy gamers" or "hardcore gamers". Social identity theory has shown that identifying with one's own group results in social comparison with other groups (Ellemers, Spears, and Doosje 2002). In the case of gaming, it enables players to set themselves apart from (groups of) people who do not play, or understand, video games. Their shared experience in the laboratory will help them solidify their social identities that are still developing since the chalk line of the magic circle does not prevent interference or ridicule from others.

In conclusion

The reception of media content is particularly profound in the case of video games, because players and game characters often merge virtually, resulting in high experiential levels of presence. The "magic circle" provides a powerful metaphor underlining that the virtual merging of player and character occurs within the boundaries of the game and is temporary (Huizinga 1955; Salen and Zimmerman 2004). Playing within the magic circle amounts to experimenting in a safe laboratory, where players can conduct personal experiments or engage in testing with fellow players. In most cases the individual and social dimension are inextricably linked. The shared experience contributes to developing and sustaining a social identity as a gamer.

The account in this chapter focused on the opportunities offered for playing out identities and emotions. In the laboratory, players can identify with avatars enacting identities, including ones that would be impossible or could be embarrassing or intolerable outside the magic circle. Additionally, players can experiment safely with a wide range of participatory emotions, including ones that are controversial in real life. Although the exploration of emotions in the game generally unfolds without many moral constraints, it may nevertheless lead players to evaluate who they are and what they feel. Emotional experiences are difficult to deny and generally invite self-reflection. For example, players may seriously wonder what the performance of atrocious acts within the game reveal about themselves as a person. In other words, the emotional experience ties in with identity work.

The theoretical argument has been embedded in empirical research where possible. There still is a lot of work to be done to gain a more profound understanding of the processes unfolding during play in the laboratory. This paper focused on entertainment games. It is an open question to what extent the processes analyzed here also occur in games with non-entertainment purposes, for example in video games that aim to communicate a political message. It is conceivable that identification and emotional arousal contribute to a deeper processing of the game's message (Neys and Jansz 2010; Raessens 2006). Moreover, it is crucial to study female player experiences in more detail. As contemporary gaming culture is very much dominated by stereotypical male interests and values, the options for experimenting with identity and emotions are profoundly gendered. This does not necessarily exclude women, as it is very well possible that female players deliberately use masculinized games in order to cross gender role boundaries in the same way as millions of male players enjoy being Lara Croft.

Notes

1. Dutch gamers were interviewed about why they liked to play video games. The quotes are translated from Dutch, the gamer's names are fictional (Jansz and Grimberg 2005).

References

Beasley, Berrin, and Tracy C. Standley. 2002. Shirts vs. skins: Clothing as an indicator of gender role stereotyping in video games. *Mass Communication and Society* 5(3): 279-93.

Blizzard Entertainment. 1996. *Diablo.* Multiplatform: Blizzard Entertainment.

Bosma, Harke A., and Saskia Kunnen. 2001. Determinants and mechanisms in ego identity development: A review and synthesis. *Developmental Review* 21: 39-66.

Cohen, Jonathan. 2001. Defining identification: A theoretical look at the identification of audiences with media characters. *Mass Communication and Society* 4(3): 245-64.

Durkin, Kevin. 2006. Game playing and adolescents' development. In *Playing video games: Motives, responses, and consequences,* eds. Peter Vorderer and Jennings Bryant, 415-28. Mahwah, NJ: Erlbaum.

Ellemers, Naomi, Russell Spears, and Bertjan Doosje. 2002. Self and social identity. *Annual Review of Psychology* 53: 161-86.

Frijda, Nico H. 1986. *The emotions.* Cambridge, MA: Cambridge University Press.

—. 1989. Aesthetic emotions and reality. *American Psychologist* 45: 1546-7.

—, Peter Kuipers, and Elisabeth ter Schure. 1989. Relations among emotion, appraisal, and emotional action readiness. *Journal of Personality and Social Psychology* 57: 212-28.

Gergen, Kenneth. 1994. *Realities and relationships: Soundings in social constructionism.* Cambridge, MA: Harvard University Press.

Goldstein, Jeffrey. 2005. Violent video games. In *Handbook of Computer Game Studies,* eds. Joost Raessens and Jeffrey Goldstein, 341–58. Cambridge, MA: The MIT Press.

Hall, Stuart. 1997. *Representation: Cultural representations and signifying practices.* London: Sage Publications.

Hermes, Joke. 1995. *Reading women's magazines: An analysis of everyday media use.* Cambridge, UK: Polity Press.

Huizinga, Johan. 1955. *Homo ludens: A study of the play-element in culture* [1938]. Boston, MA: Beacon Press.

Ivory, James D. 2006. Still a man's game: Gender representation in online reviews of video games. *Mass Communication and Society* 9(1): 103-14.

Jansz, Jeroen. 1991. *Person, self and moral demands. Individualism contested by collectivism.* Leiden: DSWO Press.

—. 2000. Masculine identity and restrictive emotionality. In *Gender and emotion: Social psychological perspectives,* ed. Agneta H. Fischer, 166-86. Cambridge, MA: Cambridge University Press.

—. 2005. The emotional appeal of violent video games for adolescent males. *Communication Theory* 15(3): 219-41.

—, Corinne Avis, and Mirjam Vosmeer. 2010. Playing The Sims2: An exploration of gender differences in players' motivations and patterns of play. *New Media and Society* 12 (2): 335-51.

—, and Maarten Grimberg. 2005. Among the LAN gamers: Men and women playing video games at a public event. Paper presented at the International Communication Association, New York City.

—, and Lonneke Martens. 2005. Gaming at a LAN event: The social context of playing video games. *New Media and Society* 7(3): 333-55.

—, and Raynel G. Martis. 2007. The Lara phenomenon: Powerful female characters in video games. *Sex Roles,* 56: 141-8.

—, and Martin Tanis. 2007. Appeal of playing online first person shooter games. *CyberPsychology and Behavior* 10(1): 133-6.

—, and Mirjam Vosmeer. 2009. Girls as serious gamers: Pitfalls and possibilities. In *Serious games: Mechanisms and effects* eds. Ute Ritterfeld, Michael Cody and Peter Vorderer, 236-48. London: Routledge, Taylor and Francis.

Jenkins, Henry, and Justine Cassell. 2008. From Quake Grrls to Desperate Housewives: A decade of gender and computergames. In *Beyond Barbie and Mortal Kombat. New perspectives on gender and gaming,* eds. Yasmin B. Kafai, Carrie Heeter, Jill Denner, and Jennifer Y. Sun, 5-20. Cambridge, MA: The MIT Press.

Kestenbaum, Gerald I., and Lissa Weinstein. 1985. Personality, psychopathology, and developmental issues in male adolescent video game use. *Journal of the American Academy of Child Psychiatry* 24(3): 329-37.

Kiousis, Spiro. 2002. Interactivity: A concept explication. *New Media and Society* 4(3): 355-83.

Klimmt, Christoph, Dorothée Hefner, and Peter Vorderer. 2009. The video game experience as "true" identification: A theory of enjoyable alterations of players' self-perception. *Communication Theory* 19(4): 351-73.

Konijn, Elly A., and Johan F. Hoorn. 2005. Some like it bad: Testing a model for perceiving and experiencing fictional characters. *Media Psychology* 7(2): 107-44.

Krotoski, Aleks 2004. *Chicks and joysticks. An exploration of women and gaming.* London: The Entertainment and Leisure Software Publishers Association.

Lazarus, Richard S. 1991. *Emotion and adaptation.* Oxford: Oxford University Press.

Lee, Kwan M. 2004. Presence, explicated. *Communication Theory* 14(1): 27-50.

Livingstone, Sonia. 2004. The challenge of changing audiences: Or, what is the audience researcher to do in the age of the internet? *European Journal of Communication* 19(1): 75-86.

Lucas, Kristen, and John L. Sherry. 2004. Sex differences in video game play: A communication-based explanation. *Communication Research* 31(5): 499-523.

McLuhan, Marshall and Quentin Fiore. 1967. *The medium is the message. An inventory of effects.* New York: Bantam Books.

Neys, Joyce, and Jeroen Jansz. 2010. Political Internet games: Engaging an audience. *European Journal of Communication* 25(3): 1-15.

Oatley, Keith. 1994. A taxonomy of the emotions of literary response and a theory of identification in fictional narrative. *Poetics* 23(1): 53-74.

Raessens, Joost. 2006. Reality play: Documentary computer games beyond fact and fiction. *Popular Communication* 4(3): 213-24.

Reijmersdal, Eva van, Jeroen Jansz, Oscar Peters, and Guda van Noort. 2010. The effects of interactive brand placements in online games on children's cognitive, affective, and conative brand responses. *Computers in Human Behavior* 26(6): 1787-94.

Roseman, Ira J., Cynthia Wiest, and Tamara S. Swartz. 1994. Phenomenology, behaviors, and goals differentiate discrete emotions. *Journal of Personality and Social Psychology* 67(2): 206-21.

Royse, Pam, Joon Lee, Baasanjav Undrahbuyan, Mark Hopson. and Mia Consalvo. 2007. Women and games: Technologies of the gendered self. *New Media and Society* 9(4): 555-76.

Ruggiero, Thomas E. 2000. Uses and gratifications theory in the 21st century. *Mass communication and society* 3(1): 3-37.

Salen, Katie, and Eric Zimmerman. 2004. *Rules of play: Game design fundamentals.* Cambridge, MA: The MIT Press.

Schneider, Edward F. 2004. Death with a story. How story impacts emotional, motivational, and physiological responses to First-person shooter video games. *Human Communication Research* 30(3): 361-75.

Schott, Gareth R., and Kirsty R. Horrell. 2000. Girl gamers and their relationship with the gaming culture, *Convergence* 6(4): 36-53.

Sherry, John L., Kristen Lucas, Bradley S. Greenberg, and Ken Lachlan. 2006. Videogame uses and gratifications as predicators of use and game preference. In *Playing video games*, eds. Peter Vorderer and Jennings Bryant, 213-24. Mahwah NJ: Erlbaum.

Steinberg, Laurence, and Amanda S. Morris. 2001. Adolescent development. *Journal of Cognitive Education and Psychology* 2(1): 55-87.

Tamborini, Ron 2003. Enjoyment and social functions of horror. In *Communication and emotion. Essays in honor of Dolf Zillmann,* eds. Jennings Bryant, David Roskos-Ewoldsen, and Joanne Cantor, 417-44. Mahwah, NJ: Erlbaum.

—, and Paul Skalski. 2006. The role of presence in the experience of electronic games. In *Playing video games,* eds. Peter Vorderer and Jennings Bryant, 225-40. Mahwah, NJ: Erlbaum.

Tan, Ed S. 1996. *Emotion and the structure of narrative film: Film as an emotion machine.* Mahwah, NJ: Erlbaum.

—. 2008. Entertainment is emotion: The functional architecture of the entertainment experience. *Media Psychology* 11(1): 28-51.

—, and Jeroen Jansz. 2008. The game experience. In *Product experience,* eds. Hendrik N.J. Schifferstein and Paul Hekkert, 531-56. San Diego: Elsevier.

Vosmeer, Mirjam. 2010. *Videogames en gender. Over spelende meiden, sexy avatars en huiselijkheid op het scherm.* PhD dissertation. Amsterdam: University of Amsterdam.

Yee, Nick. 2006. Motivations for play in online games. *CyberPsychology and Behavior* 9: 772-5.

15. Playing with others: The identity paradoxes of the web as social network

Jeroen Timmermans

The person has become the portal.
Barry Wellman (2001)

In this chapter I zoom in on one of the characteristic paradoxes of modern, mediated identities, forged from a peculiar mix of individual interests and collective behavior, that can be encountered in people's use of social network sites in particular. I tentatively explore the ramifications of the World Wide Web as a social medium, in which playful, light, frivolous self-presentation of people seems to be accompanied by the serious task of coping with social pressures induced by omnipresent (communication) media. The focus here is on social network sites and the paradox they create between being alone in front of a computer screen and talking to the world at the same time. In this context a tension is also emerging between living in a highly mediated, *globalized* world and the construction, expression, and experience of *personal* and local identities.

The paradox is that we seem to be split today more than ever between the (selfish) wish for self-expression and personal growth on the one hand, and the need for communication and community building on the other hand. I shall call this contradiction *individuality* versus *collectivity*. As Steve Jones states: "It is as if a fault line exists and two sides grate against each other; on one side is social convention, the community, the force that binds us together as social beings, and on the other is individualism, the dictum that we should just be our "selves" (provided we can discover what that is) irrespective of outside forces" (1997, 27).

In his book *The individualized society* (2001), Zygmunt Bauman addresses the same paradox. He explains in what sense we should grasp modern individuality: "What the idea of 'individualization' carries is the emancipation from the ascribed, inherited and inborn determination of his or her social character: a departure rightly seen as a most conspicuous and seminal feature of the modern condition. To put it in a nutshell, 'individualization' consists in transforming human 'identity' from a 'given' into a 'task'" (2001, 144). Ironically it is because of their "dis-embedding", the loss of traditional social and moral contexts, that individuals are prompted to a frantic search for "re-embeddedness". Identity then "owes the attention it attracts and the passions it begets to being a *surrogate of community* [...] Identity sprouts on the graveyard of communities, but flourishes thanks to its promise to resurrect the dead" (ibid., 151).

Peter Sloterdijk strikingly describes our predicament with the concept of "co-isolation" (2004, 56). Modern apartment buildings are exemplary of a life in which (in the big cities at least) we are divided by no more than a few inches of wall yet socially live miles apart. It is a common phenomenon for people living in modern cities to know their neighbors' favorite TV-shows, unsolicitedly listen to their music and smell their cooking without having so much as a clue about their names. Sloterdijk compares modern societies to *foam*, a material made of countless connected but at the same time isolated bubbles, as a metaphor for the social state of modern citizens. Equally, in his recent book on the city, Jan-Hendrik Bakker sees the modern city as the site where the opposition of the individual and the collective is materialized in the form of apartment blocks (2008, 37). Life in the cities has become more anonymous, freer, but also more individualized and lonelier. The bigger the city, the more people live together, the bigger the isolation, so it seems.

In this chapter I will show that modern communication technologies push this tension even further. The World Wide Web in particular – with its tendency to encapsulate and unite people at the same time – is a paradigmatic playground for this tension in modern morality. On the web we are more than ever caught between these two tendencies of individualization and "capsularization" on the one hand, and communication and community building on the other hand. The web will be shown to serve as a source of reflexive uncertainty and computer-mediated isolation, as well as serving as a new high-tech layer of social cement.

From a social point of view, a lot of modern technologies are highly ambivalent in their nature. For one, they provide a window to the world, they open up lives, but they also close people in and serve as capsules. Technologies such as the mobile phone, the iPod, and cars connect people and make their lives public, but they are also very private media and enable their users to shield themselves from others. I explore this paradox further by looking – among other things – at the social network site Facebook, which is not only one of the most popular sites on the web, but also constitutes a prime example of this paradox.[1] I seek to illustrate in which way Facebook reinforces the paradox by introducing aspects of playfulness.

Facebook: individualized society or social individuals?

If one wants to understand what is happening in the field of new media, then it is always insightful to look at the newest generation of users. In a double sense they are generally the "early adopters" of new media appliances. For adolescents the web serves more as a medium for communication than information, clearly in contrast to the post-war generations who – besides their professional use – still use the web predominantly as a tool for collecting information.[2] The difference between younger and older users is not so much the use of the web itself – we all *google* – but lies in the frequency of use and the multimedial combination of social media they apply. Not surprisingly, therefore, persons born after 1980 are commonly referred to as being part of the "digital generation". Journalists and scientists have given this generation many different names, ranging from "Internet generation" to "dotcom generation", "network generation", "Nintendo generation", "SMS generation", "screenagers", "generation M" (for media), and "generation C" (content) (see de Haan and van 't Hof 2006, 11). Recently, a label with very positive connotations was added to this list: "Generation Einstein".[3] One of the preeminent characteristics of this generation is their savvy use of social network sites and the impact this has on their identities. According to Jos de Haan, "Young people of the same age group give birth to peer-to-peer networks, within which youngsters discuss taboos and life choices and experiment with their identities. [...] Online "experiments" teach them who they are and what their position within the social network is" (de Haan and van 't Hof 2006, 17-18).[4]

As mentioned above, Facebook is the largest of these social network sites worldwide. Founded only in February 2004, Facebook already had more than 1.1 billion active subscribers by March 2013.[5] Due to its make-up, Facebook can be seen both as a site for individual entertainment (e.g. exploring music, Facebook games) and as a tool for maintaining and building communities. Next to the "standard" features of typical social network sites, such as creating an (elaborate) personal profile, searching for and adding friends, and communicating with them by using private messages, wall comments, pokes, or chat, Facebook also offers a range of game-like applications (micro-games) and hosts numerous groups and communities one can subscribe to.

The strength of Internet ties, a report published in 2006, shows a large advantage for users of online social networking in terms of performing their social identity (Boase et al. 2006). The authors found that using Internet and e-mail expands and strengthens the social ties people maintain in the offline world. Pay-offs especially come when people use the Internet to press their social networks into action as they face major challenges and have to make important decisions. Facebook is particularly suited for reinforcing so-called "weak ties", for example for finding old classmates or colleagues. Facebook keeps chapters open of books that otherwise would have been firmly closed, apart maybe from the occasional coincidental real-life encounter. In that sense, Facebook keeps the past alive in the present. The report strongly disputes that heavy use of the Internet might diminish people's social relations. For example, e-mail has not replaced communication with others but actually supplements it, since people can now communicate with many others in their network.

Social network sites in particular create this peculiar paradox among their users of being alone in front of a terminal and talking to buddies at the same time. The web not only brings the world into your living room; it also keeps you there.[6] Moreover, social network sites are the ultimate embodiment of the identity paradoxes caused by progressing globalization. Social network sites are prime examples of what it means to live in a highly mediated, *globalized* world, but they also provide the tools for the construction, expression, and experience of highly *personal* (and often local) identities. The global and the local intermingle in such a way as to create a "glocal" form of contemporary life, infused by multiple media, in which we chat with someone in India, but sometimes no longer even know our neighbors. On the one hand, network sites facilitate encountering the like-minded, on the other hand, they give us a platform to cross swords with intellectual opponents. In other words, it can widen our horizons, but also dangerously narrow them. The web may easily serve as a "homophilic" medium: if desired, it can be used to navigate familiar circles until such a point that mere opinions become certainties. As Kenneth Gergen observed about social technologies: "The major point here is that the technologies that bring people together also allow them to remain together, to insulate themselves in a way that permits the sacralization of a dangerously restricted view" (2000, xvi). Religious extremism is a dangerous example of this ambivalence. In doing so, a website like Facebook is in danger of creating what can be called "bounded solidarity" where groups with similar interests or ideas are reinforced to such a high degree that their "ties" become so strong it causes them to close themselves off from other parts of society.

A medium as far-reaching as the World Wide Web was simply nonexistent until two decades ago. Therefore, the task of adjusting all the possibilities in terms of communication and all the information that comes with it, presents a monumental task to its users, and forces them to reassess their identities. Not in the last place, the World Wide Web with its capacity of linking people, transactions, and money globally by a mere mouse click, contributed to, or maybe even was the final stage – the missing link so to speak – of the process that supposedly turned us into truly global citizens. Incredible for someone living a mere thirty years ago, the World Wide Web has placed the world within arm's reach. I only need to pick the right website to watch live what is happening in China, Australia, or the Americas, while I chat with a colleague in Africa and check my banking account in the Netherlands! There we see why it is called the *World Wide* Web.

In the past, several other forms of media have shown the same tendency of spurring both individualistic and social forces. Modern technologies have always advocated schizophrenic lifestyles. The novel opened up universes of the mind to its readers, but it also confined them to small reading spaces and a very constricted field of attention. The vacuum cleaner was supposed to liberate women from strenuous physical tasks, but turned them into housewives instead, as the housekeeper was no longer needed. I already mentioned modern apartment blocks housing hundreds of people in close proximity, but where front doors often remain tightly shut. A fitting early example of this paradox is the so-called *flaneur*, a typical product of the modern city: "The anonymity of the crowd provided asylum for those on the margins of society who could walk about unnoticed, observing and being observed, but never really interacting with those encountered. The *flaneur* was the modern hero, able to travel, to arrive, to gaze, to move on, to be anonymous, to be in a limited zone; in other words to be out in public and moving about in the city's paved, public spaces among strangers" (Urry 2007, 69). Paul Virilio noticed a similar phenomenon with the introduction of cinema: "This machine plunges inert cinemagoers into an unprecedented form of solitude, *multiple solitude*, since, as Marcel Pagnol so aptly puts it, a thousand spectators are reduced to one in the cinema auditorium!" (1995, 9).

Facebook not only takes Pagnol's *multiple solitude* to the next level; rather, it couples multiple solitude to the *soloist multitude*: its users are part of their own embedded in-groups. Haythornthwaite and Wellman coined an appropriate expression, "networked individualism", to explain the social consequences of social network sites. Users of modern technologies are less tied to local groups and increasingly tied to looser and more geographically scattered networks. They write:

> The personalization, portability, ubiquitous connectivity, and imminent wireless mobility of the Internet all facilitate networked individualism as the basis of community. It is the individual, and neither the household

> nor the group that is becoming the primary unit of connectivity: gleaning support, sociability, information and a sense of belonging. [...] It is I-alone that is reachable wherever I am: at a house, hotel, office, highway, or shopping center. The person has become the portal (2005, 34).

One of the distinguishing features of WEB 2.0 is its artificial intelligence. In many respects the web has become smart and it sometimes even (anticipatorily) acts instead of getting direction from its users. This smartening of the web has given users an opportunity for greater customization, for making the web not only more social but, again, also more individualistic. Let us once more take Facebook as an example. Its shareholders earn their revenue almost exclusively through advertising, which can be targeted very specifically due to data mining the users' profiles. This introduces one of the biggest downsides Facebook users face. Over the years, Facebook has developed a policy of sharing more and more information from its subscribers' profiles. Actually, its success to a large degree depends on this strategy. Facebook became really popular when its builders tweaked the site in such a way that users were given the (unasked for) functionality of tracking all their friends' moves on Facebook. A company with access to your profile may get information on who your friends are, where you live, what your hobbies are, your age, education, etc. In short: information about your identity. The debate about Facebook's "open access" policy became more heated in 2010 and its designers were forced to implement some changes to limit users' visibility for the sake of their privacy and safety.[7]

The above observations beg the question whether web communities complement traditional offline communities as a source of meaning. How much do Facebook contacts really mean to us? Has blogging and chatting replaced the local pub, school, and workplace in our lives? Philosopher of technology Albert Borgmann coined the concept of "focal object" (after Heidegger), by which he meant that technological objects "assemble" people and activities in a certain way (cf. Borgmann 1984, 196-210). In old times the fireplace ("focus" = hearth) was the designated spot for people to gather and bond by telling stories and by experiencing physical warmth and intimacy. Although Borgmann laments its loss in modern times (central heating system), the concept of "focal object" is a very fitting metaphor to describe the role of media in modern day lives. Television and radio in particular have for decades been the focal objects in homes around which families got together to watch the evening news and subsequent television shows. In this sense television is characterized by the very same paradox of making life more individualistic, as individual families withdraw from the streets into their homes. Yet this process also meant the strengthening of inner-family bonds, which is why it contributed to a stronger sense of (the nuclear) community.

The web "collects" people in an entirely different way than television does. First of all, television gathers people physically: people who watch together share a designated space together; they talk about what they see on the screen, laugh about it, sometimes even cry. A desktop computer or laptop on the other hand hampers the physical sharing of experiences. At best two people – though already uncomfortable – can watch web pages or Internet movies together. In those cases where the movie clip or site is shared with someone else, it is most likely that this person will watch the clip on his/her own computer. *Personal* computers are not designed to be used by multiple people at the same time, unlike a television that invites people to watch the TV show or movie together. In that spatio-temporal sense, PCs separate people, whereas television unites them. Communicating via social network sites on a personal computer is characterized by this paradoxical feature of isolating people (physically) and bringing them (virtually) together at the same time.

Second, another important difference between the web and television/radio as tools for social cohesion is the tailoring of information that takes place on the web (WEB 2.0). Whereas television and radio are broadcasting media, i.e. one program is sent out to a multitude of viewers or listeners who all receive the same program, the web is typically a narrowcasting medium. Users can specifically target and retrieve the information they desire. As the technology behind the web grows more sophisticated, the presentation of information and the manner of communication become ever more attuned to individual users' desires. Because of this "interactive" feature of the web, one could purport that the web's influence on users' identities is a rather conservative one, as users' interests, opinions, and desires are increasingly mirrored by the web itself. On the television, the eight o'clock news does not discriminate between its viewers, but on the smartphone someone may decide what news to download and view and what not to view. Despite the option of changing channels on television and "zapping away" a particular show, the consolidation of one's identity in terms of interests and opinions is much more likely to happen on the web than on television, which can be very shocking and confronting at times.

Serious play in the digital world?

One of the most preeminent marks of playfulness lies in the expression of the ambivalence between seriousness and non-seriousness that is constitutive of all playing. On the grounds of the analysis presented above, we can now argue that Facebook is an outstanding example of how WEB 2.0 applications hand users the tools to practice this mix that characterizes late modern identity of seriousness and frivolity. Even more so, by means of social network sites, the web provides the perfect stage for people to apply playful, light, and frivolous self-presentations as a way of dealing with the utter seriousness and social pressure underlying the process of gaining status and the building of group identities. Raessens writes: "The most important play media in this context are undoubtedly mobile telephones and so-called social media, such as weblogs and social networks, including Facebook, Hyves, LinkedIn and Twitter. These are ideal social connections that playfully express what the users think they are and how they wish to be seen by others" (2009, 68).

In the case of social network sites we come across the paradox of technology offering its users extra playroom for expressing themselves freely, but at the same time WEB 2.0 applications pre-arrange online actions more than the ideologists of freedom might wish for. In the case of Facebook, users may decide on the content of their profiles, but they are certainly not free to redesign the software or tell Facebook what advertisers to allow on the site. Moreover, strong pressure from peers is exerted to take part in social networking and to develop attractive and impressive personal profiles with preferably as many friends as possible. In this sense, users are more or less "forced" into self-reflection by means of constructing personal profiles.

Social network sites have become increasingly important within the context of leading a modern life. Ever more, people derive their sense of belonging from the "placeless" networks they create around themselves. The same can be observed in mobile devices, such as mobile phones, which for their part are said to create "lonely crowds", where people are in a public space, but are completely absorbed by their communication with someone who is physically not present. Mediated communication seems to precede physical presence, thereby creating new social effects formerly unheard of. Who we are is determined by our relations to other people we engage with. Had he known Facebook, Descartes would probably have reached the conclusion "I am linked in, therefore I am!"

Starting with written texts millennia ago, media have given an impulse to self-reflection and have thrown people on their own by creating the perfect stage for self-dialogues. The construction of weblogs, personal profiles, and homepages adds the voice of others to this process; others who comment on expressions of identity. This growing reflexivity obviously reflects on users' identities: a lack of contacts/friends on Facebook can be an important (negative) element of someone's self-understanding. In this respect Facebook resembles a competition with excellence in the social realm as a goal. In other words, the more friends people have the higher their status. Just as Twitter is all about one's followers, Facebook also has become a competition to collect online friends.

The playful character of these web applications renders this "burden" of constant reflection and updating one's social network bearable. For example, social network sites allow a playful handling of photos, pictures, and the moderation of them: they leave exuberant room for jokes, for the posting of funny messages or clips, and for the challenging and teasing of friends. The speed one can react with and the flexibility to adjust one's profile anytime renders the long-term effects of these profiles as less grave. In an article on social network sites Pearson comes to a similar conclusion: "In essence, online performative space is a deliberately playful space. The fluidity and self-conscious platforms of performance allow individuals and networks of users to play with aspects of their presentations of self, and the relationship of those online selves to others without inadvertently risking privacy" (Pearson 2009, 6). Social network sites resemble games, because acting on them is characterized by a playful mood and has playful elements to it (humor, competition, teasing), but also because they constitute a world on their own. A world in which we can experiment a bit with our identity, without suffering immediate and direct consequences outside of the cybersphere.

In an article on playful cultures, Valentina Rao calls applications such as Facebook "third places" (a concept she took from Oldenburg) due to their "networked individualistic" features. She writes: "The general mood in third places is playful and marked by frivolity, verbal wordplay, and wit" (Rao 2008, 2). Third places "exist in addition to "work" or "home", a contemporary version of the agora, the tavern, the café, where people can be together and unwind. The dichotomy between organized play (often sustained by corporate interests) and free play and playfulness as in socialization is especially visible in social networks" (ibid.). Another example of such a "third place", i.e. a novel kind of semipublic, mediated sphere, are the social websites developed and used by Dutch-Moroccans (second- and third-generation immigrants). *Maroc.nl,* for instance, is a site where an extremely playful approach is adopted to the utterly serious matter of finding one's way around Dutch culture. Dutch-Moroccans are clearly trying to steer a middle course and develop a sort of "third way", caught between two cultures. They do this by coupling self-mockery to profound discussions about who they are and where they belong. As a result, next to cartoons of Dutch right-wing politician Geert Wilders, heated discussions are being held on forums about topics they are concerned with. Again, humor and irony prove an important factor in dealing with important issues.

A well-known risk in the context of establishing group identities lies in what is called "capsularization" (De Cauter 2004). De Cauter used this term to refer to very closed, inward-looking communities of like-minded people. Without judging this development and calling this feature of social websites "right" or "wrong" – after all, technologies have always been used for the worse or the better, for war or peace – we can understand this phenomenon as an example of the ludification of the web. Similar to what happens in games, these people create meaningful worlds of their own, the logic and the sense of which is hard to understand to outsiders. Just like in-games, community members "play" these games alone in front of their terminals, but are – by virtue of playing – part of a very strong wider community.

In *Homo ludens* Dutch historian Johan Huizinga (1955) demonstrated the play-element of culture. Instead of mentioning mere practices of play *within* cultures, he convincingly presented his argument that human culture as such evolves playfully. In social reality many processes run according to the logic of "make-believe", as if all of us were playing a game. Think for example of the purchasing power of money, or the legislative powers we invest in our politicians: politicians own power because people bestow it on them. As soon as a majority of people decide to stop "playing the game", rulers lose their authority. Therefore, in many social instances the choice is not between play or non-play, serious reality, but play and reality are really one. The same goes for social network sites. Their *affordance* is their playfulness. They invite users to playfully interact with each other and with the medium, while knowing the serious social mechanisms that are at play. Social network sites are "serious games": the line between play and reality is inevitably blurred. Online, all identities are to some degree playful identities.

Notes

1. In June 2010, Alexa.com, a company that tracks rates of internet traffic, places the two best-known social network sites, Facebook and YouTube, among the top 3 sites visited. The only website that had more hits was the search engine Google. Other big social network sites include MySpace, Sugababes/Superdudes, CU2, Partypeeps.

2. See for the statistics, www.marketingfacts.nl/berichten/generatieverschil_in_internetgebruik/nl.
3. See Boschma and Groen (2009). The authors claim that in order to understand the current generation of young, techno-savvy users, we have to realize that instead of seeing them as lazy screen addicts who have forgotten how to read a book and write decent papers, we should acknowledge the fact that in terms of communication through new media they have become smarter, faster, and more social than their parents' generation.
4. Author's translation.
5. For more mind-boggling figures on Facebook, see http://newsroom.fb.com/Key-Facts.
6. One might object to this statement by referring to the portable, web-based devices people carry with them. Yet, as I see it, smartphones, laptops, and iPads only strengthen the paradox I am talking about, as in essence these devices are *personal* devices, hence they are subjected to the very same paradox of combining individual use of media and group membership.
7. Go for an overview of the debate to www.readwriteweb.com/archives/facebook_privacy_explanation_debate.php.

References

Bakker, Jan Hendrik. 2008. *Welkom in megapolis: Denken over wonen, stad en toekomst.* Amsterdam: Atlas.

Bauman, Zygmunt. 2001. *The individualized society.* Cambridge, UK: Polity Press.

Boase, Jeffrey, John B. Horrigan, Barry Wellman, and Lee Rainie. 2006. The strength of Internet ties. *Pew Internet and American Life Project,* www.pewinternet.org/~/media//Files/Reports/2006/PIP_Internet_ties.pdf.

Borgmann, Albert. 1984. *Technology and the character of contemporary life.* Chicago, IL: The University of Chicago Press.

Boschma, Jeroen, and Inez Groen. 2009. *Generatie Einstein: Slimmer, sneller en socialer,* Amsterdam: Pearson Education.

De Cauter, Lieven. 2004. *The capsular civilization: On the city in the age of fear.* Rotterdam: NAi Publishers.

Gergen, Kenneth J. 2002. The challenge of absent presence. In *Perpetual contact: Mobile communication, private talk, public performance,* eds. James Katz and Mark Aakhus. Cambridge, UK: Cambridge University Press.

Haan, Jos de, and Christian van 't Hof, eds. 2006. *Jaarboek ICT en samenleving: De digitale generatie,* Amsterdam: Boom.

Haythornthwaite, Caroline, and Barry Wellman. 2002. The Internet in everyday life: An introduction. In *The Internet in everyday life,* eds. Barry Wellman and Caroline Haythornthwaite, 3-41. Malden, MA; Oxford: Blackwell.

Huizinga, Johan. 1955. *Homo ludens: A study of the play-element in culture* [1938]. Boston, MA: Beacon Press.

Jones, Steve. 1997. *Virtual culture: Identity and communication in cybersociety.* London: Sage Publications.

Pearson, Erika. 2009. All the World Wide Web's a stage: The performance of identity in online social networks. *First Monday* 14(3). www.firstmonday.org/article/view/2162/2127.

Raessens, Joost. 2009. *Homo ludens 2.0. Metropolis M*, Amsterdam.

Rao, Valentina. 2008. Playful culture and the glamorization of everyday (virtual) life: Elements of play in Facebook applications. *Forum – University of Edinburgh postgradual journal of culture and the arts* 2. www.forumjournal.org/site/issue/special/play/valentina-rao.

Sloterdijk, Peter. 2004. *Sphären III*: Schäume. Frankfurt a. M.: Suhrkamp.

Urry, John. 2007. *Mobilities*, Cambridge, UK: Polity Press.

Virilio, Paul. 1995. *The art of the motor.* Minneapolis: University of Minnesota Press.

Wellman, Barry. 2001. Physical place and cyber-place: The rise of networked individualism. *International Journal for Urban and Regional Research*, 25(2): 227-52.

—, and Caroline Haythornthwaite, eds. 2002. *The Internet in everyday life*. Oxford: Blackwell Publishers.

16. New media, play, and social identities

Leopoldina Fortunati

Introduction[1]

In this chapter I focus on the motivations behind the current relationship between new media, play, and social identities in a framework of general, sociological categories. In particular, I intend to situate my analysis at the juncture between ludic culture, social control, and the social construction of the "ir-responsible" identity. The reason for this choice is that contemporary ludic culture can be quite well understood in light of the current imposition of social control and the mass resistance that is building against it. I am interested in answering the following research question: what is the meaning and the social function of play in postmodern society? If this question can be answered, then a different perspective from which to analyze this triple relationship will perhaps emerge.

My hypothesis is that games can currently be understood as a new "opium" of the people (to draw from a Marxian expression) and an important piece of the political economy of gender. However, for this same reason, they also offer a field of experimentation for the emergence of a new counter-power on the part of the users. The recent ludic culture, which has developed in postmodern society, might be understood as one of the outcomes of this arm-wrestling between capital and multitude.

This chapter is structured as follows. After the introduction, I will discuss the culture of games and its social meaning in the shift to the capitalist system. Then in the second section, I will analyze how ludic culture has been reorganized for reasons of social control and valorization. The third section addresses the question of the social construction of the ir-responsible identity in postmodernity. Finally, I will present and discuss some data from various research projects I carried out on new media in the last two decades and advance some concluding remarks.

Ludic culture in modernity

The history and the meaning of ludic culture owe much to Johan Huizinga's seminal work *Homo ludens* (1955). According to Umberto Eco (2002), Johan Huizinga introduces two important concepts. These are the idea that culture is a whole of different social phenomena from art to sport, and the idea of the cultural invariant. These two concepts – which for that time were revolutionary – allow us to frame the notion of game in an original way.

Games represent forms of struggle and challenges against death (for example the funeral games practiced in northern Africa), against natural elements (cross-country games), against hostile forces (war games), and, finally, against oneself (challenging personal fear, weakness, doubts, and so on). They involve fight, risk (gamble) and pretense in a framework in which somebody wins and somebody else loses (Rovatti and Zoletto 2005). The winner and the loser represent the symbol of the fight between the forces of life and, in ancient Greek culture, those of death, the cosmic and biological conflict connected to the wheat cycle, presided over by the goddess Demeter. Games are a parallel and fictitious world, built as a complex system in which the totality of figures, symbols, rules, behaviors, and instruments matter. As Eco argues, both the laws of language (Saussure) and logic as well as mathematics (from Wittgenstein to the theory of games) are based on a ludic structure (Eco 2002, xi). The various combinations of a game represent models and patterns of true life, but in a simplified fashion. However, the simplification and stability of the social order realized in the game and the sclerotization of the rule systems, action schemas, and combinatory matrixes of possible moves, which it pursues, have given support to the progression from nature to culture.

According to Chevalier and Gheerbrant (1966), since Greek and Roman times, every city has organized public games on the occasion of religious feasts, in which the allied cities participated. The ludic dimension had the function to resolve possible internal tensions, which were expressed and exteriorized through the social rite of games. The outcome was the strengthening of the unit of the group and the development of social cohesion. In the course of time, the social function of games was kept alive, by allowing the coagulation of the civic sense and the national feeling. Indeed for the inhabitants of most cities and countries, public games are still used today to build a bond which recalls common interests and origins (for example the Olympic Games or World Championships). Private children's and adult's games replicate public games, but instead of developing social cohesion they serve to create a harmonious individual. In their study of children, Piaget and Inhelder (1966) note that play is the way in which they assimilate the real to the self without constrictions and sanctions.[2] In fact, games activate the player's imagination and stimulate emotions, while the players exchange immaterial labor. For children in particular, the game is a rite of acceptation of the reality principle and it prepares their path towards adaptation to the real object. For the adult players, the game represents an occasion for investing their libido with the consequence that the game revitalizes their life.

The development of modern individuality has sacrificed the ludic aspect of life for the construction of the free and responsible individual (Huizinga 1996). In *The autumn of the Middle Ages* (1996), Huizinga describes admirably how medieval individuals with their formidable relationship with the ludic culture were obliged to make room for the modern individual. The new order of the original accumulation of capital swept away entire territories of ludic culture. The end of serfdom and the successive intervention of *habeas corpus* earned the old serf new rights, but also new responsibilities.[3] And with individual responsibility came added concerns, which are the opposite of play.

Moreover, the development of the capitalistic system and the organization of its new social order introduced the lengthening of the working day and a discipline of labor that fought violently to suppress ludic culture. The reason is evident: ludic culture was seen as an enemy of the productivity of labor.

The reproduction of the working class was seen in terms of the mere reproduction of the energies that were necessary for the worker to return to work day after day and be productive. In capitalistic society workers' games were contrasted not only at the stage of the original accumulation of capital, but also in the following stage of the development of big industry. Indeed, when the survival of the ludic culture was allowed, it was mainly for children and partly for the women of the dominant classes, while almost the entire lifespan of proletarians was reduced to working time. Ludic culture was taken away even from children of the working class, who were sent to the factory to work from an early age. Consequently, ludic culture went underground, but it was never defeated.

It was only with the great cycle of working-class struggles that reduced the hours in the working day that play re-emerged. Gradually, the working class earned a certain amount of time, subtracted from work, for personal enjoyment. The reduction of the working day opened the possibility for men in particular but also for children to enjoy time dedicated to play. The right to play became part of the struggle of the working class for improvement in their quality of life. This particular historical dynamic raises the important question about the relationship of women and games. While children re-appropriated games as a way to learn, and male adults re-appropriated games as a way to reaffirm their stronger social power over women, working class women had very little time to dedicate to play. This exclusion of women from games – more attempted than realized (see the playful component of fashion) – deserves to be stressed, because, as we will see below, the politics of games is part of the general politics in society carried out both by capital and the working class.

Strangely enough, Marx, who was a careful observer and critical analyst of capitalist society, never conceptualized the realm of the game as a field of struggle. In Marxian discourse, in fact, the game is never mentioned in the descriptions of the activities that are possible for one to experience once the revolution triumphs over the capitalistic system, that is to say, within a socialist or communist society. In his early writings, and especially in *The German ideology* (1846), Marx defines a multidimensional individual who is characterized by an exclusive sphere of activity, but who can hunt in the morning, go fishing in the afternoon, and be a critic in the evening, without becoming a professional hunter, fisherman. or critic (2005, 24). In this famous passage, Marx recalls Jonathan Swift (1677–1745), who believed that rest and amusement might be reached by changing one's activity rather than by not doing anything at all or by playing. Marx returns to this idea in the first book of *The capital* (1867) when he writes about future education. He argues that in the communist society the educational strategy for all children beyond a certain age will be to engage in productive labor alongside study and gymnastics with the purpose not only of increasing social production, but also of producing harmonious human beings (Marx 1867, 530). It is interesting to observe that children's need to play is totally ignored. Although he clearly recognizes the strategic importance of the reduction of the working day in communist society – which in the third book of *The capital* was viewed as the realm of freedom – Marx totally ignores games as this passage shows.

After his early writings – *Economic and philosophical manuscripts* (1844), *The German ideology* (1846), and *Critique of the Gotha programme* (1875) – Marx is very cautious in prefiguring the socialist (communist) society, although he frequently mentions that in a communist society there will be a free development of individuals inside a framework of rational relationships with other individuals. Even though the four books of *The capital* and also the *Grundrisse* contain very few elaborations on this topic, one concept arises very clearly: a fundamental condition for the advent of the realm of freedom is a reduction of the working day (1867, 933). The overall message of Marxian writing is that before accomplishing the revolution, there is no time to play, but only to fight. The Marxian argument that class struggle and revolution are serious matters (and not a gala dinner) is in a certain sense mirrored at the psychological level by Freud. Freud (1920) argues that children do not actually know reality because they play with things, while it is only by working with things that one can understand the world. It is only through work that one can know and meet reality. The adherence to the principle of reality requires someone to be distanced from pleasure and play which conveys that reality. Becoming an adult involves the process of separating oneself from pleasure.

Ludic culture in capitalistic societies and the theory of social control

A good starting point for understanding the game in capitalistic societies is to consider the theory of social control (Gallino 1993). According to this theory, social control usually includes the mechanisms, reactions, and sanctions that a community elaborates and applies with the intention: a) to prevent deviance; b) to eliminate an already occurring deviance (in this case the aim is to compel the social actor to behave again according to the norm); and c) to impede the act of deviance from being extended to other people (see also Ross 1901). In light of this theory, the game can be seen as Gramsci argued (1948–51) as one of the mechanisms of social control in terms of the control of social imagination or cultural hegemony. More recently, Castells (2008) stated that the power over minds is the main power in democratic systems and becomes a strategic terrain of struggle. Other authors, such as Borrelli (2000), underline that in the eighteenth and nineteenth centuries one of the most powerful and effective strategies of social control was the production of a series of cultural tools (novels, pictures, movies, and so on), which had the effect of disciplining and controlling people's imaginations. The struggles for the reduction of the working day had the effect of leaving male workers a certain amount of time liberated from the factory, while women, who were becoming increasingly "housewives", were burdened with the problem of organizing the "reproductive" working day. In other words, there was the problem of dealing with the time dedicated to the production and reproduction of the labor force. Very soon, it became clear that this "leisure" time and all the activities connected to it – the family and the education of new generations – were terrains in which the working and the ruling class would have held opposing perspectives.

The interest of the capitalist system was to take control of the social imagination and to organize all these activities in a way that had to be functional to maintain the status of the working class and social order generally. In capitalism this could only be achieved by making imagination, emotion, and affection like commodities. This strategy meant first of all the inclusion of the domestic sphere inside the overall process of valorization, by constructing a double register. This process apparently had to continue to be represented as natural, while in reality it was included in the general process of surplus value. The result was that the sphere of reproduction of the labor force grew in size and relevance. In the second volume of *Grundrisse* (160ff.), Marx argues that the costs of information and communication (as well as of transportation) and the surplus labor they require should be included in the production process. This means that they should be seen as spheres of valorization, which work as a bridge between the spheres of production and reproduction. Moreover, in the era of globalization, social, reproductive wealth is capitalized to a very high measure and almost all the individual's needs are increasingly put as social, in the sense that they have to be satisfied by means of an individual exchange. The current stage of the capitalist system describes this specific relationship between the capital and the general, collective conditions of social production (including labor force reproduction), as I argued elsewhere (Fortunati 2007). Last, but not least, immaterial labor is carried out to a different degree by men and women, and by children and adults: there are those who consume more (children, adult males, the elderly) and those who continue to perform more of this type of labor, namely women (Bonke 2004). Negotiation over the division of domestic labor continues to be open, even if in the last two decades there has been a kind of stalemate in negotiations between men and women. What I mean by "stalemate" is that negotiations between men and women have remained at an individual level, because of the decline of the feminist movement in Europe and the US. The lack of collective negotiation has meant that the division of labor inside the family has registered very slow progress, whereby in other spheres of everyday life there is a stagnation (e.g. with regard to political participation and representation), if not a regression (e.g. in relation to women's security). In this stalemate, the spread of new technologies in the home has often been used by men as a way of getting out of doing domestic work, thus establishing a kind of presence-absence in their relations with their partners and children.

Secondly, the commodification of the reproductive life has meant the reorganization of immaterial labor. Marx can help us understand the meaning of this reorganization. In the fourth book of *The capital*, Marx observes that the capitalist system does not adapt well to certain types of immaterial production such as art and poetry and he insists it is very important to conceive of material (and immaterial) production in their historical determinate forms (1867, 445). Towards the end of this book, he distinguishes two forms of immaterial production: the former consists of material goods (books, pictures, etc.), and the latter consists of final products, which are not separable from the act of production itself. Examples of this second kind of immaterial production are those performed by artists, orators, actors, teachers, doctors, priests, and so on. However, Marx concludes this discourse by stating "all these manifestations in this field are so insignificant, if we compare them to the whole of production, that they can be completely ignored" (1961, 610-1). On the contrary, if we analyze the immaterial production in the particular historical moment since the end of the Second World War, it shows that postindustrial capitalism has led to an expansion of immaterial production (Hardt and Negri 2000). Moreover, this recent expansion of immaterial labor has been characterized by a shift from the second type of immaterial production – production of material goods such as books, etc. – to the first – production of goods that are not separated from the act of production itself (Fortunati 2007). The immaterial production whose products are commodities that are acquired outside the home and consumed in the domestic sphere has become more popular. Games are a good example of this change. Games in fact, while not being inseparable from the act of production, often require support. Think, for instance, of toys that serve to sustain games. These supports have become increasingly technological devices, by means of which consistent parts of reproductive immaterial labor have been outsourced, "machinized," and industrialized.

The industrialization of cultural and entertainment products has made possible a pervasive control of the content conveyed and thus of the diffusion of the ruling-class ideology. Owning and controlling the production structures of information, communication, entertainment, and knowledge has given the ruling classes enormous power to shape the beliefs of people. On the opposite side, the interest of the working class was to use the "reproductive" time for developing a political awareness of their conditions of life and organizing struggles to improve it, for fighting and expressing their needs and desires, for gaining information and tools to develop knowledge and sociability. Ludic culture has become a field in which capital tries to use all the articulations of the process of immaterial production to its advantage, while the multitude were doing the same, but from their own point of view.

Social construction of the ir-responsible identity and the political economy of gender

After the Second World War, class struggles were so powerful that social and political control over the reproductive time of the proletariat was very difficult, although a strong development of the industrialization process of immaterial labor had taken place. One way of keeping or obtaining hegemony at the social level by capital was through the commodification of ludic culture. In the attempt to re-take social and political control over the working class, which was becoming a variable increasingly independent from economic development, ludic culture has been absorbed by the process of value production. A pivotal moment of this process has been the construction of the "ir-responsible" identity of men. If in the modern development of the capitalistic system the construction of the workers' identity was carried out in the direction of individual responsibility, at this precise moment a different identity was created, what I have termed ir-responsible. In modernity, play was reduced and disciplined, while in late modernity it has become a place of control (and re-elaboration of social conflicts), development of the capacity to work, and the shaping of ephemeral social identities. Alongside a serious worker identity, the individual – especially the male – was then allowed to cultivate a ludic pleasure during his spare time. This basically had two consequences: 1) the legitimation of the masculine right to play; 2) the re-imposition of a new lengthening of the working day for all (men and women) by using the entertainment industry.

In regard to the first aspect, an important change was affected by the social construction of gender identity. A peculiar ludic culture was in fact developed at a particular historical moment – the 1990s – in which there was a strong request by women to share with their husbands, brothers, and sons the domestic burden in a more equal way. However, the division of domestic labor in Europe, which was unequal (Bonke 2004), continued to remain that way. The information and entertainment industry was able to take advantage of men's interests in embracing the new electronic, ludic culture. These industries acted as sirens capable of attracting and legitimating, through technological charm, men's reluctant behavior towards women's requests. In reality this was not only an economic operation, which aimed to acquire new sectors for the market, but it was also a political operation. Men gained social legitimacy to play and thus did not have to share equally in the housework with women, children, ill people, and elderly. This strategy had two very important advantages: on the one hand, it kept women subordinated in society and in the family, and on the other hand, it allowed the psychic control of males. A male who plays inside an IT framework is a male who probably is less available to fight or to be supportive of the class interests of the other weak parts of the population. It is a male who probably has less time to devote to political debates and civic awareness. What is more functional to the capital of a man who defends his old social privilege of being able to dedicate part of his time to the reproduction of games (see, for example, the masculine tradition of games in pubs and bars such as cards and darts)?

In fact, electronic ludic culture also had the effect of discouraging further class solidarity between men and women. Instead of assuming an equal part of the domestic burden, many men began to dedicate much of their domestic time to games. The social legitimation of this behavior was subdued, but effective in recognizing for men the traditional "right" to dedicate part of their spare time to games, with the real consequence of a significant number of domestic labors being drawn to work in Western Europe from eastern countries. For example, migrant women from Ukraine, Moldova, and Romania have contributed to fill the holes of men's ir-responsibility at a domestic level, by caring for the elderly, children, disadvantaged people, and the sick.

In a second moment (in the last decade) the use of the entertainment industry to re-take the social and political control over the multitude was addressed more ecumenically to men as well as to women, to children as well as to adults. Capitalist penetration into the world of games has radically changed the dimension, structure, and social meaning of the game, attempting to affirm its hegemony also in this field. Private games have become isolated, sedentary, machinized, and designed with an industrial logic. This is no surprise, as Latour (1988) suggests, since technological artifacts are politics pursued by other means. In global societies the process of submission of games to the capitalist logic has been accomplished, also thanks to the fact that, as Sennett (1999) argues, the capitalistic organization of everyday life is characterized by the myth of labor as a totalizing dimension which presides all the time over life. The way in which these tools are designed also concurs with this ir-responsibility. In fact, users generally do not know how computers and the Internet work. This, of course, means a devaluation of the sophisticated intelligence that is embodied in these tools.

Contemporary society has developed a divergent view of play: the new organization of immaterial labor builds on the one related to play which is one of the most prosperous postindustrial sectors and so it has a strong interest in compelling all people to play. However, the general logic of social production requires that play is disciplined and compatible with the overall organization of everyday life, with the consequence that today individuals are subject to an ambivalent, political, and social strategy which, on the one hand, strongly stimulates them to play and, on the other hand, discourages them from doing so. This ambivalent strategy has an economic motivation that explains and supports it. As Marx argues at the end of the first volume of the *Grundrisse*, capital tends to create free time for society, minimizing the necessary labor and at the same time pushing the labor to its boundless limits (1857-58, 414-8). The pursuit of social control through games, however, is a quite complicated strategy, which risks, as we saw, becoming difficult to govern.

Ludic culture in global societies and concluding remarks

Can it then be concluded that the contemporary ludic culture represents only a capitalist initiative? Not at all. The resistance against labor and its sabotage often has a name: game. There is a large amount of literature on the fact that people at work play online games during their breaks to alleviate stressful situations. People try to transform the disciplinary world in a big play, in whose interstices unsuspected protagonists nestle, such as the group of elderly women playing with a mobile phone investigated by Carla Ganito (2007). There is in fact a liberating pleasure from the bottom up inside the game, which can also become prevalent and therefore dysfunctional. For example, as many research projects report, users have redesigned information and communication technologies, conceived and designed to inform and to communicate, for amusement. A recurrent metaphor in the research on the images of the new media was in fact the "toy" (Fortunati 1995). According to a survey, amusement is one of the three main reasons people use information and communication technologies, in addition to the organization of social relationships and time management (Fortunati 1998). A survey I carried out in 1996, and partially replicated in 2009, on the diffusion and appropriation of ICTs in the five most populous and industrialized European countries – Italy, France, Germany, Spain, and the UK –shows that the information and communication technologies are used to amuse, in addition to facilitating social relationships and helping time management. For instance, in 1996, the mobile phone was perceived by Europeans first of all as a time management aid (M=3.03, SD 1.53), then as a facilitator of social relationships (M=2.76, SD 1.54) and, finally, as an amusement tool (M=2.44, SD 1.47) (Fortunati and Manganelli 1998). While in 2009, the rankings had changed; the mobile phone was most appreciated as a facilitator of social relationships (M=3.38, SD 1.34), then as a time management aid (M=3.25, SD 1.37) and, finally, as an amusement tool (M=3.08, SD 1.38). Although the amusement use of the mobile phone had remained in third place, it must be noted that the mean increased from 2.44 to 3.08 and that this was the highest increase obtained in the evaluation of these three purposes. People, therefore, increasingly use the mobile phone in order to amuse themselves.

However, when we consider Beijing, China, the assessment of the mobile phone as a tool of amusement is lower than in Europe since it reaches a mean of 2.95 (SD 1.56) (Fortunati, Manganelli, Law, and Yang 2008a). However, in Beijing the importance of the mobile as an instrument of amusement emerges as a predictor both of the amount of mobile calls and text messages (Fortunati, Manganelli, Law, and Yang 2009). This result shows that those who play with the mobile are not subject to the danger of de-socialization, but that on the contrary gaming is an activity which is associated with a more intense relational use of this device. Other results of the regression analysis for the amusement function of the mobile phone show that as one's education level decreases, the use of this device for amusement increases. This means that lowly educated users find the mobile phone more useful to amuse themselves. If, at this point, we evaluate the Internet, for a comparison, it ranks first in terms of amusement (M=4.11, SD 1.29), given that online games are extremely popular in China. With regard to the Internet, the respondents who are most likely to rate the amusement it might offer most highly are males, including those with high levels of education, those from urban backgrounds, the young as well as the affluent.

This comparison between Europe and China shows that cultural differences should be taken into account carefully in order to understand specific approaches to new media in respect to ludic culture. Gender differences also need to be closely investigated since they cross cultural differences and are very sensitive to historical changes.

Finally, if we look at the mobile phone from a qualitative point of view, it is clear that the play component is also supported by other aspects, such as fashion (Fortunati 2005; Ling 2003, Katz and Sugjyama 2005), music (May and Hearn 2005), and games (Phillips, Butt, and Blaszczynski 2006). These playful aspects may be seen as peripheral to the mere communication process, but in reality they are structurally constitutive of the image of the mobile phone and represent a prominent part inside the construction and negotiation of contemporary human social identities.

From this analysis it can be clearly seen that a battle is underway today between capital and the multitude over the social meaning of the game. Games are now a commodity and as such their production and consumption have changed. The definition that emerged from Huizinga's work of the game as cultural invariant must come to terms with socio-economic concepts like "commodity", "immaterial labor", "capitalist system", and so on.

Notes

1. I am very grateful to Roberto Albarea for devoting time to reading this paper and giving me precious feedback on it.
2. Furthermore, they pose the problem of the rules of a game as social institutions and of their transmission from one generation to the next.
3. "The *Habeas Corpus* Act 1679 is an Act of the Parliament of England (31 Cha. 2 c. 2) passed during the reign of King Charles II by what became known as the *Habeas Corpus* Parliament to define and strengthen the ancient prerogative writ of *habeas corpus*, whereby persons unlawfully detained cannot be ordered to be prosecuted before a court of law" (from Wikipedia: http://en.wikipedia.org/wiki/Habeas_Corpus_Act_1679).

References

Arvidsson, Adam. 2006. "Quality singles": Internet dating and the work of fantasy. *New Media and Society* 8(4): 671-90.

Bonke, Jens. 2004. The modern husband/father and wife/mother – how do they spend their time? *European Observatory on the Social Situation, Demography and Family and Austrian Institute for Family Studies*, Vienna.

Borrelli, Davide. 2000. *Il filo dei discorsi: teoria e storia sociale del telefono*. Roma: Luca Sossella editore.

Chevalier, Jean, and Gheerbrant, Alain. 1966. *Dictionnaire des symboles*. Vol. II. Paris: Editions Robert Laffont S.A. e Editions Jupiter.

Eco, Umberto. 2002. Introduzione. In *Homo ludens*, Johan Huizinga, vii-xxxii. Torino: Einaudi.

Fortunati, Leopoldina. 1995. *The arcane of reproduction: housework, prostitution, labor and capital*. New York: Autonomedia.

—, ed. 1995. *Gli italiani al telefono*. Milano: Angeli.

—. 1998. *Telecomunicando in Europa*. Milano: Angeli.

—, and Anna Maria Manganelli. 1998. La comunicazione tecnologica: Comportamenti, opinioni ed emozioni degli Europei. In *Telecomunicando in Europa*, ed. Leopoldina Fortunati, 125-94. Milano: Angeli.

—. 2003. Real people, artificial bodies. In *Mediating the human body: Technology, communication and fashion*, eds. Leopoldina Fortunati, James E. Katz, and Raimonda Riccini, 61-71. Mahwah, NJ: Erlbaum.

—. 2005. Mobile phones and fashion in post-modernity. *Telektronikk*, 3/4: 35-48.

—. 2006. User design and democratization of the mobile phone. *First Monday* Special Issue 7.

—. 2007. Immaterial labor and its machinization. *Ephemera. Theory & Politics in Organization*, 7(1): 139-57.

—, and Anna Maria Manganelli, Pui-lam Law, and Shanhua Yang. 2008. Beijing calling... Modernization and the social effects of new media in China. *Knowledge, Technology, and Policy*, 21(1): 19-27.

—, and Anna Maria Manganelli, Pui-lam Law and Shanhua Yang. 2009. Practices of Mobile Phone Use in Beijing. In *Communities in action: papers in community informatics*, eds. Larry

Stillman, Graeme Johanson and Rebecca French, 163-81. Newcastle Upon Tyne: Cambridge Scholars Publishing.

Freud, Sigmund. 1920. Beyond the pleasure principle. In *The standard edition of the complete psychological works of Sigmund Freud*, Vol. 18. London: Hogarth Press.

Gallino, Luciano. 1993. *Dizionario di sociologia*. Torino: Tea, UTET.

Ganito, Carla. 2007. *Mobile phone as entertainment*. Lisbon: Paulus.

Goffman, Erving. 1961. *Encounters: Two studies in the sociology of interaction*. Indianapolis, IN: Bobbs-Merrill.

Gramsci, Antonio. 1982. Quaderni del carcere, 1948-1951, *a cura di F. Platone. Torino: Einaudi.*

Hardt, Michael and Antonio Negri. 2000. *Empire*. Cambridge, MA: Harvard University Press.

Huizinga, Johan 1996. *The autumn of the Middle Ages*. Chicago, IL: University of Chicago Press.

— 1955. *Homo ludens: a study of the play-element in culture* [1938]. Boston, MA: Beacon.

Katz, James E., and Satomi Sugiyama. 2005. Mobile phones as fashion statements: the co-creation of mobile communication's public meaning. In *Mobile communications: Re-negotiation of the social sphere*, eds. Rich Ling and Per Pedersen, 63-81. London: Springer.

Latour, Bruno. 1988. How to write "The Prince" for machines as well as machinations. In *Technology and social process*, ed. Brian Elliott, 20-43. Edinburgh: Edinburgh University Press.

Ling, Rich. 2003. Fashion and vulgarity in the adoption of the mobile telephone among teens in Norway. In *Mediating the human body: Technology, communication and fashion*, eds. Leopoldina Fortunati, James E. Katz, and Raimonda Riccini, 93-102. Mahwah, NJ: Erlbaum.

Marx, Karl. 1857-58. *Grundrisse der Kritik der politischen Ökonomie.* (It. trans. 1970. *Lineamenti fondamentali della critica dell'economia politica*, 2.vols, Firenze: La Nuova Italia).

—. 1867. *Das Kapital. Kritik der politischen Ökonomie*. Band 1. (It. trans. *Il Capitale. Critica dell'Economia Politica*, vol.1-4. Roma: Editori Riuniti. 1964).

—, and Friedrich Engels. 1846. *Deutsche Ideologie* (It. trans. *L'ideologia tedesca*. Roma: Editori Riuniti, 2005).

—. 1844. *Economic and* philosophic manuscripts *of* 1844 (It. trans. Manoscritti economico-filosofici del 1844. *In* Karl *Marx, Opere filosofiche giovanili*, a cura di G. Della Volpe. *Roma: Editori Riuniti*).

—. 1875. *Critique of the Gotha Programme* (It. trans. *Critica al programma di Gotha*. Milano: Feltrinelli, 1968).

May, Harvey, and Greg Hearn. 2005. The mobile phone as media. *International Journal of Cultural Studies*, 8(2): 195-211.

Phillips, James G., Sarah Butt, and Alex Blaszczynski. 2006. Personality and self-reported use of mobile phones for games. *CyberPsychology & Behavior* 9(6): 753-8.

Piaget, Jean, and Bärbel Inhelder. 1966. *La psychologie de l'enfant*. Paris: P.U.F.

Ross, Edward A. 1901. *Social control: A survey of the foundations of order*. New York: The MacMillan Co.

Rovatti, Pier A., and Davide Zoletto. 2005. *La scuola dei giochi*. Milano: Bompiani.

Sennett, Richard. 1999. *The corrosion of character: The personal consequences of work in new capitalism*. New York: W.W. Norton & Company.

17. Playing life in the metropolis: Mobile media and identity in Jakarta[1]

Michiel de Lange

Introduction: urban identity in Jakarta

How do mobile media technologies shape the identities of city dwellers? In Indonesia the mobile phone – or *handphone* – has rapidly gained in popularity (Figure 1). Reasons include the lagging state of fixed telephony in homes; its affordability even for low-income people; and omnipresent branding that induces an acute sense of "must have". Most importantly and central in this chapter, mobile phones offer urban Indonesians rich opportunities for identity construction and expression. In this chapter, I look at how mobile media shape the construction and performance of identities that are specific to life in Indonesia's capital city, Jakarta. Jakarta is both a city-world and a world-city (Augé 2008, xii). As "Indonesia in small", Jakarta reflects the nation's ethnic, religious, and cultural diversity. However, Jakarta's urban culture and identity transcend this mosaic. Unlike most other Indonesian cities, in Jakarta the shared symbols, interactions in public, and modes of self-presentation are not based on the rules of one traditional regional culture. Young people in particular base their identities on shared (though contested) ideas about what it means to live a "modern urban life" in the capital city. Mobile media technologies have quickly become part of this dynamic urban culture and have helped to define what it means to be a "modern Indonesian". In this chapter, based on ethnographic research, I examine two defining urban identity practices: *gengsi* (the display of prestige) and *bergaul* (the art of modern socializing), and explore some pervasive tensions that Indonesians feel between the adoption of new technologies and the construction of modern identities.

The discussion of mobile media and Indonesian urban identities revisits the idea of narrative identity that was introduced by philosopher Paul Ricoeur. According to Ricoeur, personal and group identities emerge out of ongoing processes of reflexive self-interpretation (1992). Both the interpretation of what it means to be and to have a "self" and imagining a shared sense of belonging to particular social and cultural groups are mediated. Ricoeur sees the literary narrative as the privileged medium for self-understanding, and for social and cultural identifications (ibid, 114ff.).

Storytelling mediates identity in three "mimetic" steps. People implicitly pre-understand their lives as composed of narrative elements (*mimesis*$_1$); they actively construct plotted stories about their lives and those of others (*mimesis*$_2$); and they reflexively read and understand themselves as narrative characters in these stories that come to prescribe further actions in life (*mimesis*$_3$) (Ricoeur 1984, 52-76; 1988, 248; 1992, 157-9). In this view people relate to themselves, to others, and to their environment via the media that they know and use. Although it is a tremendously powerful model it does have a number of weak aspects (de Lange 2010, 229-42). Two of these are addressed in this chapter. First, the culturally specific media and identity practices described in this chapter suggest that the notion of narrative identity is rooted in Western societies with strong literary traditions and ignores other possible cultural blueprints for identity mediation. The findings from Jakarta prompt us to revisit universalist claims about narrative as the privileged medium for identity construction. Second, various authors have proposed to use the notion of play as a heuristic lens to look at the specifics of identity construction in relation to digital media technologies (this publication; de Lange 2010; de Mul, Frissen, and Raessens 2005; de Mul 2005; Raessens 2006; 2014; Timmermans 2010). The question explored in this chapter then is how mobile media practices shape the identities of Jakarta urbanites, and how this can be understood in terms of playfulness.

Handphone *gengsi*

Gengsi means prestige or status display. It originally connoted family standing and class. Under the regime of President Suharto's New Order (1965-98) and its associated economic boom, the notion has shifted from an interior "innate" property to an image achieved by outward appearances. Appearing prestigious involves the possession and display of material goods that symbolically convey progress and cosmopolitanism. The notion regularly recurs in descriptions of Indonesian consumer society in general (van Leeuwen 1997; Sastramidjaja 2000). And it recurs in analyses of Indonesian technological culture in particular (Barendregt 2008, 164; de Lange 2001, 19, 36, 82). Indonesians rarely use *gengsi* to describe themselves, but frequently ascribe *gengsi* to other people or to indicate the general Indonesian obsession with conveying impressions through status symbols. The moral attitude towards *gengsi* is ambiguous. It is synonymous with consumptive materialistic hedonism and treated with mockery, contempt,

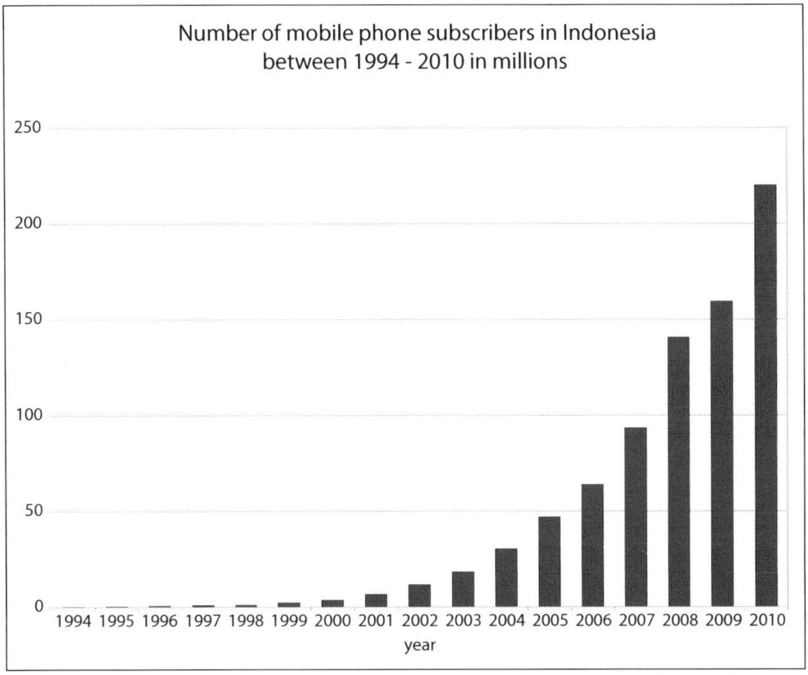

Fig. 1: Number of mobile phone subscribers in Indonesia 1994-2010 in millions (predominantly prepaid). The number of mobile phone subscriptions comprised almost 92% of the population total in 2010. This does not mean that 92% of the population own a mobile device, since many Indonesians actually have more than one subscription.[2]

or concern. It is also the measure of a "modern lifestyle" and seen as a source of pride and self-worth (Sastramidjaja 2000, 51).

Mobile media technologies have become an indispensable part of *gengsi*. Prestige can be conveyed by the mobile phone as a material artifact. The device rubs off its prestigious qualities on the individual bearer. Technology journalist Budi Putra says: "Indonesians like to possess prestigious devices. Technical specifications are not important. The phone is used to express oneself, to make one feel higher. I'd say for 80% of people the mobile phone is about *gengsi* and at most 20% really knows and uses the technology".[3] Two editors of Telset, one of the many printed glossies about the mobile phone, explain: "The mobile phone has become a kind of benchmark of the individual. The mobile phone is an object you carry with you all the time and can put on display at any moment. It is seen as part of someone's social status. Someone who doesn't have a mobile phone is thought of as backward".[4]

After choosing a brand and model, the generic stock item must be customized. The phone is dressed up, often in gendered ways. Girls and young women like danglers and sleeves. Guys often wear their phones in (fake) leather pockets. A common personalization involves picking a so-called *nomor cantik* (beautiful number). Regular SIM cards sell for 10.000 Rupiah (less than €1). A beautiful number is usually at least 125.000 Rp. Exceptionally beautiful numbers sell for 3 million or more (€250 in 2007). A website devoted to selling *nomor cantik* explains (verbatim):

> Cellphone number is your prestise [...] your number already introduce yourself first, who you are, before you introduce yourself fully. What people think with the owner phone number of 99999999? The owner must be not a common people, he must be an important people.[5]

Beautiful numbers may be chosen because they are easy to remember. They can also carry a specific personal meaning (like one's date of birth) and/or a cultural significance (Barendregt 2006b, 329; de Lange 2001, 65-6; Li 2007). Adi, who is a young marketing sales manager at the biggest and most reliable telecom operator Telkomsel, reveals another way mobile phone numbers express *gengsi*. In Indonesia's low-trust economy post-paid customers are thoroughly checked by telecoms to make sure they are creditworthy. Telkomsel post-paid numbers start with the combination 0811. Having such a number reveals that a person can afford a post-paid number, and that he or she is with what is considered the best and most expensive operator.[6]

The physical context matters also when it comes to handphone-related signifiers of prestige. One day Adi shows me around the new Telkomsel office and customer service area in a tall office building in West Jakarta. He explains that Telkomsel's "high-value customers" come here to get personal assistance. He tells me the customer service area is designed to make customers feel more important. Telkomsel recently moved to this building and redesigned its customer service interior in what Adi calls a "futuristic" style. Indeed, the space has a sterile "cool" quality that is diametrically opposed to Jakarta's chaotic, hot, and dirty streets. Even queuing up can become part of the display of prestige, Adi continues. It is quiet in the new office building because people now have to stop by at Wisma Slipi and cannot be seen by others. When Telkomsel's customer service was still located in nearby Mall Taman Anggrek (one of the biggest and most luxurious shopping malls in Jakarta), the customer desks were always busy. People had to wait in long queues and they could be seen by other people passing by. Many did not have real questions for the service desk, Adi confides, but they just wanted to be appear to belong to Telkomsel's customer base. As Adi and I have a coffee in a small café downstairs near the exit of the building, he talks about office culture in Jakarta with a generous dose of irony and self-reflection. Adi points out to me that many people walk in and out of the building with a communicator-type handphone clung to their ears and looking busy. He says there are many aspiring young executives who try to act as if they are very important and want to appear like they are successful businessmen. According to Adi, the majority of the people passing by are only pretending. He uses the phrase *hanya main-main*, "just playing". This phrase is frequently used when people talk about how others dress themselves up with their mobile phone.

Personalizing the phone quite literally changes its character from being an undetermined "wild" object to a "domesticated" companion tailored to people's individual preferences. Silverstone and Haddon call this process "appropriation" (1996, 64). In what they call "conversion", personalized phones become symbolically charged objects that "speak" for their owners. These artifacts tell other people who their owners are, and convey the message that they take care of their image. Tamed devices are also tangible everyday reminders to their owners that they are in charge of their own lives. Many Indonesians look at themselves through the eyes of others and are acutely aware that they live in an underdeveloped nation. Reflexivity, or "the turning-back of the experience of the individual upon himself", is often forwarded as a distinguishing feature of modern identity (Mead 1934, 134). Following 32 years of Suharto rule, the reform period has failed to deliver on its promises. Indonesians commonly describe the state of their country as chaotic. They say Indonesia is "still running behind" and "not advanced". Many feel that the country as a whole is hardly a source of self-pride. Showing that one is capable of at least exerting control over one's own life by taming technological artifacts offers the individual a much-coveted sense of pride and prestige. Mobile phone *gengsi* then is not just a sign or symbol of individual progress. It actualizes it. It *is* the progress. Through *gengsi* people distinguish themselves from what they call "backward people" and distance themselves from the deplorable general state of the country. This, however, is only one side of the coin. Technologically defined prestige is not a solely centrifugal force, but it can also be a way to identify with collectives. Elnar, a 23-year-old woman, was quite explicit about the potential of technologies to present a modern face of Indonesia. Elnar likes to chat online and get in touch with other people on international chat channels. Foreigners often ask her whether Indonesia has many slums. She feels that they are under the impression that Indonesia is a poor and backward country. Elnar then tries to explain: "It is modern here too. We also have factories, our own airlines, and the Internet" (de Lange 2001, 78).

Handphone *gaul*

The mobile phone is only in part a symbolic artifact used for aggrandizing individual prestige. It is also a profoundly social communication medium. Knowing how to use the mobile phone to socialize is part of *bergaul*, which can be loosely translated as the *savoir-faire* of modern socializing (Barendregt 2008, 164, 166; de Lange 2001, 30-1; Sastramidjaja 2000, 67-74). *Bergaul* consists of creative play with language. *Bahasa gaul* (*gaul* language) is the trendy language spoken by young people in Jakarta and its use has spread all over Indonesia. It borrows words from languages spoken in the capital, notably *prokem* (Jakartan lower-class vernacular), Chinese, and English. It has no fixed vocabulary. Mastery of *bahasa gaul* entails continuously inventing new words and humorously reusing existing expressions. *Bergaul* is a dynamic collection of "meta-rules" that inform not only what to say, but also how to say it and to whom, how to move around town, what to buy, and so on. One must know how to present oneself and have an opinion. It means knowing what is "now". Moreover, it is showing the knowing through speech and demeanor. It is reflexive social play in continuous flux, an infinite "metaplay" with its own rules (Sutton-Smith 1997, 147-8). If *gengsi* departs from individuality and exclusion, *bergaul* departs from social interactions and inclusiveness. Mild competition in one's self-presentation and the expression of originality should never overshadow connecting with other people and playing together. Someone who is too competitive and uses *bergaul* to increase personal *gengsi* is seen as arrogant. Newcomers to Jakarta, like young students from all over Indonesia, must quickly familiarize themselves with *bergaul* in order to link with peers and not to be considered "backward" or "from the village". *Bergaul* is an essential social skill necessary to move oneself with ease and confidence in any situation, and to be able to relate to others.

There is a lot of *gaul* talk about the handphone. People share information on the best models and providers among each other and talk about their personal relation with the phone. In late night television shows hosted by trendy young women, viewers are invited to call in and chat about such topics as "have you ever broken your handphone?" A popular blogger's "meme" at some point was writing down "ten things about my handphone" and passing these questions on to blogger friends. These were questions about brand and type of mobile phone, whether one has a special number, what kind of wallpaper is used, what the last sent text message is, where one wears the phone, and so on. Besides being a researcher's goldmine the meme shows how the mobile phone is caught up in *bergaul*. One cannot just carry any phone. One should be able to explain why one has this brand, that specific wallpaper, and a particular ringtone. The self-conscious relation to the device informs the relations with others and oneself.

In addition to being a topical item, the mobile phone as a communication medium is central to *bergaul*. Especially texting offers rich possibilities for linguistic play in socializing and self-expression. This is a text message Dewi (female, 25 years) sent to a male friend:

> Gw g taw,,c iwan jg g taw.lo cb dtg lgs di graha mobicel jl.mampang prapatan gw taw lg dah,,rabu gw lbr.ikut dunkz[7]

In English:

> I don't know. Iwan also doesn't know. Please come directly to Graha Mobicel, Mampang Prapatan road. I do know something else though. I am free on Wednesday, so come along!

This message contains several *bergaul* elements. First, this message is an ad hoc invitation to socialize and join in, without applying too much pressure ("Please come directly to Graha Mobicel").[8] Second, the message is a prelude to a possible physical encounter. Dewi is not very precise about a specific hour and location and keeps all options open ("I am free on Wednesday, come along!"). A few more messages will likely be exchanged to fine-tune the actual time and place for a meeting, if it will take place at all. Third, the message jumps into an ongoing conversation that involves multiple people ("I don't know. Iwan also doesn't know."). Fourth, the message makes creative use of abbreviated SMS language, leaving out vowels and seeking shorter alternatives for common words, and sometimes using words from other languages like English. In English the *c* in "c iwan" is pronounced *si Iwan*. *Si* is a definite article used before names of familiar people.

This example parallels mobile communication practices observed elsewhere. In the context of Norwegian teens, the use of the mobile phone to coordinate future physical meetings in sequences of increasingly precise communicative exchanges has been called "micro-coordination" (Ling and Yttri 2002, 139, 142-6). Mobile communication also involves an expressive dimension of self-presentation and a social dimension of group discussion and agreement, especially among young people. This has been called "hyper-coordination" (ibid., 140, 147-66). The use of abbreviated and foreign language in texting has also been widely described in diverse contexts. If the elements in this example parallel universal patterns, then we can ask what is particularly urban Indonesian about it. The answer, predictably, is because its language, content, and context are specifically Indonesian. It is an Indonesian expression of individual and group identities. Let's see what that means. The message may be written out as follows in *bahasa gaul*:

> Gue nggak taw, si Iwan juga nggak taw. Lu coba datang langsung di Graha Mobicel, Jl. Mampang Prapatan. Gue taw lagi deh. Rabu gue libur. Ikut donk!

In official *bahasa Indonesia* the message might be rendered as:

> Saya tidak tahu. Si Iwan juga tidak tahu. Kamu mencoba datang langsung ke Graha Mobicel, Jl. Mampang Prapatan. Saya tahu lagi. Hari Rabu saya libur. Ayo ikut!

Two steps of "encoding" occur when composing the message. First, from standard Indonesian into *bahasa gaul*, and then from *bahasa gaul* to an abbreviated SMS language. In texting almost always the national language is used, often interwoven with English words, rather than regional languages. One of the reasons is that Javanese in particular has an intricate way of establishing and expressing social standing. This is not handy when you are trying to cram a message into only 160 characters. Another reason is that *bahasa Indonesia* and international languages are considered more modern (Barendregt 2008, 166). The attempt to write down spoken *bahasa gaul* is in itself a creative play with language. People must make up their own transcriptions, since there is no standard written form. Although *bahasa gaul* is rarely found in "official" institutional publications like newspapers, books, films, and television subtitles, written *bahasa gaul* thrives where young people express themselves in informal media, including Internet blog posts, text messaging, e-mail, and youth magazines that publish letters from readers. These media offer young people play spaces to experiment with alternative identities using *bergaul* as their common distinctive feature. Many young people now own a personal communication device that enables them to bypass parental or institutional surveillance. The use of *bahasa gaul* and an abbreviated SMS language erects further boundaries. This development is of particular concern in Indonesian society characterized by its strong family ties and social hierarchies. Not surprisingly, the new liberties afforded by digital media have caused deep moral concerns, as we shall see below. The receiver on the other side must also be able to "decode" the message. This encoding/decoding is not merely a way to hide the content of the message from the prying eyes of parents or schoolteachers. It is a meta-communicative message by which both sides "perform" to one another their knowledge and versatility in playing with the rules of *bergaul*. An individual should be knowledgeable and have a personal opinion. Dewi apparently broke this rule when she started with "I don't know". But then she retook herself, saying: "I do know something else though". This negated her earlier statement, and can be interpreted as a reflexive comment on the rules of *bergaul* itself.

Questioning mobile media modernity

Despite the rich opportunities that mobile media offer for identity construction and group affiliation, Indonesians do perceive some downsides. Many feel uncertain about the compatibility of these new technologies with cultural and religious values. These technologies stir up a confusing sense of a society always on the move in which former rules and boundaries are no longer self-evident. Such uncertainties and fears come in many guises. From the use of mobile phones as detonators in Islamic terrorist attacks to alleged occurrences of the supernatural via the phone; from its presumed role in causing the general loss of moral values and cultural traditions to promoting pornography in particular (see Barendregt 2006a; 2008; Barendregt and Pertierra 2008). Discussions are very common about the compatibility of media technologies with a pious life. On the "study Islam" mailing list somebody with the nickname *antoniobandalem* expressed doubt whether Muslims are allowed to use products like mobile phones that are made by non-Muslims (*kafir*):

> As far as I know, we as Muslims are not allowed to use any products or goods made by non-Muslims [*kaum kafir*]??? Because it is said this is *haram* [not permitted by Islam], can you please clarify this?? Islamic teachers in my village often say that one becomes polluted if one uses or consumes goods that are produced by non-Muslims. The dilemma also is that on the one hand the Islamic community [*umat*] wants to commit itself to the Islamic law, however on the other hand we are also still dependent on non-Muslims like America and its allies.[9]

He received several responses on the list from people who told him it was okay to use non-Muslim products. Most of these people invoked religious argumentations. They referred to sections from the Qur'an or religious fatwas by (self-proclaimed) imams that justify the consumption of such goods. One of the most active people on the list, an IT specialist with the nickname *Chandraleka*, gave a more pragmatic reply:

> Don't be too extreme! As long as the product itself is *halal* it doesn't matter who produces it. This idea would make modern life nearly impossible: you cannot drive a car, cannot use a computer, cannot use light bulbs, and cannot use a mobile phone [...] One of the causes of extremism is ignorance about Islam. That's why it is important to study religion. Muslims are allowed to use products made by non-Muslims, thank God! It makes life much easier![10]

This example is emblematic of debates among (young) Indonesian Muslims about whether one should reject or accept technologies as part of one's religious identity. In this case technologies are understood as consumption items. In other discussions technologies are considered as media through which people relate to others, to the outside world, and ultimately, to oneself. This leads to questions like, "Is it allowed to divorce via SMS?" or, "Does the exchange of 'crazy' e-mails, SMSes, and phone calls count as adultery?"[11] In such discussions it is the dynamic boundaries of the collective playing field, the identity category itself, that are questioned instead of individual adherence to a fixed set of rules. The way *antoniobandalem* formulates his question – interspersed with religious terms – is not, "Am I a good Muslim when I use *kafir* goods?" but, "Is Islam capable of incorporating the use of these novelty products?" A term like *haram* underlines the perceived alien nature of such products as polluting not just the individual Muslim but Islam as a whole. Further, *antoniobandalem* connects his religious identity directly to issues on a global scale. In terms of we versus them, he refers to the worldwide Islamic community and the political dominance of America. He is not just questioning the identity category itself, but the relation between Islam and competing entities. Finally, the above case shows how new media technologies like Internet mailing lists are used to bypass traditional authorities on cultural and religious matters and question the rules. This can swing both ways. It can lead to a broadening or a narrowing of perspectives. *Antoniobandalem*'s Islamic teachers from the village profess one cannot use *kafir* products, but thanks to the answers he gets on the mailing list he now knows one can. It is not inconceivable, however, that these same media allow people to dig themselves in a parochial trench which can act to (re)solidify boundaries.

Concluding: playing with narratives

Narratives act as blueprints for the way people construct and interpret their identities. Indeed for Indonesians the practices of *gengsi* and *bergaul* and the debates about mobile media modernity are, in Clifford Geertz' words, "a story they tell themselves about themselves" (1975, 448). In Ricoeur's view, narrative identity aims to be a declaration of the self. It allows people after careful introspection to state: "Here I am!" and "Here is where I stand!" (1992, 167-8). An important element in Ricoeur's theory is the tension between what goes into the plot of the story (*concordance*) and what is left out (*discordance*). Nonetheless he remains silent on how this selection process occurs. Narrative theory pays no attention to the circumstances under which people make statements about themselves, the specific conditions under which they tell certain stories, and how and why they prefer or are driven to share one story but not another.

I propose to use the notion of play as a lens in order to highlight this reflexivity towards the medium and mediating process in identity construction.[12] The play perspective questions how declarations of the self come into being and shifts attention to situation-specific performances of the self. Playful identity complements narrative identity by highlighting the conditions under which particular stories are told and how identifications come into being. Play highlights the motivations behind people's choices, as well as the fact that people are driven by outside forces regardless of whether these are phrased as rules, law, fate, coincidence, or divine interventions.[13] We engage in free play and at the same time we are being played. Unlike narrative with its focus on emplotment and closure, play thus underlines the fundamental open-endedness of the question "Who am I?" The quest for identity is never finished. It is an "infinite game" (Carse 1986).

In the introduction of this chapter we have seen that identity in Ricoeur's narrative theory emerges from a threefold mimetic process. In a proposed theory of playful identities this threefold mimetics is reworked into *Play*$_{1\text{-}2\text{-}3}$ (de Lange 2010; de Mul, Frissen, and Raessens 2005). In *Play*$_1$, life's interactions are pre-understood as playful. In a dialectic between free play and rule-driven game, mobile media at once open up room to experiment with identity in the display of *gengsi* and the social play of *bergaul*, and constrain life with new burdens like forcibly having to choose the right model, to always communicate in creative ways, and to continually question pre-existing identity categories and make an effort to reconcile these with "modern" technologies. In *Play*$_2$, interactions are explicitly configured in playful ways. Sociologists such as Erving Goffman (1959) have pointed out that self-presentation in everyday social interactions involves illusory role-playing. In *gengsi*, people playfully express themselves by customizing their phones and engaging in make-believe. In *bergaul* people engage in witty to-and-fro play with language and context, as well as the deliberate coding and decoding of text messages. For *antoniobandalem* the use of Islamic terms like *haram*, *kafir*, and *umat* expresses his group affiliation in the specific context of that Islamic forum. He uses them as verbal props in his presentation of the self. In *Play*$_{3}$, people reflexively understand themselves and others as playing beings, and life as play. In the case of people who pretend to be businessmen by ostentatiously flaunting their phones, Adi comes to understand the office as a stage, the phone as a prop, and people as actors in playful performances. In *gengsi* and *bergaul* reflexive identity mediations occur via mobile media. People relate to the artifact, their communication, and to their own play. Mobile phone *gengsi* plays with the pretense involved in everyday role-playing. Mobile phone *bergaul* involves an infinite metaplay with its own rules. Identities emerge not merely in storytelling "after the fact", to borrow another one of Geertz' phrases; identities emerge by playing with narratives. From the theatrical performances of the self in *gengsi* to the social play in *bergaul*, mobile media technologies shape identities in what theater theorist Schechner calls a performative "showing of a doing" (Schechner 2003, 114-5). People come to question the pre-given rules of traditional cultural and religious narratives, and must continuously juggle the parameters. In a "mobile" world that many perceive as rapidly changing, formerly solid foundations of identification are constantly being questioned, experimented with, and transgressed. In the case of the young Muslim who questions the compatibility of mobile media with his religious identity, the quest for selfhood involves constant negotiations of boundaries between sameness and otherness, between I and we, between us and them, between the overarching structuring category and the specific self-determining instance, between local authorities and global online communities. Like an infinite game, life involves ongoing strategic decision-making at each new level.

Notes

1. This chapter is based in part on de Lange (2010 and 2013). Ethnographic fieldwork for this research was conducted in July and August 2007, with kind financial support from the Erasmus University Rotterdam Trust Fund.

2. Source: International Telecom Union statistics: www.itu.int/ITU-D/ICTEYE/Indicators/Indicators.aspx.
3. Source: interview with Budi Putra on August 3, 2007.
4. Source: interview with Telset's managing director Walid Hidayat and editor Nurhamzah on August 10, 2007.
5. Source: website www.perdanacantique.com (now offline).
6. Source: interview with Adi (alias) on August 24, 2007.
7. Source: interview with Dewi (alias) on August 25, 2007. I had asked her to show me "a typical text message".
8. Dewi literally used the words "try to come" (*coba datang*) which is a polite way to phrase an imperative in Indonesian.
9. Source: "study Islam" mailing-list, posted May 18, 2006: www.mail-archive.com/assunnah@yahoogroups.com/msg08382.html.
10. Abbreviated and translated from the "study Islam" mailing list, posted May 20, 2006: www.mail-archive.com/belajar-islam@yahoogroups.com/msg00092.html.
11. Sources: "Question: Divorce via SMS", posted April 24, 2007 www.mail-archive.com/belajar-islam@yahoogroups.com/msg00231.html (Indonesian); and "Question: do e-mail, SMS, telephone contribute to adultery?" posted April 5, 2006 www.mail-archive.com/belajar-islam@yahoogroups.com/msg00071.html (Indonesian).
12. I have worked this out elsewhere in more detail (de Lange 2010).
13. Play captures this fundamental duality between intrinsic motivations and external rules, between agency and structure, as for example in Alexander Galloway's succinct working definition: "[a] game is an activity defined by rules in which players try to reach some sort of goal" (Galloway 2006, 1).

References

Augé, Marc. 2008. *Non-places: Introduction to an anthropology of supermodernity.* London; Verso.

Barendregt, Bart. 2006a. Between m-governance and mobile anarchies: Pornoaksi and the fear of new media in present day Indonesia. *Working paper and discussion during e-seminar EASA media-anthropology list.* www.media-anthropology.net/index.php/View-document-details/Barendregt-Between-m-governance-and-mobile-anarchies.html.

—. 2006b. Mobile modernities in contemporary Indonesia: Stories from the other side of the digital divide. In *Indonesian transitions*, eds. Henk Schulte Nordholt and Ireen Hoogenboom, 327-47. Yogyakarta: Pustaka Pelajar.

—. 2008. Sex, cannibals, and the language of cool: Indonesian tales of the phone and modernity. *The Information Society* 24(3): 160-70.

—, and Raul Pertierra. 2008. Supernatural communication in the Philippines and Indonesia. In *Handbook of mobile communication studies*, ed. James E. Katz, 377-88. Cambridge, MA: The MIT Press.

Carse, James P. 1986. *Finite and infinite games: A vision of life as play and possibility*. New York: Free Press.

Galloway, Alexander R. 2006. *Gaming: Essays on algorithmic culture*. Minneapolis, MN: University of Minnesota Press.

Geertz, Clifford. 1975. Deep play: Notes on the Balinese cockfight. In *The interpretation of cultures: Selected essays*, ed. Clifford Geertz, 412-53. London: Hutchinson.

Goffman, Erving. 1959. *The presentation of self in everyday life*. Garden City, NY: Doubleday.

Lange, Michiel de. 2001. *Dunia digit@L: Internet en moderniteit in Indonesië 2000*. Amsterdam, Master's thesis, University of Amsterdam.

—. 2010. Moving circles: Mobile media and playful identities. PhD dissertation. Rotterdam: Erasmus University.

—. 2013. From *gengsi* to *gaul*: Mobile media and playful identities in Jakarta. In *Contemporary Culture: New directions in arts and humanities research*, eds. Judith Thissen, Kitty Zijlmans, and Robert Zwijnenberg, 101-9. Amsterdam: Amsterdam University Press.

Leeuwen, Lizzy van. 1997. *Airconditioned lifestyles: De nieuwe rijken in Jakarta*. Amsterdam: Het Spinhuis.

Li, Li. 2007. Superstition or modernity? On the invented tradition of lucky mobile phone numbers in China. *M/C Journal*, no. 1. www.journal.media-culture.org.au/0703/07-li.php.

Ling, Rich, and Birgitte Yttri. 2002. Hyper-coordination via mobile phones in Norway. In *Perpetual contact: Mobile communication, private talk, public performance*, eds. James Katz and Mark Aakhus, 139-69. Cambridge, UK: Cambridge University Press.

Mead, George. 1934. *Mind, self, and society: From the standpoint of a social behaviorist*. Chicago, IL: University of Chicago Press.

Mul, Jos de. 2005. The game of life. Narrative and ludic identity formation in computer games. In *Handbook of computer game studies*, eds. Joost Raessens and Jeffrey Goldstein, 251-66. Cambridge, MA: The MIT Press.

—, Valerie Frissen, and Joost Raessens. 2005. *Playful identities. From narrative to ludic self-construction*. Rotterdam. www.playful-identities.nl/HTML/downloads/2005-2010%20nwo-program%20playful%20identities.pdf.

Raessens, Joost. 2006. Playful identities, or the ludification of culture. *Games and Culture* 1(1): 52-7.

—. 2014. The ludification of culture. In: *Rethinking gamification*, eds. Mathias Fuchs, Sonia Fizek, Paolo Ruffino, and Niklas Schrape, 91-114. Lüneburg: Hybrid Publishing Lab.

Ricoeur, Paul. 1992. *Oneself as another*. Chicago, IL: University of Chicago Press.

—. 1984. *Time and Narrative*. Vol. 1. Chicago, IL: University of Chicago Press.

—. 1988. *Time and Narrative*. Vol. 3. Chicago, IL: University of Chicago Press.

Sastramidjaja, Yatun L.M. 2000. *Dromenjagers in Bandung: Twintigers in het moderne Indonesië*. Amsterdam: Het Spinhuis.

Schechner, Richard. 2003. *Performance theory*, revised and expanded edition. London: Routledge Classics.

Silverstone, Roger, and Leslie Haddon. 1996. Design and the domestication of information and communication technologies: Technical change and everyday life. In *Communication by design: The politics of information and communication technologies*, eds. Robin Mansell and Roger Silverstone, 44-74. Oxford: Oxford University Press.

Sutton-Smith, Brian. 1997. *The ambiguity of play*. Cambridge, MA: Harvard University Press.

Timmermans, Jeroen. 2010. Playing with paradoxes: Identity in the Internet era. PhD dissertation. Rotterdam: Erasmus University.

18. The conflicts within the casual: The culture and identity of casual online play

Frans Mäyrä

Introduction: the emerging culture of casual play

It is relatively easy to find examples of deep, immersive play that has effects on personal or social identity: an intensive psychodrama, live action role-play, and even some massively multiplayer online (MMO) game players report experiences that have affected the ways they perceive themselves, or human condition in general. Most of contemporary play, however, is not deep or transformative in a similar manner. This article will focus on casual gameplay that takes place in common games such as Solitaire, or more recently games such as *FarmVille* (which peaked at 80 million active players in February 2010), as well as through mobile phone applications such as *Foursquare*, a location-based game for smartphones. The aim is to discuss the significance and meaning-making activities that take place among these kinds of games, and highlight their contributions to game cultures and to our daily lives in general.

The subtitle of this article, "the culture and identity of casual online play", is wide arching and extensive, but it highlights my intention to take a look at casual play through the lens of meaning making. This involves both meanings at the level of individuals, their identities and their daily lives, but also at the level of culture where meanings are shared in a group or collective dimension, when meanings are made public. To give a quick outline, the article includes first of all a discussion of "casual" as a characteristic of games and "casual play" as a particular kind of player practice. Certain challenges in providing vocabulary and definitions will be highlighted, suggesting that we need to be able to differentiate between the casual in play, player, and in games. The key design features of "casual games" are discussed, as well as characteristics of casual play, resulting in various portraits of "casual player" being drawn. Next, the relevant findings from several research projects are summarized to showcase a research trajectory moving from more general gameplay research into specified understanding of casual games and play. The expanding range of casual experiences will be discussed making reference to *FarmVille* and similar games, and then to *Foursquare* as a casual location-based game. In the conclusion, particular cultural characteristics (and meanings derived from) casual play are tentatively forwarded.

Popularity of casual play

The popularity of "casual" is obvious in the field of gaming. While ancient in game culture, casual games first came to the attention of businesses with early successes of games such as Windows *Solitaire* (1990) and *Tetris* (1984), which became particularly popular when bundled with Nintendo GameBoy (1989), and then as a range of online games. The major expansion phase started at the end of 1990s and early 2000s, when dedicated web sites like that of PopCap Games started providing relatively small and simple Flash games that required no downloads or installation and were free to play on a web browser. The opening up of the Facebook API (Application Programming Interface) to games and other applications in 2007 was another step expanding the field of casual gaming through a popular online networking service. In the fall of 2010, it was estimated that 200 million people were playing games on Facebook alone (Alexander 2010). The growth has been fast in this field. In 2007, the Casual Games Association had estimated that the entire casual game sector attracted 200 million players a month over the Internet (Casual Games Association 2007). The economic value generated by casual games is also considerable; the revenues from connected games or from the online casual game industry was estimated to exceed three billion dollars in 2009 (Casual Games Association 2010). After major video game companies like Nintendo with its Wii console and WiiWare service, and Microsoft with its Xbox and associated Live Arcade service entered the casual games market, it has become increasingly difficult to delineate where the casual game industry starts and the "mainstream" video games industry begins. Casual has slowly become the new mainstream.

Our own research also verifies that games that are commonly classified in the casual games category are indeed among the most popular when we take a look at gaming among larger populations. The University of Tampere Games Research Lab with its partners has been carrying out nation-wide surveys of game playing in Finland in 2007, 2009, and 2010, and each time the Microsoft Windows game *Solitaire* ranked as the most popular digital game most recently played by the informants. This is also the case for online casual gaming sites where puzzle games like (digital) *Sudoku* and "classic games" like *Mahjong* and *Tetris* are regularly featured among the most popular games in these surveys. This tells us a distinctly different story about the reality of gameplay when compared to that of the game bestseller lists published by the media (see Kallio et al. 2008; Karvinen and Mäyrä 2009; Kuronen and Koskimaa 2011). While the various top 10 game lists focus on video and computer games that are either the best-selling games from various outlets or on games that receive top ratings in reviews, the most popular games in actuality are regular, older, cheaper, and less spectacular games in terms of content and technology than the more recent new blockbusters. While today they probably will not receive awards for innovation anymore, these games nevertheless form the almost unnoticed mainstream in everyday game cultures.

Casual game characteristics

But how do we define what we talk about when we talk about "casual games" – what are the main characteristics of a casual game? In our research project titled GameSpace (2006-2008; see Paavilainen et al. 2009) our research team adopted a grounded theory approach to defining the casual in games and harvested a large number of different materials related to this field before proceeding to create a synthesis. A wide selection of games literature and web page materials were analyzed and a selection of expert interviews were carried out, producing a long list of characteristics, with some of them appearing more regularly than others (see Table 1).

– **Easy to learn**	– **To mass audiences**
– Forgiving to player error	– Dominant genre of puzzle, word, arcade, and card games
– Downloadable or playable on a browser	– Generally non-violent
– Major user group is women age 40 and older	– Possibility for experimental types of games
– Players don't regard themselves as gamers	– **Low commitment and involvement**
– Inexpensive	– Short schedules of producing processes
– Try-before-you-buy	– Low production and distribution costs
– Leave and pick up easily	– Small teams in the production
– Simplistic interface	– Primary distribution source: web
– Calming effect	– Retro-games
– Keeping the mind sharp	– **Fast progress, quick rewards**
– "No casual game has ever failed by being too easy"	– Game instance and game session organization

– **Short bursts of gameplay**	– Low required investments (time, money, hardware)
– Lack of time (no time for deeper gaming experiences)	– Casual games can provide hardcore experiences (hardcore-casual)
– Game as a snack or a break	– **No advanced gaming skills**
– Educational benefits for children	– Stress-relief
– **High replay value**	– New gamer demographics: females, non-gamers, thirty-/forty-somethings, and lapsed gamers (no more time for games)
– Lapsed gamers (no more time for other games)	
– Varying player groups and different devices	

Table 1: Casual game characteristics. The list is drawn from the GameSpace project data, based on literature and web survey and expert interviews. University of Tampere, 2006-2008.

When clustered together in content analysis, there are certain key characteristics that emerge as something that people typically recognize as the features that identify "casual games" as we commonly understand them. These features include the game being easy to learn, inexpensive, supporting short bursts of gameplay, yet having a high replay value. In this sense a good casual game is much like a classic non-digital game. For example, a board game like chess has relatively simple rules. Yet it can maintain the interest of even masterful players after years of practice. It is no surprise therefore that many of the popular casual games are indeed digital versions of classic board games. The familiarity with the game rules and mechanics are also a benefit to classic games, and something that goes naturally hand-in-hand with the next key characteristic, the game being targeted at mass audiences.

Moreover, designing game features to support fast progress and quick rewards, while requiring no advanced gaming skills, are central in making a casual game and targeting large audiences. Yet such features are also something that divides the potential player base. If the game is made deliberately easy and quickly rewarding for a total novice player, then there is also considerable chance that the game will alienate advanced and challenge-driven players. This is something that is often discussed under the topic of prioritizing hardcore versus casual gamers in the game industry and in game-related media. It is not automatically clear that the interests of active, skillful players when contrasted with those who do not have much playtime or skill sets available would be compatible; indeed, some online discussions feature a clear antagonism between the two groups. The character of the "casual player" will be discussed further below.

The quality of being casual

In analysis, it soon becomes clear that "casual" in relation to games is a complex concept, and something that is linked to certain features of games, but also closely connects with certain styles of play, or even characteristics of particular game players. This is something to be expected, since the game and the player become so closely intertwined in gameplay that it is close to impossible to clearly separate the role of one from the other in the performance of play (cf. Mäyrä 2008, 17–20). Our team of GameSpace researchers published a summary of the analysis from the casual games discussion, resulting in the following network of relations (Figure 1).

The central conclusions of this analysis focus on five distinctive relationships: (1) the people who play "casual games" can adopt an attitude or playing style towards these games that is also casual, or not (e.g. it is possible to play casual games in a committed, "hardcore" manner, with substantial investments of time and energy); (2) It is possible to identify a group of players (here: "casual gamers") who dominantly play games in a "casual style" – with this relying on the notion (3) that it is possible to a certain degree to play even complex games with a casual style, attitude, or time investments. Furthermore, (4) it is important to emphasize that casual games are popular today among all kinds of people, and not all casual game players are "casual gamers" in the sense introduced above, but that dedicated game enthusiasts can often adopt casual games also in their game repertoire. And finally, (5) these relationships help to understand the characteristics of casual games as a feature set that aims to signal their primary intended role as games designed for casual use, by casual players and gamers (Kuittinen et al. 2007).

Such a conceptual analysis is useful in raising awareness about the complexity of game-player relationships when a particular area of game cultures

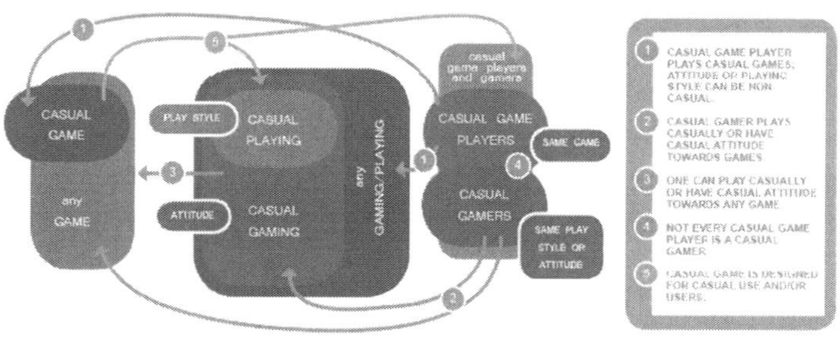

Fig. 1: Relations of the meanings of "casual" in games cultures (Kuittinen et al. 2007, 107).

is taken into consideration. The meaning of "casual" can lie in only one area of this networked phenomena, or in many of them simultaneously. It is typical to see the characteristics of games, game players, and their playing styles unproblematically interconnected and always harmoniously mirroring each other, but when examined more closely there are distinctive characteristics that can and should be separated from each other in this equation – like the not-so-hypothetical example of a "hardcore style casual gamer" points out. Looking closer at these topics in a published whitepaper, the game developer organization IGDA highlighted female players over forty who play more than nine hours per week (IGDA 2006) and the casual game company King.com also published details about some of their active female casual game players who play as much as five to ten hours per day (Norton 2008).

As they move from complex digital games to the field of casual play, players' experiences and performances commonly tend to shift from immersive to non-immersive play styles. It should be noted that immersive, dedicated play styles have a long-standing position as the standard of digital play; also our own previous work has focused on understanding players' experiences particularly through the different dimensions of immersive play (Ermi and Mäyrä 2005). Casual play is typically characterized by short sessions of playful interaction with games that are not particularly challenging, complex, or extensive. The non-immersive character of casual play allows participants to divide their attention to other activities and issues besides gameplay, suggesting that such games would be particularly suitable for various social uses and purposes. As the popularity of casual digital games has been growing, we are also witnessing an expanding range of casual game experiences, as well as an increasing range of social, entertaining, and cultural uses which the contemporary online casual games have been adapted for. Taking a closer look, casual play appears to be an enabler for different personal and social processes, sometimes momentarily moving to the center of attention, while mostly keeping in the periphery. While the vocal parts of game cultures have primarily articulated the pleasures of highly immersive gameplay, the players of contemporary casual games have started to advance an alternative view of what constitutes "good gameplay" that is based on a slightly different aesthetics of play.

Understanding casual gamers

In his book *A casual revolution* (2010), Jesper Juul proposes an argument that links playing styles to the design features of games, and what kind of time commitments they allow:

> Games as well as players can be flexible or inflexible: whereas a casual game is flexible toward different types of players and uses, a hardcore game makes inflexible and unconditional demands on the skill and commitment of a player. Conversely, where a casual player is inflexible toward doing what a game requires, a hardcore player is flexible toward making whatever commitment a game may demand. This explains the seeming paradox of the casual players making non-casual time commitments: a casual game is sufficiently flexible to be played with a hardcore time commitment, but a hardcore game is too inflexible to be played with a casual time commitment (Juul 2010, 10).

The argument is similar to the "implied player" concept forwarded by Espen Aarseth, where the game prefigures its intended players in its design, or as Aarseth puts it "the implied player [acts like] a boundary imposed on the player-subject by the game" (2007, 132). Considering Juul's argument above, the structural features of casual games appear therefore to provide more room for negotiation and more flexible boundaries for players to approach gaming.

In order to have a more comprehensive view on what the dominant daily roles of players are with regard to wider demographics, our team carried out a more thorough, three-year study of game playing and players from 2006 to 2008. Our study progressed in three stages. It included an extensive survey into game playing in the context of various other leisure activities (with 805 valid responses), followed by a smaller group selected for structured interviews (73 participants), and finally a series of 33 in-depth interviews and two focus group interviews. After quantitative and qualitative analyses, three dimensions were chosen as the key organizing principles for the data: the intensity of gaming, sociability in gaming, and the genre or nature of games played. The final outcome of the analysis was presented in the form of a heuristic model of gaming mentalities. These nine categories were created as a synthesis to suggest ways of understanding game playing that were most commonly associated with the lives of our informants:

1. Social mentality profiles:
   a. Gaming with kids
   b. Gaming with mates
   c. Gaming for company
2. Casual mentality profiles:
   a. Killing time
   b. Filling gaps
   c. Relaxing

3. Committed mentality profiles:
   a. Having fun
   b. Entertaining
   c. Immersing

(Kallio et al. 2010, 9).

This typology was not created to be an exact statistical representation of how game player mentalities are distributed in our data, but it reflects the derived, overall picture of "mainstream gaming". The deeply committed, immersive play styles are in the minority, while the motivations with social and casual, time spending related priorities are dominant. In our sample, people who were interested in games for the games' sake were in the minority, as well as those who looked for specific games and considered digital play as their primary form of entertainment. One can of course claim that there is a qualitative difference in the amount of "gaming capital" (Consalvo 2007, 186) that the dedicated game hobbyists have collected, in contrast to those people who access games principally for instrumental reasons, looking for company or just for a momentary respite from daily tasks. The cultural significance accumulated, appreciated, and shared among the gaming hobbyists is certainly a valid and important area of study on its own, but there are several other areas of signification we should be aware of and researching as well.

Cultures of casual play

Due to their nature, the cultures of casual play are somewhat challenging to study. As a phenomenon becomes increasingly non-intensive, it also becomes more difficult to perceive, detect, and analyze. While the dedicated fan of a long-standing series of strategy games, for example, might have thought about the virtues and downsides of her chosen game a lot, participated in various discussions focusing on it, and adopted a vocabulary to address its different dimensions, the casual gamer might have not done any of these things at all. The game playing might be a recurring, everyday element of her day, yet something that remains at the periphery of attention and rationalization – precisely because it is casual in character. Even admitting to another person that she plays such games in the first place might be difficult. As a side note, this is actually a reason to suspect systematic distortion in gaming surveys, for example, where many casual gamers might not participate or report anything. When the cultural status and personal investment in such games is low enough, it will also have an effect on informant motivation. "I am not a gamer", is a common first response in our interview situations, and it is only after more in-depth discussions that the full range of the informants' ludic activities starts to surface.

There are also reasons why the most commonplace elements in our lives are often the most difficult to break down analytically. Michel de Certeau (1984) has written about the everyday life in a manner that pays attention to how complex layers of meanings attach to the indeterminate areas, wastelands of our increasingly planned and regulated lives. Such "stratified places" are, according to de Certeau, "opaque and stubborn", and he goes on to describe "casual time" as the "diabolic adversary" of the system and its planning projects (1984 201-2). The casual phenomena are – paradoxically – deep in their superficiality. The non-planned moments of life, including casual gameplay, are rich in associative connections and non-verbalized personal meanings. Casual play is also often situated and contextualized in a manner that non-casual, immersive, or dedicated game playing practices are not. To use the terms of Erving Goffman (1959), rather than being played out publicly on our "front-stage" (or alone as a conscious addition to our public self-image), casual play takes place in the "back-stages" of our social and personal lives.

In addition to not being important enough to warrant attention and discussion, there remains also a deeper ambivalence that emerges from these interviews and reflections: casual play as something disgraceful and deniable. While having games as a hobby is a viable option if your time investment and effort are in harmony with the (sub)cultural frames that support the articulation of meaning in digital play, it appears that most casual game players have not adopted such values. Casual play emerges here as the unspoken "Other" of Rational Self – a waste of time and effort in an era dominated by the ideology of efficiency and productivity. The topologies of the casual and the non-casual culture of play thereby differ: while it is possible to see gaming becoming one of the pinnacles for the organization of identity, the position for casual players appears more subdued. Casual play appears more subservient to identity work, providing unspoken spaces between the outspoken areas of productivity.

Online casual play in *FarmVille*

The above discussion has highlighted some of the numerous development trends and also tensions that run through the field of casual gaming. I will

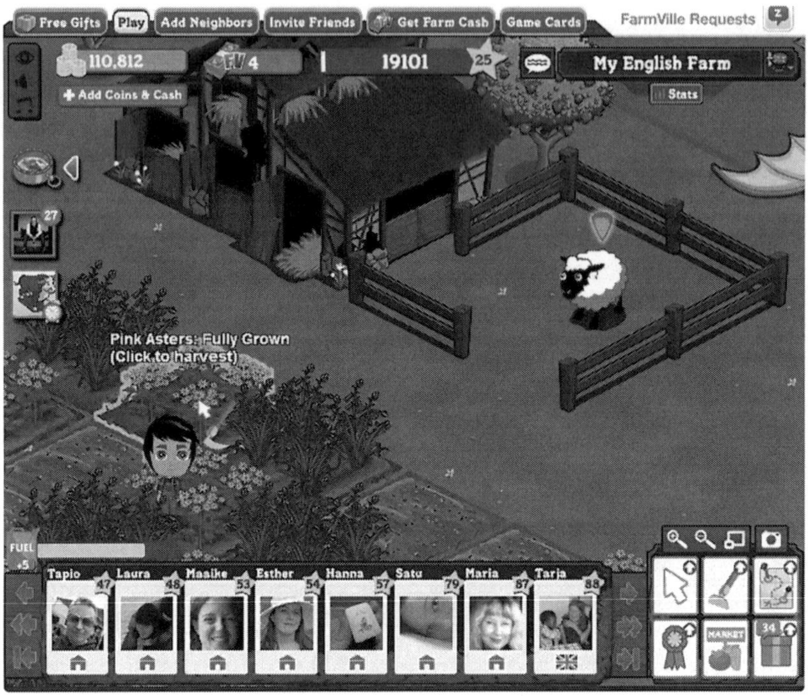

Fig. 2: The user interface of *FarmVille* (April 2011).

now illustrate the current state of casual online play with a few examples that display some typical features and developments. The first example is *FarmVille* (Zynga 2009), the archetypical "social game" that solidifies a certain set of key features in casual Facebook games.

The visual design of the game is as important as its rule set or game mechanics (Figure 2). *FarmVille* takes its players back to their childhood days of toy animals and play gardening: with their clear contours, round shapes, and big eyes, all game elements of *FarmVille* signal friendly, toy-like qualities. The theme is familiar and the processes related to farm-keeping (planting, harvesting, etc.) are easily accessible to a wide range of different potential players. Thus *FarmVille* illustrates many of the typical design goals and values of casual games: acceptability, accessibility, simplicity, and flexibility (Kultima 2009).

FarmVille is a never-ending game of resource management and gradual progression towards having and maintaining an ever-bigger and better virtual farm. All available spots of land should be ploughed, planted with fresh seeds, then harvested and planted again, in a circle of manual labor and virtual production. Every single action requires mouse-clicks, and while an advanced casual gamer might have access to tractors, feeders, or harvesting machines that speed up the process, *FarmVille* gameplay nevertheless means engaging in long sessions filled with clicking. It has been noted that it is symptomatic of *FarmVille* that some of the most coveted rewards from its gameplay are power tools that allow you to have less of *FarmVille* gameplay (Liszkiewicz 2010). Since such farming tools can also be earned by investing real money, part of *FarmVille*'s business model appears to rely on setting up artificial obstacles for players so that they will pay for their removal.

In order to reach a sense of achievement, one needs to have some challenges and investments of time and energy that justify and give meaning to that achievement. The rewards of *FarmVille* are aesthetic as well as functional, but they also reward labor by displaying the ensuing progress. It is through play that the farm expands to include more buildings, as well as more plants and decorations that reflect the taste and hard work of its player. Jason Begy and Mia Consalvo have noted how the player-preferred achievements of another casual online game, *Faunasphere* (Big Fish Games 2009), focus on completing goals and leveling up, but these can also be interpreted as "nurturing" activities within the game fiction (Begy and Consalvo 2011). There is both personal and social significance attached to gaming in a social network game like *FarmVille*; the new animals, buildings, decorations, and tools hold play value inside the game, and also display value as extensions of the player's online persona within the social exchanges of Facebook. The theme of the game is important for contextualizing the playful activities within a certain kind of referential frame – one of caretaking, culturing, and hard work in the case of *FarmVille*.

Two of the most interesting ambiguities running through *FarmVille* are related to the character of its casual play and its sociability. Casual games of this kind are most often played by middle-aged people, women and men engaged in daily routines of office work and family chores (IGDA 2006). *FarmVille* can serve as a momentary relief from the stress of having obligations. Yet it is precisely these new kinds of obligations that *FarmVille* creates for its players: planting the seeds of red currant, for example, means that I need to be back to do the harvesting in four hours, or my expensive plants will start to wither. Scott Rettberg has written how massively multiplayer role-playing games such as *World of Warcraft* serve the "corporate ideology" of our capitalistic society, by carefully modeling the workings of the market economy. The laborious routine of such online games also make them paradoxically more acceptable: "When play feels like labor, and one toils to achieve objectives, play does not feel like a waste of time. Play that feels like frivolous entertainment would be intolerable for the good capitalist.

Play that feels like *work*, on the other hand, must be *good*" (Rettberg 2008, 32). *FarmVille* adheres to the same cultural logic.

Another interesting ambiguity can be seen to operate within the role of sociability in *FarmVille*: the gift mechanism within the game is apparently enriching both for the play experience and for one's social ties by making it possible to send as gifts rare items, animals or building materials to players who belong to one's social network. However, the "gift" is also a part of the viral marketing mechanism of the game, and an important element among the devices that are intended to create a sense of social obligation to play more *FarmVille*. There is no built-in possibility for direct, simultaneous collaboration within the game, and the presence of other players can only be indirectly perceived through the traces (gifts, farm upgrades, status feed items) left in the game and elsewhere in Facebook.

Location-based casual play in Foursquare

Location-based gaming is not a new invention – one can claim that any treasure hunt game uses location-based gaming, regardless of whether digital positioning or only a paper map is being used. However, the scale of involvement in these play forms has greatly expanded, particularly as GPS has become a standard element in regular mobile phones. *Foursquare*, the service that I will use as my next example of expansion of casual play, reported to have seven million registered users (March 2011). There are also several competing services with varying feature sets, including *Google Latitude*, *Gowalla*, and *Facebook Places*. Games and services that rely on mobile and ubiquitous technologies that are a part of a wider social, practical, and ethical development where issues of power, control, identity, and privacy, among others, are in the process of becoming interconnected in new ways (see e.g. Greenfield 2006).

Foursquare is a playful, location-based social networking service, used with a smartphone client, which is focused on "checking in" at various, real-world locations, and gaining virtual rewards and recognition from them. Typical rewards are badges, for example the "Adventurer" badge is rewarded after the user has checked in at ten different venues, and the "Local" badge for checking in at the same place three times in one week. The most active recent visitor in a venue wins the "Mayor" status at that place. *Foursquare* has also opened up their system to various establishments which provide special offers to their Mayors, or to other *Foursquare* users checking in at their location (Figure 3).

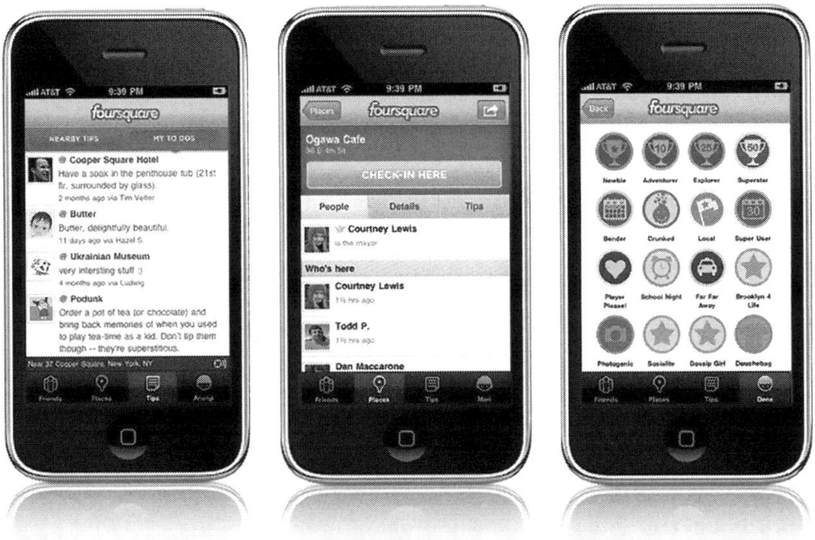

Fig. 3: *Foursquare* mobile application interface (iPhone app, Foursquare.com, 2011).

When considered as a game, *Foursquare* is a borderline case. It features points, challenges, and rewards organized in a playful manner, yet its "gameplay" is rather rudimentary. It is perhaps fair to call it a tool or service that can be used for casual play, but also for other purposes, like communicating about one's travel locations to one's social network (*Foursquare* allows status sharing via Twitter and Facebook). *Foursquare* also points towards a development where the borders between gameplay and social play start to vanish (cf. Montola et al. 2009). Rather than staying within the explicit rule set created by *Foursquare*, users can utilize the service to create playful exchanges of their own, checking in at funny places, or by framing their check-ins as joking comments to earlier check-ins by their friends or colleagues.

At its heart, the casual play in *Foursquare* carries its own ambiguities. With its links to other social networking services, *Foursquare* fits the busy lives of "urban nomads" who are constantly on the move, and want to advertise their lifestyle and location as an extension of their professional persona. On the other hand, the apparently trivial pursuit of gameplay tokens such as mayor statuses or badges sends out signals of free time and playful exploration. Taken together, these two dimensions of location-based casual play partially work against each other, allowing a dual gesture that mixes elements from one's professional and private identity into a novel kind of "multi-layered culture of casual play".

Conclusions: The conflicting culture of online casual play

The discussion and examples used above show that the evolving culture of online casual play is currently situated at the ambiguous borderlines between mundane, instrumental, and playful frames of reference. The defining feature of casual play, its non-committing character, operates as a dual gesture that identifies a casual gamer as someone who both enters the sphere of ludic playfulness, as well as maintaining some distance from it. Thus casual play can be seen as a technique of identity or self, with its simultaneous push towards both engagement and non-engagement. As such, it fits very well within the conditions of late modern societies, with their often-conflicting requirements on the lives of individuals.

The apparent simplicity combined with the complexity within the actual, underlying significance of casual online play makes it open for taking multiple routes of appropriation and sense-making. Under observation, casual online play can emerge simultaneously as something ritualistic and trivial (e.g. rote clicking), and something private and public. Involvement in simplistic gameplay in a social networking context functions socially as something that both separates and shields the player from any immediate social interaction, yet also maintains at least a superficial contact with other people, and the associated mundane realities. This internal dissonance may also explain some of its popularity, and points toward a better understanding of its specific cultural problematic dimensions.

References

Aarseth, Espen. I fought the law: Transgressive play and the implied player. *Proceedings of DiGRA 2007: Situated play.* Tokyo: DiGRA Japan.

Alexander, Leigh. 2010. Zuckerberg: Changes for Facebook, games "one of the big complaints" from users. *Gamasutra.* September 22, 2010. www.gamasutra.com/view/news/30555/Zuckerberg_Changes_For_Facebook_Games_One_Of_The_Biggest_Complaints_From_Users.php.

Begy, Jason, and Mia Consalvo. 2011. Achievements, motivations and rewards in Faunasphere. *Game Studies* 11(1) (February 2011). www.gamestudies.org/1101/articles/begy_consalvo.

Casual Games Association. 2007. *Casual games market report 2007: Business and art of games for everyone.* Layton, UT: Casual Games Association. www.casualgamesassociation.org/pdf/2007_CasualGamesMarketReport.pdf.

Casual Games Association. 2010. News: In 2009, the world wide connected casual games industry had revenues in excess of $3.0 billion on mobile, iPhone, social networks. Layton, UT: Casual Games Association. www.casualgamesassociation.org/news.php?show=1&type=news&id=15#top.

Certeau, Michel de. 1984. *The practice of everyday life.* Berkeley, CA: University of California Press.

Consalvo, Mia. 2007. *Cheating: gaining advantage in videogames.* Cambridge, MA: The MIT Press.

Greenfield, Adam. 2006. *Everyware: The dawning age of ubiquitous computing*. Berkeley, CA: New Riders.
Ermi, Laura, and Frans Mäyrä. 2005. Fundamental components of the gameplay experience: Analysing immersion. In *Proceedings of DiGRA 2005: changing views: Worlds in play*. Vancouver: University of Vancouver. www.digra.org/dl/db/06276.41516.pdf.
Foursquare Labs, Inc. 2011. *Foursquare*.
Goffman, Erving. 1959. *The presentation of self in everyday life*. Garden City, NY: Doubleday.
Gowalla. 2012. *Gowalla*.
IGDA. 2006. Casual Games Whitepaper/Wiki/Market Overview. *IGDA.org*. http://wiki.igda.org/Casual_Games_SIG/Whitepaper/Market_Overview.
Kallio, Kirsi Pauliina, Kirsikka Kaipainen, and Frans Mäyrä. 2007. *Gaming nation? Piloting the international study of games cultures in Finland*. Hypermedia Laboratory Net Series 14. Tampere: Tampereen yliopisto. tampub.uta.fi/haekokoversio.php?id=202.
—, Frans Mäyrä, and Kirsikka Kaipainen. 2010. At least nine ways to play: Approaching gamermentalities. *Games and Culture* (December 31). gac.sagepub.com/content/early/2010/11/03/1555412010391089.full.pdf+html.
Karvinen, Juho, and Frans Mäyrä. 2009. *Pelaajabarometri 2009 – Pelaaminen suomessa*. Interaktiivisen median tutkimuksia 3. Tampere: Tampereen yliopisto. tampub.uta.fi/haekokoversio.php?id=303.
Kuittinen, Jussi, Annakaisa Kultima, Johannes Niemelä, and Janne Paavilainen. 2007. Casual games discussion. In *Proceedings of the 2007 conference on future play* (Future Play '07). New York: ACM 105-12.
Kultima, Annakaisa. 2009. Casual game design values. In *MindTrek 2009 proceedings*, 58-65. Tampere: ACM.
Kuronen, Eero, and Raine Koskimaa. 2011. *Pelaajabarometri 2010*. Jyväskylä: Jyväskylän yliopisto, Agora Center. www.jyu.fi/erillis/agoracenter/tutkimus/julkaisut/elektroninen/pelaajabarometri2010.pdf.
Liszkiewicz, A.J. Patrick. 2010. Cultivated play: FarmVille. *Berfrois*, October 21, 2010. www.berfrois.com/2010/10/cultivated-play-farmville/.
Mäyrä, Frans. 2008. *An introduction to game studies: Games in culture*. London: Sage Publications.
Montola, Markus, Jaakko Stenros, and Annika Waern. 2009. *Pervasive games: theory and design*. San Francisco, CA: Morgan Kaufmann.
Norton, Robert. 2008. Games women play. *Edge Magazine Blogs*. September 18, 2008. www.next-gen.biz/blogs/games-women-play.
Paavilainen, Janne, Annakaisa Kultima, Jussi Kuittinen, Frans Mäyrä, Hannamari Saarenpää, and Johannes Niemelä. 2009. *GameSpace: Methods for design and evaluation for casual mobile multiplayer games*. Interaktiivisen median tutkimuksia 1. Tampere: University of Tampere. http://tampub.uta.fi/handle/10024/65773.
Rettberg, Scott. 2008. Corporate ideology in *World of Warcraft*. In *Digital culture, play, and identity: A World of Warcraft reader*, eds. Hilde Corneliussen and Jill Walker Rettberg, 19-38. Cambridge, MA: The MIT Press.
Zynga. 2009. *FarmVille*. PC: Zynga.

19. Afterplay

Jos de Mul

Poor me! I am a nuance.
Friedrich Nietzsche

Hurray for *Homo ludens* 2.0

In the introductory chapter of this volume we proclaimed a global "ludification of culture" and have argued that playful technologies, which have been embraced worldwide with great enthusiasm in the past decades, have profoundly affected our identities. We have demonstrated how our narrative identity, as part and parcel of a centuries-old book culture, has in the past decades been complemented, and even partly replaced by, more playful types of identities. The subsequent chapters in this volume have analyzed and interpreted *Homo ludens 2.0* by focusing on the different dimensions of our new state of play from a variety of disciplinary and interdisciplinary perspectives.

However, as we have argued with Huizinga in Chapter 1, narrative and play are no real opposites, because narrative itself can also be understood as a particular form of play. For that reason the "ludification of identity" in contemporary digital culture should be regarded as an extension of the playful dimension of human life rather than as a radical change. Taking Caillois' division once more in mind, we might say that whereas narrative, as it has been developed in writing culture, is predominantly bound to *mimicry*[1], the digital technologies that play an important role in the construction of playful identities complement this mimetic dimension with *agôn*, *alea*, and *ilinx*. As playful identities, we play many different "games" in the various domains of our everyday lives. Unlike Huizinga, who considered play and technology as complete opposites, we have shown that technologies, although they may be partly developed for dealing with "the necessities and seriousness of everyday life", nevertheless often spring from, and afford all kinds of, playful behavior. And if we look at the enthusiasm with which literally billions of people use their smartphones, tablets, and game consoles, it does not seem to be an exaggeration to assume that technology has even become one of the main domains of the ludification of our culture and identity.

Although several authors in this volume have made critical remarks about the ludification of our culture and identities, the book's primary objective was not an evaluation of this phenomenon from a normative point of view. Our main aim was to understand how the construction of playful identities through ludic media technologies takes place. Although we will not offer a detailed normative judgment in this "afterplay", we will also not finish our adventurous journey through "Playland"[2] without reflecting on some of the advantages and disadvantages of play for life.

So as not to disappoint the reader, let us make clear from the start that we do not intend to offer a univocal affirmation or rejection of the ludification of culture and identity. The choice to steer clear from such an absolute verdict is by no means primarily motivated by wanting to play our "scholarly game" according to the rules of academia, and for that reason aim at as balanced and nuanced an evaluation as possible. Instead the main reasons for this are related to the diverse character of the play phenomenon itself. Play is versatile and exists in an immense variety of types and forms, as well as appearing in an extensive variety of contexts. It is telling that Wittgenstein took the word "play" (*Spiel*) as his key example in his argument against essentialist definitions of words (1986, 31-2; cf. note 10 in Chapter 1).

Because of its immense variety, the play phenomenon is surrounded by a diversity of theoretical discourses. Brian Sutton-Smith distinguishes in his book *The ambiguity of play* no less than seven different "rhetorics", which respectively approach play from the perspective of progress, fate, power, identity, imaginary, self and frivolity. In these rhetorics we recognize many of the characteristics of play that we came across in the theories of other play scholars like Huizinga and Caillois. Sutton-Smith emphasizes that "each rhetoric applies primarily to a distinct kind of play or playfulness [and to] a distinct kind of players" (Sutton-Smith 1997, 15). Discussions about the value of play are so often confusing because the participants depart from different rhetorics, and refer to different kinds of play and players.

Because of this book's focus on identity, most of the contributions in this volume were situated in the rhetorics of self and identity, and as a result the authors have predominantly (though not exclusively) discussed kinds of play and players that are most relevant for these types of rhetorics. However, even this delineated focus does not lead to a more univocal judgment. In the introductory chapter we have pointed to the fact that play is not only characterized by immense variety, but by fundamental *ambiguities* as well.[3] Considered from a normative point of view, these ambiguities are related to as fundamental *ambivalences*. In Chapter 1 we argued that playful identity construction in the digital domain is an activity in which *reality and appearance, freedom and force, determination and change,* and *individuality and collectivism* are interconnected in complex, changeable, and often confusing ways. These ontological ambiguities and normative ambivalences often confuse our desire to get to grips with the ultimate value of the playful dimension of our lives. The same applies to ludic technologies, which are hardly ever exclusively good or bad for us. If this is simultaneously the case, ludic technologies can be called sublime (cf. de Mul 2012). Just as in the case of mountain climbing – the mother of romantic *ilinx* – ludic technologies have the power to lift us above the trivialities of everyday life, but this elevation is never without risk, and the higher we climb the greater the risks involved. Although most ludic technologies do not bring us in peril of death, they always carry the risk of aggression, alienation, addiction, commodification, and escapism, to mention just some of the possible negative effects. You simply cannot have the benefits without the costs.

However, just as modern theories and interpretations of reality often tend to be dichotomist and one-sided (cf. Latour 1993, de Mul 2014), many discourses on the ludification of culture and identity exclusively focus on the positive or negative effects and functions of play. Whereas, for example, many play scholars have followed Schiller in his claim that human freedom finds its highest realization in play, others are inclined to focus exclusively on the childish, frivolous, or addictive dimensions of play and games. In the first case, ludification is welcomed as a panacea for all the illnesses and negativities of modern culture, while the latter perceives play as irrelevant or even as undermining our very hope and "pursuit of happiness".

Curiously, we ever so often witness scholars of play oscillate from one extreme to the other at different stages of their development. Sherry Turkle is an illuminating example. In her book *Life on the screen: Identity in the age of the Internet* (1995), she appears to celebrate the unbridled possibilities of expression on the Internet and the freedom of online identity. Instead of being constrained by the responsibilities of real life, Turkle argues, people were using the web to play and experiment with their identity. However, in Turkle's more recent book *Alone together: Why we expect more from technology and less from each other* (2010), this optimism is gone and all emphasis is placed on the alienation caused by the "social" media which are controlled by commercial corporations (cf. Lehrer 2011). Turkle certainly is *not* alone in her convictions. For instance, in their recent books, "reborn" new media critics Jaron Lanier (*You are not a gadget: A manifesto,* 2010) and Nicholas Carr (*The shallows: What the Internet is doing to our brains,* 2010) also cast a rather negative light on the playful behavior allured by our digital technologies and gadgets. In Carr's view, "deep reading and other forms of calm and attentive thought" have been replaced by "the permanent state of distractedness that defines the online life" (2010, 112). Our desire for "fast-moving, kaleidoscopic diversions" has transformed us into multitasking "window jugglers" (ibid. 112-4). And according to Lanier, "smart devices" such as search engines invite you in just "playing along, lowering your standards to make it seem clever" (Lanier 2010, 32). Without a doubt, one could argue that the commercialization of Playland and the negative (side) effects of ludic technologies, such as game addiction and the celebration of violence, have only become manifest in the last decade and that the publications of Turkle, Lanier, and Carr for that reason can only now reflect on the unfortunate sides of digital culture. However, as true as their recent critiques may in part be, they now seem to overlook the positive aspects and developments that they so much overestimated during the formative years of Playland.

As we have tried to show in this volume, practices of reflexive identity construction in the digital domain take place in constant tension, and indeed interplay, between the communicative actions of free actors and the forces of commercialization, between local belonging and ongoing globalization, and between the heterogeneity of goals and means and the danger of homogenization through technology. Such oscillations and tensions may not always be symmetrical (which makes the warnings of authors like Turkle, Lanier, and Carter valuable), but we should understand such imbalances as a challenge rather than as an inescapable destiny. If life is a game, we'd better learn to play it in a skillful and informed manner instead of leaving the playfield unchallenged!

The game of life: Knowing how to play, fair play & fun

Why would living a playful life be advantageous and which dangers can we expect from such an endeavor? Let's try to sketch the most fundamental benefits and disadvantages that are at stake, with regard to the following three basic dimensions of human experience: *knowing*, *acting*, and *feeling*.

In order to be able to live our human lives in a meaningful way, we have to understand our world, our fellow men, and ourselves. Playing can help us to develop the necessary skills and insights to play "the game of life" successfully. This cognitive function of play has been studied since the 19th century by biologists and developmental psychologists (for a historical overview, see Smith 1982). Play can prepare human juveniles for adult life, and different forms of play have different functions in developing disparate spheres of adult life, varying from practicing motor skills and competition to exercises in imagination. Moreover, play both helps us to acquire specific skills and insights, as well as enhancing the flexibility of behavior, as it helps us learn to switch between and improvise with all kinds of behaviors and prepares us to deal with the unexpected. Inspired by the work of biologist Stephen Jay Gould, Sutton-Smith approaches the amazing diversity and variability functions of play from the perspective of *adaptive variability*: "If play is to be seen as some kind of adaptive variability, Gould's account provides evolutionary metaphors that certainly have some power. If quirkiness, redundancy, and flexibility are keys to evolution, then finding play to be itself quite quirky, redundant, and flexible certainly suggests that play may have a similar biological base" (Sutton-Smith 1997, 224).

Though adaptive variability may have been characteristic for (human) life and play from the very beginning, the need for it seems all the more urgent in our present age, characterized by an increasing complexity and reflective uncertainty. Exercising "world openness" and developing playful identities – and to keep playing as an adult – seem to be more crucial now than ever.

We want to clarify this a bit further by referring to Heidegger's analysis of human existence in *Being and time*.[4] For Heidegger, existing as a human being means that, while living in the present, we are always oriented toward our future possibilities, while at the same time always being constrained by the possibilities we have realized in the past. In a concise formula, Heidegger calls man a *geworfene Möglichkeit*, a "thrown possibility" (1996, 135). However, our attitudes toward our past and our future possibilities are not the same. We *narrate* and *interpret* our past and we *play* with, and *act upon*, our future projects. Of course these dimensions are not completely separate. Our past is not simply behind us, but continuously effective in our present actions, and in our interpretations we continuously revise our past. Moreover, the choices we make during our actions are always grounded in our past. This is the reason that narratives and other (interactive) forms of play are often so entangled. Although situated in the past, stories can often inspire new future possibilities, and though oriented towards the future, games can often repeat possibilities from the past. Typically, human beings tend to identify themselves with the choices made in the past and for that reason become less playful as they grow older.

Yet this does not mean that the shares of thrownness and possibility are always of equal weight. Since the beginning of modernity in Western culture there seems to be a growing dominance of the projective dimension of our existence above our thrownness. In the modern era, man understands itself predominantly as an autonomous, free acting subject. *Homo sapiens* has increasingly become *Homo volens*. Modern technology has given this autonomous subject powerful extensive means to increase the power to imagine and realize new possibilities. Interactive technologies can be regarded as derivatives of this modern ideology of autonomy. It is no coincidence that *interactivity* is one of the key concepts in the study of digital media and culture. No less in the computer game than in the "game of life", modern subjects continuously have to make choices. Whereas in premodern cultures most choices – life partner, occupation, religion – were usually made for us, in (post)modern times we continually have to choose. Whether it concerns the simple choice between taking the left or right door in a computer game and choosing a partner, profession, or lifestyle, every time the emphasis is on the *volitional* dimension of our personality. For that reason, the need for the flexibilization of ourselves is greater than it has ever been in human history. As Turkle puts it: "Not so long ago, stability was socially valued and culturally reinforced. Rigid gender roles, repetitive labor, the expectation of being in one kind of job or remaining in one town over a lifetime, all of these made consistency central to definitions of health. But these stable social worlds have broken down. In our time, health is described in terms of fluidity rather than stability. What matters most now is the ability to adapt and change – to new jobs, new career directions, new gender roles, new technologies" (1995, 255).

Of course, ludic technologies have not caused this change in identity. This transformation of the modern self is a complex process in which, among many other things, social, political, economic, and technological developments play a role. However, the massive dissemination of ludic technologies in Western and Westernized cultures is without a doubt also part of this complex process. It demonstrates that in postmodern culture there has been a major shift from representations to actions, and from interpretation of narrative meaning to reflective feedback on playful action.

Moreover, next to the cognitive and volative dimension, play also has a strong emotional dimension as it is connected with deep feelings of fear, fun, and doubt. On an existential level, play offers us a safe area to express feelings about and deal with a world which is often confusing and threatening: "All creatures, animal and human, live with some degree of existential angst, and most of them spend some portion of their existence attempting to secure themselves from this angst by controlling their circumstances. All creatures live in a world of strong feelings and are dominated by those feelings. We constantly seek to manage the variable contingencies of our lives for success over failure, for life over death. Play itself may be a model of just this everyday existentialism" (Sutton-Smith 1997, 228).

In a rapidly globalizing and increasingly multicultural world, in which different cultures and values constantly interact and not seldom clash, playing may help us to deal with such conflicting interests, attitudes, norms, and rules. As a particular kind of animal play, human play might also help us to practice conflicts in a peaceful way in order to avoid real conflicts and create new ways of cooperation. Not only by playful simulations of conflicts and reconciliation, as we find them for example in multicultural comedies and funny virals, but also by acting them out in competitive virtual worlds like *World of Warcraft*.

If Huizinga is right that "civilization arises and unfolds in and as play" (1955, foreword), it is difficult to overestimate the importance of play. By playing we both create civilization as well as foster our humanity, because humanity is deeply connected with world-openness, i.e. the ability to see the world and ourselves from a multitude of perspectives. Because of its *adaptive variability* human play constantly discloses new possibilities within the world we inhabit, but it also inexhaustibly creates new worlds, new meaningful relationships (Heidegger 1975, 42) that offer us new existential shelters and homes.

Perhaps just because play offers us all kinds of safe havens against the harshness of life, it also has such addictive qualities. Just because we play so enthusiastically, we are easily carried away by the games we play. We no longer play, but are being played, by the very rules we have party created ourselves. This is not that strange when we realize that even acts of violence and war, which we desperately try to avoid in our daily lives, often become attractive and even meaningful events in Playland, as they can be experienced without the physical risks they bring in real life. Play can help us realize goals, whereas in our offline life these goals and their realization are often denied (cf. McGonigal 2011).

When there is a danger connected to the affordances of ludic technologies, with which we create and foster ourselves and our world, it does not so much lie in the depiction of violence or other undesired behavior, or in the addictive qualities of these games, but rather in the negative impact they might have on our world openness. With Heidegger, we might describe a "world" as the all-governing expanse of an *open* relational context (1975, 42). That means that even within a strictly finite world, an infinite number of relations can be disclosed.

However, in many "digital worlds", especially those that are sheer exploratory instead of constructive, the freedom to move is rather restricted, as the field of possibilities itself is preprogrammed and finite. When we identify ourselves with these impoverished expressions, we impoverish ourselves. Although written more than twenty years ago – a long time, given the short history of digital Playland – the following warning by Provenzo is still topical:

> Bettelheim has pointed to the fact that children, as well as adults, need plenty of what in German is called *Spielraum*. Now, *Spielraum* is not primarily "a room to play in". While the word also means that, its primary meaning is "free scope, plenty of room" to move not only one's elbows but also one's mind, to experiment with things and ideas at one's leisure, or, to put it colloquially, to toy with ideas. Video games such as Nintendo, with their preprogrammed characters and their media-saturated images, present almost no opportunity to experiment or toy with ideas [...]. Compared to the worlds of imagination provided by play with dolls and blocks, games such as reviewed in this chapter [meant are a series of Nintendo games] ultimately represent impoverished cultural and sensory environments for the child (1991, 93-5).

In *The republic*, Plato banned narrative because in his view artists have a bad influence on their audiences (1974, 421ff.). If he had lived now, Plato would probably draw the same conclusion about ludic technologies. However, both with regard to narratives and ludic technologies such an argument overlooks that we derive our very identity from these playful expressions. Our humanity is closely linked to the gift of play and digital technologies offer us exciting new ways of disclosing worlds and dimensions of the self. Therefore, it would be precarious to condemn them as such. However, that does not mean that we should close our eyes to the dangers that are related to play. Playland is both ambiguous and ambivalent. It is the highest expression of human freedom, and at the same time, we are under its spell. In our acts of playing, we just act "as if" and at the same time are driven by deep earnestness. Playing satisfies our profoundest desires, but it can also be dangerous and even lethal. As life is itself.

Notes

1. For an example of this mimetic approach to narrative, see Motte 1995.
2. See the contribution by Gergen in this volume.

3. In *The ambiguity of play*, Sutton-Smith, referring to William Empson's classic *Seven types of ambiguity* (1955), even distinguishes seven types of ambiguity with regard to play, which he summarizes as follows: "1. the ambiguity of reference (is that a pretend gun shot, or are you choking?); 2. the ambiguity of the referent (is that an object or a toy?); 3. the ambiguity of intent (do you mean it, or is it pretend?); 4. the ambiguity of sense (is this serious, or is it nonsense?); 5. the ambiguity of transition (you said you were only playing); 6. the ambiguity of contradiction (a man playing at being a woman); 7. the ambiguity of meaning (is it play or playfighting?)" (1997, 2).
4. The following exposition on Heidegger is adapted from de Mul (2005).

References

Carr, Nicholas G. 2010. *The shallows: What the Internet is doing to our brains*. New York: W.W. Norton.

Empson, William. 1955. *Seven types of ambiguity*. New York: Meridian Books.

Heidegger, Martin. 1975. *Poetry, language, thought*. New York: Harper & Row.

—. 1996. *Being and time* [*Sein und Zeit*, 1927]. Albany, NY: State University of New York Press.

Lanier, Jaron. 2010. *You are not a gadget: A manifesto*. New York: Alfred A. Knopf.

Latour, Bruno. 1993. *We have never been modern*. Cambridge, MA: Harvard University Press.

Lehrer, Jonah. 2011. "We, robots." *New York Times*, January 23, 2011. Sunday Book Review, 15.

McGonigal, Jane. 2011. *Reality is broken. Why games make us better and how they can change the world*. New York: Penguin Press.

Motte, Warren F. 1995. *Playtexts: Ludics in contemporary literature*, Stages. Lincoln, NE: University of Nebraska Press.

Mul, Jos de. 2005. The game of life. Narrative and ludic identity formation in computer games. In *Handbook of computer game studies*, eds. Joost Raessens and Jeffrey Goldstein, 251-66. Cambridge, MA: The MIT Press.

—. 2012. The (bio)technological sublime. *Diogenes* 59 (1-2): 32-40.

—. 2014. *Destiny domesticated. The rebirth of tragedy out of the spirit of technology*. Albany, NY: State University of New York Press.

Plato. 1974. *The republic*. Harmondsworth: Penguin.

Provenzo, Eugene. 1991. *Video kids: Making sense of Nintendo*. Cambridge, MA: Harvard University Press.

Smith, Peter K. 1982. Does play matter? Functional and evolutionary aspects of animal and human play. *Behavioral and Brain Sciences* 5: 139-84.

Sutton-Smith, Brian. 1997. *The ambiguity of play*. Cambridge, MA: Harvard University Press.

Turkle, Sherry. 1995. *Life on the screen: Identity in the age of the Internet*. New York: Simon and Schuster.

—. 2010. *Alone together: Why we expect more from technology and less from each other*. New York: Basic Books.

Wittgenstein, Ludwig. 1986. *Philosophical investigations*. Oxford: Basil Blackwell.

About the authors

Valerie Frissen is Managing Director of the SIDN Fund and professor of ICT & Social Change at Erasmus University Rotterdam. Before she was principal scientist at TNO and managing director of CLICKNL, the Dutch research and innovation network for the creative industries. She publishes on the social impact of ICT and media. She is frequently invited as an expert and speaker in national and international fora and as an external expert in many policy oriented projects and fora. She is also member of the AWTI, an advisory board, which advises the Dutch government on Science, Technology and Innovation policy issues.
www.twitter.com/vfrissen.

Sybille Lammes is associate professor at the Centre for Interdisciplinary Methodologies at the University of Warwick. She has been a visiting Senior Research Fellow at The University of Manchester, and has worked as a researcher and lecturer at Utrecht University and the University of Amsterdam. Her background is in media-studies, which she has always approached from an interdisciplinary angle, including cultural studies, game studies, science and technology studies, gender studies and critical geography. She is the co-editor of *Digital material: Tracing new media in daily life and technology* (Amsterdam University Press, 2009), and *The playful citizen: Power, creativity, knowledge* (forthcoming). She is currently the principal investigator of the ERC project *Charting the Digital*.
www.digitalcartography.eu.

Michiel de Lange is a part-time Lecturer New Media Studies at Utrecht University. He co-founded The Mobile City, an independent research group that investigates the influence of digital media technologies on urban life, and implications for urban design. In 2010 he finished his dissertation *Moving circles: mobile media and playful identities* at the Faculty of Philosophy, Erasmus University Rotterdam. Trained as an anthropologist his research interests include mobile media, cities and urban culture, play, and identity. Recent papers and book chapters are *Owning the city: New media and citizen engagement in urban design* (2013, with Martijn de Waal) and *Executable urbanisms: Messing with ubicomp's singular future* (2013, with Marc Tuters).
blog.bijt.org.

Jos de Mul is full professor of Philosophy of Man and Culture at the Faculty of Philosophy of Erasmus University Rotterdam. He also taught at the University of Michigan (Ann Arbor) and Fudan University Shanghai. His research is located at the interface of Philosophical Anthropology, Philosophy of Technology, and Aesthetics. His book publications include *The tragedy of finitude: Dilthey's hermeneutics of life* (Yale UP, 2004) and *Destiny domesticated: The rebirth of tragedy out of the spirit of technology* (SUNY, 2014).
www.demul.nl.

Joost Raessens holds the chair of Media Theory and is the scientific director of GAP: the Center for the Study of Digital Games and Play (www.gamesandplay.nl), Faculty of Humanities, Utrecht University. Raessens' current research concerns the 'ludification of culture', focusing in particular on the playful construction of identities, on applied, serious and persuasive gaming, and on the notion of play as a conceptual framework for the analysis of media use. He was the conference chair of the first Digital Games Research Association (DiGRA) conference Level Up in Utrecht (2003). Raessens co-edited the *Handbook of computer game studies* (The MIT Press, 2005).
www.raessens.com.

Stef Aupers is a cultural sociologist and works as Associate Professor at the Centre for Rotterdam Cultural Sociology (CROCUS) at Erasmus University Rotterdam. Most of his research deals with post-Christian spirituality in modern societies and, particularly, in 'secular' and 'public' domains (i.e., business organizations, ICT, new media). He has furthermore published on conspiracy culture internet culture and game culture. Aupers has (co-)authored several books, i.e. *Religions of modernity* (Brill, 2010, with Dick Houtman) and *Paradoxes of individualization* (Ashgate, 2011, with Dick Houtman and Willem de Koster).
www.stefaupers.nl.

Tilde Bekker is Associate Professor at the Capacity Group User-Centred Engineering, of the Faculty of Industrial Design, Eindhoven University of Technology. Her research focusses on playful interactions and solutions.
http://tue.academia.edu/TildeBekker.

Gordon Calleja is Associate Professor and the Head of the Center for Computer Games Research at the IT University of Copenhagen. He currently lectures in Game Theory at Masters level at ITU. His current research

focuses on digital games and addresses three broad areas: game ontology, narrative in games, and player engagement in games and virtual worlds. Recent publications include *In-game: From immersion to incorporation* (The MIT Press, 2011).
www.gordoncalleja.com.

Daniel Cermak-Sassenrath is Assistant Professor in the Computer Games and Interaction Design (CGID) group at the ITU, Copenhagen. Daniel writes, composes, codes, reviews, builds and plays. He has experience in exploratory teaching, student projects and studio-based work, and has been teaching courses on computer games, tangible interaction, and media theory at different Universities. He is interested in theories of play, art and play, game design, phenomenology, and transmedia. Recent publications include *Interaktivität als Spiel – Neue Perspektiven auf den Alltag mit dem Computer* (Transcript , 2010, "Interactivity as play – New perspectives in everyday computing"). Currently Daniel edits a book on the playful subversion of technoculture with the (working) title *Playing the system* (Springer, forthcoming).
www.dace.de.

Patrick Crogan is Senior Lecturer in Film and Media and Cultural Studies at the University of West England. Crogan's research on topics including drones, social media, animation and film is informed by a strong engagement in critical theories of technology and media. He recently published essays on Bernard Stiegler in New Formations, Techne/Technology and Stiegler and Technics. His book *Gameplay mode: War, simulation and technoculture* was published in 2011 (University of Minnesota Press).
http://www.dcrc.org.uk/people/patrick-crogan.

Menno Deen is a PhD candidate at Fontys University of Applied Sciences. He published about serious games and education, and casual games. Deen researches motivations for games and learning. He works for game company Ranj as a game researcher.
http://nl.linkedin.com/in/mennodeen.

Leopoldina Fortunati is the chair of the Doctoral Program in Multimedia Communication at the University of Udine where she teaches Sociology of Communication. She has conducted research in the field of gender studies, cultural processes and communication and information technologies. She is the author and the (co-)editor of many books, among which *Mobile*

communication and the greater China (Routledge, 2012) and *The new television ecosystem* (Peter Lang, 2012).
http://en.wikipedia.org/wiki/Leopoldina_Fortunati.

Jordan Frith is a PhD student in Communication, Rhetoric and Digital Media at North Carolina State University. Frith's research focuses on location-aware mobile media and the constitution of public spaces of the city. Recent publications include *Mobile interfaces in public spaces: Locational privacy, control, and urban sociability* (Routledge, 2012, with Adriana de Souza e Silva).
www4.ncsu.edu/~jhfrith.

Kenneth Gergen is a Senior Research Professor of Psychology at Swarthmore College, Pennsylvania, an Affiliate Professor at Tilburg University and President of The Taos Institute. He studies social constructionist theory and relational theory, and is the (co-)author of numerous books about media and identity, among which *Playing with purpose: Adventures in performative social science* (Alta Mira Press, 2012), and *Relational being: Beyond self and community* (Oxford University Press, 2009).
http://www.swarthmore.edu/academics/kenneth-j-gergen.xml.

René Glas is Assistant Professor in New Media and Digital Culture at the Department of Media and Culture Studies at Utrecht University. Glas' current research interest focuses on notions of deviant play (including cheating) in serious games, pervasive games, gamified media and playful participatory media. Other topics of interest are the relationship between digital games and other media (most notably film), alternative pop culture, participatory culture, and digital game history. Recent publications include *Battlefields of negotiation: Control, agency, and ownership in World of Warcraft* (Amsterdam University Press, 2013).
www.reneglas.nl.

Jeroen Jansz holds the Chair of Communication and Media in the Department of Media & Communication at Erasmus University Rotterdam. He is a member of the Erasmus Research Centre for Media, Communication, and Culture. His research is about the reception of new media. The appeal of video games is a long standing research interest. He is co-founder of the Special Interest Group Game Studies in the International Communication Association, a member of PEGI's expert group (Pan European Game Information) and President of NeFCA, the Netherlands Flanders

Communication Association. Recent journal articles include *Playing The Sims2: an exploration of gender differences in players' motivations and patterns of play* (2010), with Corinne Avis and Mirjam Vosmeer, and *Political Internet games: engaging an audience* (2010) with Joyce Neys.
http://www.eshcc.eur.nl/jeroen_jansz/.

Richard Ling is Shaw Foundation Professor of Media Technology at the WKW School of Communication and Information at Nanyang Technical University in Singapore. He has been Professor at the IT University of Copenhagen, Denmark, Pohs visiting professor of communication studies at the University of Michigan in Ann Arbor, Michigan, and researcher at the Telenor research institute located near Oslo, Norway. He has (co-)authored several books, among which *New tech, new ties: How mobile communication is reshaping social cohesion* (The MIT Press, 2008).
www.richardling.com.

Frans Mäyrä is Professor of Information Studies and Interactive Media in the University of Tampere, Finland. He is the head of University of Tampere Games Research Lab, and has taught and studied digital culture and games from the early 1990s. His research interests include game cultures, meaning making through playful interaction, online social play, borderlines, identity, as well as transmedial fantasy and science fiction. He has over hundred scientific publications, including monographs *Demonic texts and textual demons* (Tampere University Press, 1999), *An introduction to game studies* (SAGE Publications, 2008) and several edited volumes and special issues in game studies journals.
www.fransmayra.fi.

Ben Schouten is Professor Playful Interaction at the Faculty of Industrial Design at Eindhoven University of Technology, and Lector Serious Game Design at Fontys University of Applied Sciences. He has worked as a professional artist for more then twenty years. His inaugural lecture in 2008 was titled *Play as a source for ambient culture.*
http://www.researchgate.net/profile/Ben_Schouten.

Adriana de Souza e Silva is Associate Professor of Communication, North Carolina State University, affiliated faculty at the Digital Games Research Center, and a faculty member of the Communication, Rhetoric and Digital Media program at NCSU. De Souza e Silva's research focuses on mobile communication and location-based networks and the question how these

shape people's interactions with public spaces and create new forms of sociability. Recent publications include *Mobile interfaces in public spaces: Locational privacy, control, and urban sociability* (Routledge, 2012, with Jordan Frith), and *Net locality: Why location matters in a networked world* (Wiley-Blackwell, 2011, with Eric Gordon).
www.souzaesilva.com/bio.htm.

Jeroen Timmermans is a senior policy advisor on research at Erasmus University Rotterdam. He participated in the NWO-funded program *Playful Identities* and completed his PhD in 2010 with the dissertation *Playing with paradoxes: Identity in the internet era.*
http://nl.linkedin.com/pub/jeroen-timmermans/26/521/816.

Index of Names

Aarseth, Espen 102, 133, 327
Ackermann, Edith 96, 172
Adams, Ernest W. 101, 103, 104, 105
Adler, Margot 78, 85
Adorno, Theodor 241, 242n
Albarea, Roberto 304n
Alexander, Leigh 334
Amerika, Mark 99
Anchor, Robert 211, 213
Anderson, Ken 179
Appadurai, Arjun 163, 208
Aristotle 32, 33
Arnheim, Rudolf 99f
Arp, Hans 102
Augé, Marc 200, 208, 307
Aupers, Stef 13, 53, 75f, 135, 348
Avedon, Elliott 12
Avis, Corinne 278, 351
Axelos, Kostas 12

Bakardjieva, Maria 208n
Bakker, Hendrik-Jan 282
Bandura, Albert 113
Banksy 140
Barendregt, Bart 308, 310, 314, 315
Barkhuus, Louise 172
Barlow, John P. 216
Barthélémy, Jean-Hugues 230, 242n
Barthes, Roland 38, 58
Bartle, Richard 79, 81, 82, 86
Bateson, Gregory 12, 19, 88, 94
Bauman, Zygmunt 10, 66, 200, 281
Baur, Timo 86
Bazin, André 100
Beasley, Berrin 270
Beck, John C. 71n, 111
Begy, Jason 331
Bekker, Tilde 22, 54, 111f, 348
Bell, Nikki 238f
Bellic, Nico 270
Benveniste, Émile 9
Berger, Arthur A. 71
Berger, Helen 78, 85, 87
Berger, Peter 190, 195
Berk, Laura E. 113, 114
Bertil, Troels 183
Bin Laden, Osama 238f, 243n
Bissell, Tom 71
Blackmore, Tim 236
Blaszczynski, Alex 303
Boase, Jeffrey 283
Bolter, Jay David 24, 25, 28, 29, 98, 101, 104, 208n, 217
Bonke, Jens 298, 300
Borgmann, Albert 36, 286
Borland, John 79
Boschma, Jeroen 291
Bosma, Harke A. 269
boyd, danah 141, 255, 257
Brereton, Pat 25
Bretthauer, David 152
Brock, Avril 120
Brown, Fraser 120
Brown, John Seely 170
Bruns, F. Wilhelm 97, 107
Bull, Michael 174
Butt, Sarah 303

Calleja, Gordon 16, 135, 168, 211f, 348f
Caillois, Roger 13, 14, 15, 19, 28, 34, 41n, 45n, 56, 242n, 243n, 337, 338
Campbell, Joseph 79
Canossa, Alessandro 120, 125
Caputo, John 81, 83
Carr, Nicholas 71n, 162, 339f
Carse, James 70, 317
Cassell, Justine 270
Castells, Manuel 43n, 114, 297
Castronova, Edward 217, 220
Cermak-Sassenrath, Daniel 21, 23, 53, 93f, 349
Chatman, Seymour 33
Chen, Sande 245, 246
Chevalier, Jean 294
Cohen, Akiba A. 192
Colbert, Stephen 140
Coleridge, Samuel Taylor 75
Collins, Randall 181, 186, 187
Collins, George 244
Consalvo, Mia 75, 76, 135, 137, 139, 328, 331
Copier, Marinka 41n, 75, 76, 85, 115, 213, 215
Crampton, Jeremy W. 200
Cranor, Lorrie Faith 172
Crawford, Chris 75, 105
Crogan, Patrick 27, 168, 205, 225f, 349
Crowley, Dennis 131, 142
Crowther, Will 79
Curry, Patrick 78

Damasio, Antonio 219
Davidson, Elizabeth 112
Dawkins, Richard 77, 88
De Certeau, Michel 199f, 329
De Paoli, Stefano 137
de Souza e Silva, Adriana 37, 167f, 169f, 350, 351f
Debord, Guy 39
Deen, Menno 22, 54, 111f, 349
DeLappe, Joseph 236, 237
Deleuze, Gilles 12, 226
DeMarco, Michael 111
Dennett, Daniel 44, 219

Depp, Johnny 269
Der Derian, James 238
Derrida, Jacques 12, 242n
Descartes, René 44, 269, 288
Deterding, Sebastian 132f, 222
Deuze, Mark 158
Dey, Anind 172
Dibbell, Julian 12, 40n, 43n, 75, 76, 209
Dixon, Dan 132
Dodge, Martin 203
Dombrower, Eddie 98, 105
Donner, Jonathan 183, 188
Doosje, Bertjan 269, 276
Dourish, Paul 94, 169, 179
Du Gay, Paul 174
Dunne, Anthony 98
Durkheim, Emile 181, 186, 187
Durkin, Kevin 275
Dyer-Witheford, Nick 61

Eberle, Gary 200, 208n
Eco, Umberto 293
Eggen, Berry 121, 122
Ehrmann, Jacques 17, 18, 211, 213
Ellemers, Naomi 269, 276
Engø-Monsen, Kenth 187, 188
Entman, Robert 171
Erickson, Erik 113
Eriksen, Thomas Hylland 160
Ermi, Laura 326

Fine, Gary Alan 135
Fink, Eugen 18, 19, 211, 213
Fiore, Quentin 268
Fischer, Aloys 94
Fjuk, Annita 186
Flusser, Vilém 97, 98
Fortunati, Leopoldina 24, 192, 264, 293f, 349f
Frasca, Gonzalo 254
Frazer, James George 79
Frens, Joep 121
Freud, Sigmund 33, 71n, 87, 296
Friedman, Ted 254
Frijda, Nico H. 271f
Frissen, Valerie 9f, 53f, 149f, 167f, 263f, 308, 317, 347
Frith, Jordan 37, 167, 168, 169f, 350, 352

Gadamer, Hans-Georg 12, 36, 42n
Galison, Peter 229
Galloway, Alexander 319n
Ganito, Carla 302
Gardner, Gerald 78
Gee, James P. 247
Geertz, Clifford 89, 317
Geirbo, Hanne Cecilie 187, 188
Gergen, Kenneth 10, 45n, 53, 55f, 269, 284, 344n, 350
Gheerbrant, Alain 294
Giddens, Anthony 35, 38, 39
Girard, René 40
Glas, René 16, 27, 54, 131f, 205, 206, 350
Glassner, Andrew 96
Goffman, Erving 42n, 111, 135, 140, 181, 186, 187, 222, 317, 329
Goggin, Gerard 183
Gold, Rich 170
Goldstein, Jeffrey 12, 58, 271, 345
Gombrich, Ernst H. 211
Gordon, Eric 175, 177
Graft, Kris 147
Graham, Stephen 175f
Gramsci, Antonio 297
Granovetter, Mark 112
Grau, Oliver 96, 100, 102, 104, 106
Greenfield, Adam 173, 332
Groen, Inez 291n
Gromala, Diane 98, 101, 104, 107n
Grusin, Richard 24f, 28f, 208n, 217
Guattari, Félix 27, 226

de Haan, Jos 113, 128, 283
Habermas, Jürgen 111
Habuchi, Ichiyo 174, 175, 196
Hackbarth, Gary 97
Hall, Stuart 26, 179, 268
Hammer, Rhonda 50
Hampton, Keith 181
Harambam, Jaron 76
Haraway, Donna 217
Hardt, Michael 299
Harley, J. Brian 200
Hayles, Katherine N. 208n
Haythornthwaite, Carolyn 158, 285
He, Wenbo 147
Hearn, Greg 303
Hebdige, Dick 151
Hefner, Dorothée 270
Heidegger, Martin 12, 44n, 234, 242n, 243n, 286, 341, 343, 345n
Heilig, Morton 100
Helmersen, Per 187, 188
Heraclitus 11
Hillebrand, Friedhelm 183
van 't Hof, Christian 283
Hong, Jason I. 172
Hoorn, Johan F. 269
Horkheimer, Max 241
Horrell, Kristy R. 271
Houtman, Dick 77, 88, 348
Huhtamo, Errki 21
Huizinga, Johan 10f, 55f, 75f, 86f, 135, 149, 154f, 211f, 227, 230f, 242n, 267, 276, 290, 293, 295, 303, 337, 338, 343
Hume, David 44
Hunicke, Robin 117, 126

Inada, Yoriko 172
Inhelder, Bärbel 294
Ishii, Kenichi 181, 187
Ito, Mizuko 112, 179, 188
Ivory, James D. 270

Jacobs, Jane 178n
Jakobsson, Peter 75, 76, 135, 213, 215, 222
Jansz, Jeroen 26, 89, 259n, 263f, 267f, 350f
Jarvis, Pam 120
Jenkins, Henry 27, 29, 78, 270
Johnson, Mark 219, 249
Johnson, Steven 125, 179
Juul, Jesper 41n, 105, 133, 135, 212, 251, 326, 327

Kaipainen, Kirsikka 335
Kalaga, Wojciech 208
Kallio, Kirsi Pauliina 323, 328
Kane, Pat 70
Kapor, Mitchell 216
Karvinen, Juho 323
Katz, James 47, 196, 291, 303, 319, 320
Kay, Alan 97, 102
Keen, Andrew 153, 154
Keller, Paula E. 97, 106
Kellner, Hansfried 190
Kempf, James 172
Kerr, Aphra 25, 137
Kestenbaum, Gerald I. 274
Khaled, Rilla 132
Kim, Hyo 181
King, Brad 79
Kiousis, Spiro 268
Kitchin, Rob 203
Klimmt, Cristoph 270, 274
Kolo, Castulus 86
Konijn, Elly A. 269
Krämer, Sybille 103
Krotoski, Aleks 270
Krueger, Myron 104, 106
Kücklich, Julian 25, 42n, 96, 97, 99, 137, 144
Kuipers, Peter 278
Kuittinen, Jussi 325
Kunnen, Saskia 269
Kunstler, James Howard 200, 208
Kupfer, Joseph H. 200, 208n

Lakoff, George 219, 245f, 257
Lamb, Roberta 112
Lammes, Sybille 9f, 37, 41n, 53f, 76, 167f, 199f, 213, 263f, 347
de Lange, Michiel 9f, 53f, 140, 167f, 207, 263f, 307f, 347
Langlands, Ben 238f
Lanier, Jaron 339f
Lardinois, André 17
Lasen, Amparo 163, 183
Latour, Bruno 76, 301, 339
Laurel, Brenda K. 101
Lave, Jean 121
Law, Pui-Lam 303
Lazarus, Richard S. 272
Le, Minh 120
Leadbeater, Charles 151
LeBlanc, Marc 117, 126
Lee, Charlotte 169
Lehrer, Jonah 339
Lehtonen, Turo-Kimo 175
Lemish, Dafna 192
van Lent, Michael 104
Leroi-Gourhan, André 233, 241n
Lesser, Eric 111
Lévi-Strauss, Claude 54, 149, 155f
Levy, Steven 98, 105, 106, 162
Li, Li 310
Licoppe, Christian 172, 187
Lievrouw, Leah A.A. 208n
Linderoth, Jonas 96
Ling, Rich 192, 303
Lister, Martin 96
Liszkiewicz, A.J. Patrick 331
Livingstone, Sonia M. 208, 268
Lo, Ven-Hwei 181
Locke, John 45n
Louis, Tristan 152
Lucas, Kristen 275
Luckmann, Thomas 190
Luhrmann, Tanya M. 78, 85, 89, 90
Lunenfeld, Peter 97, 98

Maan, Ajit 34
Mackenzie, Adrian 241n
Maeda, John 96
Maffesoli, Michel 39
Manganelli, Anna Maria 302
Malaby, Thomas M. 213, 215
Malone, Thomas W. 111
Manovich, Lev 43, 99f
Mänpää, Pasi 175
Marcia, James E. 114, 124
Martens, Lonneke 274, 275
Martis, Raynel G. 270
Marx, Karl 264, 293, 296f
Mathews, Chris 71n
Matsuda, Misa 175, 196
May, Harvey 305
Mäyrä, Frans 12, 23, 143, 144, 265, 321f, 351
McCarthy, Anna 208
McGonigal, Jane 71n, 133, 134, 200, 343
McLuhan, Marshall 102, 106, 268
Mead, George H. 31, 42n, 311
Messi, Lionel 270
Meyrowitz, Joshua 200, 208n
Michael, David 245, 246
Miki, Toshio 172
Miller, Paul 151
Minnema, Lourens 9, 12, 20
Mitchell, Elmer 12

Montola, Markus 20, 135f, 143, 144, 333
Moores, Shaun 150
Morris, Amanda S. 269
Morris, James T. 250
Motte, Warren 12, 17, 18, 344n
de Mul, Jos 9f, 53f, 160, 161, 167f, 263f, 308, 317, 337f, 348
Murray, Janet H. 219

Nardi, Bonnie A. 121
Necke, Lennart 132
Negri, Antonio 299
Neitzel, Britta 9
Neys, Joyce 259n, 277, 351
Nielsen, Petter 186
Nietzsche, Friedrich 12, 25, 337
Noelle-Neumann, Elisabeth 97
Nohr, Rolf 9
Nolan, Christopher 268
Nunes, Mark 208, 216

O'Driscoll, Tony 111
Oatley, Keith 271
Okabe, Daisuke 179, 188
Oldenburg, Ray 289
Oliver, Julian 227f
Oudemans, Theodorus C.W. 17

Paavilainen, Janne 323
Pagnol, Marcel 285
Papert, Seymour 96, 107
Pargman, Daniel 75, 76, 135, 213, 215, 222
Parkin, Simon 255
Partridge, Chris 77, 78
Paul, Hansjürgen 106
Pearson, Erika 57, 289
Pellicano, Lynn 171
Pertierra, Raul 315
de Peuter, Greg 61
Phillips, James G. 303
Piaget, Jean 96, 155, 159, 249
Pijpers, Remco 113
Plant, Sadie 28
Plato 242, 344
Plessner, Helmuth 18f, 31
Possamai, Adam 77
Poster, Mark 208
Price, Jeremy 100
Provenzo, Eugene 344
Przybylski, Andrew K. 116
Putra, Budi 309, 319n

Raby, Fiona 98
Raessens, Joost 9f, 53f, 167f, 200, 245f, 263f, 277, 288, 308, 317, 348
Rainert, Alex 133
Rao, Valentina 289
Rasmussen, David 115
Rauterberg, Matthias 106
Read, J. Leighton 68
Reagle, Joseph 172
Reeves, Byron 68, 71n, 111
Reid, Donna 181
Reid, Fraser 181
van Reijmersdal, Eva 271
Rettberg, Scott 91, 331, 332
Rheingold, Howard 100, 153, 216, 220
Richard, Jörg 97, 107
Ricoeur, Paul 11, 31f, 115, 189f, 307f, 317
Rifkin, Jeremy 9
Rigby, C. Scott 116, 128
Ritterfeld, Ute 12, 278
Robertson, Margaret 133
Rollings, Andrew 101, 103, 104, 105
Rorty, Richard 64
Roseman, Ira 272, 273
Ross, Edward A. 297
Rost, Christian 106
Rovatti, Pier A. 294
Royse, Pam 271, 275
Ruggiero, Thomas E. 268
Ruiz, Susana 247, 256, 257
Rushkoff, Douglas 216, 256
Ryan, Mary-Laure 43n, 217
Ryan, Richard M. 116

Salen, Katie 22, 23, 41, 75, 76, 81, 94f, 98, 100, 105, 133, 138, 212, 214, 267
Saler, Michael 90
Sargent, Robert G. 235
Sastramidjaja, Yatun L.M. 308f, 312
Schäfer, Tobias 27, 209
Schechner, Richard 318
Schejter, Amit M. 192
Schell, Jesse 132
Scheuerl, Hans 94, 95, 96, 99
Schiller, Friedrich 11f, 95, 339
Schneider, Edward F. 269
Schott, Gareth R. 271
Schouten, Ben 22, 54, 111f, 259n, 351
ter Schure, Elisabeth 273
Schwartz, Leigh 208n
Seeßlen, Georg 106
Selman, Robert L. 114, 119, 124
Sennett, Richard 45n, 178n, 301
Sherry, John L. 269, 271, 275
Shields, Rob 210, 217
Shklovski, Irina 169, 174
Sicart, Miguel 182
Silverstone, Roger 10, 24, 26, 311
Simmel, Georg 177, 192, 193
Simondon, Gilbert 226, 230f, 241n, 242n
Sloterdijk, Peter 282
Smith, Peter K. 340
Smoreda, Zbigniew 181
Sniderman, Stephen 95
Solove, Daniel 173
Spears, Russell 269, 276

Spengler, Oswald 15
Sprague, Rosamond Kent 11
Stack, Jack 68
Stahl, Roger 73, 236, 238
Standley, Tracy C. 270
Stapleton, Christopher 96, 97
Starr, Northon 104
Steinberg, Laurence 269
Stenros, Jaakko 134, 143, 144, 335
Stiegler, Bernard 225f, 349
Strümpel, Burkhard 97
Sturm, Janienke 121, 122
Suchman, Lucy A. 98, 121
Sugjyama, Satomi 303
Suharto 140, 308, 311
Suits, Bernard 211, 214, 215
Sundsøy, Pål Roe 183
Sutko, Daniel M. 48, 169, 175
Sutton-Smith, Brian 12, 18, 88, 200, 222, 312, 338, 341, 343, 345n
Swartout, William 104
Swartz, Tamara S. 272, 273
Swift, Jonathan 296

Tamborini, Ron 268, 273
Tan, Ed S. 271f
Tanis, Martin 269, 275
Taylor, T.L. 75, 76, 213, 215
Thimm, Caja 10
Thomas, Karin 102
Timmermans, Jeroen 23, 26, 27, 38, 57, 62, 64, 264, 281f, 308, 352
Tolkien, J.R.R. 77f
Troshynski, Emily 169
Turkle, Sherry 78, 89, 120, 155, 158, 162n, 220, 254, 339, 340, 342
Turner, Chris 243
Turner, Victor 20, 21

Urry, John 180, 285

Vaage, Kjetil O. 182
Van Buskirk, Eliot 134
Vargas, Jose A. 255
Varnelis, Kazys 112
Vattimo, Gianni 25, 45n
Verhoeff, Nanna 201
Vico, Giambattista 96
Vincent, Jane 153
Virilio, Paul 226, 238, 241n, 285
Vitz, Frank 100
Von Hippel, Eric 150f
Vorderer, Peter 12, 43n, 270
Vosmeer, Mirjam 270, 272, 275, 351
de Vries, Imar 28

Wade, Mitchell 71n, 111
Weber, Max 76, 83, 88
Weber, Sam 239, 240
Wei, Ran 181
Weinstein, Lissa 274
Weiser, Mark 170f
Wellman, Barry 71, 158, 281, 285
Wiest, Cynthia 272, 273
Wilde, Oscar 64
Wilders, Geert 290
Williams, Brett 96
Williams, Dmitri 182
Williams, Ken 98
Winter, Rainer 96
Wittgenstein, Ludwig 12, 41n, 43n, 294, 338
Wood, David 49, 176
Woodcock, Bruce 79
Woods, Donald 79

Yamauchi, Hiroshi 111
Yang, Shanhua 303
Yee, Nicholas 82, 197, 275
Yttri, Birgitte 313

Zandbergen, Dorien 90
Zimmerman, Eric 22f, 41n, 75, 76, 81, 94, 95, 98, 100, 105, 133, 138, 212, 214, 267, 276
Zoletto, Davide 294
Zubek, Robert 117, 126

Index of Subjects

Accountability 72, 112, 196
Actualization 217f
Adaptive variability 341
ADD 160
Adolescence 16, 67, 128, 270
Adult(hood) 10, 30, 59, 68, 113f, 123, 252, 294f, 297f, 301, 316, 319, 341, 344
Affordance 22, 43, 54, 136, 168, 291, 344
Agency, virtual 47, 132f, 143f, 147, 167f, 179, 218, 228, 231, 235f, 253, 319, 350
Agôn 14f, 28f, 35f, 40, 242, 338
Agonism 66, 236, 243
Alea 15, 28f, 35f, 39, 42, 45, 337
Aleatory dimension 39
Alienation 66, 229, 339
Anarchism 106, 320
Anthropology 12, 19, 46, 49, 91, 163, 208, 319, 349
Appearance 17, 28, 40, 43, 96, 114, 160, 203, 218, 229, 242, 267, 309, 339
Appraisal, primary vs secondary 272, 278
Art 13, 39, 48, 55, 70, 97, 100f, 107f, 200, 208f, 232, 243, 294, 299, 349, 351
Artifact 9, 46, 105, 194, 218, 228
Augmented reality; *see* reality
Authenticity 62f, 84, 240

Bergaul 307, 312f
Biography, cultural 157, 163
Bosnian War 45
Bounded solidarity 181, 284
Bricolage 155, 157
ButtonMashers 117

Capitalism 49, 61, 72, 83, 91, 174, 244, 297, 299, 305
Capitalism, ludo- 12
Cartography 200, 2009f, 347
Character 33f, 39, 87, 115, 120, 125, 135f, 144f, 221, 267, 269f, 274f, 305, 308, 344
Cheating, pervasive 6, 54, 131f, 144f
Citizen 45, 138, 168, 177, 240, 259, 282, 285, 347
City 22, 175f, 199, 202f, 223, 246, 259, 265, 282, 285, 291, 307f, 347
Civilization 10, 12f, 32, 154, 233, 246, 260, 291, 343
Clans, amateur vs professional 275f
Co-isolation 282
Code, open source 152, 162, 256
Collaboration 112, 149, 154, 217, 241, 332
Collective memory 191
ColorFlare 121f
Commercialization 11, 16, 340
Commitment 64f, 70, 113f
Commodification 70, 144, 174, 180, 298, 300, 339
Communication 19, 115f, 149, 167, 195, 281f, 312
communication technologies 10, 15, 21f, 61, 70, 112, 209, 235
mediated communication 178, 179, 189, 196, 313
meta-communication 19, 315
mobile communication 47, 179, 181, 197, 313f, 318f
Community 4f, 27, 57, 70, 72, 90, 119, 123, 125, 154f, 213, 212, 223, 250f, 264, 281f, 297, 315f
Complexity 20, 35, 61, 64, 144, 185, 215, 218, 257, 334, 341
Concrete, science of the 155f
Confiding 112
Conflict 7, 30, 45, 62, 94, 106, 112, 125, 134, 236f, 252, 255f, 265, 294, 300, 321f, 331f, 343
Connectivity 10, 22f, 38, 285f
Consistency 77, 102f, 342
Consumption 39, 79, 83, 174, 235, 316
Continuity, spatial and temporal 30f, 242
Control 24f, 65, 87, 94, 106, 132, 144, 161f, 169f, 188, 227, 228, 235, 240, 258, 264, 274, 293, 297f, 311, 332, 339, 342
Culture
consumer culture 151
culture as play 12
digital culture 53f, 149f
hacker culture 152, 155
ludification of culture 9, 21, 49, 53, 141, 200, 209, 265, 338f, 348
media culture 2f, 24, 26, 34, 49, 53, 143, 147, 167f, 238, 260, 264f
mythopoeic culture 88
popular culture 15, 34, 71, 73, 92, 128, 244, 256
postmodern culture 9, 12, 20, 342
transindividual culture 168
urban culture 37, 307f, 347

Darfur is Dying 24, 245f
Dark Age of Camelot 79f, 91
Database 20, 131, 141
Dating sites 36
Dead-in-Iraq 236f
Débris 159
Deconstruction 245, 251f
Demystification 254
Diachronization, Hyper- 235
Differential space 176
Discontinuous continuity 160
Discordant concordance 33
Disenchantment; *see also* enchantment 76, 78, 83, 87, 90f
Do-It-Yourself (DIY) 53f, 149f
Droemenon 235

Earnest, holy 13, 16, 48, 344
Education 9, 11, 20, 24f, 39, 49, 61, 69f, 93, 96, 118, 209, 245f, 254f, 279, 286, 291, 296f, 303, 324, 349
Emotion, participatory 272f
Enchantment; *see also* disenchantment 60, 63, 73, 80, 90
Engagement; *see also* participation 22, 58f, 66f, 84, 128, 167, 211, 215, 219f, 227f, 245, 252, 256, 259, 263, 268, 334, 347, 249
Engineer 101, 150, 155f, 244, 348
Enlightenment 11, 61, 77, 241, 244
Ennea 121
Entertainment 23, 42, 55, 58, 68, 225, 229, 235f, 256f, 271, 277f, 283, 299f
Entertainment industry 300f
Epiphylogenetic 233
Ethics 65, 190, 197, 260
Ethnography 78
Everyday, the 19, 95, 104, 153, 211, 213, 264, 329
Exclusion; *see also* inclusion 170, 176f, 219, 295, 312
Existentialism 343
Experience, aesthetic 18, 42
Experimentation 154, 220, 254, 293
Exploration 45, 49, 68, 82, 96f, 115, 119f, 124f, 203, 251, 270, 277f, 333, 351

Facebook 23, 37, 39, 56f, 57, 62, 67, 113, 126f, 140, 154, 159f, 174, 205f, 248, 253f, 259f, 322, 330f
Factuality 40, 228, 232
Farmville 37, 112, 129, 253, 321f, 329f
Fashion 28, 102, 143, 192f, 196f, 204, 234, 238, 270, 294, 296, 303f
Feedback 113f, 117f, 133f, 145, 253, 304, 342
File sharing 152
First-person shooter (FPS) 105, 227f, 275f
Flaneur 285
Flexibility 20, 25, 35, 103, 289, 330, 341
Flickr 160
Foam 282
Focal object 286
Food Force 24, 245f
Force 16f, 23f, 40, 339f
Foursquare 5, 37, 54, 131f, 167f, 201, 204f, 321f, 332f
Freedom 11, 13, 16f, 23f, 38, 40, 72, 75, 97, 264, 288, 296, 339, 343f
Fun 9, 13, 20, 25, 98, 140, 151, 200, 202f, 229f, 240f, 267, 271, 279f, 328
Fundamentalism 69

Game 41f; *see also* Location-based mobile games (LBMG), Massively multiplayer online role-playing game (MMORPG), Massively multiplayer online game (MMO)
casual game 263f, 268, 321
computer game 9f, 21f, 34, 47f, 56, 60, 76f, 88f
engagement in games 128, 215, 222
game attitude 214f
game console 9, 29, 273f, 337
game design 5, 22, 49, 54, 75, 78, 82, 91f, 109f, 223, 227, 247, 257, 267, 279, 335, 102, 105f, 147, 155, 168, 229, 243f, 251, 264f, 279, 320, 323
game mechanics 102, 107, 117, 126, 133f, 218, 324, 330
game theory 12, 48, 68, 223, 243, 258f, 278, 290, 349f
game vs play 36
location-based game 6, 54, 131, 132f
online role-playing game 24, 36, 46, 53, 79, 128, 144, 259
pervasive game 20, 48, 132, 135f, 143f, 147, 335, 350
refugee game 6, 168, 245
serious game 24, 43, 49, 245f, 257f
Gameboy 27, 128, 332
Gameplay 100, 105, 115f, 133f, 173, 211, 214f, 220f, 227f, 236, 242f, 255, 321f, 329f, 349
Games for Change 246f, 256f
GameSpace 323f, 335
Gamification 49, 132f, 144f, 200, 210, 227, 240, 320
Gaul 312f
Gender, political economy of 293
Gender roles 270, 296, 342
Gengsi 36f, 307f, 317f
Globalization 11, 298, 340
God 62, 77, 81f, 146, 210, 294, 316
Goldman Sachs 96
Google Earth 204, 207
Google Maps 37, 168, 177, 199f
Gowalla 167f, 204, 209, 332, 335
Green blogs 27

Hacking 152
Handphone 307f
Hip-hop 30f, 151
Homo ludens 10f, 32, 40f, 46f, 75, 86f, 90f, 135, 160, 211f, 223, 227, 233, 290, 292f, 304, 337
Homogenization 11, 153f, 340
Human-Computer Interaction (HCI) 172
Humanities 4, 12, 43, 213, 223, 243, 260, 320, 348
Humour 16
Hypermediacy 25, 217

ICT 10, 15, 21, 27, 35, 112, 302, 320
Identitas 29
Identity construction 11, 32f, 54, 111f, 141, 154, 189f, 257, 263f, 307f, 338f
Identity
aleatory identity 39
competitive identity 39
cultural identity 10f, 29f, 134, 225, 315f
group identity 189f
individual identity 29, 189f
ludic identity 11, 32f, 38f, 48, 115, 221, 320
narrative identity 11, 31f, 38f, 45f, 115, 128, 189f, 264, 307f, 317, 337

personal identity 29f, 45, 89, 115, 191
playful identity 9f, 54, 111f, 117f, 144, 168, 201, 245f, 317, 338
politics of identity 245, 250
religious identity 316, 318
simulational identity 39
vertigo identity 39
Ilinx 15, 28f, 34, 39, 42, 337f
Illusion 19, 77, 81, 83f, 95, 100, 106f, 243, 258
Imagination 38f, 45, 92, 152f, 156, 159, 161, 192, 210, 216, 294, 297, 341, 344
Imagination, magical 156
Immersion 20, 25, 30, 48f, 71, 79, 82, 86, 100, 108, 211, 219f, 223, 227, 268f, 335, 349
Improvisation 149f
Inception 268
Inclusion; *see also* exclusion 69, 192, 227, 298
Incorporation, logic of 168, 222
Individualism, networked 71, 73, 285, 292
Individuality versus collectivity 28, 281
Individuation 226, 230f, 240f
Indonesia 36f, 140, 142, 147, 207, 264, 307f
Industrial temporal object 27, 168, 225
Industrialization 225, 299, 300
Infantilization 200
Information 104, 160
filtering information 104, 178, 194
information asymmetry 144
information disease 160
information society 161, 169
information technologies; *see* ICT
personal information 112, 114, 126, 286
Innovation 68, 149f, 223, 323
Innovation, amateur, user driven, 150f
Interaction, ritual 181, 184f
Interactivity 10, 22f, 38, 49, 98f, 133, 225, 251, 268, 279, 342, 349
Interface 6, 9, 25, 48, 101, 105, 167f, 203, 206, 216, 218, 226f, 240, 322f, 330, 333
Internal gambling 94, 98
Intimacy 112f, 124, 286
iPhone 68, 185f, 195, 201, 208, 333f
Islam 31, 83, 315f
Isolation 113, 275, 282

Joke 35, 139, 183, 187, 190, 194, 278, 289

Kaleidoscope 155, 158

Labor 294f, 330f, 342
Laboratory 267, 274f
Language 37f, 161, 193, 213, 292, 312f, 318f
Law 20, 32, 70, 78, 103, 109, 138, 162, 178, 213, 294, 304, 315, 317, 334
Layar 37, 168, 201f
Location-based mobile games (LBMG) 169f
Lead users 152
Learning curve 116
Linux 27, 152, 161
Literacy, media 253, 260
Little Big Planet 119f, 275
Location, physical 177, 201, 207
Lord of the Rings 78f
Ludic 6, 9f, 21f, 32f, 48f, 53f, 65 69, 87, 111, 115, 136, 140f, 167f, 189, 200, 211, 213, 215f, 241, 264f, 293f, 297f, 320, 329, 334, 338f
Ludus 15, 36, 41
Lusory attitude 94, 211, 214f

Magic circle 6, 14, 19f, 41, 46f, 53, 75f, 105, 120, 127, 135, 137, 140, 159f, 168, 211f, 232, 246, 267f, 274f
Magic cycle 14, 26
Magical thinking 156
Magicians 81, 85, 87
Maps, social, digital 37, 168, 177, 199f
Massively multiplayer online game (MMO) 76, 79, 81, 90; *see also* Massively multiplayer online role-playing game
Massively multiplayer online role-playing game (MMORPG) 24, 36, 53, 79, 124f, 144, 146, 259
Mechanics; *see* game mechanics
Media culture 24, 26, 34, 49, 53, 143, 147, 167f, 238, 260, 264f
Message; *see* communication
Meta-knowledge 125
Meta-communication; *see* communication
Metaphoric drift 68
Middle Earth 77f
Militainment 73, 238, 244
Mimesis 32f, 213, 308
Mimicry 14f, 28f, 34f, 337
Mind, savage 5, 54, 149, 155f
Minecraft 121, 124f, 128
MMO; *see* Massively multiplayer online game
MMORPG; *see* Massively multiplayer online role-playing game
Mobile media; *see* mobile phones
Mobile phones 6, 9, 22f, 29, 37, 45, 167, 179f, 202, 207, 263, 288, 304f, 307f, 315, 320, 332
Mobility 168f, 175f, 180, 196, 201, 209, 285
Modernity 47, 73, 78f, 88, 90f, 196, 208, 293, 300, 304, 315, 317, 319, 320, 341, 348
Mogi 172
Monadic 270, 274
Morality 13, 46, 58, 65, 84, 111, 115f, 235, 249, 260, 277, 282, 308, 314f
MUD 79, 205
Multimediality 10, 22, 38
Multiple solitude 285
Multitude 293, 299f
soloist multitude 285
Mythology 77f, 80f, 162

Narrative 11, 17f, 25, 31f, 38f, 45f, 59f, 77f, 90, 108, 115, 119f, 189f, 199, 223, 243, 248, 264f, 268, 279f, 307f, 317f, 337, 341f
Narrative identity; *see* identity

Nature 13, 17, 24, 101
human nature 35, 47, 64
imitation of nature 102
nature vs culture 17, 294
Neopaganism 78, 86
Network
communication network 22, 25, 28, 167, 183, 186, 195, 217f, 243
social network 6, 23, 53f, 61f, 70f, 112f, 124, 127f, 140, 151f, 158f, 167, 170, 178f, 200f, 265, 281f, 269, 322, 325f, 331
Networking 67, 132, 142, 172, 201, 248, 264f, 283, 288, 322, 332, 333f
Nintendo Wii 59
Non-place 208f, 319
Norms 123, 125, 229, 332, 271, 343

Objectivity 55, 60, 78
Online 4, 7, 9, 22f, 36f, 46, 53, 56f, 72, 76f, 84f, 102, 107, 112f, 124f, 128, 133, 140, 144f, 159, 169, 174, 177, 217, 223f, 228, 230, 248, 259, 263f, 275, 278f, 283, 288f, 292, 302f, 311, 318, 321f, 334, 339, 340, 351
Ontological transformations 85f, 89
Order 13f, 19, 27, 32, 93f, 156f, 203, 212f, 253, 267, 277f, 304f

Peer-2-peer (P2P) 152, 283
Paidia 15, 36, 41
Participation; *see also* engagement *and* interactivity 22f, 27, 49, 56f, 63, 70, 101f, 131, 141, 171, 190, 231, 245, 247, 251, 258, 298
Personality 19, 71, 83, 120, 125f, 158, 239, 278f, 305, 342
Philosophy 12, 24, 47f, 92, 121, 128, 147, 228, 347
Play 11f
ambiguity of play 17f, 28, 50, 88, 92, 201, 224, 320, 338, 345
casual play 36, 47, 265, 321f
commercialization of play 11, 16, 340
competitive play; *see also agôn* 12, 57, 670, 270
culture as play 13, 16f, 32f
definition of play 13f
false play 16, 18
holy earnest of play 13, 16
immersion in play 14, 20, 25, 30, 48f, 71, 79, 86, 100, 108, 211, 219, 220, 223, 227, 268f, 335
non-serious character of play 13, 16, 38, 41, 287
play1, play2, and play3 35f, 317
play and community building 14, 16f, 27, 115, 152, 213, 264, 281f
play and technology 21f, 25f
play as determination vs change 17, 40, 339
play as freedom vs force 11, 16f, 23f, 27f, 40, 339
play as individuality vs collectivism 17, 40, 339
play as life category 14, 16
play as (only) pretending 14f, 20, 28, 39, 144, 232, 263, 294, 311, 318
play as reality vs appearance 16, 28, 40, 160, 339
play mood 14
play on, with, through, and by digital devices 23, 29
play vs game 36
play vs seriousness 13f, 24, 28, 37, 41, 50, 89, 145, 245f, 263, 264, 287f, 337
regulated play (*ludus*); *see also* game 15, 36, 41
rules of play 13, 20, 24f, 41, 54, 92, 106, 121, 138f, 223, 279
sacred play 12, 32, 42
Playfulness 9f, 14f, 20f, 35, 53, 89f, 108, 132, 144, 149, 158, 182f, 191, 264, 282, 287f, 308, 334, 338
Playland ethos 65
Playworld 13, 20
Plot (*muthos*) 33, 38, 269, 308, 317
Pointsification 133
Politics 6, 9, 20, 37f, 50, 68f, 83, 168, 231f, 243f, 260f, 296, 301, 320
Postmodernity 9f, 21, 34, 37f, 45, 65, 293, 342
Preferred readings 26
Preindividual reality 231f, 237
Pretense; *see* mimicry
Privacy 167f, 286, 289f, 332, 350f
Private vs public sphere 11, 128
Pro Am (Professional Amateur) 151f, 163
Psychoanalysis 18, 33, 71
Psychology 49, 92, 124f, 278f, 305, 350
Publics, networked 112, 128f, 146
Puerilism 16

Reality 16f, 25f, 38f, 77, 100f, 131f, 160f, 177f
augmented reality 20, 200f
virtual reality 22, 38, 49, 101, 104, 108f, 217, 243
Reflexivity 18, 31, 35, 179, 196
Representation 17, 22, 29, 33, 42, 50, 86, 95, 99f, 111, 121, 160, 200f, 218, 240, 246, 259, 265, 271, 278, 298, 328, 342
Resingularisation 27
Retention, tertiary, secondary, primary 231f
Revolution 26, 38, 40, 97, 105, 109, 133, 151, 162f, 233, 294f, 326
Ritual 5, 12f, 17, 32, 42, 50f, 70, 75f, 135, 156f, 181, 184f, 195, 213, 230f, 334, 348
Role-playing 24, 36, 40, 46, 53, 63, 78f, 82, 85f, 91, 115, 122, 124, 128, 135, 144, 146, 259, 263, 265, 318, 331
Romanticism 15, 66
Rules 13, 17, 20, 24f, 28, 49, 54f, 92f, 106f, 112, 115f, 121f, 134f, 143f, 153f, 196, 212f, 218, 223, 246, 251f, 267, 279, 294, 304, 312, 315f, 324, 338, 343

Science 76, 92
  computer science 83, 108
  human science 63
  natural science 12, 20, 32, 83f, 347
  science as a game 70
  science of the concrete 157
  social science 4, 48,87 , 213, 243
  techno-science 226
Second Life 29, 36, 124, 128, 160, 195
Second Person Shooter 227f
Second-order self 72f
Self 11f, 38, 44, 61, 307, 317
  construction of self 11, 35
  inner self 31
  playing with the self 64f, 72
  presentation of self 112, 127, 264f, 281, 288, 307, 312f
  saturated self 72
  second order self 62f
  self as another 62f
  self-awareness 31
  self-conception 68, 70
  self-esteem 113f, 123f
  self-expression 38f, 120f, 264, 281, 313
  self-identity; *see* identity
  self-image 31
  self-interpretation 307
  self-pride 311
  self-reference 76
  self-reflection 31, 311
  self-understanding 38
Serious Games Initiative 246f, 258
Seriousness, Sacred 13, 18f, 24
Sexualization 271
Simulation 14, 22, 39, 93, 103f, 220, 225f, 235f, 240, 248, 254f, 343
Situated ethics; *see also* ethics 65
Skills 15, 25, 68f, 81f, 96f, 123, 126, 324, 340f
Sleeping curve 125
Social cohesion 6, 167, 181f, 287, 294, 351
Social network; *see* network
Social status 272, 309
Social ties 283, 332
Sociology 92, 180, 195, 305
Software 27, 43, 48, 83, 896, 106, 108, 118, 127, 152, 162, 179f, 195, 218, 235, 251, 254, 260, 279, 288
Solitaire 321f
Soloist multitude; *see* multitude
Space; *see also Spielraum*
  public space 39, 112, 169f, 173f, 285f, 350
  safe space 264
  urban space 167f, 174, 176f, 307f
Spatial story 199f, 204f
Spielraum 38, 109, 233f, 344
Spirituality 13, 53, 70, 76f, 81f, 89f, 348
Sports 14f, 35f, 55f, 59, 117, 135, 138f, 270
Stakeholder 54, 132, 137f, 143f, 256
Story; *see also* narrative 31f, 39, 115, 146f, 150f, 162f, 190, 199f, 268, 279, 317f
Street sociability 175
Synchronization 234f, 240f
  hyper-synchronization 229, 236f, 243

Technology
  ludic technology 11, 22, 34, 36, 38f, 338f
  communication technology; *see* ICT
Tetris 105, 124, 128, 322, 323
Tetris trance 105
The house of Osama Bin Laden 238f
The Matrix 38, 77
Thrownness 341f
Ties, strong, weak 112, 127, 175, 284
Time 14, 26, 32, 44, 157f, 190f, 226, 235
Time Magazine 153f
Tinkering 54, 93f, 149f
Trans-individuation 230f
Transductive 230, 242
Transgression 98
Trap of realism 104
Trésor 157
Trivialization 93, 153f
Trust 138, 156, 175, 190, 310, 318, 347
Twitter 62, 126, 139, 201f, 288f, 333, 347

Urban nomad 333
User, lead 152

Values, ideological 168
Verfremdung; *see also* alienation 229
Virtuality, Real; *see also* reality 22, 38, 43
Virtualization 218, 225f, 235

War 13, 16f, 28, 32, 40, 60, 68, 226, 233f, 259, 243
Web 2.0 23f, 27, 46, 153, 159, 286f
Whrll 172
Wicca 78
Wikipedia 161, 177, 304, 350
Wishful identification 269
Women, exclusion from games; *see also* gender, gender roles 295
World of Warcraft 5, 26f, 36, 39, 43, 47, 53, 68, 75f
World Wide Web 72, 179, 281f, 292

Xbox Live 56, 116

YouTube 43, 57, 160, 290

MediaMatters

Maaike Bleeker
Anatomy Live. Performance and the Operating Theatre, 2008
ISBN 978 90 5356 516 2

Marianne van den Boomen, Sybille Lammes, Ann-Sophie Lehmann, Joost Raessens, Mirko Tobias Schäfer (eds.)
Digital Material. Tracing New Media in Everyday Life and Technology, 2009
ISBN 978 90 8964 068 0

Maaike Lauwaert
The Place of Play. Toys and Digital Cultures, 2009
ISBN 978 90 8964 080 2

Sarah Bay-Cheng, Chiel Kattenbelt, Andy Lavender, Robin Nelson (eds.)
Mapping Intermediality in Performance, 2010
ISBN 978 90 8964 255 4

Tanja Sihvonen
Players Unleashed! Modding The Sims *and the Culture of Gaming*, 2011
ISBN 978 90 8964 201 1

Mirko Tobias Schäfer
Bastard Culture! How User Participation Transforms Cultural Production, 2011
ISBN 978 90 8964 256 1

Imar O. de Vries
Tantalisingly Close. An Archaeology of Communication Desires in Discourses of Mobile Wireless Media, 2012
ISBN 978 90 8964 354 4

Nanna Verhoeff
Mobile Screens. The Visual Regime of Navigation, 2012
ISBN 978 90 8964 379 7

René Glas
Battlefields of Negotiation. Control, Agency, and Ownership in World of Warcraft, 2013
ISBN 978 90 8964 500 5

15W37250/ T4/ 9789089646392